DATE DUE

DEMCO 38-296

Although the United States has a system of law structuring a unique position for American Indians, they have been left out of U.S. legal history. Crow Dog, Crazy Snake, Sitting Bull, Bill Whaley, Tla-coo-yel-lee, Isparhecher, Lone Wolf, and others had their own jurisprudence, kept alive by their own legal traditions. *Crow Dog's Case* is the first social history of American Indians in the making of U.S. law. Crow Dog, for unknown reasons connected to a tribal dispute, shot Spotted Tail, his chief, in 1881. The families of both men settled the matter, in accordance with tribal law, for six hundred dollars in cash, eight horses, and one blanket. Nevertheless, one year later, Crow Dog was tried in the Dakota territorial court in Deadwood, convicted of murder, and sentenced to hang. He was released on appeal with a landmark U.S. Supreme Court case holding that American Indians, as one aspect of their sovereignty, were subject to their own laws, not U.S. law. In the United States of the nineteenth century, the "century of dishonor," American Indian tribes were forced onto reservations and deprived of their lands, a process marked by flagrant illegality. Within this context of domination, the tribes as well as individual Indians adopted a range of strategies to protect their sovereignty, including legal strategies. Harring describes the issues of tribal sovereignty that were brought to U.S. courts in the nineteenth century in a wide variety of contexts, illustrating a great deal about the lives of American Indians.

Crow Dog's case

CAMBRIDGE STUDIES IN
NORTH AMERICAN INDIAN HISTORY

Editors

Frederick Hoxie, The Newberry Library
Neal Salisbury, Smith College

Also in the series

RICHARD WHITE   *The Middle Ground: Indians, Empires, and
Republics in the Great Lakes Region, 1650–1815*

Crow Dog's case

American Indian sovereignty, tribal law, and United States law in the nineteenth century

SIDNEY L. HARRING

CAMBRIDGE
UNIVERSITY PRESS

icate of the University of Cambridge
ngton Street, Cambridge CB2 1RP
ew York, NY 10011-4211, USA
eigh, Melbourne 3166, Australia

© Cambridge University Press 1994

First published 1994

Printed in the United States of America

Library of Congress Cataloging-in-Publication Data

Harring, Sidney L., 1947–
Crow Dog's case : American Indian sovereignty, tribal law, and
United States law in the nineteenth century / Sidney L. Harring.
p.   cm. – (Cambridge studies in North American Indian
history)
ISBN 0-521-41563-2 (hardback)
ISBN 0-521-46716-0 (paperback)

1. Indians of North America – Legal status, laws, etc. – History.
2. Indians of North America – Government relations – History.
I. Title. II. Series.
KF8205.H37   1994
346.7301'3 – dc20
[347.30613]
                                        92-23823
                                             CIP

A catalog record for this book is available from the British Library.

ISBN 0-521-41563-2 hardback

ISBN 0-521-46716-0 paperback

To Crow Dog, Crazy Snake, Sitting Bull, Bill Whaley, Sah Quah,
Corn Tassel, White Path, Isparhecher, Spotted Tail,
Plenty Horses, Standing Bear, Bai-a-lil-le, Tla-coo-yel-lee,
Columbia George, Nynche, Red Jacket, Scun-doo,
their people, and their jurisprudence

They are strangers to the common law. They derive their jurisprudence from an entirely different source.

Ex parte Tiger 47 S.W. 304 (1898), at 305

Contents

vii

Acknowledgments

Crow Dog's Case began the first time I taught Native American law in the spring of 1985. Roberta Hunter, a member of the Shinnecock Nation, and Tonya Frichner, a member of the Onondaga Nation, decided that they were entitled to such a course. I am happy that they chose me to help them teach it. We set about examining the underlying principles of Indian law, the stories behind the cases. We found them "sovereignty stories." Criminal cases were of special interest because sovereignty was defined, ironically, in the context of so much violence. The first time that I read the *Crow Dog* "case," the published U.S. Supreme Court opinion, it occurred to me that there must be a great gulf between the case as the Supreme Court saw it and the tragic events of that August day in 1881. So I thank Roberta, Tonya, the Shinnecock elders, and the Onondaga chiefs, who painstakingly explained Indian law to me and my students. Through them I thank the native people who made this history.

The book evolved from a collection of ideas to a complete text during the four months I spent as a Rockefeller Foundation Senior Fellow at the D'Arcy McNickle Center for the History of the American Indian at the Newberry Library in Chicago in 1986. That fall Director Fred Hoxie and Associate Director Colin Calloway assembled a unique crew of fellows, including Jean O'Brien, a historian, Peter Nabokov, an anthropologist, Sonny Trimble, an archaeologist, Bill Hawk, an anthropologist, Berndt Peyer, with an interest in Native American literature, and Helen Hornbeck Tanner, whose interests are without boundaries. John Aubrey and other Newberry librarians know their collection, and with their guidance I was able to study Native American history, which provided a context for understanding the cases. Fred Hoxie and Richard Sattler suggested that the Creeks were worthy of close attention. On the Newberry fellows annual tour of Indian reservations in southern California and Arizona, I was amazed at the extent to which native people were aware of even the fine points of their legal histories. I realized that, to an extent, it was the law that defined Native American status within U.S. society, a legal recognition of a sovereignty that native people had historically defined for themselves. Each of the eight reservations we visited had its own legal history, sovereignty stories that I had never heard before.

Over the next five years the book was developed during a dozen trips to archives across the United States and Canada. These archives held almost all of the records that document the stories told here. As any historian would understand, dozens of leads failed to pan out, but I also found many transcripts of cases carefully describing the legal events that gave rise to what lawyers now know as "Indian law." I thank the keepers of those records, the archivists and libraries at the Wisconsin State Historical Society (my home library since graduate school, housing wonderful books in open stacks), the Five Civilized Tribes Archives of the Oklahoma State Historical Society, the Oregon State Historical Society, the South Dakota State Historical Society, the Alaska State Library, the National Archives, the Federal Records Centers in Denver, Kansas City, Chicago, San Francisco, Los Angeles, Seattle, and Anchorage, the Canadian National Archives, the Ontario Provincial Archives, the Alaska State Archives, the Washington State Archives, the California State Archives, the Oregon State Archives, the New Mexico State Library, and dozens of local librarians who answered questions by mail. The law libraries of the University of Wisconsin, Northwestern University, and the City University of New York supplied the hundreds of state and federal cases that I based my historical research on.

My research trips were financed by three Professional Staff Congress / City University of New York Faculty Research Grants and a National Endowment for the Humanities Travel to Collections Grant.

A number of scholars provided insight, suggestions, and comments on my work while it was in progress, including (in no particular order and in addition to those already named) William Fenton, Larry Hauptman, Rob Williams, Bob Clinton, Rennard Strickland, Fred Ragsdale, Gerda Ray, Jill Norgren, Petra Shattuck, Brad Morse, Neil Salisbury, Ray Fogelson, and James Zion. The death of Petra, a colleague at John Jay College, during the course of this research saddened me very much. I learned a great deal from her work.

Kathryn Swedlow, a law clerk at the Second Circuit U.S. Court of Appeals, served as a research assistant on the final draft of the manuscript, then applied her experience as a technical editor to the writing. Her efforts improved every page of the manuscript. She succeeded Gretchen Oberfranc, a wonderful social science editor who made the second draft into a book manuscript. Student editors of the *Arizona Law Review*, the *American Indian Law Review*, and the *Ottawa Law Review* also made improvements in the best law review tradition. The *American Journal of Legal History* published part of this work. Frank Smith, Mary Racine, and Robert Racine at Cambridge University Press further refined it.

Kim Knowles, currently public defender for the Jicarilla Apache Tribe, was my research assistant for a year while I served as a Fulbright professor at the Institut Teknologi Mara in Malaysia. Louisa Head, Betty Tabor, Joan Berke, and Pat Kennedy worked on the manuscript at different times with creativity and imagination. Marietta Filippino, Katrina Williams, and Ricardo Pla of the City University of New York Law School Library successively handled all of my interlibrary loan requests, negotiating my repeated requests for the impossible with an immense amount of good humor.

My colleagues Ruthann Robson, Joyce McConnell, Dinesh Khosla, Sharon Hom, Howard Lesnick, Homer LaRue, Ellen James, David Nadvorney, Shanara Gilbert, Peter Nimkoff, Pat Williams, Neil Gotunda, Abbe Smith, Richard Boldt, Belinda Sifford, Paula Berg, Cheryl Meyer, Tona Schmidt, Matt Wilkes, Penny Andrews, Mary Lu Bilek, Julie Lim, Bettie Scott, and Bill Mills provided a great deal of human and intellectual support in a difficult educational environment.

Michelle Harring spent an inordinate amount of time on the road, sharing in the search for obscure documents and stories, helping this all come together. Along the way, she read drafts, translated French articles into English, took notes, and helped make photocopies. I thank her and all of the others who made this book happen.

1

"This high pretension of savage sovereignty"

Early on the afternoon of August 5, 1881, on a dusty road just outside the Rosebud Indian Agency on the Great Sioux Reservation in Dakota Territory, Kan-gi-shun-ca (Crow Dog) shot to death Sin-ta-ga-le-Scka (Spotted Tail), a Brule Sioux chief.[1] Great confusion followed as Crow Dog was hunted down by Indian police on the orders of the reservation's chief clerk and locked in a military cell at Fort Niobara, Nebraska. The families of both men met and, following tribal law, settled the matter for $600 in cash, eight horses, and one blanket. A year later, Crow Dog, still in jail, was tried in the Dakota territorial court in Deadwood, convicted of murder, and sentenced to hang. In December 1883, the U.S. Supreme Court reversed the conviction, holding that the United States had no criminal jurisdiction over Indian tribes in "Indian country," because the tribes, inherently sovereign, retained the right to administer their own law as an element of that sovereignty. Crow Dog returned to his people a hero and a "troublemaker" in the eyes of his Indian agent, living out his life as a traditional leader, resisting U.S. government authority until the end, even refusing to accept his allotment until the year before he died at the age of seventy-five in 1911.

Crow Dog and the origins of U.S. Indian law

Crow Dog's case captures, in one instance, the complex and unique nature of U.S. Indian law. Based on a scant constitutional framework for a conflict over the whole of North America, nineteenth-century judges carved out federal and state Indian law one case at a time.[2] This process, often more

[1] U.S. courts referred to Indians by either their tribal names or their Anglicized names, sometimes both. The practice followed here is to use the form and spelling used in the original case, but always to indicate the tribal name (if shown in the records) at the first usage. Spellings are also often inconsistent, as court clerks phonetically spelled Indian names. These spellings of Crow Dog and Spotted Tail are as they appear in the reported opinion.
[2] The core of U.S. Indian law turns on two clauses in the Constitution. The first, the Indian Commerce Clause, grants Congress the right to "regulate Commerce ... with the Indian tribes." The second grants the president the power to "make Treaties" with the advice and

1

Sin-ta-ga-le-Scka (Spotted Tail) with three of his sons, about the time he removed his children from the Carlisle Indian School

opportunistic and pragmatic than doctrinal, provides a window into the character of nineteenth-century U.S. law, for it can be said that no area of that

consent of the Senate. A third clause, exempting "Indians not taxed" from the population base that determined the representation in the House of Representatives (contained in the same clause that counts "three-fifths" of all other persons, referring to slaves), has had less significance but clearly shows that Indians were eligible for citizenship at the time of the making of the Constitution. Kenneth W. Johnson, "Sovereignty, Citizenship, and the Indian," *Arizona Law Review* 15 (1973):973, analyzes the original constitutional language on Indians at 976–85.

Kan-gi-shun-ca (Crow Dog) posed with horse and gun

law is more uniquely American than Indian law. Opportunism and pragmatism alone cannot account for the development of U.S. Indian law, for there was a great struggle over its fundamental character, the nature of the legal doctrines that outlined the development of the government's relationship to the Indian tribes.

When the U.S. Supreme Court handed down its decision in the *Crow Dog* case, the United States was rapidly proceeding with a policy of forced assimilation, destroying the tribes as political units and incorporating individual Indians into the states as small farmers, a policy inconsistent with the

Court's holding. Crow Dog's act, in this context, was political: he had killed a "government chief," one recognized by the Bureau of Indian Affairs (BIA), which used Spotted Tail as an intermediary to persuade the Brule Sioux to adapt to reservation life and assimilate into the American nation. The federal government, which fifty years before had won a legal victory over the states, taking control over Indian affairs, was attempting to divest its authority over the tribes, even entertaining proposals to return Indians to state jurisdiction. *Crow Dog* reminded policymakers that the doctrine of tribal sovereignty was at the heart of Indian law. Although this principle had been central to the Cherokee cases, the foundation of federal Indian law, the courts had failed to develop and defend this doctrine in the years that followed.

In the fifty years between the Cherokee cases, *Cherokee Nation v. Georgia* (1831) and *Worcester v. Georgia* (1832), when the U.S. Supreme Court had first set out the "domestic dependent nations" framework for the place of the Indian tribes in relation to the United States, and *Crow Dog* (1883), the Court had failed to give significant effect to tribal sovereignty, permitting both the states and the federal government to erode the rights of the Indian tribes. Few Indian cases came before the U.S. Supreme Court during this period – perhaps twenty significant cases in fifty years – mostly involving federal claims of power over the tribes, federal–state conflict over the tribes, or legal conflicts between whites, some of whom claimed legal right by way of an Indian title or status.[3] The Court did not develop a coherent doctrine of Indian law, but applied basic doctrines of federalism.[4] During these fifty years, tribal rights were attacked on all sides: by the states, by the federal government, and by local citizens acting extralegally. Lower federal courts and state courts, facing increasing numbers of Indian cases, did not have a coherent doctrinal base to the legal decisions they applied to Indians, producing dozens of diverse and inconsistent opinions.

During the same period, Indian policy changed in ways unrelated to formal law. Dozens of Indian wars occurred as the tribes fought to defend their lands and ways of life. Congress, in 1871, unilaterally abolished the making of treaties with the Indian tribes, a fundamental change in the policy of nation-to-nation relations between the federal government and the tribes. The BIA was created to administer the assimilation of the Indian tribes into

---

[3] I have deliberately chosen to refer to "non-Indians" as "whites," unless, as in the Indian Territory, the actual context of the term referred to other races as well. My point here is that it was a particular racial group, whites, who both took Indian land and structured the federal Indian law that governed that process. When a non-Indian party to a case is not a white, that is specifically stated in the text. Only in the Indian Territory was Indian–black interaction a frequent subject of legal intervention.

[4] See Chapter 2, the section entitled "Federal Indian Law from *Worcester* to *Crow Dog*," for a discussion of U.S. Supreme Court Indian cases between 1832 and 1883.

the American nation.[5] In the midst of this legal chaos, the Supreme Court's holding in *Crow Dog* was not an abstract and vacuous one – the fate of Chief Justice John Marshall's "domestic, dependant nations" language of *Worcester* (which failed either to release a white missionary from a Georgia prison or to save the Cherokees from the loss of their lands) – but a holding that gave immediate effect to Brule Sioux sovereignty: Brule laws were recognized, as was Crow Dog's right to be free. Such a legal result, while consistent with *Worcester*, was anomalous in the context of U.S. domination of reservation life and the policy of forced assimilation.

In the fifty years between *Worcester* and *Crow Dog,* there were relatively few cases in federal Indian law. *Crow Dog,* the Major Crimes Act of 1884, which limited the application of *Crow Dog* by extending federal criminal jurisdiction to selected intra-Indian crimes, and the Dawes Act of 1886, which allotted (and alienated) much tribal land, resulted in hundreds of cases in federal courts over the next twenty years, with nearly a hundred reaching the U.S. Supreme Court by 1903. These cases collectively produced a unitary doctrine of federal Indian law, creating a new category of legal doctrine, incorporated into new sections in treatises and digests.[6] In more than a metaphorical sense, *Crow Dog* marks the beginning of the field of federal Indian law as a coherent body of legal doctrine.

It is not coincidental that the development of a body of doctrine in U.S. Indian law did not occur until after the violent and illegal conquest of the tribes. That process was still, however, a legal process because U.S. government policymakers chose to keep it beyond the reach of the law. A new ethnohistory of Indian warfare suggests that the wars were legal events to the tribes. The Indian nations resisted government illegality, attempting to enforce their legal norms on a disorderly frontier and also to protect their

---

[5] There is an extensive literature on federal Indian policy in this period. For an introduction, see F. Cohen, *Handbook of Federal Indian Law* (Washington, D.C.: U.S. Government Printing Office, 1942), Francis Paul Prucha's *Great Father: The U.S. Government and the Indians,* 2 vols. (Lincoln: University of Nebraska Press, 1984), and Frederick Hoxie, *A Final Promise: The Campaign to Assimilate the Indians, 1880–1920* (Lincoln: University of Nebraska Press, 1984).

[6] Cohen, *Handbook of Federal Indian Law,* which is clearly authoritative in the field, lists 38 U.S. Supreme Court cases before 1883 in its index, but a number only peripherally concern Indians or Indian rights, and several do not directly affect Indians at all but determine white land titles after alienation. Through 1900 this index includes 149 Supreme Court cases, or 111 in the seventeen years after 1883 – an increase from an average of less than 1 case per year to about 8 per year. In this same index are listed 296 lower federal court cases through 1900. This listing clearly does not include all federal court cases, for many, especially criminal cases, were unreported, but it does include all U.S. Supreme Court cases. The index also lists 71 state cases before 1900 but here is much less complete. For example, Cohen does not cite in his index *Tassels, Caldwell, Foreman,* or most of the state cases discussed in Chapter 2 of this volume and was clearly not intending to study state Indian law.

cultures, including their legal traditions.[7] While *Crow Dog* turns explicitly
on the U.S. Supreme Court's recognition that the Brule Sioux possessed
both their tribal law and the right to use it, neither U.S. courts nor policymakers would extend that same recognition of "Indian law" to the tribe's
collective use of violence to apply and defend that same tribal law.

The study of the legal history of "Indian law" encompasses two distinct,
though related inquiries, relating to two distinct and wholly unrelated bodies
of law. The U.S. Indian law that is studied in law schools is an evolution
of the English common law, largely federal, but also including a substantial
body of state law.[8] It originated, as a distinct area of doctrine, in a twelve-
page chapter, "Of the Foundation of Title to Land," in a larger section on
the law of real property in Chancellor James Kent's *Commentaries on the
Common Law*, dating from the first edition published in 1828, based on New
York state law (and written before the Cherokee cases). Chancellor Kent's
successors never removed U.S. Indian law from the real property section,
although by the 1880s "Indian law" had as much become a subfield of public
law as of real property, reflecting the increasing concern of the law with
matters of tribal sovereignty.[9] The American Digest (published in 1896), an
exhaustive survey of U.S. law, included a section on "Indians" running 109
pages of case summaries in fine print, divided into 66 subsections, recognizing the doctrinal complexity of late-nineteenth-century U.S. Indian law.[10]
While this framing of U.S. Indian law as a subcategory of public law focused
the doctrine on the political status of the tribes, including tribal sovereignty,
the core of doctrinal expansion was still focused on real property, as non-
Indians hired lawyers to clear Indian title in the postallotment period. Growth
of the doctrine of U.S. Indian law was so swift that in 1909 the first treatise
on U.S. Indian law was published, covering only a small portion of federal

[7] Kenneth Morrison, "The Bias of Colonial Law: English Paranoia and the Abenaki Arena
of King Philip's War, 1675–1678," *New England Quarterly* 53 (1980): 363–87. A legal history
of the Indian wars from the standpoint of Indian law has yet to be written. For a parallel
study of the conquest of the Maori, see James Belich, *The New Zealand Wars and the Victorian
Interpretation of Racial Conflict* (Aukland: University of Aukland Press, 1986).

[8] Simple nomenclature in "Indian law" is a problem. The two published casebooks in the
field are Robert Clinton, Nell Jessup Newton, and Monroe Price, *American Indian Law*
(Charlottesville, Va.: Michie, 1990), and David Getches and Charles Wilkinson, *Federal
Indian Law* (St. Paul, Minn.: West Publishing, 1986). I distinguish "U.S. Indian law" –
federal and state law defining tribal rights, rooted in the English common law – from "Indian
law" – the law of the tribes, rooted in the customary law and tribal sovereignty of the tribes
but now often adapted to the form of U.S. law.

[9] James Kent, *Commentaries on the Common Law*, vol. 3, 6th ed. (New York: Halstead, 1828);
Kent, a New York Supreme Court judge, had ridden many court circuits in the frontier
countries of western New York State in the early nineteenth century. He had lamented the
passing of the Iroquois and, a Federalist, was alarmed at the coarse frontier settlers who
replaced them. John T. Horton, *James Kent: A Study in Conservatism, 1763–1847* (1939;
New York: Da Capo, 1969), 124–6.

[10] *American Digest*, Centennial ed. (St. Paul, Minn.: West Publishing, 1896), 27:149–258.

Indian law. *Oklahoma Indian Land Laws* was narrowly concerned with post-allotment Indian title.[11] Omitted from all these legal discussions, including the *Crow Dog* case, is serious attention to the legal traditions of Indian tribes, a body of law recognized in *Crow Dog*.

U.S. Indian law is among the most historically grounded of all areas of legal doctrine.[12] The law that shaped Indian–white relations in the nineteenth century continues to influence the major cases in federal Indian law more than a hundred years later. While these nineteenth-century cases provide the grounding of federal (and state) Indian law, their legal principles arc almost always taken out of historical context. More than any other area of law, however, U.S. Indian law is the product of vivid historical events and complex historical relationships between two distinct and sovereign peoples. An ahistorical approach to the foundational U.S. Indian law cases distorts their fundamental doctrines. This is especially true of the doctrine of tribal sovereignty, buried in nineteenth-century U.S. Indian law because it was inconsistent with the policy of forced assimilation.

U.S. Indian law lacks a historical vision because it is so policy oriented and so full of contradictory objectives. At the same time that *Worcester v. Georgia* promised sovereignty to Indian tribes,[13] that sovereignty was at odds with the rapid development of the United States. At every point of conflict, the United States took some action to limit the tribes' sovereignty. The U.S. Supreme Court's *Crow Dog* opinion took the BIA and the country by surprise, for Brule Sioux sovereignty had been under forty years of U.S. encroachment, leaving the tribe on the Rosebud Reservation under the supervision of an Indian agent. The focus on the historical context of the foundation cases in U.S. Indian law is important because the concept of tribal sovereignty, as well as other doctrines, was not developed as an abstract statement of policy or principle but arose around singular events. *Worcester* can never

---

[11] S. T. Bledsoe, *Indian Land Laws* (Kansas City, Mo.: Vernon Law Book, 1909). Oklahoma Indian land law became a substantial legal specialty as whites increasingly acquired control of allotted lands. A 1913 edition was also published. A second treatise on the same subject was also written by Lawrence Mills, *Oklahoma Indian Land Laws* (Tulsa, Okla.: Lawyer's Publishing, 1924).

[12] Charles Wilkinson, *American Indians, Time, and Law* (New Haven, Conn.: Yale University Press, 1987), 13, 14. Wilkinson claims that one-fourth of the courts' decisions in Indian law refer to statutes or cases dating to the country's first century, a larger proportion than in any other area except the civil rights laws.

[13] *Cherokee Nation v. Georgia*, 30 U.S. 1 (1831). This case is considered in detail in Chapter 2. It has been the subject of considerable analysis, which is documented there. The well-known "domestic dependent nation" formulation of Chief Justice John Marshall failed to give substantive guidance to lower courts or to state and federal officials concerning the nature of tribal rights, so Marshall attempted to elaborate on the meaning of this language in *Worcester v. Georgia*, 31 U.S. 515 (1832), decided the next year. The two are always seen as companion cases, although any doctrinal meaning of the original *Cherokee Nation* has been entirely subsumed into *Worcester*.

be understood outside of the conflict between Georgia and the federal
government over domination of Indian lands, and *Crow Dog* cannot be understood outside of the factional conflict that the BIA created on its reservations.

Many legal historians have followed Alexis de Tocqueville in noting Americans' great concern with law and legality.[14] Eighteenth- and nineteenth-
century Americans were enamored of the law and wanted a legal framework
to govern their society.[15] At the same time, this legal framework came to
have an instrumental quality. Americans were not bound by Old World legal
traditions or by abstract notions of morality; they felt free to write laws that
would unleash the productive forces needed to develop a new land. The
application of this legal order to Indian tribes ranks as a test of the absolute
limits of legality and constitutionalism. De Tocqueville, who spent much of
his time as a guest of wealthy planters, did not see the dangers and the
dishonesty in the U.S. government's attempt to apply its laws to Indian tribes.
His best-known observation compared the Spanish pursuit of the Indians to
bloodhounds, and "sacking" of the New World to the Americans' "singular
attachment to the formalities of law" in their relationship to the Indian
tribes.[16]

Although the United States did not have to exercise great legal imagination
in incorporating the Indian tribes within its boundaries, it made a great effort
to do so. From the recognition of the treaty system as the most appropriate
method of legal dealings with the Indian tribes, to the early-nineteenth-
century "Cherokee cases" that gave that system legal meaning, to the "plenary power" decisions that ended the century and the notion of tribal sovereignty, U.S. law helped to structure not only U.S. Indian policy but also
Indian–white relations and, to an extent, the tribal strategies intended to
accommodate the United States. This nation's emphasis on law did not lead
to results very different from those achieved with vicious Spanish bloodhounds. Law was used to perpetrate murder and land frauds of all sorts,
and the legal rights of American Indians were ignored by state and federal

[14] Alexis de Tocqueville, *Democracy in America* (1840; New York: Knopf, 1980), 237–53.
[15] This U.S. ideal of legality received a good deal of critical attention during the bicentennial
of the Constitution in 1988. Michael Kammen, *The Machine That Would Go of Itself: The
Constitution in American Culture* (New York: Knopf, 1987), is one statement of the theme of
legality in U.S. history. James Willard Hurst, *Law and Economic Growth: The Legal History
of the Lumber Industry in Wisconsin, 1836–1915* (Cambridge, Mass.: Harvard University Press,
1964), has, as a central theme, the adherence to legality and the use of law to structure the
opening of the frontier and the expansion of the nineteenth-century U.S. economy.
[16] "The Spaniards pursued the Indians with bloodhounds, like wild beasts; they sacked the
New World like a city taken by storm with no discentment or compassion.... The conduct
of the Americans of the United States towards the aborigines is characterized ... by a singular
attachment to the formalities of law. Provided that the Indians maintain their barbarous
condition, the Americans take no part in their affairs; they treat them as independent nations
and do not possess themselves of their hunting grounds without a treaty of purchase." De
Tocqueville, *Democracy in America*, 354–5.

courts.[17] The product of the great concern with the "legality" of nineteenth-century federal Indian policy was genocide: more than 90 percent of all Native Americans died, and most native land was alienated, the balance occupied by Indians but "owned" by the United States. Indian people were under the control of Indian agents, political hacks sent out from Washington to manage the lives of native peoples and backed by the army.

The rich body of material on the history of the Indian tribes has not been incorporated into U.S. legal history. The study of U.S. Indian law should reach beyond the narrow history of U.S. laws specifically applied to the tribes. The nation's choice to simply deny that many issues of tribal sovereignty were legal issues, leaves many of the issues of U.S. expansionism, economic development, and land policy removed from the doctrine of U.S. Indian law. As a result we have the anomaly that, while U.S. Indian law is among the most historically grounded of doctrinal areas of U.S. law, we lack an Indian presence in other areas of legal history. Surveys of U.S. legal history either leave this unique Indian legal history out or lament the lack of scholarship in the area.[18] Even classic legal histories of areas of law that might include some analysis of Indian legal history often do not. Willard Hurst's *Law and Economic Growth: The Legal History of the Lumber Industry in Wisconsin, 1836–1915*, a detailed legal history of the role of law in structuring the economic development of half of Wisconsin pays scant attention to the ownership of this land by Indian tribes, who continued to live there during the entire period of the study.[19] Omitted is any discussion of the forced removal of the Winnebago, fraudulent timber contracts on Chippewa and Menominee lands (frauds that led to hearings by the U.S. Senate in 1889), a lawsuit over state title to timber on school lands on the Menominee Reservation that reached the U.S. Supreme Court in 1877, deprivation of Indian hunting and fishing rights reserved by treaty, and an extensive legal conflict over basic issues of federalism as the state resisted federal jurisdiction over the tribes resulting in at least ten reported cases.[20] There is no need

---

[17] There were two main themes in nineteenth-century Indian law. A line of cases affirming sovereignty runs through *Worcester, Crow Dog,* and *Talton v. Mayes,* 163 U.S. 376 (1895), while an opposing line of cases denying that sovereignty and giving the United States "plenary power" over the Indian tribes begins with *Kagama* and *Lone Wolf* and dominates Indian law in the first half of the twentieth century. See Wilkinson, *American Indians, Time, and the Law,* 24.

[18] See, e.g., Kermit Hall, *The Magic Mirror: Law in American History* (New York: Oxford University Press, 1989), 146–8, 371; and Lawrence Friedman, *A History of American Law* (New York: Simon & Schuster, 1986).

[19] Cambridge, Mass.: Harvard University Press, 1964. Hurst discusses "Indian titles" at 9, 20, 28, 95, 119.

[20] U.S. Congress, Senate, 50th Congress, 2d session, Report no. 2710, March 2, 1889; *Beecher v. Wetherby,* 95 U.S. 517 (1877); Richard N. Current, *Pine Logs and Politics: A Life of Philetus Sawyer* (Madison: State Historical Society of Wisconsin Press, 1950), 72–3, 211–12; Horace S. Merrill, *William Freeman Vilas: Doctrinaire Democrat* (Madison: Wisconsin State Historical

to belabor the point that Indians occupy an important place in U.S. legal history that has not been adequately studied.

Indians and their law

The scope of the legal issues defined thus far are traditionally the subject of legal history, a study of courts and cases, creating a set of doctrines unique to U.S. law. This, however, is only a portion of the study of Indians under U.S. law, for as *Crow Dog* makes clear, there were two laws, two legal traditions that were absolutely unrelated. The Indian tribes had their own laws, evolved through generations of living together, to solve the ordinary problems of social conflict. This legal tradition is very rich, reflecting the great diversity of Indian peoples in North America. Yet this law was seldom analyzed in U.S. Indian law, even when it was recognized. When it was discussed, as in *Crow Dog*, is was often treated contemptuously, dismissed there as "a case of Red man's revenge," a racist and false description of Sioux law.[21] The legal history of Indians and their incorporation into the United States is the history of the meeting of these two legal traditions.

Tribal political structures, based variously on the extended family, clan, band, village, tribe, or other unit, met in many different kinds of contexts to make legal decisions.[22] These legal decisions were based on the collective

Society Press, 1954), 141–50. The denial of Chippewa hunting and fishing rights underlies ten federal court cases in the 1970s and 1980s; see Kenneth Nelson, "Wisconsin, Walleye, and the Supreme Law of the Land: An Overview of the Chippewa Indian Treaty Rights Dispute in Northern Wisconsin," *Hamline Journal of Public Law and Policy* 11 (1991):381–416. Wisconsin's legal conflict with the United States over its jurisdiction over Indians within the state is discussed in detail in Chapter 2, the section entitled "The North and West, 1835–1880."

21 Even the labels often given the laws of Native people, "customary law" or "traditional law," imply that it is inferior to the state law of Anglo-American nations. Here I refer to the laws of the Indian tribes as "tribal law," just as I would call the law of Wisconsin "state law." When I refer to the collective laws of Indian America I use the term "Indian law" representing the law of Indian people. Correspondingly, when I am referring to United States law defining legal matters with the Indian tribes, I use the term "U.S. Indian law" or "federal Indian law." This language treats the two legal traditions as equals. The English common law is every bit as "customary" or "traditional" as the laws of the Indian tribes. The only context where I use "traditional" to refer to a body of Indian law is when an Indian nation had two sets of laws, one the original tribal laws, which I call "traditional," and one a formally enacted code of written laws, intended to assist the tribe in governing itself in the context of a larger U.S. nation. This form of legal dualism was common in the Indian nations of what is now Oklahoma.

22 There are ten full-length monographs or dissertations on the traditional law of Indian people, works that are rarely cited in legal scholarship. Karl Llewellyn and E. A. Hoebel *The Cheyenne Way: Conflict and Case Law in Primitive Jurisprudence* (Norman: University of Oklahoma Press, 1941); E. A. Hoebbel, "The Political Organization and Law Ways of the Comanche Indians," *Memoirs of the American Anthropological Association*, no. 54 (1940); John Phillip Reid, *A Law of Blood: The Primitive Law of the Cherokee Nation* (New York: New York University Press, 1970); Rennard Strickland, *Fire and the Spirits: Cherokee Law from Clan to Court* (Norman:

social experiences of the tribe, often individualizing decisions in ways very different than is common under U.S. law. Even more important, tribal law was not static, but underwent great change following contact with whites, adapting to changing social, economic, and political situations. The Creek law that confronted forced removal in 1820s and 1830s Alabama was a very different law than had existed when white traders first met the Creek a hundred years before. Creek law in the Creek Nation after the U.S. Civil War reflected a complex meeting of this tribal law and a formal set of laws adopted by a bicameral legislature, a House of Warriors and a House of Kings. It cannot be a coincidence that the laws adopted by this legislative body most often avoided areas covered by traditional tribal law, deliberately leaving two sets of Creek law in force, a complex policy of legal dualism designed to enable the Creek Nation to function within the broader context of U.S. hegemony.[23]

Such elaborate forms of legal adaptation were not the norm of the Indian tribes. By and large, tribal law operated informally within very small social units. Most tribal legal actions were invisible; others appeared to whites as individual actions. The scale of tribal law made it flexible and efficient but also vulnerable to the social disorganization introduced by the cataclysmic social change that accompanied the military defeat or forced removal to reservations far away, fates that befell most of the tribes. Michael Green, in a sensitive analysis of the nature of Creek law in the 1820s, reminds us that by that time, even before removal, the Creek people had been decimated, the population reduced to a tiny percentage of a once powerful nation.[24] The whole social order of the Plains tribes was scarcely a hundred years old when whites arrived in the early nineteenth century, reflecting a legal order adapted to a nomadic life-style and highly organized buffalo hunts. The transitory nature of these societies required well-structured police so-cieties not found among other Indian tribes.[25] Through the work of Karl

---

University of Oklahoma Press, 1975); Julius Lips, "Naskapi Law," *Transactions of the American Philosophical Society*, vol. 37, p. 4 (1947); Jane Richardson, "Law and Status Among the Kiowa Indians," *Monographs of the American Ethnological Society*, no. 1. (1940); Bruce A. Cox, "Law and Conflict Management Among the Hopi," Ph.D. dissertation, University of California, Berkeley, 1968; John Provisne, "The Underlying Sanctions of Plains Indian Culture: An Approach to the Study of Primitive Law," Ph.D. dissertation, University of Chicago, 1934; John A. Noon, "Law and Government of the Grand River Iroquois," *Viking Fund Publications in Anthropology* 12 (1949); William A. Newell, *Crime and Justice Among the Iroquois Nations* (Montreal: Caughnawaga Historical Society, 1965). My own survey of ethnographies of various Indian tribes has produced more than seventy sections or chapters describing the operation of tribal law.

[23] The Five Civilized Tribes of the Indian Territory, the Cherokee, Creek, Choctaw, Chickasaw, and Seminole, used similar versions of this strategy of legal dualism (discussed in Chapter 3).

[24] Michael Green, *The Politics of Creek Removal* (Lincoln: University of Nebraska Press, 1983).

[25] Provisne, "The Underlying Sanctions of Plains Indian Culture."

Llewellen and E. A. Hoebel, we have a sensitive picture of the complexity of the substantive law of two Plains tribes, the Cheyenne and the Comanche. There is no question that these societies had sophisticated legal traditions, bodies of unwritten law that were understood by all the people and applied through tribal legal processes.[26] While these tribal laws were under great pressure because of the rapid social change that followed contact with white people, tribal law often adapted to these changes, continuing to govern increasingly complex social relations. *Crow Dog* itself demonstrates the effectiveness of Brule tribal law after repeated tribal adaptations to white domination.

The Pueblos, Iroquoan, and Algonquin peoples, Northwest Coast tribes, California tribes, and Great Basin desert tribes add even greater legal diversity to those discussed. Each of these legal traditions was changing in the face of contact with whites, helping to structure interpersonal relations within the tribes, as well as to accommodate white pressure on tribal society. Tribal law did not disappear. Rather, it did much to help structure the position of Indians in U.S. society, preserving traditional tribal cultures and protecting traditional political orders. Still, tribal law was in conflict with U.S. law, and the violent exercise of U.S. power did great damage to tribal legal orders. A full understanding of the Indian in U.S. legal history requires a parallel study of the meeting of these two laws, tribal law and U.S. law.

Legal pluralism: the meaning of sovereignty in U.S. Indian law

The doctrine proclaimed in Crow Dog's case should have the same meaning for all Indian people that it had for Crow Dog. He went free because the U.S. Supreme Court recognized the sovereign right of the Brule Sioux to have their own law in their own land. The *Crow Dog* doctrine provides the clearest recognition under U.S. law of a pluralist legal tradition in the United States.[27] This legal pluralism not only benefited native peoples, but

---

[26] Llewellyn and Hoebbel, *Cheyenne Way;* Hoebbel, "Law Ways of the Comanche Indians."

[27] H. M. Hooker, *Legal Pluralism* (Oxford: Oxford University Press, 1974), analyzes the different models for recognizing legal pluralism present in the world today. The dominant model in Western industrial societies has been to incorporate minority legal systems into the dominant system. Colonial legal systems, however, often left the preexisting local systems alone, keeping the law of the colonial power for its own nationals and for matters affecting them. Today, in southern Africa, such countries as Lesotho, Botswana, and Malawi have a system of legal dualism, where a citizen may choose between a common law and a customary law resolution of a conflict. Canada, Australia, New Zealand, and Latin American countries have not recognized the traditional law of native people in their legal systems. This is now an issue of controversy in some of those countries. Australia has considered these questions in great detail in a two-volume report of its Law Reform Commission: *The Recognition of Aboriginal Customary Laws* (Canberra: Australian Government Printing Service, 1986). New

as Robert Williams has shown, also provided a great opportunity to enrich the legal culture of the United States: a chance to "Americanize" U.S. law, to infuse it with tribal legal traditions.[28]

That opportunity has substantially been lost. After the *Crow Dog* decision of 1883, an aggressive policy of assimilation sought to "Americanize" the Indian.[29] This process ranks as one of the great legal atrocities in the United States, equal to the *Dred Scott* case and the internment of U.S. citizens of Japanese descent in concentration camps. Assimilation was implemented by a draconian system of laws. "Law for the Indian" became a slogan of Indian reformers and the BIA. This slogan referred to a violent process of imposing an external law, either state or federal, on the tribes for the express purpose of forcing their assimilation into the United States, deliberately destroying tribal law in the process. As U.S. courts came to hold that the reservation jail was "analogous to a school," the law overshadowed the army as the method of choice to force assimilation.[30]

The image of U.S. law replacing the gun as the agent of civilization reveals the coercive core of the application of criminal law to Indians. Even if the law could not accomplish this end, it was inextricably intertwined with other assimilationist institutions. BIA schools could not function without compulsory attendance laws and BIA police to arrest or threaten parents for not sending children to school. BIA farmers could not teach the Indians to farm without laws and police to prevent Indians from killing their stock for food. Christian churches could not convert without laws to ban traditional ceremonial activities. Land could not be allotted without laws to punish Indians who resisted.[31]

In this process, traditional tribal law yielded. It did not disappear, but it was seriously weakened and, beginning in the 1880s, lost much of its au-

Zealand's Maori land court, restricted under New Zealand law to jurisdiction over customary land titles, is now aggressively stretching its jurisdiction into other areas. Several Canadian tribes, although they have no right to their own law, simply defy Canadian authority and apply customary law in matters where they believe it appropriate.

[28] Robert Williams, "The Algebra of Indian Law: The Hard Trail of Decolonizing and Americanizing the White Man's Indian Jurisprudence," *Wisconsin Law Review* (1986):219.

[29] This process is well documented in Hoxie, *The Final Promise*. The process of assimilation is analyzed and the vast literature cited in Prucha, *The Great Father*, p. 6, "Americanizing the American Indians," 609–757. Prucha has also published an edited collection of primary documents on this process: *Americanizing the American Indian* (Lincoln: University of Nebraska Press, 1966).

[30] Prucha, *The Great Father*, 676–81, analyzes the "law for the Indians" position. It is considered here in Chapter 4. The analogy between the prison and the school was the basis for the holding of *United States v. Clapox*, 33 F. 575 (D.C. Or. 1888), discussed in Chapter 6.

[31] Both Hoxie and Prucha offer numerous examples of forced assimilation, and tribal histories contain additional testimony. The best single source of information is the annual report of the BIA. The reports for each year after the Civil War are full of detail, organized on a reservation-by-reservation basis, with each agent proudly, and undoubtedly with exaggeration, reporting the progress in Americanizing "his" Indians.

thority to a BIA legal order composed of an all-powerful Indian agent backed by a "code of indian offenses," Indian police, and agency-appointed chiefs and judges.[32] Later, the Indian Reorganization Act of 1934 empowered the tribes to establish tribal governments that were copies of white local governments, complete with local laws, local police, and even a local "justice of the peace" in the form of a tribal judge.[33] Although both of these models were called "Indian courts" and the law that was applied was called "Indian law," they were a form of U.S. law and not the tribal law that the U.S. Supreme Court had found Crow Dog entitled to be judged by.[34]

Yet the sharpest observers of tribal courts have pointed out that the Indian judges of these courts preserved much tribal common law; therefore, these "courts of Indian offenses" should not be dismissed as simply copies of white courts.[35] Rather, they were a foundation for building a pluralist legal tradition in the United States. In these tribal courts and in their tribal governments, native people in the United States have the political foundation for the broad application of whatever tribal law they want to use. *Crow Dog* recognized that right.

A more detailed understanding of the context of nineteenth-century federal Indian cases helps to clarify the doctrine of federal Indian law in another way: Indian people understood themselves to be sovereign, acted as if they were sovereign in the most responsible way they could under the circumstances, made judgments concerning ways to defend their sovereignty, and

---

[32] William T. Hagan, *Indian Police and Judges: Experiments in Acculturation and Control* (New Haven, Conn.: Yale University Press, 1966).

[33] Samuel Brakel, *American Indian Tribal Courts: The Costs of Separate Justice* (Chicago: American Bar Foundation, 1978), gives a brief history of the system of tribal courts, as does Hagan, *Indian Police and Judges.*

[34] L. Meriam, *The Problem of Indian Administration* (Cleveland, Ohio: Meriam, 1928), analyzes the problems in the courts of Indian offenses just prior to the passage of the Indian Reorganization Act. Kirke Kickingbird, "In Our Own Image..., After Our Likeness: The Drive for Assimilation of Indian Court Systems," *American Criminal Law Review* 13 (1976):675, offers a historical overview of the entire process.

[35] Brakel, *American Indian Tribal Courts*, criticizes tribal courts for not measuring up to white standards of due process, although his findings (and even his examples) could well have come from the courts of New York City. William J. Lawrence, "Tribal Injustice: The Red Lake Court of Indian Offenses," *North Dakota Law Review* 48 (1968):639–59, finds parallel criticisms of one tribal court. The problem with both studies is that they compare the reality of tribal justice with an idealized view of U.S. justice. James Zion's two studies come to sharply different conclusions and are based on much more careful work with the tribal courts. See Zion, "The Navajo Peacemaker Court: Deference to the Old and Accommodation to the New," *American Indian Law Review* 11 (1985):89–110, and "Harmony Among the People: Torts and Indian Courts," *Montana Law Review* 45 (1984):265–79. Zion establishes convincingly that there is a Native American common law that has survived imposed U.S. law and nearly one hundred years of BIA-imposed courts and that is practiced in the existing tribal courts. D'Arcy McNickle, in a short story surely based on his boyhood experiences on the Flathead Reservation in Montana, shows how the Flatheads used the agent's court to outwit the Indian agent.

both retained Indian law and used that law to structure their actions. Therefore, the record of Indian peoples' attempts to protect their sovereignty defines the legal concept of sovereignty more accurately than does a long line of ambiguous federal cases, and the history of this struggle is a vital part of the U.S. legal tradition.

An inquiry into this record can strengthen contemporary critiques of federal Indian law in at least two ways. First, the doctrine of federal Indian law preserves only a white peoples' interpretation of the legal reality of Indian–white relations. No Indian participated in the lawmaking, and rarely could Indians assist in the preparation of arguments in cases involving Native Americans.[36] Moreover, Indians, like blacks, were frequently the subject of statutory discrimination, denying them even the right to appear at witnesses against white people.[37] Nineteenth-century interpretations of Indian legal status might be dismissed as both illegitimate and illegal. If we accept them, however, as a modern legal and political reality, these historical cases can still be viewed as both Indians and whites understood them. In this way, modern federal Indian law can be seen in the context of both tribal history and the tribal understanding of the meaning of sovereignty.

Second, analysis of the context of nineteenth-century Indian cases shows that they are misunderstood in their modern applications. All first-year law students are taught that the holding of a case cannot be separated from its facts. But what happens when the facts of the case are thoughtlessly or deliberately distorted? The principle of tribal sovereignty at the heart of modern *Crow Dog* doctrine is undermined in federal Indian law because the image of Crow Dog as a murderer who escaped punishment marks the case as a kind of legal atrocity rather than as an important statement of doctrine.

The century of dishonor

The full bloody history of nineteenth-century Indian–white relations, although not recounted here, underscores Rennard Strickland's statement that we are dealing with "genocide at law," a legal history of a million deaths and the violent dispossession of several hundred distinct native

---

[36] Native Americans were accorded citizenship by a 1924 act of Congress. A variety of earlier federal statutes had afforded citizenship to individual Indians who applied for it and met certain standards. One Indian leader's struggle against citizenship is reported in Clinton Rickard, *Fighting Tuscarora* (Syracuse, N.Y.: Syracuse University Press, 1973). In only a few cases at the beginning and end of the nineteenth century did natives actively shape their position, chiefly in cases involving Cherokees, who worked with their lawyers in a very astute way.

[37] Christian Fritz, *Federal Justice: The California Court of Ogden Hoffman, 1851–1891* (Lincoln: University of Nebraska Press, 1991), 211.

peoples from their lands over an area five thousand miles wide.[38] The legal core of this genocide begins with the constitutionally enshrined treaty process, the nation-to-nation compacts that set out binding legal obligations on the United States and on the Indian tribes. Through these treaties, the United States bought land for expansion and settlement and secured peace and political stability on its frontiers. In exchange, the Indian tribes secured the rest of their lands in perpetuity, the legal recognition of their ways of life and their right to continue those traditions, and political stability on their frontiers.[39]

When the United States refused to enforce Indian treaty rights against its own citizens, leaving the tribes open to all forms of violent encroachment, the tribes often tried to enforce the treaties themselves. White history now recounts these events as the "Indian wars." There is no accurate count of them, for there is no common agreement of what constitutes an Indian war, but they number more than a hundred.[40] This process of systematic treaty violation, backed by a ready willingness to engage in military action against Indians, defined for Helen Hunt Jackson the "century of dishonor."[41] She, like many Americans, did not see Indian wars as the result of the tribes' attacks on innocent settlers. Rather, she saw them as defensive actions, engaged in reluctantly by tribes pushed beyond all limits by greedy whites with the tacit approval of the government. U.S. law has yet to redress these legal wrongs. Chief Justice William Rehnquist has dismissed these violations of law as "historical and not legal matters," beyond the scope of modern law.[42]

The U.S. courts never developed a consistent theory for the legal structuring of the Indian wars. International law was never applied, and Congress, with the sole power to declare war under the Constitution, never declared a war against an Indian tribe.[43] After these wars, the tribes were often dealt with by military action that lacked any legal pretext at all; military trials and executions of Indians for murder and other offenses resulting from these

---

[38] Rennard Strickland, "Genocide at Law: An Historic and Contemporary View of the Native American Experience," *Kansas Law Review* 34 (1986):713–55.

[39] The Indian treaties are collected in Charles Kappler, *Indian Laws and Treaties* (Washington: U.S. Government Printing Office, 1904). There is an elaborate law of treaties. A good discussion of the current legal status of treaties is Charles Wilkinson and John Volkman, "Judicial Review of Indian Treaty Abrogation: As Long as Water Flows, or Grass Grows upon the Earth – How Long a Time Is That," *California Law Review* 63 (1972):601–61.

[40] Robert Utley, *The Indian Frontier of the American West, 1846–1890* (Albuquerque: University of New Mexico Press, 1984), is one account of the final fifty years of this process.

[41] Helen Hunt Jackson, *Century of Dishonor* (1881; New York: Harper & Row, 1965).

[42] *United States v. Sioux Nation*, 448 U.S. 371 (1980), at 435. Rehnquist was dissenting in this particular case, although the Chief Justice's distortion of history is often at the heart of court opinions. See, e.g., *Oliphant v. Suquamish Indian Tribe*, 435 U.S. 191 (1978).

[43] This was a major argument for the conclusion in *Caldwell v. State*, 6 Peter 327 (1832), that the Indian tribes are not sovereign. See Chapter 2.

wars occurred. Whole peoples were removed hundreds or thousands of miles from their homelands, held in concentration camps, and deprived of their lands without trial. Legal recognition of the Indian wars did not occur until the 1890s in federal court interpretations of the Indian Depredations Act of 1891. The purpose of this act, passed after the Indian wars were over, was to force the tribes to pay for damages to property, largely the property of whites, resulting from Indian "depredations." Dozens of these cases were decided in federal courts, with the U.S. Supreme Court finally passing on the legal status of an Indian war.[44]

This systematic abrogation of the law in the U.S. treatment of Indians cannot be explained without reference to racism and legal imperialism. Many nineteenth-century whites did not regard agreements with Indians as serious undertakings to be respected because they believed that Indians were not the same kind of human beings and that their political and legal institutions merited no recognition.[45] The laws of the Creek people, for example, were dismissed as "a high pretension of savage sovereignty" in *Caldwell v. State* (1833), an Alabama Supreme Court case that is the most detailed pronouncement of the states' position on Indian rights in the nineteenth century. This language was not an aberration: racist language describing Indians was routine in judicial opinions, BIA reports, and legislative hearings.[46]

Images of the American Indian and the tribal relationship to U.S. society are deeply ingrained in our culture. The Indian symbolically stands for many different things in the United States, many having nothing at all to do with Indians themselves. The conquest of the Indian on the frontier was a powerful rite of passage for whites, perhaps equal in importance to the Civil War. The resistance of the Indian to forced assimilation marked a rejection of white values that were seen as universal, even divine. Indian law reflected this imagery as much as it did economic and political interests, as whites destroyed the tribes because their sovereignty rejected universal Anglo-American cultural values.[47]

---

[44] The Indian Depredations Act is discussed in Chapter 8, the section entitled "The Legal Recognition of Indian Wars."

[45] Yasuhide Kawashima makes this clear in his study of the Puritans and their legal relations with Indians: *Puritan Justice and the Indian: White Man's Law in Massachusetts, 1630–1763* (Middleton, Conn.: Wesleyan University Press, 1986). See also Reginald Horsman, *Race and Manifest Destiny: The Origins of American Racial Anglo-Saxonism* (Cambridge, Mass.: Harvard University Press, 1981); Richard Drinnon, *Facing West: The Metaphysics of Indian Hating and Empire Building* (Minneapolis: University of Minnesota Press, 1980); and Ronald Takaki, *Iron Cages: Race and Culture in 19th Century America* (New York: Knopf, 1979).

[46] Edmund Morgan, *American Slavery, American Freedom: The Ordeal of Colonial Virginia* (New York: Norton, 1975), esp. 316–37.

[47] On the image of the Indian in U.S. culture, see Richard Slotkin, *The Fatal Environment: The Myth of the Frontier in the Age of Industrialization, 1800–1900* (New York: Atheneum, 1985), and Robert Berkhofer, Jr., *The White Man's Indian* (New York: Knopf, 1978).

Of red, black, and yellow: the relationship of U.S. Indian law to the legal oppression of other racial minorities

The doctrines of Indian law have been kept far removed from civil rights law, and the legal struggles of Indian people have involved different cases and distinct legal issues from the legal struggles of other racial minorities. While Indian law is based primarily on tribal status, not on racial status, it is clear that the genocide perpetrated against Indians and the denial of Indian humanity inherent in the "plenary power doctrine" would not have been perpetrated against white people. Late-nineteenth-century attempts to apply the Fourteenth Amendment and extend U.S. citizenship to Indians failed.[48] Ironically, this benefited the tribes because attempts to impose citizenship on Indians, originating with eastern liberal Indian reformers, were inconsistent with the tribes status as nations. Only Justice John Harlan, the "great dissenter" who believed that the Constitution followed the flag, would have applied U.S. citizenship to the Indian tribes and the Fourteenth Amendment to tribal institutions, just as it applied to state institutions.[49]

The same Supreme Court that "buried" the civil rights acts in the 1880s and 1890s also created the plenary power doctrine, allowing the federal government virtually unlimited power in suppressing the rights of tribal Indians, clearly consistent policies. Just as blacks were put at the mercy of state and local authorities, tribal Indians were turned over to BIA bureaucrats, with both races kept from self-determination, their cultures smashed and effective participation in the American nation thwarted. As late as 1879 a U.S. attorney argued that Indians were not even "persons," entitled to a writ of habeas corpus, citing *Dred Scott*, an infamous U.S. Supreme Court case holding that blacks were an inferior class of person, unable ever to be citizens of the United States, for the proposition.[50]

Dred Scott is revealing in another respect, for in it Chief Justice Roger Taney distinguished Indians from blacks doctrinally, the earliest the Court ever attempted to do so. Taney had dealt with the legal status of Indians only once before in his twenty-one years as chief justice. In *United States v. Rogers*, an 1846 case involving a white man claiming Cherokee citizenship

---

[48] R. Alton Lee, "Indian Citizenship and the Fourteenth Amendment," *South Dakota History* 4 (Spring 1974):198–221.

[49] See Harlan's dissent in *Talton v. Mayes*, 163 U.S. 376 (1896). The "Constitution following the flag metaphor" comes from the "insular cases," where Harlan powerfully argued that the Constitution extended to the rights of colonized peoples in Puerto Rico. *Downes v. Bidwell*, 182 U.S. 244 (1901).

[50] This occurred in the case of *United States ex rel. Standing Bear v. Crook*, 25 Fed. Cas. 695 (C.C.D. Neb., 1879), a case discussed in Thomas Henry Tibbles, *The Ponca Chiefs: An Account of the Trial of Standing Bear* (Lincoln: University of Nebraska Press, 1972). *Dred Scott v. Sandford*, 60 U.S. (19 How.) 393 (1857).

(in many nineteenth-century cases, Indian rights were legally defined in cases where no Indian was a party), Taney had simplistically followed John Marshall's "domestic dependent nations" analysis, but had rejected the notion that the Cherokee was a foreign nation, emphasizing the tribes dependent status.[51] In *Dred Scott* Taney ignored this reasoning, distinguishing Indians from blacks (important in his racist argument that blacks could never become citizens while Indians could) by stating that Indians were in law equivalent to foreign nations, and when the government extended citizenship to Indians it did so by its power to naturalize foreigners.[52] Later in the opinion Taney forgot this distinction, referring to blacks as "this unfortunate race," the same phrase he had used to refer to Indians in *Rogers*.[53]

Nor can there be any question that issues of race underlay the Cherokee cases, even though Marshall was careful to keep such issues out of his opinion, focusing instead on the political status of the Cherokee Nation.[54] This distinction, that the Indian tribes were in a unique political relationship with the United States, has survived and is still the fundamental reason why civil rights laws do not apply to Indian tribes: civil rights are personal rights, extending to individuals, not to tribes. Georgia, and southerners generally, were outraged by the interference of northerners in Cherokee affairs, a danger equally likely if northern missionaries or teachers came to work with black people. Georgia also feared the consequences of an egalitarian relationship between blacks and Indians that might promote slave unrest. Finally, the whole concept of state's rights, the right of Georgia to regulate its own affairs, was fundamental to protecting slavery as an institution, and any undermining of that right, by Indians or anyone else, threatened that institution.

In the West, later in the nineteenth century, Chinese and Indians were involved in numerous court cases, but again, the legal doctrines were kept distinct. Illustrative of the nature of these distinctions Federal District Judge Matthew Deady of Oregon simultaneously wrote opinions very sensitive to the rights of Chinese while dismissive of the rights of the Indian tribes. For Deady it seems the distinction was not racial but turned on policy. The Chinese sought the chance to participate in the American nation, to work

[51] *United States v. Rogers*, 4 How. 567, 572 (1846). The significance of this case is discussed in Marvin L. Winitsky, "The Jurisprudence of Roger B. Taney," Ph.D. dissertation, UCLA, 1973, 84–5.

[52] Don H. Fehrenbacher, *The Dred Scott Case: Its Significance in American Law and Politics* (New York: Oxford University Press, 1978).

[53] *Dred Scott v. Sanford*, 60 U.S. (19 How.) 393 (1857), at 426; *United States v. Rogers, 4 How.* 567 (1846), at 572.

[54] Chief Justice John Marshall, a Virginian, clearly kept legal issues surrounding blacks far from legal issues relating to Indians. G. Edward White, *The Marshall Court and Cultural Change, 1815–35* (New York: Macmillan, 1988).

hard and occupy commercial positions in American communities. Indians sought to remain outside of the American nation, openly challenging U.S. authority whenever it intruded on tribal sovereignty. Deady's opinions all undermine tribal sovereignty, promoting a policy of forced assimilation, while at the same time requiring the federal government to respect the civil rights of Chinese. Following Marshall's original distinction that relations with Indian tribes were political and not personal, it was tribal status as much as race that accounts for the distinct Indian policy of the nineteenth century. While issues of race and racism underlie Indian law, these issues were subordinated to a political status, derived from the original nation-to-nation treaty status. The fact that Indians owned so much land forced the United States to recognize their political status as nations, a status at the core of treaty negotiations for the alienation of Indian lands.

Legal history and legal doctrine

The emergence of new fields of legal doctrine characterizes the United States in the nineteenth century: torts, labor law, and commercial law all developed virtually anew in response to social and economic growth. Indian law, however, is uniquely American: no other nation with an indigenous population incorporated them so determinedly through legal means, developing a vast body of new law for the purpose. By and large U.S. Indian law is judge made law. Chief Justice John Marshall's domestic dependent nations framework from the first half of the century structured legal reasoning concerning the place of the tribes in America, informing the opinions that succeeded *Worcester* whether local judges followed Marshall's reasoning or distinguished it. The plenary power doctrine of Justice Samuel Miller, while less original and imaginative than Marshall's, was every bit as judicially created.[55] Both doctrines struck political compromises that both justices believed would allow the law to structure the complex relationship between the United States and the tribes. Local judges – federal, state, and territorial – had to apply these general frameworks, and the continuous judge-made modifications to them, in a variety of situations that was almost unimaginable: the frontier gave rise to all manner of schemes, all manner of human choices.

The social nature of legal doctrine, "black letter law," divides scholars. There is no question that the detailed development of legal doctrine to structure social life, and formalistic styles of judicial reasoning that follows from the development of black letter law accompanied the rapid social change of nineteenth-century industrialization, allowing various groups of land-

---

[55] Nell Jessup Newton, "Federal Power over Indians: Its Source, Scope and Limitations," *Pennsylvania Law Review* 132 (1984):195–288, offers an excellent introduction to the origin of the major doctrines of federal Indian law, focusing on the nature of federal power.

owners, industrialists, and commercial entrepreneurs to build a legal frame-work that would, even if left alone, protect their interests as "neutral" judges applied black letter law to the increasing numbers of cases that came before them.[56] There is no agreement as to the meaning of this expanded doctrine, however. For some the development of legal doctrine was largely indepen-dent of direct political and economic structuring, as judges, acting as legal scientists, struggled to strike appropriate doctrinal balances among com-peting forces, looking for guidance to basic principles of the common law. For others the development of these new legal doctrines was much more explicitly political, representing the interests of the dominant political forces of the day. Still others struggle to define more complex relationships, in-volving the interplay of various social, economic, and political forces, with the law, to a greater or lesser extent, mediating and structuring social development.[57]

The rise of judicial formalism permitted judges to deny the value choices that underlay difficult, even inhuman, decision. A. E. Kier Nash argues that southern judges came to rely on legal formalism, the idea that reference to black letter doctrine was a neutral inquiry, as slave law became more complex and more repressive, denying the basic immorality of the whole system of law they enforced.[58] We know less about the motivations of western judges in federal Indian law decisions. Many, for example Matthew Deady of Port-land, Oregon, and Isaac Parker of Fort Smith, Arkansas, wrote a number of major opinions in federal Indian law, relying on legal formalism, borrowing widely from different areas of common law to find doctrinally based "so-lutions" to legal problems brought to their courts. Of other judges, even well-known ones, we know nothing beyond the text of the opinions them-selves, usually competently drafted with routine citations to a few cases, masking obvious policy choices behind legal formality.

The plan of the study

There were at least four distinct legal models for the structuring of Indian–white relations in the nineteenth century. Each is the subject of one part of

[56] David Sugarman, "A Hatred of Disorder: Legal Science, Liberalism and Imperialism," in Peter Fitzpatrick (ed.), *Dangerous Supplements: Resistance and Renewal in Jurisprudence* (Dur-ham, N.C.: Duke University Press, 1991).

[57] Mark Kelman, *A Guide to Critical Legal Studies* (Cambridge, Mass.: Harvard University Press, 1987). See esp. chap. 7, "Visions of History," for an introduction to this debate. See also the special issue of *Wisconsin Law Review* 4 (1985), "Legal Histories from Below," for three approaches to the new legal history.

[58] A. E. Kier Nash, "Reason of Slavery: Understanding the Judicial Role in the Peculiar Institution," *Vanderbilt Law Review* 32 (1979):7–218, and idem, "Fairness and Formalism in the State Supreme Courts of the Old South," *Virginia Law Review* 56 (1970):64–100.

this study, with the focus on a particular Indian people and the legal structuring of their incorporation into the United States, considering both tribal law and U.S. law. Federal Indian law begins with the Cherokee cases. Instead of focusing on *Worcester v. Georgia* – John Marshall's classic, but so ambiguous as to be almost meaningless, statement of the status of American Indians under the laws of the United States – I look first at a case that represents a great loss. Corn Tassel was tried and sentenced under Georgia law for a crime committed on Cherokee lands. His appeal to the U.S. Supreme Court led to a hasty hanging and arrogant state defiance of federal law and the right of federal authorities to regulate Indian affairs. Georgia's actions, and the state court decisions that legalized them, survived as precedent in state cases until 1931, when a Wisconsin decision, *State v. Rufus*, abandoned the doctrine that states, as an attribute of state sovereignty, have full jurisdiction over Indians within their boundaries.

The second model of Indian–white relations, and the greatest U.S. experiment with tribal sovereignty, was the federal recognition of the Indian nations as "domestic nations," incorporating them within the scheme of constitutional federalism. In the Indian Territory – modern-day Oklahoma – the Cherokees, Creeks, Choctaws, Chickasaws, and Seminoles had constituted themselves as Indian nations in the 1850s and built sophisticated political systems modeled, at least in form, after the United States. The United States, through treaties, guaranteed the sovereignty of these nations, and the legal status of these Indian nations was repeatedly recognized by the federal government. There, with judges, sheriffs, courts, appellate courts, juries, and jails, Indians administered their own legal systems virtually free of federal authority. This situation continued until 1898, when the last tribal murder trials and executions were carried out – legal actions upheld by the U.S. Supreme Court in *Talton v. Mayes* (1896). Although the major cases are primarily Cherokee, the legal doctrine covers equally all of the Five Civilized Tribes. The focus here is on the meaning of sovereignty in the Creek Nation and in Creek law through the *Talton* decision and the termination of the nation in 1898. The legal history of the Creeks, struggling to build a nation that honored the legal traditions of the people but also accommodated a changing Creek society and an encroaching American nation, shows both the great capacity of the Indian people to adjust to change and the limitations of tribal sovereignty within the United States.

The third model followed from Crow Dog's case. Congress and the BIA rejected the application of tribal sovereignty to reservation Indians, imposing instead a policy of forced assimilation, backed by the extension of federal law to tribal Indians for serious offenses under the Major Crimes Act, and a repressive system of administrative justice for lesser offenses. A full range of federal cases gave effect to this policy of forced assimilation, giving rise to a new doctrine in federal Indian law, the plenary power doctrine holding that federal power over tribal Indians was essentially unlimited. *Crow Dog* was still good law, however, and the *Crow Dog* doctrine that tribes had sovereign right to their own law – unless limited by federal authority – survived. Still, the plenary power doctrine, the legal foundation of a national policy of forced assimilation of the tribes, represents the deliberate use of U.S. law to destroy the Indian tribes.

Alaska was left outside the preceding legal models because of a district court decision, *United States v. Seveloff,* rendered by Judge Matthew Deady of Portland, Oregon, in 1872 and clarified in four successive opinions. Deady denied that the federal Indian law operant in the rest of the United States applied to Alaska. In giving Alaskan Indians the same legal status as white people, these decisions at the same time accorded no recognition of any form of tribal legal or political institutions, a parallel of the legal models of Canada and Australia. Ironically, this was the legal model that Georgia wanted to apply to the Cherokees in the 1820s. The federal government, by the 1870s, had come full circle on its own legal policy toward American Indians and was trying to divest the tribes of their legal sovereignty, even turning tribal Indians over to states for criminal trial and punishment. Hence, the tribal sovereignty of Alaskan natives was not recognized because that recognition had come to pose so many legal problems in the rest of the United States. The fourth model I will discuss is the complete extension of U.S. law in the 1880s and 1890s to the Tlingit, the dominant tribe in the southeastern Alaskan panhandle. These were the first American Indians put under the full authority of state or territorial law by the federal government in a direct attempt to extinguish tribal sovereignty and force assimilation.[59]

For each of these studies, although the full range of legal issues structuring Indians will be considered, the focus, for reasons given, is on the criminal law. The tribes' right to their own law as an attribute of tribal sovereignty, the core of *Crow Dog* doctrine, specifically concerned criminal law. The tribes' right to structure their own social orders required the right to their own criminal law. While Indian traditional landholding laws were characterized as "communistic" by whites, tribal criminal law was called "barbaric," and tribal sovereignty in that area was subject to the worst attack, being called "a high pretension of savage sovereignty." Moreover, the U.S. criminal law that was imposed on the tribes has played, both historically and at the present, a disproportionate role in shaping Indian tribes in the U.S. image.

---

[59] The Pueblo's of New Mexico were put under territorial authority in *United States v. Joseph*, 94 U.S. 614 (1876), but on the theory that they already were assimilated, having held Mexican citizenship. Many other states had taken jurisdiction over Indian tribes through federal acquiescence.

The criminalization of American Indians and other native peoples has largely been ignored by scholars. American Indians, along with Canadian Indians, New Zealand Maories, and Australian Aborigines share the awful distinction of being the most arrested and jailed peoples in the world. American Indians are arrested at a rate that approaches 40 per 100 of population per year, compared to about 5 per 100 for black Americans and just over 1 per 100 for white Americans.[60]

This study is more thematic than temporal, with the core legal process of the imposition of federal law on the Indian tribes occurring in the late nineteenth century. Because of this thematic focus, rigid time frames are not adhered to, and a number of times doctrinal evolution is followed into the early twentieth century. Study of the development and change of the doctrine of Indian law between *Worcester* and *Crow Dog*, the period between 1832 and 1883, dominates one chapter. Because U.S. Indian law is so deeply rooted in history, most of the doctrinal discussions have relevance in current U.S., now largely federal, Indian law. While occasionally these linkages are pointed out, generally they are not because such references cannot be made without extensive citation to complex bodies of doctrine. This study, although it considers the evolution of legal doctrine, is not primarily a history of legal doctrine. Rather, it is a social history of Indian law.

With this focus on the legal structuring of violence throughout these parallel studies, my concern is the incorporation of the tribes under U.S. law in each of these contexts, the evolution of U.S. law and legal doctrine, the changing law of the Indian tribes, and the legal structuring of the meeting of these two systems of law. Indian law played a vital role in the structuring of U.S. law. Nineteenth-century Indian tribes had a distinct legal culture, which, though it changed continually, was distinct from non-Indian legal culture and deeply held in the hearts of Indian people – so deeply held, in fact, that this legal culture was retained in the face of U.S. legal imperialism, creating a foundation for a pluralist legal system in the United States today.

---

[60] Arrest rates on Indian reservations, while there are enormous variations, include some statistics that are among the highest in the world, exceeding rates of 100%. Sidney L. Harring, "Native American Crime in the United States," in Laurence French (ed.), *Indians and Criminal Justice* (Montclair, N.J.: Allenheld-Osmun, 1983), 93–108.

2

Corn Tassel

State and federal conflict over tribal sovereignty

The foundational case in federal Indian law is *Worcester v. Georgia* (1832). Known collectively with *Cherokee Nation v. Georgia* (1831) as one of the "Cherokee cases," it has been the subject of much analysis, particularly for its formulation of tribal sovereignty.[1] The case precipitated a famous constitutional crisis when President Andrew Jackson remarked, "John Marshall has made his decision, now let him enforce it," and refused to use federal power to protect Cherokee rights against Georgians.[2] This conflict itself illustrates the core contradiction in Indian law cases during most of the nineteenth century: federal Indian law evolved in a legal battle with the states over federal control of Indians and Indian lands, with tribal sovereignty or the legal rights of native people often not even of secondary concern. Hence, Chief Justice John Marshall's famous pronouncements of Indian rights were virtually meaningless to the tribes.

All modern legal discussions of the Cherokee cases omit consideration of the first such case, *Corn Tassel*, which, although known to legal scholars because it establishes the context for the more famous cases, is never seen as having doctrinal meaning.[3] In addition to demonstrating the wholesale federal abandonment of treaty obligations toward the Cherokee, the case represents a cowardly cession of both federal power and tribal sovereignty

---

[1] The best summaries of the context of these cases are Joseph Burke, "The Cherokee Cases: A Study in Law, Politics, and Morality," *Stanford Law Review* 21 (1969):500, and G. Edward White, *The Marshall Court and Cultural Change, 1815–35*, (New York: Macmillan, 1988), especially chap. 10, "Natural Law and Facial Minorities: The Court's Response to Slaves and Indians." The best discussion of their current legal meaning is Charles Wilkinson, *American Indians, Time, and the Law* (New Haven, Conn.: Yale University Press, 1987), 14–26. See also Robert Williams, *The American Indian in Western Legal Thought*. (Oxford: Oxford University Press, 1990), esp. chap. 7, "The Colonists' War for America," which presents a compelling argument that the real foundational cases in federal Indian law are *Fletcher v. Peck* and *Johnson v. McIntosh*.

[2] There is some question whether Jackson actually made this statement, but his actions clearly indicate his intention. See F. Cohen, *Handbook of Federal Indian Law* (Charlottesville, Va.: Michie, 1982), 3d ed., 83, 173.

[3] *State v. George Tassels*, 1 Dud. 229 (1830). As was common practice in many Indian criminal cases, Corn Tassel's name was put in an English form.

to the states. This action dominates early- to mid-nineteenth-century Indian law.[4]

Corn Tassel's case

All of the Cherokee cases arose from the same tragic violation of tribal rights. The impact of the American Revolution, extensive trading, and white settlement had substantially reduced the Cherokees' traditional homelands in Georgia, Tennessee, North Carolina, and Alabama and had fundamentally changed the basis of Cherokee society.[5] The tribe adapted to white ways, but within a context that protected Cherokee values, creating a model of multiculturalism and legal pluralism that could have transformed nineteenth-century U.S. society. Many became successful farmers or merchants and converted to Christianity. The tribe changed its method of government in favor of a republican form featuring elected chiefs and elected representatives to a tribal council, which adopted a code of laws based largely on U.S. law.[6] The tribe published a newspaper, the *Cherokee Phoenix*, that communicated Cherokee views throughout the country.[7]

Although a number of Americans, especially in the North, supported the Cherokee model of adapting to U.S. society, there was a great deal of trouble with local whites and with the state of Georgia, mainly because the Cherokees kept from white ownership and state control millions of acres of prime farmland and forests.[8] After the revolutionary war there was an endless series

[4] The policy of Indian removal was not limited to southern Indians but was widely enforced through 1861 as new states were admitted to the union. Often as a precursor of statehood, Indians would remove themselves beyond the reach of white settlement. See Grant Forman, *Indian Removal* (Norman: University of Oklahoma Press, 1932).

[5] Betty Anderson Smith, "Distribution of Eighteenth-Century Cherokee Settlements," and William C. Sturtevant, "The Cherokee Frontiers, the French Revolution and William Augustus Bowles," both in Duane H. King (ed.), *The Cherokee Indian Nation* (Knoxville: University of Tennessee Press, 1979).

[6] V. Richard Persico, Jr., "Early Nineteenth-Century Political Organization," and Theda Perdue, "Cherokee Planters: The Development of Plantation Slavery Before Removal," in King (ed.), *Cherokee Indian Nation;* Grace S. Woodward, *The Cherokees* (Norman: University of Oklahoma Press, 1963); John Eaton, *The Life of John Ross* (Chicago: n.p., 1921); William G. McLoughlin, *Cherokees and Missionaries, 1789–1839* (New Haven, Conn.: Yale University Press, 1984); idem, *Cherokee Renascence, 1789–1833* (Princeton, N.J.: Princeton University Press, 1986); and Rennard Strickland, *Fire and Spirits: Cherokee Law from Clan to Court* (Norman: University of Oklahoma Press, 1975), esp. chaps. 2, 3, 4, and 5.

[7] Theda Perdue, *Cherokee Editor, The Writings of Elias Boudinot* (Knoxville: University of Tennessee Press, 1983).

[8] The Georgia position is best stated in a two-volume defense of the state's actions by Governor Wilson P. Lumpkin, *The Removal of the Cherokee from Georgia*, (Wormsloe, GA: n.p., 1907). Ulrich B. Phillips, "Georgia and States Rights," *Annual Report of the American Historical Association* 2 (1902): 75–81, also presents the Georgia position. Support from the North was organized primarily by missionaries. See McLoughlin, *Cherokees and Missionaries*, chaps. 10,

of encroachments on the lands of the Cherokees, neighboring Creeks, and all other southern tribes. As U.S. population pressure increased, so did killings on both sides.[9] The discovery of gold in North Georgia in 1829, together with national political changes in the election of 1828, permanently altered an already fragile balance of power. Georgia acted to incorporate the Cherokee lands, and late in 1829 the state legislature extended full state jurisdiction, both civil and criminal, to the Cherokee Nation. Further state laws prohibited any Cherokee from acting as a tribal judge or meeting as a member of the national council, effectively outlawing Cherokee self-government.[10] To Georgians, the very existence of a distinct tribal community within the state's boundaries was a threat to the sovereignty that they believed to be a state's natural right following from political dominion.

The Cherokees were not caught off guard. In 1827, they had adopted a new constitution proclaiming themselves to be the Cherokee Nation in direct defiance of Georgia's imperialism.[11] The Cherokee National Council, faced with the threat of individual land sales that would undermine the collective will, passed a law carrying the death sentence for any member of the tribe who sold land to whites.[12] The Cherokees also sought the legal protection of the United States and in 1830 set out to retain the best legal talent in the country to defend their interests. Chief John Ross hired the Georgia firm of Underwood and Harris and also the Baltimore firm of William Wirt, former attorney general and perhaps the country's greatest expert in Indian law.[13] Since President Jackson had cut off the Cherokees' annuity as a part of the pressure to move them West – and to impede their access to the federal courts – the fees had to be paid by individual Cherokees.

Wirt, who as attorney general had issued two opinions holding that the tribes had an independent national status and who had urged the Cherokees to test their rights in the U.S. Supreme Court, moved quickly to file a test case.[14] The first action at hand was that of Corn Tassel, variously called in court documents George Tassels and George Corn Tassel. We know little

11, and 12. A series of essays written by Jeremiah Evarts and published as the "William Penn Essays" in the *National Intelligencer* were a powerful defense of Cherokee rights. See Francis Paul Prucha, *Cherokee Removal: The William Penn Essays and Other Writings by Jeremiah Evarts* (Knoxville: University of Tennessee Press, 1981). See also Eaton, *Life of John Ross*, chap. 4.

[9] Kenneth Penn Davis, "Chaos in the Indian Country: The Cherokee Nation, 1828–1835," in King (ed.), *Cherokee Indian Nation*.

[10] B. J. Ramage, "Georgia and the Cherokees," *American Historical Magazine* 199 (July 1902):202–4. These were aggressive laws designed to force the Cherokees to move westward by making any kind of continued tribal existence impossible.

[11] McLoughlin, *Cherokee Renascence*, 388–410.

[12] Strickland, *Fire and Spirits*, 76–8.

[13] Charles Warren, *The Supreme Court in United States History* (Boston: Little, Brown, 1923), 2:191–2; Woodward, *Cherokees*, 162–7.

[14] 1 Op. Att'y Gen. 465 (1821); 2 Op. Att'y Gen. 110 (1828).

about Corn Tassel and his crime.[15] He was accused of having "waylaid and killed an Indian named Sanders, Talking Rockford" in what is now Pickens County, then in the Cherokee Nation. Although this intratribal crime was under Cherokee jurisdiction, Tassel was tried in the September 1830 term of the Hall County Superior Court before Judge Charles Dougherty, found guilty, and sentenced to hang.[16]

Attorney Underwood appealed Corn Tassel's case to the superior court. In a hasty opinion designed to preempt federal action, the panel of judges produced a ten-page decision that was to be cited often by state courts during the mid-nineteenth century.[17] *State v. George Tassels* begins an important chain of case law that predated *Worcester* and came to the opposite conclusion: it held that states have full criminal and civil jurisdiction over the Indian tribes within their boundaries as a matter of state sovereignty.

The court began by noting the "excitement" of the Indians and their advocates and by claiming that the Tassel case was "interposed" – put forward by northern reformers – because of its political significance, an observation that denied Cherokee integrity in defending tribal rights. The court went on to note that many different types of relations with Indians had existed in U.S. history and that many changes of public opinion and public policy had taken place. Beginning its survey with the British occupation of North America, the court found that exclusive land title was held by the British by right of discovery but that the Indians retained some rights with a legal, as well as just, claim to possession. The rights of Indians to complete sovereignty as independent nations, however, was "necessarily impaired," and their power to dispose of their lands however they wish denied. The 1807 case of *Fletcher v. Peck* was cited for the proposition that

[15] 30 U.S. (5 Pet.) 1831; 31 U.S. (6 Pet.) 1832. I have had both the National Archives and the Georgia State Archives searched for records of Corn Tassel's case, and I have personally searched the extensive primary collections on the Cherokees at the Newberry Library as well as all extant Georgia newspapers for that period. Corn Tassel's unreported federal case survives only as a one-page writ of error by John Marshall, a copy of which I obtained from the Georgia State Archives, Atlanta. Jill Norgren and Petra Shattuck, "Limits of Legal Action: The Cherokee Cases," *American Indian Culture and Research Journal* 14 (1978): 14–25, contains the most detailed analysis of the legal structuring of the case. McLoughlin, *Cherokee Renascence,* chap. 21, also discusses the case.

[16] Belle K. Abbot, *The Cherokee Indians of North Georgia* (University, Ala.: Confederate Publishing, n.d.), 42. Abbot provides the text of a one-paragraph newspaper article published in the 1880s. Although it contains no documentation, it is the most detailed account of Corn Tassel's crime and trial. A copy of Abbot is held in the Pamphlet Collections of the Wisconsin State Historical Society, Madison.

[17] *State v. George Tassels,* 1 Dud. 229 (1830). The dicta referring to the matter as a test case is found at 230. As far as I can determine, no analysis of U.S. Indian law has ever cited this case to stand for doctrine. Considering that it was more than a hundred years before the states finally abandoned the doctrine of *State v. Tassels,* that states had criminal jurisdiction over Indians residing on Indian lands within their borders, this neglect leaves out an important chain of analysis in the history of U.S. Indian law.

recognition of a state's title to land was not inconsistent with the recognition that Indian rights had not yet been extinguished, one step toward the argument that state jurisdiction was not inconsistent with Indian rights.[18]

Having established state sovereignty over the land of the Cherokees, the court turned to the question of federalism. It noted that although Congress had the power to declare war, no president had ever asked Congress to do so and no member of Congress had ever complained that the president had usurped the power of Congress by declaring an Indian war.[19] By this logic, the Indian tribes were not sovereign nations. This point was reinforced by noting that the state of New York had vested itself with criminal jurisdiction over Indians in 1822 and faced no federal remonstrance, although the Seneca objected bitterly and eloquently. The court's final argument about political sovereignty ended with the issue that had begun the whole matter: control over land. It was impossible for a sovereign nation to exist that could not hold land in fee simple but only by right of occupancy.

> The court then offered a racist and distorted history of pre-existing treaty law: The habits, manners, imbecile intellect of the Indians, opposed impracticable barriers to either of these modes of procedure. They could neither sink into the common mass of their discoverers or conquerers, or be governed as a separate, dependent people. They were judged incapable of complying with the obligations which the laws of civilized society imposed, or of being subjected to any code of laws which therefore required that they should be sanctioned by any Christian community. Humanity therefore required that they should be protected in their existence, under these customs and usages, as long as they chose to adhere to them.[20]

The court, as expected, upheld the Georgia law extending criminal jurisdiction over the Cherokees and thus the death sentence against Corn Tassel.

This decision had been expected by Wirt, who immediately appealed to Chief Justice John Marshall for a writ of error. Marshall granted the writ on December 12, 1830, and ordered the state to appear before the Supreme Court in Washington on "the second Monday in January next ... to show cause if any there be why judgement rendered against the said George as in the said writ of error mentioned should not be corrected."[21] The Georgia legislature was called into special session on December 22 and voted to defy

---

[18] 5 Cranch. 87 (1807) at 232.

[19] Ibid., 234.

[20] Ibid., 236.

[21] United States of America to the State of Georgia, December 12, 1830. This language is quoted from a photocopy of the writ, obtained from the Georgia Department of Archives and History, "File II – Names, Marshall, John." The text of the writ, together with an account of the proceedings and Georgia's defiance, is found in the *Niles Daily Register*, January 8, 1831, 338 and 339.

the writ and proceed with the execution. Corn Tassel was hung on December 24. He rode up to the gallows seated on his coffin, mounted the scaffold without assistance, and spoke calmly to the crowd below, which included about five hundred Cherokees, whose presence had necessitated calling out the Georgia guard in anticipation of conflict. Corn Tassel's body was turned over to his people, and he was buried nearby.[22]

Three days later, on December 27, Wirt served on the state of Georgia a subpoena for a second test case, that of *Cherokee Nation v. Georgia.*[23] This was a bold jurisdictional move: Wirt filed the original action in the U.S. Supreme Court as a lawsuit between a foreign nation and a state. He asked for an injunction "to restrain the State of Georgia, the Governor, Attorney General, Judges, justices of the peace, sheriffs, deputy sheriffs, constables and others, officers, agents, and servants of that State, from executing and enforcing the laws of Georgia, or any of these laws, or serving process, or doing anything toward the execution or enforcement of those laws within the Cherokee territory."[24] *Cherokee Nation*, then, was filed explicitly to vindicate the legal right of Corn Tassel to a trial by his own people.

This was too bold a move for Chief Justice John Marshall. With the same caution he had used in another challenge to the jurisdiction of the Court, *Marbury v. Madison* (1803), Marshall chose a conservative approach that undermined tribal sovereignty. The Court lacked a clear analysis of the position of the Cherokees within the United States and offered three interpretations that represented the possible options.[25] Marshall, together with Justice John McLean, took a middle position that is seen today as the holding of the case. He found that the Cherokee Nation was not a foreign nation but a domestic nation, therefore the Court lacked original jurisdiction.[26]

---

[22] See Warren, *The Supreme Court in United States History*, 2:192–4, n. 39. "Indian Affairs," *Annual Register* 5 (1830–1): 27–9. The only details of the hanging are in Abbot, *Cherokee Indians of North Georgia*, 42. See also the *Richmond Enquirer* (Virginia), January 8, 1831.

[23] Woodward, *Cherokees*, 165.

[24] Ibid., 165–6. The full record of documents and arguments of the case was published in Richard Peters, *The Case of the Cherokee Nation Against the State of Georgia* (Philadelphia: n.p., 1831). The major scholarly analyses of the context of the case are J. Burke, "The Cherokee Cases: A Study in Law, Politics, and Morality," *Stanford Law Review* 21 (1969): 500–31, and G. Edward White, *The Marshall Court and Cultural Change, 1815–35* (New York: Macmillan, 1988), chap. 10, "Natural Law and Racial Minorities: The Court's Response to Slaves and Indians."

[25] In *Marbury*, Marshall held that Marbury was entitled to his commission as a federal magistrate but found that the Court had no power to give it to him. Thus, when faced with a difficult political case where the Court ran a risk of being defied, Marshall developed the method of boldly laying the foundation for an important constitutional principle but then failing to grant a real remedy that he knew would be resisted. In a sense, this strategy gave a victory to both sides, but it also avoided a direct crisis. On the context of *Marbury v. Madison*, see Charles Warren, *The Supreme Court in United States History* (Boston: Little, Brown, 1926), vol. 1.

[26] *Cherokee Nation v. Georgia*, 30 U.S. (5 Pet) 1 (1831), at 16–20.

This was a clear victory for Georgia and those states whose support for Georgia had provoked a nullification crisis that threatened the Court as well as the whole federal system. Justices Smith Thompson and Joseph Story believed that the Cherokees were a foreign nation.[27] The two remaining justices, Henry Baldwin and William Johnson, believed that the Cherokees were a conquered people with no status as a nation at all, either foreign or domestic.[28]

In dicta, however, Marshall went on to lay the foundation for his future decisions on the rights of Indians. His views are typical of his policy of using the court to promote federal power nationally and his acute sense of political compromise.[29] Recognizing that the legal status of the Indian tribes had to be developed beyond *Johnson v. McIntosh,* he defined the Indian tribes as "domestic dependent nations" and described their relationship to the United States as one that "resembles that of a ward to his guardian."[30] This paternalistic statement of Indian dependency defined the authority of the federal government in Indian affairs, the purpose Marshall intended, but left the Indian nations with an undermined and ambiguous legal status. Marshall's views represented the legal analysis of only two members of a divided Court and left no clear guidance for lower courts on the legal status of Indian tribes under U.S. law. Rather, it was a compromise between the positions of Story, Wirt, Adams, and northern Whigs who, for reasons based on both natural law and resistance to the power of southern slaveholders, wanted to accord substantial sovereignty rights to Indian nations, and the states-rights, antisovereignty position of Jackson and southern Democrats.[31] Marshall probably believed that this compromise represented a framework within which Indians could live, but without a strong show of federal power to enforce U.S. laws protecting tribal sovereignty, the strong antisovereignty position of Georgia represented a great threat to Indians at the local level, far dispersed from centers of federal power. The threat was soon realized in a vicious attack by Alabama and Georgia on the Creeks and Cherokees following the Cherokee cases.

Modern scholars of Indian law look at *Cherokee Nation* as the beginning

---

[27] Ibid., 50–80.

[28] Ibid. Justice Baldwin's opinion is at 31–50, Justice Johnson's at 21–31. Johnson asked rhetorically, "Must every petty kraal of Indians designating themselves a tribe or nation, and having a few hundred acres of land to hunt on exclusively, be recognized as a state?" He then compared the Cherokees to European sovereign states and concluded that he had "strong reasons for doubting the applicability of the epithet 'state' to a people so low on the grade of organized society as our Indian tribes." The three-way split on the Court occurred because Justice Gabriel Duval took no part in any of the Cherokee decisions.

[29] There is a large body of analysis of the jurisprudence of John Marshall, "the great federalist." For an introduction, see White, *The Marshall Court and Cultural Change.*

[30] Ibid., 17.

[31] Ibid., chap. 10.

of a long chain of federal efforts to assert power over Indians. Marshall's opinion was a feeble gesture compared with Georgia's dramatic assertion of state power when it hung Corn Tassel. There was no federal protection of Cherokee rights because the Court was divided and the executive did not act. Furthermore, by holding that the Cherokees were not a foreign nation and by ruling against them on jurisdictional grounds, the Court impaired the tribes' legal access to the protection of the highest federal tribunal. Georgia, on the other hand, following the principles stated in *State v. Tassels*, acted decisively and with great force. There can be no clearer symbol of where the political power over the Cherokees lay than the brave image of Corn Tassel ignobly hung by the state of Georgia in bold defiance of the federal law.

This pattern of federal cession of authority over Indian tribes continued even more dramatically in *Worcester v. Georgia*, the third of the Cherokee cases.[32] The laws that Georgia had extended to the Cherokee Nation were more than simply the general laws governing the rest of the people of Georgia. Through the passage of special laws aimed only at the Cherokee, there was a direct intent to destroy the political, economic, and social infrastructure of the nation. For example, meetings of the tribal council were forbidden, and any Cherokee who acted as a judge in tribal courts was to be punished as a criminal. Further, to prevent northern missionaries from stirring up dissent against state authority, no non-Indian could enter Cherokee lands without a license issued by the state. Those already on Cherokee lands were obliged to take an oath of allegiance to the state of Georgia.[33]

Eleven missionaries arrested under this last law were tried in the Superior Court of Gwinnett County and sentenced to four years at hard labor in the Georgia penitentiary. Offered pardon and release if they swore the oath of allegiance and left Cherokee country, nine did so. The Reverend Samuel Worcester and Elizur Butler refused and went to prison.[34] Attorney Wirt appealed to the U.S. Supreme Court for a writ of error on October 27, 1831. For the third time in a year, the state of Georgia refused to recognize the authority of federal law and took no part in the proceedings on the ground that the Supreme Court had no jurisdiction.[35]

Marshall responded to Georgia's challenge to federal authority over the Indian nations. Using the Constitution, the history of Indian treaties, and international law as a foundation, he found that the Cherokees were a domestic dependent nation constituting a distinct community and occupying

---

[32] 31 U.S. (6 Pet.) 515 (1832).
[33] Woodward, *Cherokees*, 158–9.
[34] Moulton, *John Ross*, 45–6. For a biography of Worcester, see Althea Bass, *Cherokee Messenger* (Norman: University of Oklahoma Press, 1936), esp. 115–60.
[35] Warren, *The Supreme Court in United States History*, 1:213–15.

their own territory with primary responsibility for their own affairs. But, Marshall qualified, they were not fully independent as a nation, for they were under the protection of the United States in a complex way.[36] The federal government, under both its powers in foreign affairs and its power to regulate trade with the Indian tribes, had exclusive authority in Indian affairs. Cherokee lands were entirely outside of the political control of the state of Georgia. This holding was an important victory for the Cherokees: the laws of Georgia had no force in Cherokee country, and the convictions of Worcester and Butler were reversed and annulled.[37]

Georgia refused to release the missionaries and openly defied the court, provoking what was perhaps the most serious constitutional crisis prior to the *Dred Scott* decision. The Jackson administration refused to enforce the Supreme Court's order against the state, and the Cherokees were defeated. The two missionaries abandoned the Cherokee cause, took the oath of allegiance to the state, and were pardoned by Governor Lumpkin on January 10, 1833, after a year and a half in prison.[38] *Worcester* and *Cherokee Nation,* although foundational in current U.S. Indian law, signaled defeat for the Indian tribes and victory for those who sought to enforce state laws on Indian lands and deny any form of legal recognition to the Indian nations.[39]

Worcester cannot be understood apart from *Cherokee Nation.* Although it did not produce a 2–2–2 split of the justices (the two justices who believed the Cherokees a foreign nation and the two who believed them a domestic nation agreed that Georgia lacked authority over them, producing a 4–2 decision), *Worcester* turned on a much narrower issue. Georgia had sought to criminalize under state law the mere presence without permit of a missionary – who also happened to be the local postmaster, a federal appointment. Under the Constitution, a federal official cannot be required to hold a state permit. Georgia's egregious conduct in the face of constitutionally mandated federal prerogatives underlay the final holding. The impact of *Worcester,* like *Cherokee Nation,* not only was very limited, but also left the

---

[36] 31 U.S. (6 Pet.) 515 (1832), at 559–60.

[37] Ibid., 560–2. Justice Baldwin, who in *Cherokee Nation* had thought the Cherokees a conquered people with no sovereign status at all, still thought so and believed that the Supreme Court lacked jurisdiction in the case.

[38] Warren, *The Supreme Court in United States History,* 1:215–19, n. 63; Bass, *Cherokee Messenger,* 157–9 n. 46.

[39] *Worcester v. Georgia,* 31 U.S. 515 (1832), like *Crow Dog,* both expands the rights of tribes and narrows them at the same time. Although *Worcester* attributes a kind of sovereignty to Indian tribes, it also clearly defines the tribes as within the domain of federal, not state, law and in a dependent relationship to the federal government (559–60). Thus, the Cherokee cases on the whole are clearly rooted in a broad notion of tribal sovereignty, but they are also the origin of the plenary power doctrine that later permitted Congress unilaterally to terminate many tribal rights. See Nell Jessup Newton, "Federal Power over Indians: Its Sources, Scope, and Limitations," *University of Pennsylvania Law Review,* 132 (1984):199.

Cherokees in such a weak position in the South that many of them "consented" to removal to the Indian Territory. *Worcester*, therefore, was a weak and ambiguous precedent as a tribal sovereignty case. Language that is read strongly in the late twentieth century was not understood so clearly in the early nineteenth.

State v. George Tassels, however, was widely cited in state cases throughout the nineteenth century for the principle that statehood automatically conferred full jurisdiction over Indian tribes – the opposite of the holding in *Worcester*. Most states with substantial Indian populations, when faced with the question of criminal jurisdiction over those tribes, held that they had such jurisdiction and that it was sound public policy that they exercise it.[40] The analysis that follows will outline this pattern of state jurisdiction through the major cases. It must be remembered, however, that the majority of American Indian criminal cases, like Corn Tassel's trial, are unreported. During the nineteenth century, thousands of Indians were hailed into local courts, tried, and sentenced to prison or hung. Were it not for his famous and futile appeal, financed by his tribe, which had previously hired one of the best lawyers in the country to defend tribal interests, Corn Tassel would have hung without legal notice. With great local prejudice, little money, and few lawyers willing to make jurisdictional appeals, most Indians served their state sentences.[41] The reported cases provide only the barest outline of this injustice.

State criminal jurisdiction over Indians

The nineteenth-century dispute between the federal government and the states over jurisdiction of the Indian nations was fought in two distinct stages. The first involved the states that were heavily settled by whites at the time of the Cherokee cases. Within this group the states that were among the

---

[40] As nearly as I can determine with a state-by-state analysis of Indian criminal cases, all of the states east of the Mississippi with substantial Indian populations claimed jurisdiction over the tribes within their boundaries, except Minnesota. This method cannot tell the full extent of state jurisdiction over Indians because they often did not have access to courts in which to raise jurisdictional issues. Thus, if a state was silent on the matter of jurisdiction over Indians, in the absence of cases we cannot know whether this means the state claimed or did not claim jurisdiction over Indians within its boundaries.

[41] Chief Justice Cuthbert Pound of the New York State Court of Appeals admitted as much in "Nationals Without a Nation: The New York State Tribal Indians," *Columbia Law Review* 22 (1924):98–9. The relatively small number of cases that survive reflect the poor quality of criminal justice in the United States of the nineteenth century. Criminal defendants had no right to defense counsel, and it seems clear that most Indians hailed into state criminal courts had no means to raise any jurisdictional defense at all. It might be noted here that Corn Tassel did not speak English, and there is no record that he was represented by counsel. Had his case not been put forth on appeal as a test, his death would have gone completely unnoted.

original thirteen colonies presented special legal issues because they had a history of relations with the tribes before they were a part of the United States, that is, preceding any federal relations with the tribes. The remaining states of the South and old Northwest often claimed some authority over the tribes descended from the rights of the original colonies but also relied on simple pragmatism or natural law. States further west were created in a context of more recognition of federal authority and in (or after) the Civil War era when federal hegemony over both the states and the tribes was established. Still, even these states made arguments defending state sovereignty over the tribes.

While these jurisdictional disputes often turned on criminal jurisdiction, there can be no question that the real issue was the control of tribal lands. The ownership of the western lands had been a difficult issue at the Constitutional Convention, and it seems likely that the dearth of constitutional references to the Indian tribes was precisely because the status of the Indian tribes was inextricably intertwined with the vast areas of land that they occupied.[42] As part of the constitutional compromise the federal government gained ownership of the western lands.[43] This put federal land title in conflict with huge syndicates of land speculators that owned titles derived from both Indian nations and the states.[44] The first of the "Indian law" cases that reached the U.S. Supreme Court were brought by these syndicates of speculators. Thus, the first important legal decisions on tribal sovereignty did not even involve the tribes as parties.

The ownership by the Cherokee Nation of the land claimed by both sides in *Fletcher v. Peck* was ignored by Chief Justice Marshall, a land speculator himself, in his opinion, although the case can be seen as the first tribal rights case to reach the court.[45] *Johnson v. McIntosh*, the first U.S. Supreme Court case to directly consider tribal rights, again was one in which the parties were both land speculators, one of whom claimed title through a direct sale of land by certain chiefs of the Illinois and Piankeshaw nations and the other who held a title through the federal government.[46] Marshall's opinion, at least partially inconsistent with his *Worcester* opinion, relies on the doctrine of conquest to extinguish tribal rights to the ownership of land, defining the Indians as "an inferior race of people ... under the perpetual protection and pupilage of the government" who "could have acquired no proprietary in-

[42] See Chapter 1, note 2.
[43] C. Peter Magrath, *Yazoo: The Case of Fletcher v. Peck* (New York: Norton, 1966); Williams, *The American Indian in Western Legal Thought*, chap. 7, "The Colonists War for America."
[44] Ibid.
[45] 6 Cranch 87 (1810).
[46] 21 U.S. (8 Wheat.) 543 (1823). The significance of the case is discussed in Williams, *The American Indian in Western Legal Thought*.

terest" in the vast lands that they "wandered over."[47] It would be the 1880s before such language would again dominate the U.S. Supreme Court's reasoning in an Indian rights case, in large part because federal hegemony over the tribes and against the states before the "plenary power era" of the late nineteenth century was based on their status as Indian nations, a status that required treating Indian rights with respect. Marshall himself found this view in *Worcester*: the tribes were nations with a measure of sovereignty, but not in the traditional international sense. Rather, tribal nationhood was a more limited type of sovereignty, that of "domestic, dependant nations." The sovereignty over tribal lands that was juridically extinguished in *Johnson* was replaced with a political sovereignty, limited in theory only by the power of the federal government but capable of resisting the encroachments of the states, which were also "domestic and dependant," a fact southern states were unaware of until the Civil War.

The Northeast and South, 1822–35

Georgia repeatedly protested that *Corn Tassel* and the state assumption of criminal jurisdiction that had preceded it were not unique to the state but reflected both law and de facto practice in the original thirteen colonies. The federal courts were singling out Georgia and ignoring similar problems in the North. A small but growing literature on colonial criminal jurisdiction over Indians reflects the legal contradictions inherent in this argument.[48] On the one hand, both the colonies and the states believed that criminal jurisdiction followed sovereignty over land; therefore numerous colonies and later states enacted this belief into law and extended their jurisdiction over the Indians within their boundaries.[49] On the other hand, colonial treaty

---

[47] See Williams's trenchant commentary on this case in ibid.

[48] In addition to Yasuhide Kawashima, *Puritan Justice and the Indian: White Man's Law in Massachusetts, 1630–1738* (Middletown, Conn.: Wesleyan University Press, 1986), see Kathleen Joan Bragdon, "Crime and Punishment Among the Indians of Massachusetts, 1675–1750," *Ethnohistory* 28 (Winter 1981):23; James Rhonda, "Red and White at the Bench: Indians and the Law in Plymouth Colony, 1620–1691," *Essex Institute Historical Collections* 110 (July 1974):200; Lyle Koehler, "Red/White Relations and Justice in the Courts of 17th Century New England," *American Indian Culture and Research Journal* 3 (1979):1; William Stitt Robinson, "The Legal Status of the Indian in Colonial Virginia," *Virginia Magazine of History and Biography* 61 (July 1953):247; Kenneth Morrison, "The Bias of Colonial Law: English Paranoia and the Abenaki Arena of King Philip's War, 1675–1678," *New England Quarterly* 53 (1980):363.

[49] These colonial statutes were compiled by the Committee on Indian Affairs of the U.S. House of Representatives and are printed as Report no. 319 of the 21st Congress, 1st session, March 19, 1830. The timing of the research and publication indicates that it must have been done at the behest of Georgia or parties sympathetic to Georgia's position.

after treaty left the tribes with the right to make and enforce their own laws.[50] To an extent this contradiction reflects a local colonial claim of sovereignty against the British, whose attempt to keep direct control over relations with Indians was bitterly resented by the colonists and was among the causes of the American Revolution.[51]

This contradiction in law was generally not a significant contradiction in practice. Most cases involving the application of tribal law in Indian country occurred beyond the reach, if not the jurisdiction, of the law of colonies or states. It was the extension of white settlement deep into western lands occupied by Indians and the refusal of Indians to keep moving beyond the range of white law that provoked the jurisdictional conflict, making a dispute like *Corn Tassel* inevitable.

New York, as the Georgia courts pointed out, was the first state to assign itself jurisdiction over Indian tribes by specific statute after adoption of the Constitution.[52] Therefore, the first New York case under that law is important because it directly interposed New York State criminal law into a Seneca tribal killing, exactly as Georgia later did in the case of Corn Tassel. Caugh-quaw-taugh, a Seneca woman living on the Buffalo Creek Reservation, was, under Seneca law, guilty of witchcraft. She was killed by a blow to the head with a hatchet by Soo-non-gize, who carried out the execution with the full authority of the tribal government. He was then indicted for murder by the state of New York under the name of Tommy Jemmy and was represented in court by his chief, Red Jacket. Red Jacket advanced the

---

[50] The best discussion of the status of criminal jurisdiction in treaty law is Robert N. Clinton, "Development of Criminal Jurisdiction over Indian Lands: The Historical Perspective," *Arizona Law Review* 17 (1975):951.

[51] Robert Clinton, "State Power over Indians: A Critical Comment on Burger Court Doctrine," *South Dakota Law Review* 26 (1981): 434–446; Douglas E. Leach, *The Northern Colonial Frontier, 1607–1763* (New York: Rinehart & Winston, 1966); and W. Stitt Robinson, *The Southern Colonial Frontier, 1607–1763* (Albuquerque: University of New Mexico Press, 1979).

[52] Rhode Island had, in 1803, enacted a statute indirectly asserting criminal and civil jurisdiction over the Narragansett Indians, providing that any Indian committed to jail for debt should be considered a "poor prisoner" entitled to statutory relief. This statute is cited in *The Narragansett Indians*, 20 R.I. 713 (1898), at 751. Maine also asserted full state jurisdiction over Indians, its courts holding in 1842 that a provision in the Maine Constitution providing that "all men are born equally, free, and independent" meant that the Penobscot tribe could not be a "nation by themselves," going on to assert that it was obvious that if one of them committed a crime, he or she was under full state jurisdiction. *Murch v. Tomer*, 21 Me. 535 (1842), at 537. *State v. Newell*, 24 At. 943 (1898), holds that Indians in Massachusetts and Maine have always been bound by the laws of the states in which they live. A detailed discussion of the rights of Maine's Passamaquoddy tribe is Francis J. O'Toole and Thomas N. Tureen, "State Power and the Passamaquoddy Tribe: A Gross National Hypocrisy?" *Maine Law Review* 23, 1 (1971):1–4. Massachusetts followed the same policy. *Danzell v. Webquish*, 108 Mass. 133 (1871) at 134, simply states that "the remnants of the Indians tribes, residing within the limits of Massachusetts, having never been recognized by any treaties or executive or legislative acts of the government of the United States as independent political communities," were under the control of the legislature of the state.

supremacy of treaty law in arguing that New York State had no jurisdiction over Seneca tribal matters and ended his defense with a stirring condemnation of the barbarity of U.S. justice that included a reference to the Salem witchcraft trials.[53]

The state legislature settled the dispute in a novel and decisive way. Since the law was unclear, it passed a statute that asserted state criminal jurisdiction over Indian tribes and at the same time pardoned Jemmy. The language and reasoning were straightforward:

> Whereas the Seneca, and other tribes of Indians residing within this state, have assumed the power and authority of trying and punishing, and in some cases capitally, members of their respective tribes for supposed crimes by them done and committed in their respective reservations, and within this state. And whereas the sole and exclusive cognizance of all crimes and offences committed within this state, belongs of right to courts holden under the constitution and laws thereof, as a necessary attribute of sovereignty, except only crimes and offenses cognizable in the courts deriving jurisdiction under the constitution and laws of the United States.[54]

The statute went on to extend state law to Indians for their "protection," as well as to defend state sovereignty. New York exercised this jurisdiction unchallenged until a state court of appeals, in *Cusick v. Daly*, a felony assault case occurring on the Tuscarora Reservation in 1914, found *Crow Dog* to have preempted New York State in the area of criminal jurisdiction over Indian reservations.[55] Still, state authorities were reluctant to give up jurisdiction over Indians, and state officials and state courts still took jurisdiction over tribal Indians.[56]

The failure of New York's assumption of criminal jurisdiction over Indian tribes to provoke a nationwide crisis struck Georgia as discriminatory, but there were differences. Georgia went beyond the assertion of criminal jurisdiction and engaged in harsh and punitive measures designed to force

---

[53] William L. Stone, *The Life and Times of Sa-Go-Ye-Wat-Ha, or Red Jacket* (Albany: J. Munsell, 1866), 383–7; Robert W. Bingham, *The Cradle of the Queen City: A History of Buffalo* (Buffalo: Buffalo Historical Society, 1931), 386–8.

[54] Quoted in Stone, *Life and Times of Red Jacket*.

[55] *People ex rel Cusick v. Daly*, 212 NY 183 (1914).

[56] New York has an extensive body of state Indian law, illustrating the state's desire to maintain jurisdiction over tribal Indians. See Cuthbert Pound, "Nationals Without a Nation: The New York State Tribal Indians," *Columbia Law Review* 29 (1922):97; Gerald Gunther, "Governmental Power and New York Indian Lands: A Reassessment of a Persistent Problem of Federal State Relations," *Buffalo Law Review* 8 (1958):1; and Robert B. Porter, "The Jurisdictional Relationship Between the Iroquois and New York State: An Analysis of 25 U.S.C. 232, 233," *Harvard Journal of Legislation* 27 (1990):497. State Indian policy is discussed in Helen M. Upton, *The Everett Report in Historical Perspective* (Albany: New York State Bicentennial Commission, 1980).

the Cherokee to move west.[57] It should not be surprising that the next four states to claim jurisdiction over Indian tribes were Alabama, Tennessee, Mississippi, and North Carolina, representing an extension of Georgia's conflict with federal authority over the lands of the southern tribes.

The situation in Alabama was perhaps even more corrupt and brutal than that in Georgia. The Creek lands there had been the scene of violent struggle. The Creeks had been the victims of a massive land fraud perpetrated by Alabamans but actively abetted by some Creek leaders, including Robert McIntosh, a principal chief. When it became clear that McIntosh had sold Creek lands in 1825 in violation of tribal law and had accepted bribes from whites to move the tribe west, a tribal council ordered him executed. The death sentence was carried out by a force of more than a hundred "law-menders," who attacked McIntosh's heavily guarded plantation, released innocent visitors, burned his large house, and shot McIntosh as he emerged. President John Quincy Adams, saddened by McIntosh's death, nevertheless believed it was a legal execution. Over the next seven years, the situation deteriorated to such an extent that President Jackson ordered federal troops and marshals to protect the Creeks from the Alabamans, an action he had been unwilling to take for the Cherokees in Georgia.[58]

Alabama and Mississippi had, in the meantime, assumed full jurisdiction over the Creeks and Choctaws and their lands by statutes in 1829. Alabama's action was upheld by the Alabama Supreme Court in *Caldwell v. State*.[59] Caldwell, a white man, was under a state sentence of death for murdering a Creek Indian on Creek lands.[60] His enterprising attorney argued that Alabama had no jurisdiction over Caldwell because his crime occurred in the Creek Nation. The court instead found the Creeks had no criminal jurisdiction over anyone, either white or Indian, and that Alabama had complete civil and criminal jurisdiction over Creek lands. Whereas Cherokee legal rights in Georgia had been lost by some of the best lawyers in the country, hired by the Cherokees themselves and representing their interests,

---

[57] Georgia and the other southern states appear to have tacitly supported and encouraged white violence against Indian people in order to force the tribes to agree to "voluntary" removal. There is no real disagreement among scholars on this point. See, e.g., McLoughlin, *Cherokees and Missionaries;* Michael Green, *The Politics of Indian Removal* (Lincoln: University of Nebraska Press, 1982), 141–86; and Mary Young, *Rednecks, Ruffleshirts, and Redskins: Indian Allotments in Alabama and Mississippi, 1830–1860* (Norman: University of Oklahoma Press, 1961).

[58] Green, *Politics of Indian Removal*, 56–68, 95–6, 100, 174–5.

[59] 6 Peter 327 (1832).

[60] We know even less about Caldwell and his crime than we know about Corn Tassel. Michael Green, who read all of the Alabama papers extant on Creek–white relations at the time, found no newspaper account of the case at all (Green, private correspondence, 1987). We do not even know whether Caldwell was ultimately executed for his crime after the court upheld state jurisdiction. On the general context of Indian–white relations in Alabama at the time, see Green, *Politics of Indian Removal*, 141–86.

Creek legal rights in Alabama were lost in a case in which the tribe was not even a party.

Caldwell is closely related to the Cherokee cases. Alabama extended its jurisdiction over Indians a year after Georgia led the way. *Caldwell* was decided two years after *Corn Tassel,* a year after the Supreme Court's *Cherokee Nation* decision, but before *Worcester.* The well-reasoned, 118-page opinion is important as the best single judicial statement of the southern position on state jurisdiction over Indian lands, essentially contemporaneous with *Worcester.*

Chief Justice Abner Lipscomb, writing for the court, began with the idea that state jurisdiction was a "shield of protection" over Indians, not only from crimes commited against each other but also from the encroachments of whites – here referring to Caldwell personally as an example of the kind of bad white man against whom Indians needed state protection.[61] The court then took up the issue of the Constitution's commerce clause. The Indian Trade and Intercourse Act of 1834, enacted by Congress under the authority of the commerce clause to "regulate Commerce with foreign Nations, and among the several states, and with the Indian tribes," gave the federal government broad criminal jurisdiction over the tribes and over whites on tribal lands. Whereas the issue in the Cherokee cases had been the effect of treaty rights on criminal jurisdiction, *Caldwell* was the first judicial opinion to consider whether the commerce clause could extend that jurisdiction. Although under modern U.S. Indian law the Indian commerce clause is as important as the Constitution's treaty clause in granting exclusive power to the federal government in Indian affairs, Alabama did not then accept this interpretation. According to Lipscomb, power to regulate Indian trade did no more to confer federal criminal jurisdiction over Indians than did the power to regulate commerce between the states. In fact, such an extension of federal power under the commerce clause in the case of Indians could deprive the states of all jurisdiction.[62]

The court then turned to the major issue in the Corn Tassel case: the question of what it called "this high pretension of savage sovereignty." The court defined Indians as "wildmen" and described their customary law as "adventitious and temporary, passing from one warrior to another, as accident might determine."[63] Indian treaties were labeled "quasi-treaties" and held to be political in character, a mere public policy choice of Congress to be passed on to the states with statehood and not international in character with rights to be determined under international law.[64]

[61] 6 Peter 329 (1832).
[62] Ibid., 330.
[63] Ibid., 334.
[64] Ibid., 340.

Justice Reuben Saffold, in a concurrent opinion, offered an extensive history of colonial jurisdiction over Indians, finding that the colonies had indeed exercised criminal jurisdiction over the Indian tribes.[65] In his analysis, the state of Alabama, not the federal government, inherited this power. Georgia, one of the original thirteen colonies, enjoyed such jurisdiction. Under the Constitution, each new state was admitted on an equal footing with the original thirteen, and therefore Alabama had jurisdiction over its Indian tribes just as Georgia did.

This view was repeated by Justice John Taylor in a concurring opinion that presented yet another argument: if the tribes had sovereignty co-equal with the states, what was to keep the tribes from asserting sovereignty over the states? The idea that

> to secure the "rights" of the Indians, the state was to relinquish some of those most important to her, and place herself in something of a state of pupilage to, and dependance upon the savage tribes within her boundary, can not be tolerated for a moment. We are almost surrounded by these children of the forest; were we to yield all that is claimed for them, in a short time we might...feel the effects of their "independence." Our citizens might be prohibited by these new sovereigns from carrying on intercourse with several of the neighboring states.... For offences, either pretended or real, charged to be committed by them while journeying through the dominions of these sovereigns, they might be dragged before their chiefs and other head men, and upon the most crude and unsatisfactory testimony, be consigned to ignominious or fatal punishments.[66]

Taylor and Saffold were correct in their historical analyses of the position of Indians in colonial society but wrong in their view that treaty rights were simply a matter of policy. The judges were evidently unaware of, or unwilling to give state effect to, the fact that the constitutional system had struck a balance between the rights of sovereign states, sovereign tribes, and the federal government. The specter of whites subject to the ignoble justice of Indian tribes was a fiction. Although early treaties often recognized tribal jurisdiction over non-Indians in Indian country, treaties after the early nineteenth century required that non-Indians who committed crimes on Indian lands be given up to U.S. authorities.[67] In any case, it is doubtful that the

---

[65] Ibid., 343–53. It should be noted that Saffold cites *Cherokee Nation v. Georgia*, 355, for the proposition that jurisdiction over Indian tribes is a matter of political character, not for the courts to decide.

[66] Ibid., 442–3.

[67] Kawashima, *Puritan Justice and the Indian*, 28. For a full discussion of criminal jurisdiction in the treaty period, see Clinton, "Development of Criminal Jurisdiction over Indian Lands," 951.

Creeks could have given any white a more ignoble trial than Georgia had
provided Corn Tassel.

The 1833 Tennessee statute that extended state criminal jurisdiction over
the Cherokee Nation was a model of moderation when compared with those
of Alabama and Georgia. As the federal government would later do in the
Major Crimes Act of 1885, Tennessee limited its criminal jurisdiction over
Indians to the specific crimes of murder, rape, and larceny. The statute
specifically recognized "all other usages and customs of the Cherokee,"
granting legitimacy to Indian customary law by statute. The law went on to
prohibit settlement by whites "on the lands of the Indians" and required
that the act not be construed "to invalidate any law or treaty of the United
States made in pursuance of the constitution thereof."[68] The latter provision
represents an explicit acknowledgment of the *Worcester* case and distinguishes
Tennessee from Georgia and Alabama in the state's unwillingness to defy
federal authority directly.

State v. Forman, Tennessee's parallel case to *Caldwell* and *Corn Tassel,*
followed those cases' same general arguments, but it was handed down in
1835 and was therefore the first case to confirm state criminal jurisdiction
over Indian tribes in direct contradiction to the clear holding of *Worcester.*[69]
Since President Andrew Jackson was Tennessee's most dominant political
figure and at that time was anxious to avoid the constitutional crisis that the
Cherokee cases had created, it is not inconceivable that *Forman* represents
an effort by southern nationalists to find a middle ground between *Corn
Tassel* and *Caldwell* on the one hand and *Worcester* on the other and thereby
avoid the sectional strife the Cherokee cases had caused.[70]

James Forman, a Cherokee, was indicted for killing John Walker, another
Cherokee, within the boundaries of the Cherokee Nation. Forman's defense
was that he was a Cherokee and not under the jurisdiction of Tennessee.
The local state court rejected this argument and convicted him. Forman's
appeal, like Caldwell's, resulted in a lengthy analysis of the state's claims to
jurisdiction over the Indian nations. Nearly half of the Tennessee Supreme
Court's 115-page opinion is a historical analysis of the history of Indian–
white relations in North America that closely follows the interpretation of
Caldwell. It further provides a detailed history of Cherokee–white relations

---

[68] *State v. Forman,* 8 Yerg. 256 (1835).
[69] Ibid.
[70] Michael Green argues that President Jackson's role in these southern Indian matters was a
complex one. While fully agreeing with Georgia that no Cherokee Nation could be allowed
to function within Georgia's borders, he later used federal troops to protect the rights of
Creeks in Alabama against white encroachment. The key difference was that the Creeks
had ceded their lands to the whites and had agreed to move West; hence Jackson was
protecting Indians who were not challenging the authority of any state. Green, *Politics of
Indian Removal,* 174–81.

specifically for the purpose of contradicting the historical analysis of *Worces-ter*.[71] The major thrust is that the Cherokees had surrendered all political power to the British and that the colony of North Carolina had inherited British sovereignty over the Cherokees.

It is important to note that the court in *Forman* believed that the result in *Worcester*, the release of the missionaries, was correct, since missionary work came under the heading "intercourse with Indians" and therefore was a federal matter because of the Indian commerce clause. Beyond that result, however, the court believed not only that *Worcester* misread the history of Indian–white relations, but that it was constitutionally unsound for other reasons. The Constitution guaranteed the states a republican form of government, but that republican form became "a dead letter at the Indian boundary."[72]

The court then offered a more detailed analysis of the history of state jurisdiction over Indians than did *Caldwell*.[73] It found support for its interpretation in two federal circuit court decisions on the legal status of Ohio Indians by Supreme Court Justice John McLean. McLean had written a concurrent opinion as part of the *Worcester* majority but had never fully agreed with Marshall's view that the Cherokees were entitled to sovereign status under the Constitution. Later, sitting as a circuit judge, McLean wrote two opinions that undermined that decision. In *United States v. Bailey*, he found that although the commerce clause had wide scope, it did not extend federal criminal jurisdiction over Indian tribes.[74] This action created a jurisdictional void: it left no authority over Indian lands other than Indian jurisdiction, a result that would place local whites under Indian law or no law at all. A year later in *United States v. Cisna*, McLean came to the same holding, but this time he invited Ohio to pass legislation to extend the state's criminal jurisdiction over the Wyandot Reservation.[75] Both of these cases

---

[71] *State v. Forman*, 8 Yerg. 256 (1835), at 257–306.

[72] The court goes to great lengths to cover much the same historical ground as *Worcester* in finding the opposite conclusion – that the Indians had not historically been treated as sovereign nations and had always been subject to the authority of the colonies. See ibid., 299, 300, 304, 311, 334–5. Here again is a clear notion of compromise in the writing of the opinion, seeing in *Worcester* the right result but the wrong reading of the sovereignty issue. Since Georgia did not represent itself at the argument in *Worcester*, *Forman* may be the best Jacksonian rebuttal of Marshall's reasoning. The case does not appear in any of the major treatments of U.S. Indian law.

[73] Ibid., 316–24. At 320 the court states that Massachusetts, Maine, Rhode Island, Connecticut, New Jersey, Virginia, the Carolinas, and New York all had a long-standing practice of jurisdiction over Indian tribes and that North Carolina, Georgia, Tennessee, Alabama, New York, and Ohio had "recently" extended their laws over Indian tribes within their boundaries. At 304 the court had listed the same states, with the addition of Maine.

[74] 24 F. Cas. 422 (C.C.D. Ohio, 1834). Bailey is discussed in *State v. Forman*, 8 Yerg. 256 (1835), at 317.

[75] A discussion of the context of McLean's *Cisna* decision, 25 F. Cas. 422 (C.C.D. Ohio,

had involved whites but, like *Caldwell*, were used to bring Indians under state criminal jurisdiction. Tennessee had taken its cue directly from Bailey and passed state legislation to fill a jurisdictional void, although obviously not one that the Cherokee recognized.

Mississippi's statute survived until 1978, when the U.S. Supreme Court found that Mississippi lacked jurisdiction over reservation Choctaws.[76] Convicted of aggravated assault in a county court and sentenced to two years in the state prison, Smith John, descendent of Choctaws who had resisted removal to the Indian Territory, appealed his conviction to the Mississippi Supreme Court, arguing that the Choctaw Reservation was "Indian country" and that therefore the state lacked jurisdiction. The Mississippi court held that it had always had jurisdiction over the Choctaws and that the reservation had never been considered "Indian country" under federal law. The U.S. Supreme Court reversed John's conviction in a lengthy opinion recalling the injustice of the state's assertion of jurisdiction over the southern Indians and the violence of their forced removal. John, like his ancestors, was free in his own country.

The North and West, 1835–80

The legal positions set forth in *Corn Tassel, Tommy Jemmy, Forman,* and *Caldwell* are the most complete statements of mid-nineteenth-century state Indian law. Maine, Mississippi, Ohio, Indiana, North Carolina, and Arkansas took similar positions without elaboration in the 1830s and 1840s – the law was so settled that no argument needed to be made.[77] Later in the century, as more new states were admitted farther to the west, the issue was resolved in consistent ways, incorporating both the Corn Tassel doctrine, the state claim that criminal jurisdiction over all lands within the state was inherent in state sovereignty, as well as the assimilationist idea that as tribal Indians domesticated and lived closer to white people, they placed themselves under state law. Kansas, Nebraska, Wisconsin, and California extended state law over Indian reservations before *Crow Dog.*[78] Cases based on these laws lack

---

1835), is in Monroe Price, *American Indian Law* (Indianapolis: Bobbs-Merrill, 1973), 6–7. *Cisna* is considered in *State v. Forman,* 8 Yerg. 256 (1835), at 317–19.

76 *United States v. John,* 437 U.S. 634 (1975). The opinion at 652–3 notes that, in light of Indian history, a tribe's failure to challenge state jurisdiction does not waive its rights.

77 These states simply passed statutes, often never challenged, asserting criminal jurisdiction. A typical state process can be found in one line in *State v. Ta-Cha-Na-Tah* (64 N.C. 614 [1870]), in which North Carolina upheld its statute extending criminal jurisdiction over Indians (Rev. Code, chap. 50, sec. 16 [1838]): "Unless expressly excepted, our laws apply equally to all persons, irrespective of race."

78 Kansas asserted general jurisdiction over all persons in the state and argued that the federal government lacked the right to enact criminal legislation over reservation Indians. See *United States v. John Ward,* 1 Kansas 601 (1863), and *United States v. George Stahl,* 1 Kansas 606

the formal historical analysis of *Forman* or *Caldwell* but speak to a straight-forward public policy of state sovereignty, as well as a perceived need for local law and order. These states also acted in a void where there was no clear federal policy. Although the federal government claimed criminal ju-risdiction through the Trade and Intercourse Act of 1834, it rarely asserted this jurisdiction over the states prior to *Crow Dog.*

In 1850, California passed a law providing "for the protection and pun-ishment of Indians." In seventeen sections the act gave local justices of the peace jurisdiction over all Indians within their districts and provided for whippings of up to twenty-five lashes for "an Indian convicted of stealing horses, mules, cattle, or any valuable thing." The same act also made pro-vision for indenturing Indian children as servants and curtailed tribal land rights.[79] The statute was upheld by the California Supreme Court in *The People v. Juan Antonio,* an 1863 case arising from a theft that occurred in Santa Cruz County. No federal court ever passed on the issue, although the law was intended to apply to Indians living tribally and in distinct Indian communities as well as to Indians living among whites.[80] This left California Indians at the mercy of the local population. California was particularly aggressive because tribal Indians came into direct conflict with the expansion of the gold-based economy, which depended on legal control of the frontier.[81]

If federal courts had ever passed on the status of the California Indians, they might well have carved out the kind of exception for "civilized Indians" that the U.S. Supreme Court found applicable to the Pueblo Indians of New Mexico in *United States v. Joseph* (1876). The Court decided that the Pueblos

(1868). Although both cases actually involved whites, the claim of jurisdiction extended to tribal Indians. Nebraska relied on similar reasoning; see *State v. Hunt,* 4 Kansas 65 (1868). Wisconsin, in *State v. Doxtater,* 47 Wis. 278 (1879), presented the most elaborate of the post-*Caldwell* claims to criminal jurisdiction over Indian reservations. California passed a statute claiming criminal jurisdiction over Indians in 1850, upholding it in *People v. Juan Antonio,* 27 Calif. 404 (1865).

[79] Albert Hurtado, *Indian Survival on the California Frontier* (New Haven, Conn.: Yale University Press, 1988), chap. 7, "The Dilemma of California Indian Policy," contains a discussion of the context of this law.

[80] *The People v. Juan Antonio,* 27 Calif. 404 (1865). This case is discussed in Chauncey Goodrich, "The Legal Status of the California Indian," *California Law Review* 14, no. 2 (19236), 83–100 (pt. 1), and 14, no. 3 (1926), 157–87 (pt. 2).

[81] Frontier California produced one of the most violent of white attacks on Native Americans. See Sherburne Friend Cooke, *The Conflict Between the California Indian and White Civilization* (Berkeley: Ibero-American, nos. 21–4, 1943), esp. chap. 1, and Albert Hurtado, *Indian Survival.* Michigan, also in 1850, took the opposite tack in taking full civil and criminal jurisdiction over Indians. It amended its constitution to extend full state citizenship to Indians. This included the right to serve on juries and to sue and be sued in any of Michigan's courts. This juridical equality, however, did not gain justice for the Indians because of extensive local racism and the domination of the courts by timber and real estate interests. Bruce A. Rubenstein, "Justice Denied: An Analysis of American Indian–White Relations in Michigan, 1855–1889," Ph.D. dissertation, Michigan State University, 1974. See es-pecially chap. 5, "Separate but Unequal: Survival in White Society."

had a settled, domestic existence and were therefore not subject to the same laws passed for the protection and civilization of "wild tribes." The laws of New Mexico Territory applied to the Pueblo just as they applied to other people in the state. This distinction was based on the creation of a false dichotomy between stationary agricultural tribes and nomadic tribes that was rooted in a conception of agriculture as the distinguishing characteristic of a civilized versus a barbarian people.[82]

In *Joseph*, the Supreme Court followed the lead of New Mexico's territorial court in *United States v. Lucero* (1869). In a lengthy analysis of the legal status of New Mexico's Indians, the court found that Spanish and Mexican law distinguished between settled, agricultural Indians and "wild tribes" and had conferred citizenship on the Pueblo, which the United States was bound to respect because it had extended U.S. citizenship to all Mexican citizens in the Gadsden Territory at the time of acquisition. Beyond this reasoning, however, *Lucero* reflected rising local prejudice against tribal sovereignty. Territorial Chief Justice Watts opined that "Providence made this world for the use of the man who had the energy and industry to pull off his coat, roll up his sleeves, and go to work on the land, cut down the trees, grub up the brush and briars, and stay there on it and work it for the support of himself and his family" – a test the Pueblo met, although the law made no distinctions between them and the nomadic Navajo and Apache. This case makes it clear that territorial courts, although under federal authority, could also challenge federal–tribal relations and, for the same reasons, local interests in conflict with tribal rights.[83] The question of jurisdiction over the Apaches was settled by the New Mexico Supreme Court in 1884 without reference to *Lucero*. Carpio Monte, a Mescalero Apache, killed a white man on the reservation. Charged in federal district and sentenced to death, Monte challenged federal jurisdiction, claiming that he should be prosecuted under territorial law. The court, citing *Crow Dog*, held that jurisdiction was federal, upholding Monte's death sentence.[84] New Mexico held criminal jurisdiction over the Pueblo Indians, but not over the Mescalero, based on its own

---

[82] *United States v. Joseph*, 94 U.S. 614 (1876), was overruled in *United States v. Sandoval*, 231 U.S. 28 (1913). The idea that the Pueblo were somehow racially unlike all other native people and therefore needed no legal protection from the United States was not unique to the *Joseph* opinion: it was also a part of the rationale for a separate Indian policy for Alaska. See Chapter 8.

[83] Under various "organic acts" the territories enjoyed a form of home rule that created local control of many governmental institutions, including courts. The question of the jurisdiction of territorial courts over Indians was specifically decided by the U.S. Supreme Court in *ex parte Gon-Shay-ee*, 130 U.S. 348 (1889).

[84] *United States v. Monte*, 3 N.M. 173 (1884).

distinction between Indians who tilled the soil and those who were "nomads."

An 1879 Wisconsin Supreme Court decision in the case of an Oneida Indian indicted for adultery committed on the Oneida Reservation cites this abdication of federal jurisdiction in Indian matters. The court in *State v. Doxtater* defined the issue simply: when a defendant challenges the authority of the state to punish him, the burden is on him or her to show why the state does not have jurisdiction. In a confused decision, the court noted that many states had taken jurisdiction over crimes committed by Indians on reservations and that criminal jurisdiction is one aspect of a state's sovereignty. The court then reasoned that since it was uncontested that the federal government exercised criminal jurisdiction over Indian reservations in a territory before statehood (here the court cited a federal trial of a Winnebago at Green Bay in the early nineteenth century),[85] power passed to the state at the time of statehood unless specifically reserved. The court held that the state had received criminal jurisdiction over Indian reservations upon statehood.[86] Wisconsin was acting in the tradition of California and New Mexico and doubtlessly expected the federal courts to similarly acquiesce to the state's jurisdiction. It almost succeeded: Wisconsin exercised jurisdiction over tribal Indians until 1931, often in conflict with federal courts.[87]

This line of reasoning was rejected in only a few western states.[88] The most important of the rare state cases upholding Indians' right to apply

---

[85] The cited case, *Mau-zau-mau-ne-kah v. The United States*, 1 Pin. 124 (1841), legendary in Wisconsin history, involved the killing of French trader Pierre Pauquette in a dispute with a Winnebago in which Pauquette pulled open his shirt, challenging his opponent to "strike, and see a brave man die." Convicted and sentenced to death in a territorial court, Mau-zau-mau-ne-kah challenged the court's jurisdiction on the ground that the crime had been committed on the lands of the Winnebago and was therefore under the exclusive jurisdiction of the United States. The Wisconsin Supreme Court overturned his conviction. There is no further record of this case, so it appears that he was not retried in federal court.

[86] *State v. Doxtater*, 47 Wis. 278 (1879), at 283, 293–4, 295, 296, 297.

[87] *State v. Rufus*, 237 N.W. 70 (1931).

[88] Besides Nevada, only the supreme courts of Minnesota and Nebraska specifically reject state jurisdiction over the tribes and then only after *Crow Dog* and *Kagama*, raising a serious question of why no cases involving tribal Indians were reported earlier, as well as the question of why county authorities believed they had the legal power to arrest and try reservation Indians. The Minnesota Supreme Court, in *State v. Campbell*, 53 Minn. 354 (1893), reasoned that ordinarily the state would acquire jurisdiction over the tribes at the time of statehood but must defer to the power of the federal government to "regulate commerce" with the tribes, thus the state deferred to *Kagama* (at 357–8). The Nebraska Supreme Court, in *ex parte Jesse Cross*, 18 Nebr. 417 (1886), does virtually the same thing. Both cases raise an inference that tribal Indians tried in state courts *before* the government directly asserted its jurisdiction over tribal crimes in "Indian country" would have been held under state jurisdiction. Obviously, the passage of many years between statehood and these decisions means that some cases involving tribal Indians must have been prosecuted in local courts.

their own law in crimes between Indians is Nevada's *State v. McKenney* (1883), the last state case on the issue preceding *Crow Dog*. Spanish Jim, a Shoshone, killed a woman belonging to the same nation in Nye County, Nevada. The case attracted a great deal of local attention, as a posse chased and caught the "murderous redskin," who was reported in the local press to have killed six people. This reputation for violence was heightened when Jim broke out of prison and led another posse on a lengthy chase before he was finally recaptured and tried. At his trial, the local judge ruled that the state courts had no jurisdiction over Indians and dismissed the murder charge. Attorneys representing Nye County and the state of Nevada, as well as the U.S. attorney, then appealed the dismissal to the Nevada Supreme Court.[89]

Perhaps the most significant outcome of the trial was that the U.S. attorney, who carried a legal duty to protect the jurisdictional interests of the federal government, conceded state jurisdiction over the Shoshones. His legal analysis, concurrent with the appeal of Crow Dog, was completely inconsistent with all existing federal doctrine in the area but in broad agreement with the predominant line of state cases. His first argument, taken straight from Alabama's position in *Caldwell*, was a position that federal courts had never upheld: the Indian commerce clause could not reach the matter of criminal jurisdiction over Indian tribes. He went on to deny that federal treaties with the Shoshone had any effect on criminal jurisdiction and further argued that in any case such treaties were abrogated by statehood. He ended with Alabama's argument that each state was admitted on an equal footing with the original states and that the original states had complete criminal jurisdiction over the Indian tribes.[90] This case is closely linked to *Crow Dog* and other cases by which federal authorities were searching for ways to extend state and territorial criminal law to Indians. The major legal reason that the U.S. attorney gave for abandoning jurisdiction over Spanish Jim was that he was not on a reservation at the time of the killing. This reasoning in the context of the western Shoshone was disingenuous, however, and was soon to be rejected by the U.S. Supreme Court in its expansive definition of "Indian country" in *Crow Dog*. Finally, one part of the federal strategy here appears to have been drawn from Andrew Jackson: subjecting the Shoshone to the authority

---

[89] Brief of the State of Nevada, Respondent, *State v. McKenney*, 18 Nev. 82 (1883). This information is found in the original case file, held in the Nevada State Archives, Carson City. An account of the events leading up to the case can be found in the *Belmont Courier*, March 17, 24, April 7, 14, May 12, September 8, 1883.

[90] Attorney General of Nevada, "Relators Points and Authorities," 24–30. Printed brief, contained in the case file.

of state law might force them to abandon their traditional lands and move to the Duck Valley Reservation under federal protection.[91]

In what is the strongest state court opinion denying state jurisdiction, the Nevada Supreme Court rejected the U.S. attorney's arguments. Its opinion that the state had no jurisdiction left a de facto holding of the sovereign right of the Shoshone to their own law, since it was clear to the state court that the federal government not only did not exercise jurisdiction over the dispersed traditional Shoshone but did not want to. The court's exhaustive analysis of state jurisdiction over Indians found that Nevada's Organic Act of 1861 specifically reserved all rights held by Indians within the state and recognized full federal authority over those Indians.[92] This principle was often followed by the western states, where the question of the rights of the Indian tribes was specifically dealt with in the original statehood legislation.

We know nothing about the motivation of the state judges in *McKenney*. Given that an impressive array of lawyers representing both state and federal interests argued that Nevada had jurisdiction over the Shoshone and that obvious local jurisdictional problems would be created by any holding that a Shoshone off the reservation was under federal jurisdiction, their opinion is remarkable. Still at issue then was whether the Nevada Organic Act's explicit federal reservation of authority over the tribes covered Indians off reservations, and it would have been easy for the judges to decide in favor of the state. It seems likely that the issue of state sovereignty had been replaced by a more pressing economic concern: criminal jurisdiction or any other state responsibility over the Shoshone would be expensive. Moreover, the federal government now saw criminal jurisdiction over the tribes as a liability that it would willingly divest. In fact, the U.S. attorney argued that Nevada had jurisdiction, a position that the Oregon U.S. attorney took as well.[93] It is also possible that the Nevada court deliberately released a Shoshone murderer in order to provoke a federal reaction, either congressional legislation or a federal court decision, a result parallel to the political use made of the U.S. Supreme Court's *Crow Dog* decision. No direct evidence supports either interpretation.

The formal jurisdictional battle did not end the subjection of reservation Indians to state criminal jurisdiction. Most states with significant Indian

---

[91] Nevada's Shoshone Indians roamed their traditional lands, refusing to settle on reservations. A general history of the status of Indians in Nevada is Elmer R. Rusco, "Early Nevada and Indian Law," *Western Legal History* 2, no. 2 (1989): 163.

[92] *State v. McKenney*, 18 Nev. 82 (1983) at 84–6.

[93] See Chapter 4, the section entitled "Early BIA Attempts to Prosecute Indians Under State or Territorial Law."

populations had by the 1880s already asserted such criminal jurisdiction and simply continued to exercise it. Many states, like California, did so expressly by statute; others, like Wisconsin and New Mexico, did so by judicial opinions of the legal status of Indians under existing state law. This written record of cases and statutes is deceiving because it is based on legal activity to which few tribal Indians had access. Without specific legislation or appellate test cases, there is no record of the extent of the application of state law to tribal Indians. Indians were arrested and punished under local law at the discretion of local authorities under existing state laws generally applicable to all persons. There is no question that large numbers of Indians were prosecuted in local courts with no reference to their formal legal rights as tribal Indians. Without money, lawyers, or an articulable right to the writ of habeas corpus, Indians had few defenses against such practices. And as the Wisconsin Supreme Court put the matter in *Doxtater*, a defense of lack of jurisdiction must be proved by the party raising such a legal claim, putting the burden of such a defense squarely on Indian defendants.

It is clear that the states did not stop asserting jurisdiction over tribal Indians even after the *Crow Dog* and *Kagama* decisions, which, without citing *Corn Tassel*, clearly put an end to any legal pretense of state jurisdiction over intra-Indian crimes in Indian country. For example, it was 1914 before New York deferred to federal authority.[94] Wisconsin was even slower. The state supreme court, citing *Crow Dog* as binding precedent, finally overruled *Doxtater* in 1931.[95] During all this time, there were few federal challenges to state jurisdiction, even though the issues were the same as those of the Cherokee cases. This federal deference to state courts left the tribes unprotected against the encroachments of local whites.

In 1894, Michel Thomas, a Chippewa convicted in state court of murdering another Chippewa on Lac Courtes Oreilles Reservation, appealed his conviction in federal court, arguing that Wisconsin lacked jurisdiction. The U.S. Supreme Court ultimately held that criminal jurisdiction on the reservation was federal but then became confused by a state argument that Thomas's crime had occurred a few feet off the reservation. The case was remanded to the Wisconsin Supreme Court to determine where the crime had occurred, which resulted in returning jurisdiction over the case to the state.[96]

Wisconsin continued to arrest and jail Indians for state offenses committed on reservations. John Blackbird, a Chippewa living on the Bad River Reservation, was arrested in 1901 for setting a net for suckers on a creek within

---

[94] *People ex rel Cusick v. Daley*, 212 N.Y. 183 (1914).
[95] *State v. Rufus*, 237 N.W. 70 (1931).
[96] *United States v. Thomas*, 151 U.S. 577 (1894).

the reservation. He was given thirty days in jail by the county court.[97] Moving to the federal district court on a writ of habeas corpus, the federal judge ordered him released. Not only did *Crow Dog* give the tribes jurisdiction over tribal Indians, but *Kagama* and the Major Crimes Act provided that only the federal government had limited jurisdiction. Moreover, Chippewa treaties gave members of the tribe the right to hunt and fish. But, in dicta, Judge Romanzo Bunn stated the reality as few judges would:

> After taking from them the great body of their lands...it would be adding insult as well as injustice now to deprive them of the poor privilege of fishing with a seine for suckers in a little red marsh water stream upon their own reservation. These lands have long been their hunting and fishing ground. When an Indian cannot get a morsel of port and white flour, a...sucker from some stream where brook trout would never abide, boiled or roasted by a camp fire, is sometimes a luxury, to deprive him of which would be ungrateful in the extreme. I feel confident that neither the state nor congress ever mediated any such cruelty.

The judge went on to blame the arrest on the overzealousness of a local game warden but overlooked the fact that the sentence of jail had been passed by a state judge.[98]

Judge Bunn's guarded comment on local prejudice was a statement of the obvious that seldom reached the printed opinions in Indian cases. Federal authority over Indians, from the time of the Cherokee cases, did conceal the unpleasant reality of racial prejudice by local authorities from the main thrust of developments in Indian law. *Blackbird*, however, did not put an end to state arrests on the Bad River Reservation. Finally, in 1931, the Wisconsin Supreme Court in *State v. Rufus* addressed the issue. Frank Rufus, also a Chippewa Indian, was convicted in the county court of statutory rape. He objected to the proceedings, arguing that the court lacked jurisdiction over Indians on the reservation, but was overruled by the court. On appeal the Wisconsin Supreme Court overruled *Doxtater*, holding that *Crow Dog* and *Kagama* made it clear that the states lacked criminal jurisdiction over Indians on reservations.[99] The process of simple recognition of an elementary principle of tribal rights had taken the Wisconsin courts fifty years. But the struggle was not over. Jerry Pero was a Chippewa also living on the Bad River Reservation. He was convicted of a murder on the reservation in 1927 in county court, receiving a life sentence in the Wisconsin State Prison. Under federal law that court

---

[97] *In re Blackbird*, 109 Fed. 139 (1901).
[98] Ibid., 145.
[99] *State v. Rufus*, 237 N.W. 70 (1931).

lacked jurisdiction, but it was 1938 before Pero brought a writ of habeas corpus in federal court. The federal district court ordered Pero released, holding that since his mother was a full-blooded Chippewa, his father half-blooded, and that he was recognized as a Chippewa and lived on the reservation, he was an Indian even though he was not an enrolled member of the Bad River band. The state of Wisconsin refused to free him and appealed the ruling to the Circuit Court of Appeals. The Court upheld the lower court's ruling and freed Pero.[100] Wisconsin's claims to criminal jurisdiction over reservation Indians, firmly grounded in Georgia's hanging of Corn Tassel, were over.

The language of John Marshall in *Worcester* was largely irrelevant to Indians confronted with the power of the states in the nineteenth century. There were two opposing lines of decisions on the extension of criminal law to crimes between Indians living in "Indian country." The strongest line, both in terms of the number of cases and in terms of the prevailing legal analysis of the day, was deeply entrenched in state law. It denied the vitality of tribal law and sovereignty, dismissing tribal society as "savage," fit only to be pushed aside by the forces of white civilization. In this view criminal law was a matter reserved to the states by the Constitution as routine police powers, an essential element of state sovereignty. Accordingly, it was not sound public policy to extend any notion of sovereignty or law to the Indian tribes because that would lead to violence, disorder, and jurisdictional confusion and also serve the fiction of assigning some legitimacy to political structures that were primitive and uncivilized.

This view coincided with the outlook of the strongest critics of federal Indian policy, the assimilationist Indian reformers centered around the Indian Rights Association after the 1880s.[101] Their "law for the Indians" slogan presumed the tribes to be lawless and offered full extension of state law over Indian tribes as one powerful mechanism for transforming Indian society. It is important to see the power and consistency of these state cases as setting the stage for the *Crow Dog* decision and for the changes in the application of criminal law to Indians that followed. By the time of Nevada's *McKenney* case, this line of state cases had become entrenched in federal doctrine itself. The decision to prosecute Crow Dog reflected a fundamental change in the traditional federal understanding of tribal sovereignty, as that understanding had evolved in federal cases since *Worcester*. Simply put, federal authorities were no longer committed to the doctrine of tribal sovereignty and, in furtherance of assimilationist goals, were willing to cede their criminal juris-

---

[100] *Ex Parte Pero et al.*, 99 Fed. 2nd. 28 (1938).
[101] William T. Hagan, *The Indian Rights Association: The Herbert Welsh Years, 1882–1904* (Tucson: University of Arizona Press, 1985).

diction back to the states, a process begun in Oklahoma in 1898. This cessation of jurisdiction was consistent with state doctrines, following from *Corn Tassel* and *Caldwell*, that tribal sovereignty was inimical to both state sovereignty and the ultimate development of the country by white people.

Federal Indian law from *Worcester* to *Crow Dog*

In contrast to this fifty-year line of state cases denying tribal sovereignty was a series of federal cases weakly following *Worcester*. Federal Indian law between *Worcester* and *Crow Dog* was simple and clear on the level of doctrine, but hollow and abstract in practice. The tribes, as "domestic dependent nations," had a sovereign right to their self-government, including all matters of criminal law in relation to tribe members. The principle was so clear that it produced little federal litigation. The major decisions of the era primarily determined either tribal rights against the government of the United States or preserved exclusive federal authority over the tribes at the expense of the states.

Even this small amount of litigation revealed some of the weakness in the federal doctrine of Indian law. First, it was always clear that even when the federal government, following *Worcester*, was vigorous – and it not always was – in denying the states the right to encroach on tribal lands, the same did not apply to federal encroachment. The major issue in *Worcester* was federalism and not tribal sovereignty. In *United States v. Rogers* (1846), the first tribal rights case decided after *Worcester*, a white man who married a Cherokee woman, held Cherokee citizenship, and lived in the Cherokee Nation argued that he could not be charged by federal authorities for an offense committed on Cherokee lands because he was a Cherokee and under tribal jurisdiction. Chief Justice Roger Taney emphasized the dependent status of the tribes in his opinion and held that while the Cherokees could grant Rogers citizenship, the United States could still recognize and prosecute him as a U.S. citizen. The sovereignty of the Cherokee Nation was not equal to that of the American nation.[102]

The 1866 "Cherokee Tobacco" cases made this distinction clear. A federal tax was imposed on all tobacco products manufactured "within the United States." Cherokee entrepreneurs, facing a nation devastated by the Civil War, began producing tobacco in earnest and, believing themselves not a part of the U.S. nation, making large profits on tax-free tobacco. The U.S. Supreme Court held that the Cherokee Nation was within the United States, again emphasizing its dependent relationship.[103] *The Kansas Indians*

---

[102] *United States v. Rogers*, 45 U.S. (4 How.) 567 (1846).
[103] *Cherokee Tobacco*, 78 U.S. (11 Wall.) 616 (1871). Robert K. Heimann, "The Cherokee Tobacco Case," *Chronicles of Oklahoma* 41 (Fall 1963): 299–322.

and *The New York Indians* similarly were taxation cases but primarily concerned federal jurisdiction over the tribes, holding that the states had no
right to tax reservation Indians.[104]

A number of cases involving the expansion of federal criminal jurisdiction
into the states in the area of the enforcement of liquor control laws in Indian
commerce also reflect an expansion of federal power over the states, often
moving far beyond the boundaries of Indian country.[105] Congress passed a
number of laws prohibiting the introduction of alcohol into Indian country
or the selling of liquor to Indians.[106] Much of the prohibited behavior occurred, not on federal lands or tribal lands, but within the states. This area
of federal law enforcement put federal power in opposition to local business
interests with a good deal of power in state politics. Federal courts consistently supported this extension of federal power under the Indian commerce
clause, regulating "commerce with the Indian tribes" irrespective of where
such commerce was located. The two leading cases, *United States v. Holliday*
and *United States v. Forty-Three Gallons of Whiskey*, pitted local merchants
in Minnesota and Michigan against claims of Indian agents to jurisdiction
over liquor sales off the reservation.[107]

United States v. McBratney went even further, undermining the very fabric
of Marshall's *Worcester* opinion – and here again no Indians were parties to
the case.[108] McBratney, a white man, killed another white on the Ute Reservation in Colorado. The state tried him for his crime under state law and
sentenced him to hang. McBratney appealed, arguing that his crime occurred
under federal jurisdiction. The U.S. Supreme Court held that because
Colorado had been admitted to the Union "on equal footing" with the other
states, and because Congress had not explicitly reserved jurisdiction over
whites on Indian reservations, the state held jurisdiction as an attribute of
its sovereignty.

> The Supreme Court's equal-footing argument ignored Marshall's lan-
> guage in *Worcester:* The Cherokee Nation, then, is a distinct community,

---

[104] *The Kansas Indians,* 72 U.S. (5 Wall.) 737 (1867); *The New York Indians* 72 U.S. (5 Wall.)
761 (1867).
[105] Cohen, *Handbook of Federal Indian Law,* 1st ed., chap. 17, "Indian Liquor Laws."
[106] Ibid.
[107] *United States v. Holliday,* 70 U.S. (3 Wall.) 407 (1866); *United States v. Forty-Three Gallons
of Whiskey,* 108 U.S. 491 (1883) and 93 U.S. 188 (1876). The latter case involved liquor
brought in 1872 into Crookston, a white farming village on lands ceded by the Chippewa
and, by treaty, to be kept free of liquor. Needless to say, considerable local white interest
was behind eleven years of protracted litigation, including two trips to the U.S. Supreme
Court.
[108] *United States v. McBratney,* 104 U.S. 621 (1882), is generally seen as unfathomable to experts
in Indian law. Some have argued that the result is simply a mistake. It has also been stated
that the result may have been dictated by purely racial policies. See Cohen, *Handbook of
Federal Indian Law,* 3d ed., 264–6.

occupying its own territory, with boundaries accurately described, in which the laws of Georgia can have no force, and which the citizens of Georgia have no right to enter, but with the assent of the Cherokees themselves.[109]

If Colorado had equal footing with Georgia under this analysis, it would have no jurisdiction over any Indian lands at all, and the requirement of an express reservation of jurisdiction was unnecessary. *McBratney* stands today as good law, testimony to the weak impact of *Worcester* in actual practice.[110]

Although these cases significantly restricted tribal sovereignty in a few areas, the U.S. Supreme Court avoided major statements on the nature of tribal rights through the mid-nineteenth century, deferring without opinion to a status quo recognizing tribal law in offenses among Indians as a treaty right. Both treaty law and the Trade and Intercourse Acts laid out the doctrine clearly and unambiguously. The Jacksonian policy of forced Indian removal pushed many tribes beyond the effective legal reach of either the states or the federal government.[111] The original tribes that agreed to removal to the Indian Territory often did so to flee the jurisdiction of state courts and to accept the promise of the right to live under their own laws.[112] Those living in the western territories, beyond the reach of white society, had never recognized the authority of U.S. law and were free of encroachment by the states because they lived in federal territories, but even there they lived in remote areas. The expansion of both railroads

---

[109] 31 U.S. (5 Pet.) 515 (1831), at 561.

[110] *Oliphant v. Suquamish Indian Tribe,* 435 U.S. 191 (1978), among the Supreme Court cases most restrictive of tribal sovereignty in recent years, finishes the job that *McBratney* began and deprives tribal court systems of any criminal jurisdiction over non-Indians.

[111] The policy of "Indian removal" meant different things to different interest groups, centering only on the common core of the physical movement of the tribes to lands in the West. The most ambitious of reformers believed that ultimately, beyond the threat of local whites, the tribes would become assimilated. For others, not aware that ultimately whites would claim all lands in the United States, removal was a solution in itself: the Indians would simply be gone and therefore no longer any kind of an issue. See Ronald N. Satz, *American Indian Policy in the Jacksonian Era* (Lincoln: University of Nebraska Press, 1975); Michael Rogin, *Fathers and Children: Andrew Jackson and the Subjugation of the American Indian* (New York: Random House, 1975); Robert A. Trennert, *Alternative to Extinction: Federal Indian Policy and the Beginnings of the Reservation System, 1846–51* (Philadelphia, Pa.: Temple University Press, 1975). Trennert, at chap. 1, "The Barrier and the Indian," argues that the idea of the "barrier" on the frontier represented a permanent solution in which racially inferior Indians would simply remain out of the way. Obviously, in such a context, Jacksonians simply weren't threatened by tribal sovereignty because it was meaningless.

[112] There is no question that this is true for the Five Civilized Tribes. Dozens of tribes, however, were removed, and many of their experiences were very different. A survey of some of the other removal efforts is Jay P. Kinney, *A Continent Lost – A Civilization Won: Indian Land Tenure in America* (Baltimore: Johns Hopkins University Press, 1937). A discussion of the full range of provisions of the Indian removal treaties is found in Cohen, *Handbook of Federal Indian Law,* 1st ed., 53–62.

and a land-hungry population across the country ended this isolation. The last wave of major Indian wars in the 1870s and 1880s put all of the tribes within the reach of U.S. law. The next attacks on tribal lands faced by the Indian nations did not involve the states, for the federal government had seized plenary power over the tribes.[113] Rather, it pitted the Indian nations against a federal government determined to destroy tribal sovereignty.

[113] Nell Jessup Newton, "Federal Power over Indians: Its Sources, Scope, and Limitations," *University of Pennsylvania Law Review* 132 (1984): 195, offers a complete survey of the legal basis of the expansion of federal power over Indians. The plenary power doctrine means that federal power over the tribes is complete and unrestricted in any area that the government chooses to extend it. Accordingly, the tribes would retain only such powers as the federal government chose to permit them to retain. Newton discusses the legal basis of this doctrine at 207–28, properly describing the period 1877 to the 1930s as the "plenary power era." This is undoubtedly true, but from the standpoint of the tribes.

3

U.S. Indian law and the Indian nations

The Creek Nation, 1870–1900

The contradiction between tribal sovereignty and a colonial model of imposed law was nowhere more publicly debated than in U.S. policy toward the Indian nations in eastern Oklahoma. The Cherokee, Creek, Choctaw, Chickasaw, and Seminole – the Five Civilized Tribes – all had purchased their lands in fee simple from the government of the United States in the 1830s (1850s in the case of the Seminole) as a part of complex treaty negotiations accompanying the surrender of their southeastern lands.[1] Even Andrew Jackson had argued that only by moving beyond the boundaries of the United States to the Indian Territory could the tribes be "perpetuated as Nations and enjoy the right of living under their own law."[2] The tribes' right to maintain their own laws forever was deeply embedded in the consciousness of the Indian people, who all knew by the time of removal that only through strong defense of their traditions would they survive.[3]

All of these tribes, following the Cherokee model, constituted themselves as "nations" in the West, and that usage became common in the white press and in government relations with them.[4] The question of tribal sovereignty

---

[1] The Indian nations, referred to as "nations" routinely in their nineteenth-century dealings with the United States, clearly enjoyed a special status distinct from tribes in the remainder of the United States. See F. Cohen, *Handbook of Federal Indian Law* (Washington, D.C.: U.S. Government Printing Office, 1942) at chap. 23, "Special Laws Relating to Oklahoma."

[2] Francis Paul Prucha, *American Indian Policy in the Formative Years: The Indian Trade and Intercourse Acts, 1790–1834* (Cambridge, Mass.: Harvard University Press, 1962), chap. 9, and Ronald N. Satz, *American Indian Policy in the Jacksonian Era* (Lincoln: University of Nebraska Press, 1975), chap. 5; the quotation is at 126.

[3] Two recent ethnohistories of the Creeks and Cherokees before removal make clear the role of traditional legal culture in their struggle to resist but also to adapt to white political and economic pressure on traditional native society: William G. McLoughlin, *Cherokee Renascence, 1789–1833* (Princeton, N.J.: Princeton University Press, 1986), and Michael Green, *The Politics of Creek Removal* (Lincoln: University of Nebraska Press, 1982). Those familiar with these works can see how both have influenced my thinking on related issues.

[4] The origin of the term "Indian nations" was in numerous treaties negotiated between the Indian nations and British, colonial, and U.S. authorities. This usage by the executive branch was adopted by U.S. judges even in the earliest Indian rights cases. While Chief Justice John Marshall appears to have deliberately avoided using the term in *Fletcher v. Peck* and *Johnson v. McIntosh*, he deliberately used it repeatedly in both *Cherokee Nation v. Georgia* and in

that later emerged in *Crow Dog* had already been settled in these Indian nations. The state's greed for tribal lands and Andrew Jackson's "Indian removal" policy therefore indirectly reinforced mid-nineteenth-century tribal sovereignty in three ways: first, the Five Civilized Tribes, as well as other eastern tribes, acquired political experience in dealing with the United States that they used as the theoretical foundation for their nations in the West, not only calling themselves "nations" but getting treaties from the United States that recognized that status. Second, the tribes created living models of that sovereignty in the form of effectively functioning Indian nations with unique Indian political and social institutions. Third, these removed southern Indian nations created models of sovereignty that were racially based, ones that influenced both western Indian nations as well as U.S. Indian policy.

While initially it was thought that these Indian nations would be a permanent feature of the frontier, as tribal societies acculturated at their own pace, the creation of these nations soon became a political liability to the United States, as white settlement encroached on Indian lands after the Civil War.[5] In response to federal pressure, internal disagreement spread within the tribes over a wide variety of issues, including the relationship between traditional tribal laws and new laws needed to accommodate the rapid social change occurring within the Indian nations.[6] We know about the dissension and factionalism that occurred within the Cherokee Nation,[7]

Worcester v. Georgia. Attorney General William Wirt in an 1828 opinion, responding to the argument that the Indian nations had a limited independence, was clear: "Nor can it be conceded that their independence as a nation is a limited independence. Like all other independent nations, they are governed solely by their own laws. Like all other independent nations, they have the absolute power of war and peace. Like all other independent nations, their territory is inviolable by any other sovereignty" (2 Op. Att'y Gen. 110 [1828]). While Wirt's views on the matter were clearly in dispute, the usage "Indian nation" became general when referring to the Civilized Tribes, a usage occurring hundreds of times in congressional documents, court cases, executive matters, and in the popular press. By the 1880s, in the assimilationist era when federal authorities were trying to force the Indian nations from their lands, the usage became a topic of controversy. But that does not change, after the fact, the universal legal recognition that the Indian nations had in the mid-nineteenth century.

[5] Among the models for this arrangement was the admission of an Indian state or states. See Annie Abel, "Proposals for an Indian State, 1778–1878," *Annual Report of the American Historical Association* 1 (1907):89–104. On the permanent "Indian barrier" on the frontier, see Robert Trennert, Jr., *Alternative To Extinction: Federal Indian Policy and the Beginnings of the Reservation System, 1846–1851* (Philadelphia, Pa.: Temple University Press, 1975), esp. chap. 1, "The Barrier and the Indian," 1–15.

[6] While in general I refer to the laws of the Indian tribes as "tribal law," rather than customary or traditional law, in this chapter we need to distinguish between two kinds of tribal law, the traditional law of the Creek and Cherokee people and the statutory law adopted by the legislatures of the Creek and Cherokee national governments. Therefore, I use the term "traditional law" to refer to the body of tribal common law that preexisted those legislative enactments.

[7] The process called "factionalization" by anthropologists has produced a large literature; see

which, along with the Choctaw Nation,[8] most readily adapted to the creation of new legal institutions to parallel those in the United States. Indeed, perhaps the best student of Cherokee law reports that their appellate decisions by the 1880s were comparable to those of appellate courts in neighboring states.[9]

Much less is known about the legal institutions of the Creek Nation. A complex balance between traditional law and various pieces of borrowed U.S. law emerges at the center of a factional struggle that repeatedly divided Creek society between the Civil War and 1909. Of all the nations of the Indian Territory, the Creeks and Seminoles most successfully excluded whites and preserved their traditional ways.[10]

Although some observers might argue that Cherokee legal institutions were "civilized," a term that describes only the degree to which Cherokees copied the form of U.S. law, few would say the same of the Creeks. Creek legal institutions retained many traditional ways. Where some version of borrowed U.S. law was applied, it was most often just a thin veneer. In other areas the Creeks refused to compromise. The Cherokees built a modern prison at Tahlequah that was better than the federal prison at Fort Smith; the Creeks held to the end that imprisonment was not a fit punishment for Creek people.[11] The Cherokees readily adopted the U.S. gallows for their executions; the Creeks stubbornly held to a quick and bloody gun blast to the chest.[12] When the final U.S. assault on the lands of the Five Civilized Tribes came, it was justified under a general attack on the "lawlessness" endemic in the Indian Territory and the injustice and barbarity of the Indian

---

Chapter 4, the section entitled "The Trial of Crow Dog." This literature is extremely important for the study of U.S. Indian law because it encompasses the obvious conflict between traditional law and various adaptations modeled after U.S. law. The usually cited traditional–progressive dichotomy does not adequately reflect the complexity of Native American adaptation mechanisms, a point that is well documented in McLoughlin, *Cherokee Renascence*. Rather, there was political conflict within Indian tribes as individuals and groups made difficult political choices, using traditional and progressive strategies.

[8] Angie Debo, *The Rise and Fall of the Choctaw Republic* (Norman: University of Oklahoma Press, 1934).

[9] Rennard Strickland, *Fire and Spirits: Cherokee Law from Clan to Court* (Norman: University of Oklahoma Press, 1975).

[10] The best comparative analysis of the Five Civilized Tribes at the point of liquidation is Angie Debo, *And Still the Waters Run: The Betrayal of the Five Civilized Tribes* (Norman: University of Oklahoma Press, 1940), chap. 1. Grant Foreman, *The Five Civilized Tribes* (Norman: University of Oklahoma Press, 1934), also offers a comparative analysis of the experiences of the Indian nations. Perhaps the best evidence of the success of the Creeks and Seminoles at preserving their old ways is population statistics. According to Debo, 13, by 1890 the Cherokees, Choctaws, and Chickasaws all had white majority populations in their nations. The Creeks and Seminoles retained large Indian majorities: 9,999 Creeks to 3,387 whites; 1,761 Seminoles to 172 whites.

[11] Strickland, *Fire and Spirits*.

[12] For a report of one Creek execution, see "Heart Pierced," *Daily Oklahoman* (Guthrie), October 10, 1893, 1.

courts. From the beginning, the Indian nations were in the way of white settlement and subject to assault on all sides, including from federal law.

The legal status of the Indian Territory, 1865–1900

Beginning in the 1870s, the "lawlessness" of the Indian Territory became a national issue often debated on the floor of Congress and in the press.[13] From that time on, a persistent effort was made – primarily by local white businessmen and western politicians – to restrict the legal sovereignty of the Indian nations, one step at a time.

The legal foundation for that encroachment had been laid in John Marshall's ambiguous language in *Worcester*. So long as the Indian nations were "domestic dependent nations," they were subject to some measure of federal authority, but Marshall had given no hint of the legal framework for that relationship. *United States v. Rogers* (1846), the first U.S. Supreme Court decision on Indian rights following *Worcester*, addressed precisely the issue of how much authority the federal government retained in the Indian Territory. William Rogers, a white man, married a Cherokee woman and was adopted into the Cherokee Nation, living there for nine years. Section 25 of the Indian Trade and Intercourse Act of 1834 gave the United States jurisdiction for the punishment of crimes in "Indian country" but expressly provided that such jurisdiction "shall not extend to crimes committed by one Indian against another."[14] When Rogers was indicted in federal court for the murder of another white man who had become a citizen of the Cherokee Nation, he argued that the federal court lacked jurisdiction because the crime was between two citizens of the Cherokee Nation.

The statute left the courts of the United States to determine whether Rogers was an Indian. Chief Justice Roger Taney seized on the "domestic dependent" condition of Marshall's opinion and held that the Cherokees were not an "independent nation," but their lands were under the power of the United States; thus Rogers had committed his crime within the United States. As though this limitation on the political sovereignty of the Cherokee Nation was not dispositive, Taney further included a racial limitation of

---

[13]   See Francis Paul Prucha, *American Indian Policy in Crisis* (Norman: University of Oklahoma Press, 1976), 379; U.S. Congress, Senate, "Memorial of the Members of the Bar of Muscogee and the Northern District of the Indian Territory...," 54th Congress, 2d session, Doc. 164, February 27, 1897 (Serial Set, v. 3471), 3,6,7,14; U.S. Congress, House of Representatives, "Offenders to be Arrested in the Indian Territory," 50th Congress, 1st session, Report 1016, March 12, 1888 (Serial Set, 2601), 1; U.S. Congress, Senate, "Memorial of C. Brownell," in "Memorial on Bill Creating and Establishing United States Courts of Indian Territory," 50th Congress, 1st session, Misc. doc. 153 (1888; Serial Set, v. 2517), 6,7,9; and J. H. Moore, *The Political Condition of the Indians and the Resources of the Indian Territory* (St. Louis, Mo.: Southwestern Book, 1874).

[14]   Prucha, *American Indian Policy in the Formative Years*, chap. 8.

Cherokee sovereignty. Rogers could not become an Indian under U.S. law, because the status referred to in the act was not a national status activated by the political process of the Cherokee Nation. Rather, it was a racial status: while a white man might acquire some privileges through membership in an Indian tribe and in return be under tribal law for some purposes, "he is not an Indian."[15]

This logic had other implications. It established the right of the federal government to limit Cherokee sovereignty within the Cherokee Nation. The Cherokees could recognize Rogers as a citizen for purposes of conferring the benefits of tribal membership on him, but Cherokee citizenship did not alter Rogers's status as a U.S. citizen. The relationship that Taney defined between federal and tribal authority, based on the Indian Trade and Intercourse Act, holds through to the present day: tribes in Indian Territory might have authority over Indians within their lands, but the United States has authority over whites, as well as the right to determine who belongs to which racial category.[16] Therefore, two criminal jurisdictions coexisted side by side in Indian country, with the United States exercising the power to determine which people fell under each jurisdiction.[17]

Within five years of Taney's decision, Congress took the first of a series of actions to extend U.S. law to the Indian nations. The District of Arkansas was divided in two in 1851, with a Western District Court sitting at Van Buren and having full federal jurisdiction over the Indian Territory. While the court had jurisdiction only over whites, this expansion of federal jurisdiction into the Indian nations still threatened tribal sovereignty. Only one judge served both districts, however, and cases were few with the Civil War and Reconstruction greatly slowing the expansion of federal law into the

[15] *United States v. Rogers*, 45 U.S. (4 How.) 567 (1846), at 572, 573. Obviously, leaving the decision of who is legally entitled to claim the status of an Indian under federal law has the potential to restrict tribal sovereignty. This issue is discussed in Chapter 5, the section entitled "The Racial Geography of Federal Indian Law."

[16] The *Rogers* case is not particularly significant in federal Indian law, and then primarily as Chief Justice Roger Taney's major Indian law opinion that can be juxtaposed against his infamous *Dred Scott* opinion. No Indians were even parties to the case, and William Rogers, a white man and a citizen of the United States, was trying to escape a murder indictment by arguing that his Cherokee citizenship made him subject to Cherokee rather than federal laws. Taney held that both Rogers and Jacob Nicholson, his victim, in effect retained dual citizenship, a decision that did not do great injury to Cherokee sovereignty in itself. More damaging in the case is Taney's reasoning that emphasized the "domestic dependent" language of *Worcester* rather than the "nations" language of the same case. Taney, a Jacksonian, goes to great lengths in his opinion not to refer to the Cherokee nation as a "nation," calling it "the Cherokee country" instead.

[17] This is still the case. The doctrinal history of this distinction is summarized in F. Cohen, (Washington, D.C.: U.S. Government Printing Office, 1942), *Handbook of Federal Indian Law*, 363–5. Chief Justice William Rehnquist has added the latest layer to this problem of the coexistence of two distinct systems in *Oliphant v. Suquamish Indian Tribe*, 435 U.S. 191 (1978).

territory.[18] With the end of the Civil War and the expansion that followed, the pace of white encroachment increased, with the regular appearance of cattle drives through Indian land and the beginnings of railroad construction. In 1871, Congress created a separate judgeship for the Western District and moved the court to Fort Smith. Already the Indian Territory had the beginnings of a "lawless" reputation caused by white horse and cattle thieves fleeing state jurisdiction.[19]

Between 1871 and 1875, four judges presided in this new district, including one carpetbagger who served fourteen months, tried few cases, and ran up a $40,000 bill for court costs. This situation ended in 1875 with the appointment of Judge Isaac Parker and the beginning of U.S. legend. In his thirty-one years on the bench, Parker tried thousands of criminal cases, sentenced more than two hundred men to the gallows, and personally watched seventy-nine hang. With his filthy jail often filled with several hundred men awaiting trial, Parker became popularly known as "the law West of Fort Smith."[20] Furthermore, even though Indians were a minority of the criminals convicted in the Fort Smith court and the court lacked jurisdiction over most activities involving Indians,[21] the overall effect of Parker's administration was a significant extension of U.S. power into the Indian nations.

His most important jurisdictional ruling in this respect was *ex parte Kenyon*. Kenyon, the white husband of a Cherokee, was serving five years in the Cherokee Nation's prison for stealing a horse belonging to his deceased wife. Arguing that the Cherokees had no jurisdiction over Kenyon because he was white, his attorney filed a writ of habeas corpus in Parker's court. The Cherokees countered that Parker had no jurisdiction over the Cherokee Nation and could not issue the writ. Parker held that the entire Indian Territory was within his jurisdiction. His logic was simple and not of the kind often applied to jurisdiction over Indians: he had authority to issue the writ against a state court, and clearly the Cherokee Nation "does not possess a higher right of sovereignty than the several states of the union." Parker issued the writ and Kenyon was freed.[22]

---

[18] G. Bryan Dobbs, "Murder in the Supreme Court: Appeals from the Hanging Judge," *Arkansas Law Review* 29 (1975):47–70, at 47–8.

[19] Glenn Shirley, *Law West of Fort Smith* (Lincoln: University of Nebraska Press, 1957), 14–15. There exists a rich mine of primary source materials for a legal history of the federal court at Fort Smith.

[20] See ibid., 17–24, for a history of the court prior to Parker's appointment. Statistics on executions are cited at ix and a detailed listing of Parker's hangings at 209–43.

[21] The Indian majority of 1880 was lost at some point before the 1890 census, and whites became a majority of the population of Parker's district. His criminal jurisdiction covered the Indian Territory – all of present-day Oklahoma – although the size of that territory had been reduced by the late 1880s. Jurisdictional issues are treated throughout Shirley, *Law West of Fort Smith*.

[22] *Ex parte Kenyon*, 14 F.Cas. 353 (1878). Judge Parker's decision followed logically from the

This case followed the U.S. Supreme Court's *Cherokee Tobacco* (1871) case, the second of its efforts to clarify the legal status of the Five Civilized Tribes. This case also extended federal power over the Indian nations, although it used a different legal basis. To evade a federal tax passed in 1868 on distilled spirits, fermented liquors, tobacco, snuff, and cigars produced "anywhere within the exterior boundaries of the United States," a number of speculators, both Cherokee and white, began to produce tobacco in the Cherokee Nation, convinced that it was not within the boundaries of the United States. The resulting lawsuit presents a striking parallel to the original attempts of Georgia to extend its jurisdiction over the Cherokee. The Cherokee Nation recognized as much, appropriating $1,500 to hire the best legal counsel available, Albert Pike, the former Confederacy's Commissioner of Indian Affairs, and Senator Robert W. Johnson.[23] The Court's majority, relying on Chief Justice Taney's language in *Rogers*, held that the Cherokee Nation was within the limits of the United States.[24] Justices Joseph Bradley and David Davis dissented, believing that it was not. Since Congress had the power to pass laws specifically affecting the Cherokee Nation and had done so at other times, they argued, the Indian nations were in all ordinary cases "autonomies" and did not fall within the general laws of the United States unless expressly mentioned.[25] Whatever the external status of these nations, there can be no question of their internal status: they exercised complete internal sovereignty.

The courts of the Indian nations were left with full jurisdiction, both civil and criminal, over the citizens of their own nations and over all other Indians within their territory. The Federal District Court in Fort Smith had criminal jurisdiction in the Indian Territory over whites and over Indians who committed crimes against whites. This system might have been clear enough in the early 1870s, but the rapid commercial expansion within the Indian Ter-

---

Supreme Court's *Cherokee Tobacco* case: if the Cherokee Nation was somehow within the United States, yet not a state, nor obviously a territory, it must at least be in some kind of similar status. The fact that this case was heard forty years after the Cherokee's moved west, indicates that the federal government had given little thought to the legal status of the Indian nations. It also indicates that the Indian nations had taken criminal jurisdiction over whites as an attribute of their sovereignty up to this time.

[23] Robert K. Heimann, "The Cherokee Tobacco Case," *Chronicles of Oklahoma* 41 (Fall 1963):299–322, at 317–19. *The Cherokee Tobacco*, 78 U.S. (11 Wall) 616 (1871).

[24] Ibid., 619–21.

[25] Ibid., 622–4. This dissent represents the last time that a U.S. Supreme Court justice followed the lead of justices Story and McClean in holding the Indian nations as outside the limits of U.S. authority, albeit with the analogy of "foreign nations" of the 1830s now replaced by the language of "autonomies." In the decade following the Civil War, in which the Indian nations actively participated, the idea that the Indian nations were "foreign" was beyond the comprehension of any U.S. policymakers. Still, this idea that the Indian nations were autonomies gave effect to Marshall's domestic, dependent nations framework in a way that did far less violence to Indian sovereignty than the *Rogers* emphasis on their domestic and dependent status.

ritory, especially in the Choctaw and Cherokee nations, left U.S. commercial interests lobbying for an adequate system of civil court jurisdiction. Some civil matters fell under the jurisdiction of the federal district court, but many were left to the civil jurisdiction of the Indian nations, which often lacked adequate civil laws to govern commercial activity.[26] Some of the nations, particularly the Cherokee and Choctaw, responded to this problem by establishing elaborate civil codes to regulate commerce within their territory, but the Creeks did not.[27]

Congress, in 1889, created a Federal District Court for the Indian Territory, sitting in Muskogee, a railroad town in the Creek Nation. The court held civil jurisdiction in all controversies over $100 but not in civil suits between Indians. Initially, the Muskogee court could try only minor criminal cases; full jurisdiction remained at Fort Smith.[28] The next year the criminal jurisdiction of the Muskogee court was expanded, and branches of the court were created later in the other Indian nations.[29] In 1896, Congress granted full criminal jurisdiction to these courts, and the federal court at Fort Smith ceased to function.[30]

In a very real sense, the "law and order" problem of the Indian nations was the product of U.S. politics and not of Indian sovereignty. The jurisdictional void created when the Indian nations were denied criminal jurisdiction over their own land and when U.S. courts were established a hundred

[26] The jurisdictional reach (and corresponding limitations) of civil courts was of great importance to white businessmen and lawyers living in the Indian Territory; hence, there were many memorials to Congress on the subject. See, e.g., U.S. Congress, Senate, "Memorial of C. Brownell," 50th Congress, 1st session, Misc. doc. 153 (1888; Serial Set, v. 2517), and "Additional Judge of the United States Court in Indian Territory," 54th Congress, 2d session, Doc. 164 (1897; Serial Set, v. 3471).

[27] Strickland, *Fire and Spirits;* Angie Debo, *The Rise and Fall of the Choctaw Republic* (Norman: University of Oklahoma Press, 1934), chap. 7; Oliver Knight, "Fifty Years of Choctaw Law, 1834–1884," *Chronicles of Oklahoma* 31 (1953):76–95.

[28] "Memorial of C. Brownell," outlines the history of federal jurisdiction in the Indian Territory. It is important to note that all of the Indian nations consistently resisted the extention of federal jurisdiction into their territory. See, e.g., U.S. Congress, House of Representatives, "Protest of the Creek Delegates Against the Expansion of the Jurisdiction of the United States Court in the Indian Territory," 51st Congress, 2d session, Misc. doc 104 (1891; Serial Set, v. 2869). So important was the creation of this court to white commercial interests that a new reporter, the *Indian Territory Reporter,* was established to publish the cases of this court.

[29] Angie Debo, *The Road to Disappearance: A History of the Creek Indians* (Norman: University of Oklahoma Press, 1941), 326. Debo shows how the Indians' fears of the impact of federal courts in their territory were correct. White residents found protection and expansion of their rights in federal courts, where judges sympathetic to white expansionist interest generated ruling after ruling favorable to those interests. Those rulings undermined Creek prohibition laws (327), interpreted Creek inheritance laws in such a way as to allow whites to inherit Indian property (334), and in 1895, allowed white citizens to create municipal governments under Arkansas statutes, independent of tribal authority (364–5).

[30] Shirley, *Law West of Fort Smith,* 199–206.

miles or more away attracted non-Indian criminals from throughout the West. Subjecting those whites to tribal courts might well have both kept white outlaws out of the Indian nations and effectively punished those who either committed crimes or fled there. As it was, even ineffective cooperation between U.S. marshalls and tribal police led to hundreds of arrests of criminal whites.[31] Few whites wanted to make this distinction.[32]

The tribes recognized that extension of federal jurisdiction over their lands would be accompanied by a vigorous white assault on them. Therefore, the tribes organized an effective resistance that repeatedly delayed Congress's attempts to expand federal jurisdiction. Senate Bill 679, for example, which proposed to organize a Territory of Oklahoma and to create a new federal court with jurisdiction there in 1870, brought a large delegation from the Five Civilized Tribes to Washington. Their twelve-page remonstrance was prophetic:

> They are swift to hunt up every fragment of record which they suppose will militate against the Indians, distort its meaning, and parade it before the public gaze, but suppress every particle of record which is favorable to the Indians...
> However much our people might want to avoid difficulty, their [squatters' and speculators'] object and interest would be to provoke it. We think we hazard nothing in saying that in nineteen out of twenty cases of hostility between Indians and Whites, it was engendered by the class of persons just described, or the failure of the government to keep its treaty stipulations.[33]

The Creeks sent a number of protests and remonstrances to Congress. These most often included lengthy quotations from their treaties to prove their right to self-government. For example, Article 15 of the Creek and Seminole Treaty of 1856 specifically stated, "So far as may be compatible with the Constitution of the United States . . . the Creek and Seminoles shall be secured in the unrestricted right of self-government, and full jurisdiction over persons and property within their respective limits."[34] Article 10 of the Creek Treaty of 1866 went more directly to the matter of federal courts in the Indian nation:

> The Creek agree to such legislation as the Congress and President . . .
> may deem necessary for the better administration of justice and the

---

[31] In one well-known incident, Cherokee lighthorsemen engaged in a gun battle with U.S. marshals, but by and large the relationship was much more cooperative, especially given the racism and corruption of many of the marshals. Shirley, *Law West of Fort Smith.*

[32] Debo, *Road to Disappearance,* 326–8.

[33] U.S. Congress, Senate, "Memorial of the Delegates of the Cherokee, Creek, and Choctaw Nations of Indians," misc. doc. 143 (1870; Serial Set, v. 1408), 4.

[34] U.S. Congress, House of Representatives, 51st Congress, 2d session, Misc. doc. 2869 (1891; Serial Set, v. 2517), 1.

protection of all rights of person and property within the Indian Territory: provided, however, that said legislation shall not in any manner interfere with or annul their present tribal organizations, rights, laws, privileges or customs.[35]

From the standpoint of U.S. law, this treaty merely created a set of interests to be balanced by either Congress or the courts. The Creeks had had enough experience with that kind of balancing. A federal court within their territory was not substantially different from a federal court in Arkansas with jurisdiction over the Creek Nation. There was more than a symbolic objection to the creation of federal courts sitting within the Creek Nation. The Creeks, as a matter of national policy, deliberately chose not to make Creek law available to non-Indians who wanted to do business in their nation. This was one way to keep the population of white intruders low – a Creek strategy that largely succeeded.[36]

The united efforts of the Five Civilized Tribes, together with the strong language of their treaty rights, carried substantial weight in Washington and doubtlessly influenced Congress's decision in 1885 not to extend the Major Crimes Act to the Indian Territory. Although the tribes effectively blocked the creation of a state from their lands until 1907, nine years after the liquidation of the Indian nations, they were not so long successful in blocking the extension of federal legal jurisdiction.

Well-organized whites in the Indian Territory and their powerful allies around the country petitioned Congress. Perhaps the strongest appeal came in 1891 from Governor William Fishback of Arkansas. In a letter to President Grover Cleveland, Fishback pronounced the Indian Territory a great "school of crime" and a danger to neighboring states. He cited the example of a gang of bank robbers arrested in Arkansas with a map showing their route from the Indian Territory to Chattanooga, Tennessee, as proof that "a very large percentage of the bank robberies which take place between the Rockies and the Alleghenies are organized in the Indian Territory." Moreover, the outlaws had a bad influence "stirring up the young Indians to deeds of blood and theft." Citing an unnamed Muskogee newspaper for the statistic of two hundred murders in one year beyond the jurisdiction of U.S. courts, Fishback argued that the federal government should exercise its power of eminent domain over the Indian nations because they were a "constant menace to the peace and order of all the states of the Mississippi Valley."[37]

---

[35] Ibid.

[36] There was considerable intertribal dispute over Creek policy toward noncitizen whites who needed permits to work in the Creek Nation. Wealthy Creeks favored a liberal permit system, but most of the tribe was against it. Creek law on these matters was changed several times; finally all permits were abolished in 1893, an action that should have removed all whites from Creek lands but obviously did not. See Debo, *Road to Disappearance*, 329–30.

[37] Governor Fishback's letter, evidently widely circulated at the time, is found in W. J. Watts,

The newly appointed federal judges in the Indian Territory participated in the campaign to discredit the tribal courts and used their positions to damage tribal institutions. In 1897 all three federal judges in the Indian Territory wrote detailed letters to Congress echoing the views of Governor Fishback. Judge William Springer of Muskogee pointed out that his court had disposed of 3,817 criminal and 3,146 civil cases since 1889. In addition, Springer claimed that 80 percent of the 1,202 criminal cases disposed of in the federal district courts of Fort Smith and Paris, Texas (which had federal criminal jurisdiction over the Choctaw and Chickasaw nations), were from the Indian Territory.

Springer repeated two common arguments. First, he claimed that most of the citizens of the Indian nations were whites (including those claiming to be of Indian blood). This argument, which dated back to Cherokee and Creek claims for tribal sovereignty against Georgia and Alabama, implied both that Indian law no longer existed, because the Indian nations were controlled by white or mixed-blood people, and that the Indians had voluntarily given up their sovereignty by inviting whites to live in their lands. Second, he claimed that Indian justice was "exceedingly expensive per capita and notoriously inefficient," that is, Indians guilty of crime went free because their legal systems did not function effectively.

Finally, in a backhanded compliment, Springer said he believed that "the degree of civilization which has been attained by the citizens of the Five Civilized Tribes is far in advance of the crude and inefficient jurisdiction exercised by the tribal courts." Continuing, he argued that "the judicial anomaly existing in the Indian Territory is without any precedent in civilized countries. There are two sets of laws operating upon two classes of people who live in the same locality." It was possible to have a business partnership between two people, one of whom was subject to one law, and one to another.[38]

By the 1880s and 1890s, the U.S. Supreme Court was regularly taking

Cherokee Citizenship and a Brief History of Internal Affairs in the Cherokee Nation (Muldrow, Indian Territory: Register Print, 1895), 133. The context of its use by Watts is important. A number of whites launched an attack on the government and legal system of the Cherokee Nation by claiming to be Cherokees and thus demanding access to Cherokee lands. Since the courts of the Indian nations had exclusive jurisdiction in matters of tribal citizenship, the whites, not unexpectedly, lost in the Cherokee courts. This example of the injustice of the Cherokee courts then became one argument used by whites who wished to abolish the court system of the Indian nations because, they claimed, it was under the control of a few wealthy and self-interested Indians. The Dawes Commission later accepted part of this reasoning; see later this section. The Cherokee side of this controversy can be found in Morris L. Wardell, *A Political History of the Cherokee Nation, 1838–1907* (Norman: University of Oklahoma Press, 1938), 277–9. Although the Creeks never had an intruder problem as did the Choctaws, Chickasaws, and Cherokees, the fates of the Five Civilized Tribes were interrelated.

[38] "Additional Judge of United States Court in the Indian Territory," 9, 11–14.

cases from the Indian Territory that raised the full range of these jurisdictional problems.[39] Whites hoped that the Court would act to end the special status of the Indian nations. The Court closely following its logic in the plenary power doctrine of *United States v. Kagama*, indicated that only Congress could take such action. Consistent with this position, the Court handed down a series of opinions upholding the criminal jurisdiction of the Indian nations.

Famous Smith, a Cherokee convicted and sentenced to death by Judge Parker, appealed his conviction on the ground that the person he was convicted of killing was not a white but a fellow Cherokee and that the federal courts therefore had no jurisdiction over his crime. Although the issue of the victim's race was a matter of law, burdening the government to prove the victim was white in order have jurisdiction over Smith, Parker sent the question to the jury as a part of its deliberative process. Not surprisingly, it decided the victim was white and that Smith was guilty of murder. The Supreme Court in *Famous Smith v. United States* (1894) found Smith's victim to be Cherokee and ruled that Parker had erred in letting the jury decide this issue. The verdict was set aside, upholding the jurisdiction of the courts of the Cherokee Nation.[40]

An earlier, more direct attempt by Parker to use federal criminal law to intervene in Cherokee society and undermine tribal self-government occurred in *in re Mayfield* (1891). Mayfield, a Cherokee man, was convicted in Parker's court of adultery with a white woman and sentenced to three years in the Detroit House of Correction. Mayfield petitioned for a writ of habeas corpus on the ground that Cherokee courts had exclusive jurisdiction over all crimes committed in their nation "in which members of the nation ... shall be the only parties." Because the woman was not married and not indicted, Mayfield argued that he was the "only party" and, therefore, under Cherokee jurisdiction. Unlike the case of Famous Smith, in which the Cher-

---

[39] While an extensive system of appellate review characterizes the modern U.S. legal system, this was not true in the nineteenth century, particularly in the area of federal criminal law. Until 1889, for example, there were no criminal appeals from Judge Parker's court. G. Bryan Dobbs, "Murder in the Supreme Court: Appeals from the Hanging Judge," *Arkansas Law Review* 29 (1975):46. More generally, see David Rossman, "Were There No Appeal: The History of Review in American Criminal Courts," *Journal of Criminal Law and Criminology* 81 (1990):518. Obviously, this lack of access to appellate review in criminal law until very late in the nineteenth century is part of the reason that there are so few Indian rights cases earlier in the century.

[40] *Famous Smith v. United States*, 151 U.S. 50 (1894). The Court's willingness to give the Cherokees the benefit of the doubt as to race did not extend to black citizens of the Indian nations. In a closely parallel murder case, *Alberty v. United States*, 153 U.S. 499 (1896), the Court decided that Alberty, a former slave who became a citizen of the Cherokee Nation, must be legally treated as a member of the tribe even though he was not an Indian and that his victim, the illegitimate child of a Choctaw and a Negro woman, was not an Indian; therefore, jurisdiction over the crime was in the federal courts.

okees, like the United States, had a murder statute, the Cherokee Nation never had an adultery statute. The U.S. Supreme Court accordingly granted the writ and set Mayfield free.[41]

In *Talton v. Mayes* (1896), the Court let a Cherokee murder conviction and death sentence stand. Bob Talton appealed to the Court that he had not had a fair trial because he had not been indicted by a grand jury as required by the Fifth Amendment of the U.S. Constitution. The Court held that "the powers of local self government enjoyed by the Cherokee Nation existed prior to the Constitution ... they are not operated upon by the Fifth Amendment."[42] Without even citing *Kagama* or the Major Crimes Act, the opinion held firmly to the view that the Cherokees had a right to their own laws because their inherent sovereignty preceded the Constitution and because their treaties with the United States gave them the right to maintain their own legal systems. The same principle held true in the Creek Nation. Shortly after *Talton* was decided, William Tiger was sentenced by a Creek court to be shot for the murder of another Creek. He appealed to a federal court for a writ of habeas corpus, arguing that the Creek prosecutor had not followed the proper procedures in his indictment of Tiger under Creek law.[43]

Rejecting a common law argument about the meaning of the term "indictment," the court in *ex parte Tiger* (1898) clearly recognized the autonomy of Creek law: "If the Creek Nation derived its system of jurisprudence through the common law, there would be much plausibility in this reasoning. But they are strangers to the common law. They derive their jurisprudence from an entirely different source."[44] This recognition not only of Creek sovereignty, but of the integrity of Creek jurisprudence and the court's refusal to apply common law reasoning to Creek law characterize the legal recognition of the legal sovereignty of the Indian nations, even at the end of the nineteenth century. Even twenty years later, the U.S. Supreme Court heard the appeal of a lawsuit against the Creek Nation for an 1890 attack by hundreds of Creek citizens against eighty miles of fence erected within the nation by a cattle company composed of wealthy Creeks in league with Texas cattlemen in violation of the nation's "mile-square" pasture law. Dismissing evidence that the Creek government had acted improperly in refusing responsibility for the damage under Creek law, the Court held that "the Creek Nation was recognized by the United States as a distinct political community

---

[41] *In re Mayfield*, 141 U.S. 112 (1891). Strickland, *Fire and Spirits*, 31.
[42] *Talton v. Mayes*, 163 U.S. 376 (1896).
[43] *Ex parte Tiger*, 47 S.W. 304 (1898). This case was in the newly created federal court of appeals for the Indian Territory, hearing an appeal from the federal district court for the northern district of the Indian Territory. This special appellate court was created to handle the great volume of appeals from the district courts.
[44] Ibid., 305.

with which it made treaties and which within its own territory administered its internal affairs."[45]

Notwithstanding this case, *Talton* and *Tiger* were among the last cases that left the Indian nations with any measure of sovereignty in the area of criminal jurisdiction over major offenses. Congress, in part directly responding to the problems that tribal sovereignty created within the white conception of the American nation and also as part of a broader Indian policy of land allotment, finally terminated the Indian nations. The tribes of the Indian Territory had exercised sufficient political strength to exempt themselves from the provisions of the Dawes Act of 1887,[46] just as they had escaped the provisions of the Major Crimes Act of 1885. Even the Oklahoma Organic Act had been blocked by a strong faction in Congress upholding traditional treaty rights until, as a compromise, the Indian nations were left outside of the boundaries of the territory. This opposition had within it the seeds of its own undoing because its argument was based on traditional contract theory. Treaties "freely" negotiated between equal parties could be changed by the "consent" of the tribes.[47]

---

[45] *Turner v. United States and Creek Nation of Indians*, 284 U.S. 354 (1918), at 357. On the mile-square pasture law, see pages 91–3 below.

[46] The full history of the Dawes Act has yet to be written, but it clearly represented the union of two opposing white strategies for the domination of the tribes. The assimilationist organization Friends of the Indian saw allotment as the only way to force assimilation of the tribes. Those who wanted tribal lands saw allotment as the only way to wrest the tribes' remaining lands from them. D. S Otis, *The Dawes Act and the Allotment of Indian Lands* (Norman: University of Oklahoma Press, 1934; 1973). Otis, in discussing the motivations of the Indian nations in opposing allotment, incredibly leaves out tribal sovereignty and focuses on the influence of Texas cattlemen with substantial leased grazing interests (43).

[47] For the Indian position on their treaty rights, see U.S. Congress, Senate, "Memorial from the Delegates from the Indian Territory Protesting the Passage of the Bill to Organize the Territory of Oklahoma," 45th Congress, 1st session, Misc. doc. 82 (1878; Serial Set, v. 1786), and "Memorial of the Delegates of the Cherokee, Creek and Choctaw Nations of Indians," 41st Congress, 2d session, Misc. doc. 143 (1870; Serial v. 1408). The influence of these Indian arguments can be seen in congressional debate on the Dawes Act and the Major Crimes Act. See U.S. Congress, House of Representatives, "Organization of the Territory of Oklahoma," 45th Congress, 3d session, Doc. 188 (1879; Serial Set, v. 1867); "The Territory of Oklahoma," 44th Congress, 2d session Report 82 (1877; Serial Set, v. 1769); and "Organization of the Territory of Oklahoma," 50th Congress, 1st session Report 263 (1888; Serial Set, v. 2599). The latter report recommended to the full House for the first time that the Territory of Oklahoma be incorporated. The section entitled "Views of the Minority" (16–30) is a strong statement of the Indian's position. The compromise Oklahoma Organic Act, passed on May 2, 1890, created an Oklahoma Territory of former Indian lands alienated after the Civil War and largely settled by whites, and it removed western tribes west of the Indian Territory. A revealing look at what was in store for the Indians placed within the boundaries of this new territory can be had from the report (chart, 2), which lists the population and land base of each of the tribes in Oklahoma and, after calculating "acreage required by Indians and allowing them 160 acres for a family of four," concludes that the Indians required only 462,949 acres and that 11,582,684 acres were

Congress was determined to end forever the sovereignty of the Indian nations, and that is what was at stake for those nations in their resistance to allotment. In the fall of 1893, Congress appointed a special commission to negotiate with the tribes, particularly the Cherokees, for surplus lands in the Indian Territory for white settlement. These negotiations opened up many Oklahoma tracts and the famous land rush in the Cherokee outlet. With these negotiations finished, Congress mandated the commission to stay in operation and oversee the allotment of the Indian nations themselves. Although allotment did not inherently require the abolition of the governments and institutions of the Indian nations, that was the clear course of action followed by the Commission to the Five Civilized Tribes, more often called the Dawes Commission.[48]

The commission's 1894 annual report sounded the theme for its work and set out its legal theory for the liquidation of the Indian nations. Indian political structure was subjected to merciless attack: "Justice has been utterly perverted in the hands of those who have thus laid hold of the forms of administration in this Territory and who have inflicted irreparable wrongs and outrages upon a helpless people for their own gain." It followed from this subversion of justice that the treaty rights of the Five Civilized Tribes were nullified. The government of the United States had, through the various treaties, given the tribal governments a trust responsibility to administer the nations for "the use and enjoyment in common by each and every citizen of his tribe." By granting mining and grazing rights, the tribal governments exceeded their power and violated their trust. It was therefore the "plain duty of the United States to enforce the trust it had so created and recover for its original uses the domain and all the gains derived from the perversions of the trust or discharge the trustee."[49]

In a related argument, the commission claimed that the United States had granted the tribes the power of self-government but that the tribes had so failed to exercise that right capably that the government had the duty to revoke the power.[50] This argument, of course, falsely assumes that tribal

"surplus." The members of the Five Civilized Tribes had no illusions about the meaning of being incorporated into the Oklahoma Territory.

[48] Prucha, *American Indian Policy in Crisis*, 388–94.

[49] The best source on the work of the Dawes Commission is the exhaustive commission reports themselves. The process of negotiations is covered in detail in Commission to the Five Civilized Tribes, *Annual Report*, 1894, 1895, 1896 (Washington, D.C.: U.S. Government Printing Office). The quotations are from the 1894 report, 19–20. The federal trusteeship doctrine in Indian affairs descends deductively from the tribes' domestic dependent status and was first applied by the U.S. Supreme Court in *Kagama* and *Lone Wolf*. Robert Clinton, Nell Jessup Newton, and Monroe E. Price, *American Indian Law* (3d. ed. Charlottesville, Va.: Michie, 1991), at 15–18.

[50] Commission to the Five Civilized Tribes, *Annual Report*, 1894, 19–20.

sovereignty derives from a grant of power by the United States and was not an inherent attribute of Indian nations before they entered into treaties with the United States.[51]

The Dawes Commission increased its attacks on Indian "misrule" in succeeding years. The *Annual Report, 1895* concluded:

> All of the functions of the so-called governments of these five tribes have become utterly unable to protect life or property rights of the citizen. Their courts of justice have become powerless and paralyzed. Violence, robbery, and murder have become almost of a daily occurrence, and no effective measures of restraint or punishment are put forth by these governments and courts to suppress crime.... A reign of terror exists, and barbarous outrages almost impossible of belief are enacted, and the perpetrators hardly find it necessary to shun daily intercourse with their victims.[52]

Allegations of terrorism and the routine threatening of witnesses appearing before the commission filled out the report.

The process of U.S. exploitation of the lands of the southern tribes had come full circle. The Dawes Commission "negotiated" with a coercive message to the Indian nations: either agree to allotment and the termination of the functions of their national governments or the federal government would do it involuntarily on less favorable terms. The issue divided the Indian nations and caused considerable unrest. Finally, the nations were forced to cede their lands "voluntarily."[53]

The Creeks, in confronting the hostility of the Dawes Commission, had come full circle as well, back to the "law of Polecat Springs" of seventy years before, which had made the alienation of Creek land the foundation of tribal law. The members of the Dawes Commission were unaware of the functioning of tribal law just beyond their sight:

[51] Commission to the Five Civilized Tribes, *Annual Report, 1894*, 20. The evidence supporting this conclusion is summarized at 15–18. Senator Dawes, in common with most other white Indian reformers, believed in the necessity of forced assimilation of the Indian tribes in the the mainstream of U.S. life, thus the whole idea of tribal sovereignty and the Indian nations was inconsistent with this approach. He believed that the original creation of the Indian nations had been a step toward that goal. But since those nations had not, in fact, assimilated, there had been a case of "arrested progress," so that "Indians living in the woods... were less civilized and fit for citizenship than they were twenty years ago" (15). Dawes is here admitting that the Indian nations had successfully managed to preserve tribal culture and institutions. This logic is clearly opposed to his own argument three pages later that a "few mixed bloods and adopted whites" had taken control of the tribal governments for "their own gain" (16, 18).

[52] Commission to the Five Civilized Tribes, *Annual Report, 1895*, 15.

[53] The best single account of the coercive context of this negotiation is Debo, *And Still the Waters Run*, who would agree that Dawes and his commission were essentially concerned with the destruction of tribal sovereignty in the Indian nations.

A man of known integrity and irreproachable character, appeared before
the Commission and presented his knowledge of the condition of affairs
and views for change. In a few days, the Commission were in receipt
of a letter from him informing him that he had been followed in Missouri,
where he went on business, by two armed Indians, who informed him
that he would be killed if he returned home through the Territory.[54]

The Creeks did not consent to the allotment of their lands, so Congress
acted unilaterally. On July 1, 1898, the national governments of the Five
Civilized Tribes were stripped of their powers, ending the hundred-year-
old U.S. policy of recognizing, if not always encouraging, tribal sovereignty
outside of the boundaries of U.S. society.

We are the poorer for what the Dawes Commission failed to understand
of the vitality of the law of the Indian nations. The tribes of the Indian
Territory became subject to the full jurisdiction of the territorial courts of
Oklahoma. No reservations were created, and the allotted (and soon to be
largely stolen and alienated) land was not defined as "Indian country."
Therefore, *Crow Dog* and the Major Crimes Act did not reach the Creeks
or any of the other Five Civilized Tribes. In 1907, at the creation of the
new state of Oklahoma, full state civil and criminal jurisdiction was extended
over the Five Civilized Tribes, intending to end any remnant of their sov-
ereignty-based right to their own laws.[55]

Creek legal culture, 1870–1900

Creek law operated with little reference to U.S. law and legal institutions,
taking Creek nationhood and tribal sovereignty as its starting point. The
Creek warriors who tore down Turner's eighty miles of fence because it
violated their conception of Creek property law were unconcerned with U.S.
law governing such actions. An understanding of the operation of Creek law
and legal institutions in the Indian Territory in the late nineteenth century
requires the recognition that two parallel legal institutions operated side by
side. One system of laws was traditional, with roots running back to the
original Creek towns in Georgia and Alabama. The other system was the
set of "adaptive" laws copied from U.S. legal institutions or from Cherokee
or Choctaw models and formally adopted by the Creek National Council.[56]

---

[54] Ibid., 76.

[55] It is now clear that this did not occur and that the Indian nations of Oklahoma retain much
of their tribal sovereignty. F. Cohen, *Handbook of Federal Indian Law* (Charlottesville, Va.:
Michie, 1982), summarizes the current status of the Five Civilized Tribes.

[56] The key to understanding tribal legal systems in the nineteenth century is in this understanding that the ethnographic accounts of traditional tribal law so popular in late-nineteenth
and early-twentieth-century anthropology present static, traditional legal orders that could
not adapt to the rapid social change introduced by white contact. In reality these traditional

The interaction of these institutions can be seen in a brief history of the factional struggles that characterized Creek politics between the Civil War and 1908. Although serious factional struggle troubled Indian political life throughout the United States and existed in all of the Indian nations in Oklahoma, the Creek Nation probably suffered the most serious factional rifts of any American Indian tribe.[57]

After their removal from Georgia in the 1830s, the Upper and Lower Creeks reconstituted their towns in a close approximation of their original spatial relationships, with the more acculturated Lower Creeks along the Arkansas River and the more traditional Upper Creeks along the Canadian River. The towns (forty-six were enumerated in the census of 1890) had a total population of about ten thousand Creeks. With each town having well under one hundred adults, these were very small, well-ordered units. Unlike the ancestral towns in the South, however, in which dwellings were concentrated around a small square, the new towns were dispersed over an area of at least several miles, with each family unit living in a small cabin on a plot of communally owned farmland. Plots were not so far-flung, however, as to disrupt the traditional face-to-face network of interrelationships that had characterized life in the towns.

The Creeks were never a single tribe but a loose confederacy of towns interlinked through a complex clan structure. Each Creek citizen belonged to his or her town for life. A hundred years of white contact, deaths through war and disease, internal migration within Georgia and Alabama, and removal had altered traditional social structures, but they still functioned effectively. In the 1840s and 1850s, the traditional town councils operated in the Indian Territory as both political and legal bodies as they always had, dispensing justice in traditional ways.[58]

legal orders were all in transition, accommodating traditional legal orders inside a framework of adapting political and legal structures. Debo, *The Road to Disappearance*, shows this for the Creek Nation. Peter Whiteley, *Deliberate Acts: Changing Hopi Culture Through the Oraibi Split* (Tucson: University of Arizona Press, 1988), imaginatively shows the same process for the Hopi. Karl N. Llewellyn and E. Adamson Hoebel, *The Cheyenne Way* (Norman: University of Oklahoma Press, 1941), a study intending to show that traditional Cheyenne law had many of the elements of jurisprudence as it is understood in Western law, also shows how Cheyenne law adapted to social change. Ironically, the Plains Indian legal orders of the mid-nineteenth century were themselves the products of rapid legal change and were less than a hundred years old, reflecting the influence of the horse and rapid mobility on tribal culture and social organization.

[57] I base this judgment on the simple fact that no tribe fought internal wars as frequently as the Creeks did after contact with whites. This nation of perhaps ten thousand people had five civil wars between 1860 and 1908 – roughly one per decade – and on several other occasions two Creek governments functioned simultaneously and contentiously.

[58] On the transition of traditional Creek society in the Southeast, see Green, *Politics of Creek Removal*, chaps. 1–2, and Debo, *Road to Disappearance*, chaps. 1–3. The classic ethnohistory of Creek society is John Swanton, *Social Organization and Social Usages of the Creek Confederacy*, Bureau of American Ethnology, no. 42 (Washington, D.C.: 1924–5). Another early eth-

Little is known of traditional Creek law. By the time white observers recorded anything of Creek society, it had already undergone cataclysmic social change. The Creek population at the end of the eighteenth century may have been reduced by 90 percent from the level of one hundred years before. Moreover, white observers did not fully understand what they saw. Early descriptions of Creek law focused on a relentless pursuit of blood revenge as the basis of the legal culture, even to the point of barbarity: for example, a boy who accidentally killed another boy had to suffer death.[59]

Creek laws were reduced to writing in Alabama in the 1820s and remained in effect until the liquidation of the nation. Virtually all of the early laws concerned crime and punishment, perhaps in a graphic way illustrating what the major issues were. Trials were held, with a minimum of procedural formality, before the whole council. Witnesses were seldom called, as the accused most often admitted his guilt, a form of courage expected from a warrior. Punishment – and shooting and whipping were the only punishments – was carried out almost immediately. This law was simple and direct, with a strong sense of accountability to the community and of personal responsibility for harm done to others.[60]

The early codification of Creek law was the result of two forces. First, the complexity of relations with whites put the Creeks, like the Cherokees, on notice that they had to act as a sovereign nation to forestall the white

---

nohistory is Ohland Morton, "The Government of the Creek Indians," *Chronicles of Oklahoma* 8 (1930):42–64, 189–225.

[59] On changes in Creek society during the seventeenth and eighteenth centuries, see Green, *Politics of Creek Removal*, 1–44. John Swanton, "Social Organization and Social Usages of the Creek Confederacy," 42nd Annual Report of the Bureau of American Ethnology, 1924–5, quotes much of the early material. See, e.g., James Adair's influential *History of the American Indians* (1775; rpt. New York: Johnson Reprint, 1969): "The American Indians are more eager to revenge blood, than any other people on the whole face of the earth" (340).

[60] The only account of this early legal process is Green, *Politics of Creek Removal*, chap. 4. The text of these early Creek laws, evidently first written down in 1818, is available in Antonio J. Waring (ed.), *Laws of the Creek Nation*, University of Georgia Libraries Miscellania Publications, no. 1 (Athens, 1960). Evidently, the law was originally laid down by the council at a treaty negotiation with whites in July 1817. At that time the council agreed to a small land cessation to whites, but perhaps as a part of a compromise to get that cessation approved, the council proclaimed a law: "Anyone, however great he might be, even Big Warrior, Little Prince, or McIntosh [specifically naming existing chiefs] should he sell another foot of land to the Georgians would be put to death" (5). This law remained unwritten until reported in the white press in 1824 in an account of a talk given by a Creek leader (5). Swanton, *Creek Confederacy*, 338–58, offers a complete account of the operation of Creek law in the nineteenth century, based on early accounts of white travelers. For example, he quotes Josiah Gregg's famous *Commerce of the Prairies* on a Creek trial Gregg witnessed: "They have no trial by jury, and their judicial proceedings are exceedingly summary – frequently without witnesses; for the warriors are generally too proud to deny a charge, lest it be construed as cowardice. Executions sometimes take place within an hour after the commencement of a trial. Murder, rape, and a third conviction of stealing are punished with death" (344). Also see Debo, *Road to Disappearance*, 125–8.

onslaught. A code of laws was an important part of this effort. Second, the increased mobility of early-nineteenth-century society and heightened divisions between Upper and Lower Creeks weakened traditional town-based tribal legal structures, especially in intertown matters. Although most of the early written laws were simple codifications of well-understood traditional laws, there were two exceptions. The law of Polecat Springs forbade the selling of Creek lands, the possibility of which only the pressure of U.S. society had introduced. Creeks also passed a law outlawing blood revenge when a person was punished by the nation for violations of its criminal law. This law is instructive because the need for it shows that the nation was potentially hampered in its law enforcement by prior legal obligations at the clan and town level to such an extent that it was not clear that the nation could order a punishment without running the risk that the national officer carrying out the punishment might be executed in return.[61]

Yet even in early descriptions there is evidence that other social mechanisms structured Creek legal culture and that blood revenge was not unleashed and out of control. The right to blood revenge was held by the family and the clan, not by the town or nation. This right did not follow automatically from a killing. Rather, the family had to "collect, consult, and decide." Only if a broader tribal interest was at stake did they consult with tribal authorities. In some cases, the family of the person doing the injury made restitution, a result incompatible with a simple "blood revenge" analysis of Creek law because a law based on restitution necessarily requires a socially structured negotiation process that aims at reconciliation of the parties and restoration of the status quo after an injury.[62]

This law had impressed many white observers. In 1897, even as he condemned the national courts of the Indian nations, Federal District Judge Charles Stuart respected their traditional law: "When the Indians determined their controversies among themselves, according to their customs and unwritten laws, there was something sturdy and honest about their methods and judgements."[63]

The Civil War disrupted the Creek Nation. The Lower Creeks generally sided with the Confederacy, the Upper Creeks with the Union, and the two factions fought their own civil war. The end of the American Civil War brought a quick peace and an end to the isolation of the earlier years.[64] In 1867, the Creeks adopted a constitution that created a Creek national gov-

---

[61] Waring (ed.), *Laws of the Creek Nation*, 17 and 18; see esp. Law 2d, Law 4th, Law 6th, Law 7th. The fact that four early laws were directed at the abolition of blood revenge indicates that the practice was still prevalent in the early nineteenth century.

[62] Swanton, *Creek Confederacy*, 343.

[63] U.S. Congress, Senate, Doc. 164 (1897; Serial Set, v. 3471), 14.

[64] Debo, *Road to Disappearance*, 184–9.

ernment, which lasted until 1898. That government was based on a legislature with two houses – a House of Kings and a House of Warriors – both
elected in the towns by universal male suffrage. The town remained the
basis of elective government but with no formal role in the national government. The principal chief and second chief, again following the traditional
two-chief structure of the towns, were elected by direct popular vote for
four-year terms. The court structure was also determined by the same constitution and remained unchanged for the life of the Creek Nation.[65]

Like similar structures in the other Indian nations, this national government did not directly address the traditional town political structures. The
traditional governments based on the towns lost none of their powers; rather,
they were simply not mentioned except as electoral units.[66] There was an
unwritten division of powers between the two systems of government. It is
clear, for example, that the town councils processed criminal cases and
interpersonal disputes in the early years of the constitution, but it is not
known to what extent they continued to do so in later years.[67]

There is evidence that the Creeks had two parallel criminal justice systems
operating at the same time, one traditional and one the formal legal system
of the Creek Nation. If this is so, the Creeks were using an adaptive mechanism parallel to the one documented for the Cherokees in the Old South:
not only did the operation of two systems satisfy powerful white observers,
including the U.S. government and some acculturing Creeks who wanted a
more "progressive" legal system, but it also protected the sacred laws of the
traditional Creeks. These parallel systems were secretly linked both through
traditional town and clan structures and through a nationally shared understanding of the complexity of the task that the Creeks faced in surviving
as a nation and accommodating the powerful United States.

This unwritten understanding between the traditional and constitutional
structures broke down during the civil wars that divided the Creek Nation.
An upheaval occurred in 1869–70, almost immediately after the creation of
the first Creek constitutional government, over the distribution of government moneys, which had always occurred in the towns. The traditionals
were enraged when the national government kept the money for distribution.
They argued that the treaty of 1866, which ended the Civil War in the Indian
nations and redefined their relations with the United States, had "given
them their old law back," including the right to distribute annuity money in

[65] Ibid., 179–82.
[66] See the Creek Constitution, published in *Acts and Resolutions of the National Council of the Creek Nation* (Muskogee, Okla.: Phoenix Printing, 1900). We have one ethnography of the function of Creek institutions, including political institutions, at the town level in the 1930s: Frank Speck, *The Creek Indians of Taskigi Town*, Memoirs of the American Anthropological Association, no. 2 (Menasha, Wis.: 1931).
[67] Speck, *Creek Indians of Taskigi Town*, 113–15.

the traditional way.[68] The matter was made worse by the failure of the Creek
government to settle advantageously the Creek claims against the United
States for war losses, leaving many Creeks owed a total of several million
dollars.[69] By the winter of 1869–70, the Creeks had two national governments, one constitutional and one traditional, both with armed lighthorsemen
attempting to enforce their laws against each other.

The Creek election of 1870 was a referendum on the future of Creek
constitutionalism. All parties understood that a victory for the traditional
side meant a return to the old laws; a victory for the progressives meant the
full implementation of new laws by the national government under the constitution. The Indian agent and the U.S. government took an active interest,
viewing a progressive victory as essential for the eventual assimilation of the
Creeks.[70]

The election could not be held because the competing governments had
inconsistent electoral rules. The traditionals rejected the whole notion of
the secret paper ballot: Creeks, they insisted, must vote as they always had,
by "standing on their feet" in open town councils.[71] Ultimately, there were
two elections. The traditionals called all Creeks to come to the council
ground at Okmulgee and vote "standing on their feet." The progressives
voted by secret ballot according to their new election law. Two sets of chiefs
were elected. The Indian agent announced that the U.S. government would
recognize only the constitutional government and that the traditional faction's
election was illegal.[72] Although each side then took up arms to defend its
government, a compromise was arranged, partly through the auspices of the

---

[68] Debo, *Road to Disappearance*, 184–9. My discussion of Creek factional wars is based on
Angie Debo's analysis of these events. Her history of the Creek people not only is a model
of what a good ethnohistory should be, but also sets the standard for what good legal history
should be. She integrates traditional legal source materials into a social history of the life
of the people and makes clear the impact of law on both daily life and social change in the
Creek Nation. One major theme of her history of the Creek Nation is the struggle between
traditional and acculturating Creek factions, with power being shared between them for the
entire period.

[69] Ibid., 189–94. The total value of the Creek claims that were lost amounted to nearly $200
per capita, representing a lifetime's work for the average Creek citizen. The government's
failure to negotiate this claim successfully was more than a serious political defeat for the
nation; it brought real hardship on every Creek family.

[70] Ibid., 191.

[71] Ibid., 182–3, 192–4. Here we have a rare glimpse of Creek struggle over the political process
itself, as opposed to the political ends that the process might produce. This would suggest
a parallel struggle over the written law that implies a law existing in unwritten form at the
town level.

[72] Debo, *Road to Disappearance*, 193. This direct interference in Creek national politics by the
Indian agent alerts us to recognize that Creeks, both traditional and progressive, must always
have engaged in political activity with one eye on the United States and its political forces.
For this reason, the Creeks' adoption of U.S.-based political forms cannot be judged simply
as a case of traditionals versus progressives: often the traditionals engaged in such maneuvering to protect other aspects of their culture.

Indian agent but also because the Creeks had a powerful tradition of negotiation. Both sides would vote according to their ways, but the traditionals
would make a paper record of the votes from each village. All the votes
would be counted in the open, with six men from each side monitoring the
count.

The election of a progressive candidate as chief settled nothing, however.
Within a year a traditional leader was signing papers as "principal chief,"
and again the Creek Nation had two governments. This unstable political
life produced a situation already common to the Creek Nation and one that
recurred to the end of the nation's life: the traditionals gave refuge to young
men, both Indian and black, who made their living as horse thieves and fled
to the traditional faction to escape the reach of the Creek national courts.
The government reacted by passing a new treason law at a session addressed
by the Indian agent. It went far beyond the old law of Polecat Springs, which
had made the alienation of Creek land the foundation of treason law. It
forbade any Creek citizen to petition a "foreign power" – an attempt to cut
off the traditionals' access to the government of the United States – or to
carry any subversive message, and it prescribed a penalty of fifty to one
hundred lashes for each offense. The lighthorse was also increased to enforce
the law.[73]

Creek politics became increasingly complex during the next ten years.
The issues were still the same: the traditional Creeks had a view of their
society that they refused to give up. Their legal culture gave them a personal
responsibility for their traditional laws that they could not, in good con-
science, yield to the constitutional government. In 1880, however, it was the
operation of the constitutional legal system itself that sparked rebellion. The
newly elected progressive chief, Checote, permitted district judges to use
their power to punish his political opponents. Then his court system brought
charges against the traditional chief Isparhecher for taking his cousin as his
wife in violation of an 1874 law against incest passed by the constitutional
government. This law was rooted in the constitutional government's attempt
to look respectable in the eyes of Christian missionaries and the U.S. government and had no roots in Creek culture.[74]

The arrest of several of Isparhecher's men for violations of another dis-
respected new law, one that forbade warriors to go about armed, set off
armed clashes. Eventually, U.S. troops were ordered into the nation to
maintain peace. Negotiations between the two factions went badly, and in-
surgent forces fled west to the Sac and Fox Nation. There they remained,
making sporadic attacks on the constitutional government, until in the spring

[73] Debo, *Road to Disappearance*, 200–1.
[74] Ibid., 270.

Isparhecher, traditional Creek leader during the "Green Peach" war, later elected
principal chief of the Creek Nation

of 1882 federal troops were sent to capture them. Isparhecher's men fled
across the Indian Territory and took up a defensive position on a hill in the
Wichita Agency, apparently ready to fight. Instead, they broke and ran, and
their leaders were captured and returned to the Creek Nation, guarded by
the military. Once back, the insurgents refused to leave military protection
and demanded that the nation be divided and that the army protect the
traditionals.[75]

Carrying on a tradition of political balance and reconciliation, Checote
pardoned most of the insurgents. Moreover, Isparhecher was elected chief
in 1883. The close election was contested, and the Indian agent declared
L. C. Perryman the winner. Isparhecher stepped down from national government but remained a traditional leader.[76]

Perryman proceeded to give the nation away to Texas cattlemen and
merchants, making himself rich in the process. Among the most unpopular
of his actions was the leasing of huge tracts of tribal land to ranchers for
grazing, leading to an attack on their fences by hundreds of armed tradi-

[75] Ibid., 274–9.
[76] Ibid., 281–4.

tionals.[77] Once more, the Creeks had two sets of chiefs. Perryman was rumored to have lost thousands of dollars of the nation's funds to embezzlers working for him. Armed traditionals came to Okmulgee and dragged Perryman into the square, shouting angry questions and accusations at him. He was allowed to return to his hotel for the night, but the next day he fled the Creek Nation. The second chief, following Creek custom in balancing the national government between traditional and progressive factions, was a traditional who did not speak English. On Perryman's absence, this second chief legally assumed the duties of the principal chief. The National Council then impeached Perryman, suspending him as chief pending his impeachment trial. The Creek Supreme Court made two contradictory rulings: first, that Perryman could be suspended prior to trial, but later that his suspension was illegal. In effect, the court restored the still absent Perryman as chief. The court clerk, adding to this constitutional crisis, refused to enter the second order in the record, letting the original suspension stand. Both Perryman and the second chief continued to act as chief and issue orders.[78]

The Creeks resolved this crisis by electing Isparhecher chief in 1895, uniting traditional and constitutional in one leader. Under Isparhecher, however, there was really only one issue: the forced allotment of Creek lands and the political abolition of the nation. Isparhecher polled his people twice on the issue; the Creeks stood firmly against allotment and did not treat with the Dawes Commission. The commission was incensed at the irreconcilability of the Creeks (as well as of other tribes) and put an end to the fiction that the U.S. government would negotiate with the tribes for the voluntary cessation of their lands. Congress then unilaterally legislated the end of the Indian nations. The Creeks were told that if they did not accept allotment voluntarily, their lands would be allotted involuntarily, and individuals would either be assigned lands or be denied their allotments altogether.[79]

When the lands were finally allotted, beginning in 1899, it was done by Chief Pleasant Porter without the cooperation of the traditionals. Porter, elected chief in 1899, was understood to favor a compromise with federal authorities, believing that the Creek cause was lost. The traditionals still favored holding their ground and resisting. The continued rebellion of Chitto Harjo (Crazy Snake) after 1901 was the sixth time in less than fifty years that the Creeks once again had two governments, one constitutional and one traditional.[80]

---

[77] These attacks gave rise to the cattlemen's lawsuit against the Creek Nation for damages, ultimately decided in *Turner v. United States and Creek Nation of Indians.*

[78] Ibid., 355–9.

[79] Ibid., 361–76.

[80] Ibid., 376–7.

The Creeks always maintained two laws: one their traditional law embodied in the old treason law of Polecat Springs, the other a constitutional legal order enacted by the National Council under the supervision of the BIA. These legal orders could be seen as opposites, but that was not their true relationship. Rather, they represented a balanced strategy to preserve the tribe. At the same time, this strategy struck an accommodation with the United States, which respected only legal institutions resembling its own. This thin veneer of U.S. legal culture never entirely effaced the legal culture of the Creek Nation.

The constitutional legal system of the Creek Nation

How was the traditional legal culture of the Creek people embodied in the formal legal institutions created by the constitution of 1867? What role did these formal court structures play in a social context that was deeply rooted in traditional ways that would not yield to a constitutional order based on U.S. law? There is ample evidence that the Cherokee Nation's court system was as sophisticated in its legal reasoning as any of the U.S. courts in the surrounding states, but the same cannot be said of Creek courts. At most, individual features of U.S. law were imposed over local Creek traditions, but more often they worked hand in hand with traditional legal mechanisms.

The court records of the Creek Nation have been substantially preserved, along with similar records for other Indian nations. These accounts are in very rudimentary form, recorded by a court clerk, almost always in English, in a simple bound record book. The information provided on each case is most often sparse: charge, name of defendant, witnesses or jurors called, disposition. Often some of this information is missing; many cases, for example, list no dispositions. Other cases, however, include simple transcripts or much more detailed accounts. In whatever form, these little-used documents are a rich repository of information on Creek society.[81]

The district courts met as needed, usually four times a year, and presented the opportunity for major gatherings of local Creeks. Most of the cases tried in all six districts involved criminal offenses, and most of these concerned thefts of various sorts. Traditional Creek society knew very little property crime. Yet judging from the case flow, theft became epidemic in the Creek

---

[81] The court records of the Creek Nation have been microfilmed, making them easily accessible to researchers. The originals are held in the Oklahoma State Historical Society, Oklahoma City. These extensive records are largely complete, although there are substantial gaps, probably owing to the technology of the day rather than to lost records. For example, it seems clear that few Creek chiefs kept copies of their pardons. The pardon itself was sent to the court with authority over the defendant. Thus, the pardon papers of the Creek Nation comprise not copies of the pardons but the correspondence pertaining to them. Still, we have many of the pardon applications, which can tell us much about the process.

Nation by the late 1870s.[82] These cases were often redefined from criminal to civil and back again because the Creek courts were not bound by such distinctions and because new forms of property produced confusion of legal ownership.[83] For example, many property cases stemmed from the new, nontraditional line of succession introduced in the civil law of inheritance. Under traditional Creek law, property stayed within the clans. Marriages were always outside of the clan; hence wives and the children of wives by other marriages received nothing from a husband's estate. New Creek inheritance laws guaranteed wives some measure of support from a husband's estate. The resulting property disputes between a widow and members of her husband's clan often ended up in criminal court with mutual accusations of theft, particularly of livestock.[84]

The case of Jim Easy, a black citizen of the Creek Nation,[85] could be considered a typical example of a criminal case of theft. The case is unusual in that there is a transcript of the trial in a crude handwriting, full of misspellings, but clearly showing the course of the proceedings. Easy was charged with stealing a hog from Stephen Colbert. The case was called on the morning of January 3, 1882, but three potential jurors were missing. It was not until late the next day that twenty-four jurymen were finally present. Both the prosecuting attorney and the prisoner announced that they were ready to proceed, and they selected a panel of twelve jurors. By then, it was late evening, and the court adjourned until the next day.[86]

Four witnesses were called, two for each side. All saw Easy with a freshly butchered hog, but they disagreed over the "mark" on the hog. Mose Standford reported seeing a "smoothcrop" earmark he recognized as Colbert's; but when he looked later, it had been changed. Colbert testified that one of his hogs was missing and that Easy told him he took it. For the defense, Willie Marshall testified the mark he had seen was a "squarefork." Marshall

---

[82] Swanton, *Creek Confederacy*, 356–7. Debo, *Road to Disappearance*, 230, reports that property crime had become frequent. She attributes this to several reasons: the immoral influence of white criminals around Fort Gibson, the development of Creek criminal gangs that specialized in horse stealing, and the existence of "turbulent" black communities in the nation.

[83] In the 1870s, criminal and civil cases were most often kept in the same book. By the middle to late 1880s, the district courts uniformly used separate books labeled "civil" and "criminal," but cases regularly appear in the wrong book. Frequently, a jury would bring in a civil verdict in a criminal case, usually in finding money damages in a theft case. This illustrates sound common sense: a missing hog may be either lost or stolen; a dispute over a horse could involve theft or a confusion over ownership.

[84] An unusually large number of cases of theft involve disputes over ownership of livestock between family members, cases that ordinary would not be referred to courts.

[85] The Creeks, like most other nations of the Indian Territory, were required to make black residents citizens in treaties with the United States ending the tribes participation in the Civil War. See Debo, *Road to Disappearance*, 164–74.

[86] Creek Nation Archives, reel 18, Coweta District Court records, vol. 5, Oklahoma State Historical Society, Oklahoma City.

also stated that a year before he had "let Easy have a hog" but that he did
not know if this was the same one. Easy did not take the stand in his own
defense.

On the fourth day of the trial, "after the lawyers were through talking on
the case," Judge Coweta Micco called one of the jurors forward, pronounced
him the foreman of the jury, and charged all to decide the case according
to the evidence and Creek law. Later that same day, the jury found Easy
not guilty of the crime, and Micco ordered the captain of lighthorse to
release him from custody.

We know what this trial cost because the court issued "warrants" to
witnesses and jurors, each of whom was paid one dollar a day (judges,
prosecutors, and lighthorsemen were salaried). Six men received one dollar
each; eight, two dollars each; and fifteen, including the victim, four dollars
each. In total, the warrants, excluding payment to one person not located,
came to eighty-two dollars.[87] Surely a major source of cash income for the
people of Coweta District in January 1882 was Jim Easy's trial.

The meaning of such a careful trial for an accused thief is difficult to
deduce. On the one hand, it shows enormous attention to fundamental
notions of fairness and due process. On the other hand, both Angie Debo
and contemporary white historians have criticized Creek justice as "too
lenient" and unable to punish offenders. In fact, regular references in court
records to whippings proves that the Creek system of justice was not reluctant
to punish. Perhaps also the traditional Creek sense of honor and individual
responsibility that placed a heavy pressure on offenders to plead guilty and
take their punishment worked the opposite way with an offender who denied
responsibility. In a society that placed heavy weight on a man's word, Creek
courts could not easily convict when the offender, as Easy did, offered a
plausible defense.

The Coweta District Court processed fifteen criminal indictments in 1882,
including Jim Easy's. Seven defendants were charged with theft of cattle,
hogs, and pistols. Three were charged with disturbing the peace and one
with resisting arrest. Two separate indictments for treason resulting from
the Creek civil wars – one with three defendants and one with eight defen-

---

[87] Ibid. Federal District Judge William Springer cites the high cost of the courts of the Indian
Nations as evidence of bad government; U.S. Congress, Senate, "Memorial for Additional
Judge of U.S. Court in Indian Territory," (54th Congress, 2d session, Doc. 164 (1897;
Serial 3471), 18. Springer's data on the fixed costs of Creek justice (exclusive of the juror
and witness fees listed here) are as follows: judges, $400 per year; prosecuting attorneys,
$200 per year plus $25 per conviction; captain of lighthorse, $300 per year; privates in
lighthorse, $275. With four privates per district, fixed salaries cost $2,000 per year, plus
$25 per conviction, for each of six districts. Witness and juror fees were also substantial; in
the Deep Fork District in the 1870s, for example, they amounted to about $1,000 per year.
It is important to note here that these legal institutions were only on the district level in
Creek constitutional government. All other institutions existed on the national level.

dants – were dropped without trial.[88] Only three indictments led to criminal convictions, with two of the defendants receiving fifty lashes each, one for rape and one for stealing a yearling.

Between 1882 and 1895, the Coweta District Court heard 163 criminal cases. More than 80 percent of them were like Jim Easy's case: small-scale theft, primarily of livestock. The only other offense that brought a significant number of cases, 17, was disturbing the peace, a category that included both minor and dangerous behavior. There were 5 murder indictments in the fourteen years, leading to 3 acquittals, 1 verdict of guilty, and 1 defendant who fled the court's jurisdiction. The remaining cases involved: rape, 2; treason, 2; perjury, 2; violating pasture laws, 3; mayhem, 2; resisting an officer, 3. Forty of the 163 defendants were acquitted, and 33 were found guilty. A variety of factors led to the abandonment of the remaining cases. For a few, no disposition is evident.[89]

We can compare the court records of Eufala District for a similar period. With a population of just over two thousand Upper Creeks, as opposed to Coweta's fewer than one thousand Lower Creeks, Eufala nevertheless shows a surprisingly similar pattern of crime. In 450 criminal cases indicted between 1889 and 1897, a total of 130 defendants were found guilty, 114 not guilty. Again, about half the cases were dismissed or nolle prossed for unknown reasons.[90]

Using a base line of 350 thefts for the eight-year period, nearly 20 percent of the district's population suffered theft at the hands of someone later indicted for the crime. Few people were indicted twice – the records note second and third offenders for sentencing purposes – which means that nearly 20 percent of the population was indicted for theft. The pervasiveness of this crime seems to indicate the ineffectiveness of both traditional social control mechanisms and the formal criminal justice institution of the Creek Nation.[91]

The Eufala docket books list the type of property stolen and generally

[88] Creek Nation Archives, reel 18, Coweta District Court records, vol. 5.
[89] These data are based on my analysis of the court records, held in the Creek Nation Archives in the Oklahoma State Historical Society, Oklahoma City.
[90] Creek Nation Archive, reel 19, Eufala District Court records.
[91] Without more extensive analysis of crime patterns, no explantion is possible. One avenue for investigation lies in the fact that the Creeks were a loose confederacy of related and unrelated peoples, with social mechanisms based in the towns. As activity moved beyond the towns, intertown social control mechanisms may not have been as effective as intratown ones had been, particularly as dispersed settlement patterns took hold and people from different towns lived in close proximity to one another. The familiar white explanation of jurisdictional problems may also apply: while the nations had jurisdiction over all Indians within their borders, regardless of tribal affiliation, the lighthorsemen of each nation could not cross into the territory of other nations but had to go through a cumbersome extradition process that gradually broke down. Finally, Debo, *Road to Disappearance*, 226, 285, suggests that the quality of Creek law enforcement was poor and politicized.

offer a brief description of every crime. Besides the obvious attractions of livestock – hogs were far and away the most commonly stolen property – almost everything that could be owned could also be stolen: guns of all kind, money, plows, apples, cotton, and other farm produce, items of clothing, sewing machines, spools of thread, even a "diamond broach" valued at ten dollars. Although most of the property seems to have been taken from the outdoors, thefts from enclosed buildings and stores were not uncommon.

With at least double the population of Coweta, Eufala had more crime (and more murders) but shows an equally high rate of acquittals and dismissed cases. Twenty murders occurred in an eight-year period, with 6 convictions, 4 acquittals, and 10 cases nolle prossed for diverse and often unclear reasons. Once again, other than property crime, disturbing the peace was the only offense that resulted in a significant number of cases: 16 indictments. Other cases included: rape, 3; attempted rape, 2; mayhem or assault, 5; trespassing, 2; arson, 3 (two houses and one haystack); interfering with an officer, 2; taking down timber to sell to the railroad, 1; profane language, 1; disturbing a religious service, 3; perjury, 2; employing noncitizens of the nation without a permit, 2; carrying a pistol, 5; and leasing land to noncitizens, 7. A scattering of other offenses appeared as well: one indictment for "carrying a pistol and shooting a person," a curious combination of a petty offense and a serious one; one charge for incest (brother–sister, which conformed to Creek traditional law, rather than between cousins, which did not); and "setting the woods on fire."[92]

This pattern of crimes, not a surprising one for eight years in a diverse frontier community, shows a curious mix of offenses against both traditional law and new laws designed to protect the Creek Nation in its complex relationship with U.S. society. Laws passed by traditionals and designed to exclude whites from the Creek Nation by prohibiting the hiring of "noncitizens" or the leasing of land to them were rarely enforced. Similarly, 5 indictments for "carrying a pistol" must reflect selective arrests, for the carrying of weapons was common.

Even if the murder rate in Eufala was high, it bears no relation to the 257 murders a year that the white press claimed were perpetrated in the Indian nations in the 1890s.[93] Projecting Eufala's rate on all of the Creek districts would produce no more than 10 murders a year throughout a Creek Nation with a total population of perhaps ten thousand Creeks and six thousand persons of other races. Creek courts handed down no more than two or three murder convictions per year, and federal convictions did not add significantly to this total.[94] This statistic still requires explanation, how-

[92] Creek Nation Archives, reel 19, Eufala District Court records.
[93] Commission to the Five Civilized Tribes, *Annual Report, 1895*, 76.
[94] The estimate of ten murders per year is derived by assuming that the Eufala rate was average

ever; for in the context of the level of frontier violence and disorder, it is difficult to explain why there were more murders than all other forms of nonfatal assault combined. Even in the most violent context, many more people should have been injured than killed. There can be no logical explanation for this anomaly other than that serious assaults were probably not prosecuted or punished.

Execution for murder came to symbolize the barbarism of the Creeks. Creek execution has a special fascination in a country infatuated by executions and lynchings. The image of the condemned, paroled to go home to get his affairs in order, returning to an appointed ground for his execution, checking his coffin, making a speech to the assembled crowd, facing his chosen executioner, pinning a piece of paper over his heart, and being dispatched with one shot at close range had a great deal of drama.[95] That a society's mode of execution makes a powerful statement about its law is basic to the sociology of law. These executions, however, have been exaggerated out of proportion to their occurrence. There were few murder indictments, fewer convictions, and even fewer executions.

Those sentenced to death had no right to appeal, because the Creek Supreme Court had no criminal jurisdiction whatever. That a supreme court could possess considerable appellate power in the civil area and none in the area of criminal law may seem an anomaly, but it made sense to the Creeks and reveals much about the role of the formal courts of the Creek Nation in relation to traditional Creek law. The traditional councils had long decided criminal cases with a right of pardon by the chief as the remedy for any potential injustice, and this model was incorporated in the formal law of the Creek Nation.[96]

Every defendant sentenced to death was entitled to petition for a pardon from the principal chief, and the "pardon papers" offer one way of looking more systematically at the processing of serious crimes. These are far less

and ran about two per year and that the population of Eufala District was about one-fourth of the Creek Nation. Not included in these data are killings involving whites, which were never under the jurisdiction of the Creek courts. The famous court at Fort Smith, with federal criminal jurisdiction over the Creek Nation as well as most of the rest of the Indian Territory, averaged about eight murders a year from the whole territory, more coming from the Choctaw and Cherokee nations than from the Creek because they had much larger white populations. See Shirley, *Law West of Fort Smith*, ix.

95 "Last Execution Under Creek Law," *Muskogee Daily Phoenix*, September 29, 1935. This same execution is described in R. L. Williams, "A Trial and Execution Among the Creeks," *Chronicles of Oklahoma* 2 (1933):142. Another execution is described in "Heart Pierced," *Daily Oklahoman* (Guthrie), October 10, 1893, 1, col. 2.

96 The supreme court was left with an appellate function in civil law. Most civil law lacked traditional roots in Creek law, yet the nation needed to develop a commercial law and accommodate some measure of economic development well beyond the poorly educated and often remote district court judges. The supreme court was also an important political institution, with a regular role in reconciling the nation after its repeated constitutional crises.

complete than the court records but provide more information on individual cases. In all, parts of 131 pardon applications can be found in the pardon files of the Creek Nation Archive, covering the period from 1870 to 1896. Although we have no systematic data on the total number of murder convictions in the Creek courts during this period, the 27 pardon applications that involve murder cases must represent a significant proportion of all murder convictions occurring in the nation. Based on Eufala's and Coweta's total of 7 convictions during a twenty-year period, the remaining four districts, in a slightly expanded time period, should have produced no more than 25 to 30 convictions. Adding to the uncertainty, court records do not report executions, only murder convictions, perhaps because the pardon application was understood and because the execution was carried out by lighthorsemen and not the court. To make interpretation even more difficult, there was never any written record of actual pardons awarded in response to the applications. This appears to have been a deliberate choice, not an inadvertent mistake, and shows the traditional quality of the Creek pardon.

The lack of a written record led some criminal defendants to claim falsely that they had been pardoned. A chief cause of this confusion was the death penalty for a third conviction of theft. A good number of people reached this limit, but few were executed. Instead, pardon meant that an offender began the cycle over again, subject to fifty lashes for his next conviction as a "first" offender. Judges often exhibited confusion at the number of times a person had actually been convicted and sentenced, necessitating more pardon applications. One ingenious prosecuting attorney even tried to secure the death penalty for a horse thief by charging him with a first offense for stealing the saddle, a second for the bridle, and a third offense for the horse. The death penalty was imposed, but the principal chief pardoned the offender for two of the convictions. In effect, then, the pardon power reached only death sentences and political disabilities, because whippings were carried out on the spot. One Creek court story has a lawyer making an eloquent argument for a stay of execution of a sentence until the judge informed him that he could stop because they were done whipping his client.[97]

The pardon power was also used to bring Creek justice in line with the traditional expectations of town and clan. The pardon papers contain lengthy petitions, often signed by dozens of people, offering every conceivable explanation and excuse for criminal conduct. For example, one series of petitions alleged the murder victim was of "bad character." Others emphasized that convicted killers were "family men" who were needed to support their children.[98]

---

[97] "Pardon papers," Creek Nation Archive, reel 24. Debo, *Road to Disappearance*, 228–9, discusses the problem of the death sentence for the third theft conviction.
[98] Ibid.

In Creek society, as in tribal societies generally, the fundamental purpose of the law was the reintegration of the community. The death penalty was never automatic, but was the subject of complex negotiations between clans, with the chief or elders having a mediating function. In the modern legal system of the Creek Nation, this function was embodied in the principal chief, with the Supreme Court specifically denied a role. Although the Creek Supreme Court might apply uncertain legal norms – a complex mix of Creek and U.S. laws – the principal chief could use his pardon power with no legal restrictions of any kind, even to the extent that he did not keep records of the process.

Other pardons and pardon applications are more in character with traditional U.S. conceptions of the pardon power: they asked for mercy or commutations in the interest of justice. One petition on behalf of an elderly horse thief pointed out that he was so ill with consumption that whipping would amount to a death sentence. Many other pardons were formalities aimed at nothing other than the removal of political disability following conviction of a crime. This penalty followed from the Creek civil wars, when some participants were afterward denied the right to engage in politics or hold office. Many treason convictions were pardoned after the Creek civil wars as part of a process of national healing.[99]

Although we do not know how many pardons were granted, it is clear that they were granted freely for almost any reason. Principal Chief Perryman, attempting to make Creek practice more like that of the United States and perhaps to defend Creek justice against charges of laxness, wrote some petitioners that they had to have a valid reason for asking for a pardon, that one could not be granted on general terms. By the 1890s, most of the pardons appear to have been for third-offense theft convictions, a category of capital conviction that was not consistent with Creek notions of justice.[100] In fact, the whole idea of property crime was foreign to Creek traditional law. The application of the death sentence to third-offense theft was the result of the Creeks' refusal to construct a jail. Indeed, Creek law never incorporated imprisonment as punishment.

The operation of the courts themselves raises more question concerning Creek justice. About 147 men served in the nine Creek judicial positions – six district judges and three supreme court judges – during the last thirty years of the Creek Nation. With a Creek adult male population of not much more than two thousand, this means that perhaps 5 percent of the men served as judges, rotating the job through a good proportion of the politically active male population.[101] Judges needed no special education

[99] Ibid.
[100] Ibid.
[101] A complete list of Creek judges is found in the Creek Nation Archive verticle files under

and were often illiterate in English, although English was well understood by the clerks. They were almost totally ignorant of common legal principles but were equipped to apply their own understanding of traditional Creek law. Short terms kept most judges from ever becoming self-taught through continued exposure to lawyers or from developing reasoning from lines of related case.

The judges were deeply embedded in the political life of their nation.[102] They were elected to four-year terms at the same time that the chiefs and delegates to the House of Warriors and House of Kings were elected. This meant that traditional leaders out of power in the central government could be in power at the district level. Judges were the highest political officers in their respective districts and were often called on by the chief to perform such political duties as raising temporary lighthorse to put down insurrection.

The district courts played an important political function in mediation between the national government and the towns. Trials like that of Jim Easy became a common form of traditional gathering where important matters could be discussed. Moreover, the liberal payment of witness and juror fees probably fed the entire gathering. The reliance on jury trials meant that even the most ordinary case took at least a day, with dozens of people called into attendance. Thus, the jury exercised considerable flexibility in applying the law and protected traditional Creeks from the full application of the laws of the Creek Nation. Finally, prosecutions after the numerous internal conflicts were virtually impossible because of the popularity of the traditionals and their access to the court system. Once again, the lack of any appeal to the supreme court protected the local character of the district courts.

Creek law, unlike that of the Cherokees, involved little of the analytical form that characterized the positivism of U.S. law. Rather, judges operated within the political constraints of their culture and rendered fair decisions as they saw them. In some cases, judges resorted to basic principles of law adopted from U.S. legal doctrine, but their rulings often coincide with

---

the heading "Courts." A few names appear twice, and several men appear under two names. Thus, we cannot be sure exactly how many men served as judges, but my point remains the same: the positions were freely rotated within the politically active population. Some judges, nevertheless, enjoyed long tenures; Coweta Micco of Coweta District, for example, served for nearly twenty years.

[102] The Creek court system is provided for in *Acts and Resolutions of the National Council.* See also Debo, *Road to Disappearance,* 246, 269, 273, 281, 285. As an example of their involvement in broader political and economic roles, as well as the weak administrative infrastructure of the Creek Nation, judges were given the authority to issue permits for enclosing large pastures with wire fence – a lucrative prerogative that enriched several Creek families and obviously created opportunities for corruption (336).

simple common sense. There was no Creek law based on written precedent, and there was no arguing a Creek case based on preexisting cases.[103]

A remarkable feature of Creek law is the high number of acquittals, running roughly 50 percent of all cases. It is difficult to speculate on their significance. On the one hand, the lighthorse were by no means an efficient police force and seem to have brought many weak cases. On the other hand, the juries were composed of friends and neighbors who knew the cases well and were often inclined to believe defendants who denied guilt, consistent with the "beyond a reasonable doubt" standard of Anglo-American law. The large number of nolle prossed and dismissed cases, just over 50 percent of the total, may well be meaningless, reflecting the difference between the discretion of officers and the legal standards applied by judges and prosecutors.[104]

When political pressure on the Creek Nation became more powerful in the 1880s and 1890s, the national legislature passed laws to deal with these new situations. The mile-square pasture law and laws prohibiting leasing land to noncitizens were sound and sensible measures promoted by traditional Creeks, rationally geared toward the preservation of Creek society and the exclusion of non-Indian economic influences from Creek politics.[105] From hundreds of violations, however, only a handful of cases came to the courts, and most of those were nolle prossed or led to verdicts of not guilty. The Creek lighthorse force seems to have been at least partially successful in bringing in common property criminals, but it was never able to enforce this critical economic legislation. The legal history of the mile-square pasture law indicates that the administration of the law was inextricably bound up with Creek factional politics. This can be seen in the *Turner* case, when the U.S. Supreme Court denied cattlemen's claims for damages against the Creek Nation for failing to protect their property.[106]

The case arose from an attempt of wealthy Creeks to circumvent the mile-square pasture law. Clarence Turner, a white, and Pleasant Blackstone, a Cherokee, organized a firm, Blackstone and Turner, in the business of raising and selling cattle. As noncitizens, they could not hold pastureland

---

[103] Rennard Strickland argues that the Cherokees did develop a sufficient legal tradition so that cases could be based on precedent. Strickland, *Fire and Spirits*, 161–5.

[104] The figure of 50 percent is based on analysis of all criminal cases from Coweta and Eufala districts.

[105] The mile-square pasture law, approved by the National Council on November 10, 1896, represented a victory over the few wealthy Creeks who leased large pastures to whites. It made all pastures over a mile square – 640 acres – illegal and subject to removal unless approved by a majority of local residents in an election. *Acts and Resolutions of the National Council*, sec. 240–5. Similarly, the law forbidding permits for noncitizens was aimed at wealthy Creeks. Ibid., secs. 223–30.

[106] *Turner v. United States and Creek Nation*, 248 U.S. 354 (1919), affirming 51 C.Cls. 125 (1916). The case file is held in Record Group 267, National Archives.

in the Creek Nation, so they organized a second firm, Pussy, Tiger and Company, to fence off a large pasture. Pussy and Tiger were prominent Creeks, associated with ninety-eight other Creeks, each of whom was to be paid $100 per year under their contract with Blackstone and Turner. Pussy, Tiger and Company, following the mile-square pasture law, filed a petition with Judge Jacob Knight of the Deep Fork District of the Creek court to hold an election of local residents, required if a pasture larger than a mile square was to be fenced off. Initially, the measure lost, but Judge Knight was presuaded to call a second election, in which the pasture was approved.[107]

Incensed traditional Creeks, charging that those voting for approval were bribed, threatened to tear down the fence if an attempt was made to build it. Blackstone and Turner leased the pasture, an area twenty-five miles square, to white cattlemen for $27,000 a year, including a $10,000 advance to build a four strand wire fence around this huge tract. Hearing this, traditional Creeks induced Creek National Treasurer N. B. Moore to approach Chief Perryman to ask him to halt construction of the fence, threatening to destroy it if it were built. Turner, hearing of the plan to destroy the fence, sought, in federal district court, an injunction against tearing down the fence. Creeks, ignoring the injunction, posted notices that the fence would be destroyed. As workmen began to build the fence, they were threatened with violence. The traditional leader, Isparhecher, approached the fence crew, informing them that he would tear down the fence if they continued. Several days later, three groups of twenty-five Creeks, proceeding from different points along the sixty completed miles of fence, cut the wire and scattered the staples along its entire length. Although ample notice of this action was given, no Creek Nation officials attempted to stop this destruction, which was well organized and carried out in broad daylight.[108] The only reasonable conclusion is that this action was carried out by traditional Creeks, taking the enforcement of the mile-square pasture law into their own hands. Officials of the Creek national government, after they had declared that the fence was "legal," were powerless to intervene, not even making a symbolic effort to arrest the perpetrators. Turner's lawsuit, asking for $194,729 in damages, mostly for lost profits, went to the U.S. Supreme Court, which held that the Creek government held sovereign immunity and was not responsible for damages without its consent.[109]

In conclusion, there is no question that the Creeks, unlike the Cherokees, lacked a legal system that conformed to U.S. notions of law. Meeting the

---

[107] Case file, *Turner v. United States and Creek Nation*, 50–2.
[108] Ibid., 54–5.
[109] *Turner v. United States* 248 U.S. 354 (1919), 357–9.

U.S. legal standard did not protect the Cherokees from U.S. distortions of their law and legal culture. It is clear that the Creeks imposed a thin veneer of a constitutional legal order over a deeply rooted traditional legal order. That constitutional order seems to have operated largely in the area of theft and the counting of estates, cases that were both beyond the scope of the traditional legal order. Homicide cases, because of their seriousness and because they often cut across clan and town lines, also came within the jurisdiction of the constitutional government.

The Creeks never thought they needed a legal system like that of the Cherokees, let alone that of the United States. The breakdown in law and order that the Dawes Commission seized on was based on some readily observed disorder and social decay, but it was exaggerated beyond all proportion.[110] To the extent that it represented observed criminal activity, much of that activity had more to do with the ineptness of U.S. jurisdictional frameworks than with any failure of Creek justice. However, Creek justice, individualized and deeply rooted in traditional town and clan systems, also failed to adapt to the demands put on Creek society by political and economic pressure from U.S. society. The mile-square pasture law was necessary to the continued vitality of Creek political life, but it was not enforced. Yet U.S. law regulating Creek–white relations on the frontier also proved unenforceable. The Creeks were not left in perpetuity to their own political community in the hills of their nation and therefore cannot be judged by a standard that proved no more adaptable to their situation.

Crazy Snake's rebellion

The legal struggle over the future of the Creek Nation did not end with the liquidation of the national government and the resulting cessation of all its legal functions in July 1898. The traditionals did not recognize the allotment of their lands because it was contrary to their old law. Within less than two years, a traditional Creek government met on Hickory Ground, in the heart of their nation. Traditional Creek government, not having been created by U.S. laws, could not be liquidated by them.[111] This reconstitution of their old law was based on a letter from the acting secretary of the interior in which he promised to honor all Indian treaties. This, to the traditional

---

[110] Here it might be useful to suggest that the relevant comparison is between the quality of Creek justice and that found in racially diverse rural areas of the southern and western United States. No one would suggest that those areas had systems of justice superior to that of the Creeks.

[111] *Indian Journal* (Muskogee, Okla.), February 1, 1901, 4, cols. 1, 2, 3.

Creeks, was an admission that the liquidation of their national government was illegal.

Lahtah Mekko was named principal chief by the council at Hickory Ground, but Chitto Harjo, Crazy Snake, was regarded as the leader of the traditional Creeks.[112] As if the act of re-creating the Creek government was not sufficiently defiant, the new government, called the Snakes in the press, passed a new land law and posted it all over the Creek Nation:

> Hickorytown, Oct. 11th, 1900
>
> From this day on, the citizen or Creek citizen in the Creek National as far as the Creek line extend and also there shall be no laborers employed. This law created according to treaty any person violating this law shall be fined the sum of $100 ... and shall be payed to the Nation also shall receive fifty lashes on his bare back. Any person who was employed shall be removed by the principal Chief.... Also any person ...should interfere such notice shall be fined the sum of $50 fifty dollars.[113]

Lighthorsemen were sent out to post this notice and to enforce it. An unknown number of Creeks were whipped for leasing their lands to whites.

This continuation of the Creek civil wars was directed not against the law of the Creek Nation but against U.S. laws, and the uprising caused considerable alarm in Oklahoma. Federal troops were dispatched and Chitto Harjo and other leaders were captured and jailed. In March 1901, 253 Creeks were indicated for conspiracy to deprive unknown members of the Muskogee tribe of their personal liberty and to "detain them without lawful authority." The federal grand jury went on to find that these Creeks had "willfully and feloniously formed a certain government ... purporting to be the legal and lawful government of the Muskogee tribe of Indians." They had elected a chief, a second chief, a twelve-member cabinet to advise the chiefs, members of the House of Warriors and the House of Kings, and they had appointed a judicial branch and lighthorsemen.[114]

In a plea bargain arrangement, all the arrested Creeks admitted their guilt in a detailed statement:

---

[112] Unpaginated document in case file, *United States v. Chitto Harjo et al.*, Mar. 2, 1901. I photocopied this indictment from an original in the National Archives, Fort Worth Branch. It is held as "U.S. Court in Indian Territory – Muskogee. Criminal Case 5581–5584," Record Group 21.

[113] This notice was reprinted in the indictment at 6. The spelling and punctuation are left unchanged because it is instructive to see how difficult it was for these Creeks to prepare a notice in the English language, which was almost unused among the traditionals.

[114] *United States v. Chitto Harjo et al.*, criminal case no. 5584. This file is held in Record Group 21, National Archives, Fort Worth. Quoted at 4. This 253-person indictment, that of an entire band of Indians, may be unique in federal law, representing the criminalization of an Indian uprising. But politically, the specter of an Indian war in 1907 was an embarrassment.

We state that as citizens of the Creek Nation we have been opposed to the abolition of our courts by any act of Congress and to any change in our tribal form of government, and that, in October 1900, we met together and agreed to form a government of our own.... That it was our intention and purpose to pass laws and to execute the same upon all citizens of the Creek Nation without regard to any act of Congress in force in the Creek Nation. That said government was formed for the purpose of causing the arrest, imprisonment, and punishment of all persons, citizens of the Creek Nation, who should take any allotment of lands or rent any lands to non-citizens of this Creek Nation, or employ any White non-citizens in any capacity whatsoever.[115]

The spirit of the original law of Polecat Springs emerged in this action of the traditional Creek council. The federal government, not relishing the prospect of a trial and recognizing that locking up more than two hundred Creeks for these crimes admitted the failure of the allotment policy, pardoned all of the convicted Creeks after a few months in prison.[116] Those arrested amounted to about 10 percent of the adult male Creek population.

Chitto Harjo returned to his extended family in the hills of the central part of the Creek Nation. He does not appear to have had a major political role in the earlier constitutional government of the Creek Nation, having only held a seat in the House of Kings. His sudden emergence as a leader at age fifty-four in 1900 testifies to the continued existence of two political traditions: the Creeks always had traditional leaders, often without formal power in the national government, as well as constitutional leaders. When the constitutional government consented to its own dissolution and its leadership persuaded the tribe to sell its lands, a traditional leadership emerged to challenge these developments. This traditional leadership operated entirely within the Creek Nation and did not directly engage U.S. authorities on any level, as before, abdicating those political relationships to other Creeks. The critical difference now was that the former Creek constitutional government had revealed itself impotent and had put itself out of existence.

The attempt of the Creeks to restore their government did not end with the abortive rebellion of 1900–1. Little is known of the activities of Chitto Harjo and his people in the ensuing years, but regular encampments of the traditionals on Hickory Ground continued. Accounts of more Creek uprisings appeared in the press in 1902 and 1907, small actions by armed traditionals. It appears that traditional Creek government was functioning at

[115] Unpaginated document in case file, case no. 5584.
[116] "Crazy Snake...Will Be Released," *Chieftain* (Vinita, Okla.), February 28, 1901, 1. The Apache warrior Geronimo and members of his band were still interned at Fort Sill, Oklahoma, twenty years after their uprising.

Chitto Harjo (Crazy Snake), traditional Creek leader who attempted to restore traditional Creek law in two twentieth-century uprisings

this time without the direct challenges to state authority that had resulted
in the arrests of 1901.[117]

In 1906, Chitto Harjo testified before a committee of Congress that
came to Tulsa to investigate conditions in the Indian Territory. His speech,
given in Creek, was an eloquent plea for recognition of the treaty rights
of the Creek people, a simple plea for justice. It began with a recital of
the whole history of Creek–white relations and was based on his own
experience with the Union Army in the Civil War. It ended with a call
to honor the treaties. In response to a question, Chitto Harjo explained
that he was a farmer and that, although he "used to have horses and hogs

---

[117] The press reported Snake rebellions in 1902 and 1907, giving some indication of the
continuity of events between the 1900 and 1908 uprisings. See "Snakes in Rebellion," *Alva
Review* (Alva, Okla.), July 31, 1902, 1, and "Creeks are Arming," *Muskogee Times-Democrat*,
November 7, 1907, 1.

and cattle," he had precious few left because of the depredations of neighboring whites.[118]

With the creation of the state of Oklahoma in 1907 and the full extension of Oklahoma law over all of the former Indian nations, the condition of the traditional Creeks, as well as of other Indians, was one of bitterness and poverty.[119] In 1907, a large number of traditional Creeks were once again encamped on Hickory Ground. They had refused allotment and rejected all forms of authority that were not their own. The situation at Hickory Ground was made more complicated by the presence of a large black population, which in turn was divided into two groups. One was composed of Creek freedmen who had a long history of alliance with the Creek traditionals; the others were unemployed blacks who had turned to various lawless activities in order to survive and to escape white racism and the reach of state law.[120] The Creeks remained at Hickory Ground for two more years, until the outbreak of the "smoked meat rebellion" of 1909.

Complaints from local whites about the theft of hams from smokehouses offered a pretext for state intervention. The traditional Creeks had already moved their encampment a short distance away on the advice of the Indian agent that their close association with blacks was politically unwise. When an inept sheriff's posse was discovered, gunfire broke out, and an unknown number of blacks were killed, one white was seriously injured, and forty blacks, one white, and one Creek mixed-blood were captured. Other blacks escaped, and the sheriff took possession of the grounds. The next day parties unknown burned the Snake council house.

On the pretext that the Snake leadership was responsible for these events, the sheriff secured an arrest warrant for Chitto Harjo on the charge of conspiracy. Upon arriving at Harjo's log house, the sheriff and his deputies found at least nine other traditional Creeks assembled there for

---

[118] John Bartlett Meserve, "The Plea of Crazy Snake," *Chronicles of Oklahoma* 11 (1933):910–11.

[119] The two best accounts of the 1908 uprising are Daniel F. Littlefield and Lonnie Underhill, "The Crazy Snake Uprising of 1909: A Red, Black or White Affair?" *Arizona and the West* 20 (1978):307–24; and F. S. Barde, untitled manuscript, dated Apr. 16 [1908], in F. S. Barde Papers, Oklahoma State Historical Society Archives, Tulsa. See also Mel Bolster, "The Smoked Meat Rebellion," *Chronicles of Oklahoma* 31 (1953):37–55, and Eleanor Patricia Atwood, "The Crazy Snake Rebellions: A Study in the Breakdown of Tribal Government," *Vassar Journal of Undergraduate Studies* 15 (May 1942):44–60.

[120] An attempt to sort out the role of blacks in the uprising has been the major focus of most analyses. See Littlefield and Underwood, "Crazy Snake Uprising." This dimension of the events is an important one and there can be no question that the Creek Nation's traditionally open policy toward black membership had become an issue injurous to Creeks in a segregated society. But this emphasis obscures the fact that the core of the movement at Hickory Ground was a continuation of traditional Creek government from the 1900–1 uprising and that the alliance between traditional Creeks and blacks was an old one, mutually beneficial to both groups. Debo, *The Road to Disappearance*, 249–84.

the purpose of escorting him to Hickory Ground. Although it is not clear who fired first, gunfire erupted, and two deputies were killed. By the time the posse returned, Harjo had fled, a wanted murderer. The state of Oklahoma, anxious to exercise its newly acquired sovereignty, raised more than a thousand militiamen to put down the rebellion. Several blacks were killed as the militia attacked the camp at Hickory Ground, although most of the Creeks had dispersed. Chitto Harjo lived the remaining three years of his life a hunted man, hiding in the hills with Choctaw friends. With him, the traditional laws of the Creek people also went underground, protected in the hearts of people who would not accept the liquidation of their nations and the allotment of their lands.[121]

It is clear that this forcible breakup of the last Creek traditional government on Hickory Ground was not the end of an unbroken chain of traditional Creek governments. If any government was extinguished on Hickory Ground, it was the last of the attempts of the Creeks to maintain a national government. When anthropologist Morris Opler studied Creek political organization in Oklahoma in 1937, he reported the town governments still strong and vital. The base of traditional Creek law had moved from the national council back to the towns after the legal suppression of the last traditional governments.[122]

There is more than a little irony in the federal indictment of the last of the Creek governments for "purporting to organize a government and make laws for the Creek people"; for this, as we know from the historical context of *Worcester v. Georgia*, is the same type of law that Georgia attempted to make and enforce against the Cherokees, an arrogant usurpation not only of federal authority but also of the legal authority of the Indian tribes. In a long, convoluted chain of events, *Worcester* – so far as it defended the sovereign right of the Indian tribes to have their own political communities, governed by their own laws – became a dead letter under U.S. law, abandoned by the same federal government that under Andrew Jackson had refused to protect the rights of the Creeks and Cherokees in the South seventy years before. Native people never gave up their old laws and the sovereignty that protected those laws.

The abandonment of the federal government's relationship with the Creek Nation as an "autonomy" marked an abandonment of its own policy. While the Creek Nation was a sovereign nation, not in any way created by the

---

[121] Federal investigators later determined that Oklahoma state authorities had overreacted. See Littlefield and Underwood, "Crazy Snake Uprising," 322.

[122] Marvin Opler, "The Creek Town and the Problem of Creek Indian Political Reorganization," in Edward Spicer (ed.), *Human Problems and Technological Change* (New York: Russell Sage Foundation, 1952). Frank Speck, "Creek Indians of Taskigi Town," *Memoirs of the American Anthropological Association*, 2, pt. 2 (1907), confirmed this analysis.

United States, the Indian nations of Oklahoma had been placed there by the federal government, directly as a consequence of its removal policy. Creek sovereignty there, an extension of natural law and recognized by the Indian reformers of the 1830s, had, by its very success and preservation, become unacceptable to white Americans fifty years later.

4

Crow Dog's case

Although the Supreme Court's holding in *Crow Dog* was a striking recognition of the Brule's retention of tribal law as an element of tribal sovereignty, whites deliberately misrepresented the case as a simple one of factional politics and murder, thereby demeaning all elements of the Brule Sioux society and culture, including their law.[1] Accompanying a parallel attempt to discredit the tribal laws of the Indian nations in Oklahoma, the BIA successfully created a brutal image of the tribal law of reservation Indians. While the Indian nations had gone to great lengths to establish the legitimacy of their legal orders in relation to the American nation, the same was not true for the tribes in the West, who remained independent and carried on traditional ways in their ancestral lands. Crow Dog's Brule people were among these so-called wild tribes.[2]

In *ex parte Crow Dog*, the U.S. Supreme Court reversed Crow Dog's conviction for the 1881 shooting death of his chief, Spotted Tail. The court did not address the substantive grounds of the case but held that, following *Worcester*, Indian tribes retained the right to their own tribal law as an inherent

---

[1] Ethnographers do not agree on the tribal composition of the Sioux Nation. The Sioux people consisted of three distinct tribes: the Eastern or Santee Sioux, consisting of four bands, the Middle or Wichileya, composed of two bands, and the Western or Teton Sioux, composed of seven bands. Of the latter tribe, the Oglalla band occupied the Black Hills, while the Brule band occupied central South Dakota. Ernest L. Schusky, *The Forgotten Sioux: An Ethnography of the Lower Brule Reservation* (Chicago: Nelson-Hall, 1975), 14.

[2] Indian policy in the post–Civil War period was complicated by the vastly different forms of tribal adaptation to federal power. While a large number of removed tribes had peaceably settled down as small farmers in Oklahoma and Kansas or continued their traditional farming and fishing practices on their own lands in New Mexico and Washington, others engaged in extensive armed resistance, which in turn was variously categorized by the United States as acts of insurrection, war, or merely banditry. A pejorative term that denies the legitimacy of their resistance, "wild" was commonly applied to those tribes that resisted U.S. government authority. It is useful to remember that tribal peoples at this time all over the world were violently resisting European colonialism as that process encroached on tribal lands. There is a growing literature on this process of resistance. See, e.g., Ranajit Guha, *Elementary Aspects of Peasant Insurgency in Colonial India* (Delhi: Oxford University Press, 1983), which creates a framework for analyzing different types of tribal resistance.

attribute of sovereignty; therefore, the courts of the United States lacked criminal jurisdiction over crimes committed between Indians in Indian country. By all accounts, this decision aroused such a popular outcry that Congress was compelled to enact the Major Crimes Act of 1885 extending federal jurisdiction to major felonies occurring between Indians in Indian country.[3] The case never comes to mind without at least an unconscious thought that the holding allowed a killer to escape punishment, perpetrating an injustice that a popular reaction caused Congress to remedy through the imposition of federal law. This "tribal injustice" view of the case has undermined the doctrine of tribal sovereignty and continues to overshadow the true meaning of the case. It is necessary to clarify the factual context of the case so that a *"Crow Dog* doctrine" of Native American sovereignty can emerge from the lawbooks.

Crow Dog's case is important because it is a bridge between the ambiguous and ineffective sovereignty language of *Worcester* and the complete subjugation of tribal sovereignty during the late nineteenth century. The congressional passage of the Major Crimes Act in response to *Crow Dog* was a keystone in the development of the new plenary power doctrine that put the tribes completely under the control of Congress and the U.S. political process.[4] The parallel undermining of the customary social control mechanisms of tribal society weakened not only law and social cohesion but also all other tribal relationships, including marriage, family and clan interactions, the distribution of property, and social and political organization.[5] The U.S. Supreme Court colluded in this destruction of tribal institutions by creating the plenary power doctrine, legally justifying Congress's assertion of total power over the tribes.

A closer analysis of *Crow Dog* and the Major Crimes Act reveals that

---

[3] *Ex parte Crow Dog*, 109 U.S. 556 (1883); chap. 341, 23 Stat. 362, 385 (1885). The Major Crimes Act is now codified as 18 U.S.C. Sec. 153 and has been expanded to fourteen felonies from the original seven.

[4] The plenary power doctrine begins with *United States v. Kagama* (1886), a case that upheld the legality of the Major Crimes Act, and will be considered in Chapter 5.

[5] We are just beginning to see a renewed interest in the customary law of American Indians, a subject universally left out of Indian law casebooks. There is an earlier small literature on Sioux customary law. See, e.g., Norman D. Humphrey, "Police and Tribal Welfare in Plains Indian Cultures," *Journal of Criminal Law, Criminology, and Police Science* 33 (1942):147; William Christie MacLeod, "Police and Punishment Among Native Americans of the Plains," *Journal of Criminal Law, Criminology, and Police Science* 27 (1937):181; John Provisne, "The Underlying Sanctions of Plains Indian Culture: An Approach to the Study of Primitive Law," Ph.D. diss., University of Chicago, 1934; and Ella Cara Deloria, "Dakota Treatment of Murderers," *Proceedings of the American Philosophical Society* 66 (November 1944):368. Currently, some lawyers and legal scholars working with Indian tribes are concerned to revitalize customary law so that tribal court systems might better serve Indian communities. See James Zion, "Harmony Among the People: Torts and Indian Courts," *Montana Law Review* 45 (1984):265.

extension of criminal law over reservation Indians was the product of a broad national movement toward an assimilationist Indian policy that had, since the 1870s, come to dominate the Indian policy of both Congress and the BIA. "Popular outcry" does not explain either the decision to prosecute Crow Dog (under existing law there should have been no prosecution) or the passage of the Major Crimes Act. Rather, the BIA cultivated *Crow Dog* as a test case and tried to create other test cases both before and after to gain precisely the end that was won: federal criminal jurisdiction over the Indian tribes. The Supreme Court in reversing Crow Dog's conviction had adopted this view, mischaracterizing the case as one of "red man's revenge," a racist and false statement that conjured up the "blood revenge" image of tribal law and invited federal intervention to "civilize" the Sioux.[6]

BIA officials had been attempting to acquire such jurisdiction since at least 1874, because they needed the coercive power of the criminal law as one means to force the assimilation of the Indians.[7] It is clear that beginning the day after Spotted Tail's killing, the BIA engaged in a systematic distortion of the facts of the case. Officials claimed that a popular outcry among local whites necessitated the arrest, even though the Indian agent (the BIA official locally in charge) at the Rosebud Agency, home of Spotted Tail and Crow Dog, had immediately ordered the arrest, well before the killing was known off the reservation.[8] Likewise, the outrage provoked by the Supreme Court's reversal of the case came primarily from BIA officials and Indian reformers. The Major Crimes Act was thereupon tacked to the end of an annual Indian appropriations bill, where it produced less debate than the liquor regulations included in the same measure.[9]

Between *Worcester* and *Crow Dog*, U.S. Supreme Court cases on Indian law skirted the issue of tribal sovereignty, focusing instead on expanding the power of the federal government and limiting the power of the states. Since the courts had failed to deal with larger questions of tribal rights, the sovereign right of Indians to maintain their own law was intact in federal Indian law at the time of *Crow Dog*, except in the de facto removal of virtually all tribal jurisdiction over whites, mostly by treaty.[10] The tribes held rights as

---

[6] *Ex parte Crow Dog*, 571. This language recalls Chief Justice Lipscomb's analysis of the character of tribal law in *Caldwell v. the State*, the first time a U.S. court analyzed the character of the laws of American Indians. "Whatever authority exercised was adventitious and temporary, passing from one warrior to another, as accident might determine" (333–4).

[7] U.S. Congress, Senate, 43d Congress, 1st session, Report 367, 2 (1874). A discussion of the course of this BIA lobbying for "criminal law for the Indians" follows.

[8] The Rosebud Agency was on a site selected by Spotted Tail in 1878 for his people on the Great Sioux Reservation. In 1889, after allotment, the Great Sioux Reservation was broken up into smaller reservations, and the Rosebud Agency became the much smaller Rosebud Reservation, which it remains today.

[9] On the debate over the Major Crimes Act, see *Congressional Record* (1885), 934–6.

[10] In *United States v. McBratney*, 104 U.S. 621 (1882), the U.S. Supreme Court gave the states

sovereign political communities from time immemorial with or without treaty recognition. This principle, though denied by BIA administrators in the aftermath of *Crow Dog*, was clearly understood by the Brule.

Brule law

Neither Justice Stanley Matthew's decision in *Crow Dog* nor the later debate in Congress over the Major Crimes Act was informed by actual knowledge of Sioux law. Although the Supreme Court understood that Crow Dog's case had been processed under the tribal law, nothing in the Court's decision indicated anything but the most superficial comprehension of that law. Still, it was a rare event for the court to even acknowledge the existence of the tribal law of the Indian nations.

The eighteen Plains tribes, diverse peoples speaking ten languages, developed a remarkable system of laws, very similar from tribe to tribe.[11] Much of what is known today about their legal systems in the nineteenth century dates from ethnographic studies of the late nineteenth and early twentieth centuries, some of the classic works in American anthropology. Unfortunately, the political and legal structures of Indian people were not as important to the ethnographers as ceremonial matters, and so while knowledge of their legal processes is substantial, it is not as complete as modern knowledge of other aspects of tribal culture. None of these studies directly describes the legal processes of the Brule Sioux, which must be inferred from general knowledge of the Oglalla Sioux and other northern Plains tribes.[12]

jurisdiction over crimes committed by whites on Indian reservations. While such jurisdiction interfered with tribal sovereignty, this was a cession of federal jurisdiction, not tribal jurisdiction, because federal law governed crimes committed by whites on federal land. *McBratney* is discussed in Chapter 2, the section entitled "Federal Indian law from *Worcester to Crow Dog*."

[11] The Plains Indians captured the imagination of the American people in the late nineteenth century, with their 1876 defeat of General George Armstrong Custer at the Battle of Little Big Horn. Stories of the battle were widely circulated in the popular press. Popularly called a "massacre," Sioux and Cheyenne warriors met Custer's surprise attack of their village on open ground, soundly defeating his professional troops. Richard Slotkin, *The Fatal Environment: The Myth of the Frontier in the Age of Industralization, 1800–1890* (New York: Atheneum, 1984), discusses the impact of this event on U.S. culture at 371–498. There are a number of anthropological and historical works on Plains Indian culture. See, e.g., Clark Wissler, "Indians of the Plains," in *Handbook* (New York: American Museum of Natural History, 1927).

[12] In the early 1930s, John Provinse found that, of the Plains tribes, only five had sufficient ethnographic data for a study of their legal processes: Dakota Sioux, Crow, Blackfoot, Assiniboine, and Omaha. "The Underlying Sanctions of Plains Indian Cultures," 28–9. A complete list of these ethnographic studies may be found in Provinse's bibliography, 192–7. See also E. Adamson Hoebel, *The Political Organization and Law Ways of the Comanche Indians*, Memoirs of the American Anthropological Association, no. 54 (1940); E. Adamson Hoebel and Karl N. Llewellyn, *The Cheyenne Way* (Norman: University of Oklahoma Press, 1941), and Jane Richardson, "Law and Status Among the Kiowa Indians," *Monographs of the American Ethnological Society*, no. 1 (1940). Together these works provide a substantial

The primary social unit in Sioux society was the band. These bands survived entirely by hunting, which required a migratory camp life. The political structure was based on a chief's council, which appointed head men for each band. The headmen selected two bodies of police, one for war and one for hunting. These police functionaries were chosen as individuals and not on the basis of membership in particular warrior societies. Membership in the police societies cut across all of the warrior societies to ensure fairness.[13] Characteristic of the Plains Indians were well-developed police societies with broad-based power to perform a wide range of social functions.

Most often these functions were not permanently accorded to individuals but were assigned on a seasonal or some other temporary basis, so that this responsibility was ordinarily held by a large proportion of the males in a band over time. Many ethnographers saw the necessity of the successful hunt as the common core to the universality of these police institutions among the Plains tribes. Anthropologist John Provisne deemphasized the importance of the hunt, however, finding that these legal structures pervaded all elements of band life and were as much devoted to the resolution of ordinary disputes. The exact legal process of these interventions is not clear. For example, the police societies may have coerced disputants into arriving at a private settlement rather than investigating the incident and applying tribal law to decide the case.[14] The primary value in settling these disputes differed sharply from U.S. law. There was little concern with punishment, retribution, or applying any abstract notions of justice or morality. The goal was the termination of the conflict and the reintegration of all persons involved into the tribal body. For the hunt, and the perpetual migration that it entailed, to succeed, all people had to work together and to conform to one system of rules. This process runs counter to a system based on blood revenge.[15]

The process that occurred in the homicide case of Crow Dog, that of a tribal council meeting to arrange for a peaceful reconciliation of the parties with an ordered gift of horses, blankets, money, or other property, was one of a number of conflict resolution mechanisms available to the Sioux. Ap-

---

picture of the traditional laws of the Plains Indians, although it is largely reconstructed from the recollections of tribal informants in the early twentieth century.

[13] Provinse, "Underlying Sanctions of Plains Indian Cultures," 34.

[14] Ibid., 60–1.

[15] Most preliterate legal systems purported to be based on "blood revenge" appear, on closer examination, to carefully structure such revenge in a number of ways. See William Ian Miller, *Blood-Taking and Peacemaking: Feud, Law, and Society in Saga Iceland* (Chicago: University of Chicago Press, 1990), and P. K. Nayak, *Blood, Women and Territory: An Analysis of Clan Feuds of Dongria Konds* (New Delhi: Reliance Publishing House, 1989). Sidney L. Harring, "The Rich Men of the Country: Canadian Law in the Land of the Copper Inuit," *Ottawa Law Review* 21(1988):1, analyzes a string of blood revenge killings that served as a pretext for the imposition of Canadian law on an Inuit people.

parently it was used only after the most serious of tribal disturbances. The council met not to adjudicate the dispute but to reconcile the parties involved. Hence, the result of the case – the offering of property to one side by the other – does not indicate any substantive resolution of the merits of the case: Crow Dog had been in no way "convicted" by a tribal council. Nor was the offered property "blood money," a payment to relatives to atone for the killing in a substantive way or to take the place of blood revenge. It was an offer of reconciliation and a symbolic commitment to continuation of tribal social relations. Although the family of Spotted Tail accepted the offer, this was not necessary to resolve the conflict. Often the recipients refused to take the offered property, a position that showed the tribe both their pride and their wealth.[16]

The police societies played a complex role in this council-based process, acting as peacemakers and undertaking the preliminary negotiations that made the reconciliation possible. They approached both parties to determine willingness to make a settlement and enforced the settlement that was ultimately reached if voluntary compliance was not secured. Although often the police societies acted independently of direct council authority, they also worked as the enforcement arm of the council when the council carried out legal functions.[17]

This is the legal system that the Supreme Court found the Brule had a sovereign right to use to settle their internal disputes. It was obviously operating in the 1880s, even though factionalism is often thought to have destroyed the ability of tribal political processes to function. Tribal law, however, had to have a tribal legitimacy in order to exist. It depended on the maintenance of the authority of traditional structures that could use traditional legal norms to resolve disputes between opposing factions. Most tribes had such processes functioning effectively in spite of years of factional struggle, as the Brule showed by settling two complex killings in three years through tribal law.

Spotted Tail and Crow Dog: Brule Sioux society in 1881

Both Spotted Tail and Crow Dog still, in the late twentieth century, live in the hearts of the Brule people. The life of each, for different reasons, has assumed legendary proportions. Spotted Tail is seen by many on the Rosebud Reservation as a great statesman who kept his people out of war and attempted to secure Brule sovereignty in the face of U.S. imperialism. Crow Dog, to these people, was an outcast, killing his chief for personal glory.

---

[16] Provinse, "Underlying Sanctions of Plains Indian Culture," 67.
[17] Ibid.

This view was clearly put forward by the BIA and has been adopted by most whites: Crow Dog is described as an "ambitious and resentful" plotter in a late-twentieth-century legal history.[18]

Spotted Tail, born in 1823 and fifty-eight years old when he died, in a short lifetime saw the Great Sioux Nation dismembered by the United States, its people made dependents and virtual prisoners on a handful of reservations. He had been a warrior and a war chief, seriously wounded fighting U.S. troops at Bluewater, Nebraska, in the Sioux War of 1855. For his part in this war he was imprisoned at Fort Leavenworth, Kansas, for four months and, in the process of being transported to Kansas through hundreds of miles of white farms, had realized that the Sioux could never defeat the whites. After his release he devoted his considerable political abilities to avoiding further conflict with the whites. By 1865 he was clearly recognized as the head chief of the Brules, leading the tribe in all treaty negotiations at Fort Laramie and making several trips to Washington. While he did not trust the whites, he steadfastly kept the Brule at peace in the Sioux War of 1876.[19]

Spotted Tail's efforts secured him first an agency for the Brules, then a reservation, a portion of their traditional homelands in central South Dakota. Here at the Rosebud Agency he attempted to preserve a homeland for his people under U.S. hegemony. He intimidated the weak and corrupt Indian agents sent to the reservation, once even moving the agency to his own location. His independent ways put him in frequent conflict with BIA bureaucrats. He would have nothing to do with various schemes to make his people farmers. When the BIA built him a three-story house at a cost of $40,000, he refused to occupy it, living in his traditional camp a few miles from the agency. Although he sent a number of his children east to the Carlisle Boarding School, he angrily removed them because, instead of learning to read and write, they were made to learn farming skills and to march around "like soldiers." He had blocked the surveying of a railroad line across his reservation by refusing them protection. Still, Spotted Tail's political options were sharply limited in such a context: he was negotiating what concessions he could under conditions of military and political domination.[20]

Traditionally, the Sioux did not have strong head chiefs but were governed by councils composed of numerous band chiefs. These leadership positions were not hereditary but fluid, deferring to individual ability and changing

[18] Edward Lazarus, *Black Hills, White Justice: The Sioux Nation Versus the United States, 1775 to the Present* (New York: Harper/Collins, 1991), 99–100.
[19] George E. Hyde, *Spotted Tail's Folk: A History of the Brule Sioux* (Norman: University of Oklahoma Press, 1961), 73–8, 127.
[20] Ibid., 293–4, 317–18; 322–4, 335–6, 327.

tribal structures. Crow Dog's place in this structure can be inferred from several sources. He was clearly a leader of the Orphan band, one of the traditional Brule bands that took its name from an 1844 tragedy. In a war against the Shoshones, the band's chief, Big Raven, and all the able-bodied men in his camp were killed. Crow Dog, born in 1834, had lived through the same transformation of his tribe that Spotted Tail had. His name came from a vision: one night a Coyote warned him of an impending white attack. His band prepared for the attack, just in time to defend themselves against white settlers and Crow Indian scouts. Crow Dog was badly injured but was cared for by two Coyotes, who brought him food and kept him warm. When he had recovered, a Crow showed him the way back to his people.[21]

Apparently Crow Dog had once been an Orphan band chief but was still a leader identified with Brule who were more willing than Spotted Tail to resist federal authority. He was closely associated with Crazy Horse, accompanying the war chief when he surrendered in 1877, only to be brutally bayoneted by a soldier. That day, Crow Dog asserted his leadership, preventing bloodshed by riding between the soldiers and angry Sioux prepared to avenge Crazy Horse's murder.[22] He had also journeyed to Canada to briefly join Sitting Bull's band in exile.[23] Crow Dog was solidly in the center of traditional Sioux, refusing to accommodate the U.S. government.

This, on its face, appears to be inconsistent with his role as chief of the Indian police at Rosebud Agency. The police were chosen by the Indian agent and were responsible to the BIA, not to the tribe. There is some evidence that traditional warriors attempted to gain control of the reservation police forces, and Crow Dog may have had this in mind.[24] Rosebud traditionals may have been concerned that, in view of Spotted Tail's immense power, they needed to seize power over reservation institutions wherever they could. The Indian agents, also concerned about Spotted Tail's power, may have deliberately appointed police officers opposed to Spotted Tail. In any case, Crow Dog did not last long as police chief: appointed in the fall of 1879, he was removed in the winter of 1879–80, serving an even shorter second term later in 1880.[25]

The dispute between Spotted Tail and Crow Dog cannot be understood in contemporary U.S. cultural terms. The 1881 world of two warriors, cast in leadership positions at an Indian agency established only in 1878, must have involved complex cultural, religious, social, and political forces. Nearly

---

[21] Mary Crow Dog, *Lakota Woman* (New York: Harper, 1991), 178–80. Ms. Crow Dog, granddaughter-in-law of Crow Dog, presents this story as told by Crow Dog's son, Henry.
[22] Ibid., 178, 181; Hyde, *Spotted Tail's Folk*, 285.
[23] Mary Crow Dog, *Lakota Woman*, 180.
[24] This is discussed in Chapter 6, the section entitled "The Indian Police."
[25] Hyde, *Spotted Tail's Folk*, 312–16.

ten thousand Brules lived in traditional camps, scattered for miles around the agency. These camps would have physically resembled the camps of fifty years before, but Brule society was irretrievably changed. While the Brule lived in tipis in sprawling camps surrounded by thousands of fine ponies, there was little for them to do there. Some of the men still roamed parts of their traditional hunting grounds, a practice carried on well into the twentieth century. In 1880 some Brule who had escaped to Canada with Sitting Bull returned. The Brule had hosted a traditional Sun Dance in the summer of 1879, attracting thousands of Sioux from other reservations who attended, with or without the passes that the Indian agents claimed they required. But the economy was largely one of dependency, and factional politics probably became increasingly concerned with structuring this new relationship with the United States.[26]

The killing of Spotted Tail

The killing of Spotted Tail reveals a great deal about late-nineteenth-century reservation life. While the killing can be located in intense factional struggle, it is impossible to know what the inner workings of Brule tribal politics were in the summer of 1881 or to reconstruct exactly what happened the day that Crow Dog shot Spotted Tail. The common version of the incident is narrated by the popular historian George E. Hyde in the final chapter, entitled "The Betrayal," of his heroic study, *Spotted Tail's Folk: A History of the Brule Sioux.* Hyde relates that Spotted Tail had appointed Crow Dog chief of the Indian police at the Rosebud Agency. Crow Dog, a subchief and leader of a traditional faction, was jealous of Spotted Tail and greedy for the spoils of power available on the reservation. From his position as chief, he had stirred up discord over Spotted Tail's leadership and had tried unsuccessfully to elect a member of his faction as chief.[27]

To this "jealous factional rivalry," Hyde incorporated three more reasons for the killing, completely confusing the political motivation. First, Spotted Tail had twice removed Crow Dog from his position as chief of police, leaving Crow Dog bitter over his loss of personal power. Then Hyde adds a dispute over a woman, Light-in-the-Lodge, the wife of a disabled old man. Spotted Tail had taken Light-in-the-Lodge as his second wife. Crow Dog thereupon took up her first husband's cause as part of a deliberate

---

[26] Ibid., 302–31.

[27] Hyde, *Spotted Tail's Folk,* 308–36. Hyde's work is an example of traditional tribal histories, which rely primarily on white sources to create an "Indian history." Another popular history, one that is consistent with Hyde but far more anti-Indian, is Doane Robinson, "A History of the Dakota or Sioux Indians," *South Dakota Department of History Collections* 2 (1904), 444.

Brule police from Rosebud Agency

effort to portray himself as the champion of traditional Brules against the arbitrary power of Spotted Tail, an "agency chief" installed by the U.S. Army.[28] Finally, Spotted Tail had apparently personally been paid "grazing fees" from white ranchers, money that Crow Dog had also tried to collect.[29]

For Hyde, primarily political reasons led Crow Dog to assassinate his chief. On August 5, 1881, Crow Dog brought a load of wood to the agency from his camp nine miles away. He sold the wood, a major source of his income, and began the return trip home in midafternoon, just after the tribal council had broken up. He may have known that Spotted Tail would leave the council at this time and ride two miles to his newly built government house on the same road. As Spotted Tail rode toward him, Crow Dog stopped his buckboard and crouched low on the ground beside it as if to repair a wheel. When Spotted Tail approached within fifteen feet, Crow Dog sprang up with his rifle and shot him in the side, the bullet exiting through his chest. Spotted Tail fell from his horse, rose, took a step or two toward Crow Dog, attempted to draw his pistol, but fell dead. Crow Dog then leapt onto his buckboard and drove off at high speed toward his camp.

[28] The exact status of Spotted Tail's chieftainship is still the subject of debate. It is clear that he occupied a traditional chieftainship in the Brule tribe, but it is also clear that whites recognized him as the Brule chief because he kept the tribe out of warfare. On November 24, 1876, General George Crook had appointed him chief of both the Pine Ridge and Rosebud reservations. Hyde, *Spotted Tail's Folk*, 115, 127.

[29] Ibid., 313, 314, 317.

The aftermath described in the usual account of this case is as important as the killing itself, for this is where both the "popular outcry" distortion first emerges and where the "red man's revenge" view of Brule law enters. Eagle Hawk, the current head of the Indian police, "did not dare arrest Crow Dog," according to Hyde. This left the Rosebud Agency's chief clerk, Henry Lelar, acting Indian agent in the absence of agent John Cook, to wait until the day after the killing, when the "first fury of the Sioux" had worn off, to call a tribal council meeting. This council followed Brule law and ordered an end to the trouble, sending peacemakers to both families. The families in turn, also following Brule law, agreed to a payment of $600, eight horses, and one blanket, which Crow Dog's people promptly paid to Spotted Tail's people. Brule law effectively and quickly redressed the killing and restored tribal harmony, a point that even the U.S. Supreme Court later recognized.[30]

In describing the "popular outcry" that necessitated the arrest and trial of Crow Dog, Hyde's account merges with the official report of the BIA, which is the basis of discussion of the case in legal texts and scholarly articles. By that account, when Indian Agent John Cook returned from a Chicago business trip to the reservation on August 10 "he seems to have been contented with this [customary] settlement, but the public was now aroused and the officials in Washington demanded action at Rosebud."[31] Accordingly, Cook "got the council to act again." Crow Dog and Black Crow, a son-in-law of Spotted Tail who was thought by Cook to be the instigator of the conspiracy, "were induced to submit to arrest and were taken in charge" by Indian police, under the authority of the agent, not the tribe, and sent to Fort Niobara, Nebraska, to be held for trial.

This account is wrong. In fact, Crow Dog had been arrested and conveyed with all deliberate speed three days earlier, on August 7, on the authority of an Indian agent who was fully aware that the Brule had already settled the case according to tribal law. A telegram from Lieutenant James Paddock at Fort Niobara informed Acting Agent Lelar that "Hollow Horn Bear has this day turned over to the C.O. [commanding officer] of this Post Crow Dog and Black Crow – and that they are now held here under the charge of the guards."[32] We know from Crow Dog's trial how the arrest occurred, for both Hollow Horn Bear and Agent Lelar gave testimony. According to Lelar, "I sent Eagle Hawk to arrest defendant. When he failed, I sent Hollow

---

[30] Hyde, *Spotted Tail's Folk*, 332–4. This account of the process of customary Sioux law is corroborated by a story in the *Black Hills Daily Times*, August 9, 1881, reporting that the killing had been settled according to Brule law.

[31] Hyde, *Spotted Tail's Folk*, 333.

[32] Lt. James Paddock to Henry Lelar, August 7, 1881, Records of the BIA, Special Case 91, Record Group 75, National Archives.

Eagle Hawk, chief of police at Rosebud Agency and witness at Crow Dog's trial

Horn Bear, who made the arrest." Hollow Horn Bear, chief of the Orphan band and not a police officer,[33] described the arrest in detail:

> Mr. Lelar gave me a paper for the arrest of Crow Dog. Found defendant on a hill between White River and Rosebud Creek, where I made the arrest. Defendant had no clothes at the time, except a blanket, breech-clout, and leggings and was on horseback. I did as I was ordered and took defendant to Fort Niobara.[34]

[33] Hyde, *Spotted Tail's Folk*, 316.
[34] *Black Hills Daily Times*, March 25, 1882. Although there obviously was a transcript made of the trial, none turned up in my search. Fortunately, the *Black Hills Daily Times* ran a day-by-day account of the trial, including detailed quotations of testimony from the witness stand, evidently recorded by a shorthand stenographer in the courtroom. This account is not official, but I believe it to be accurate. Crow Dog's appeal brief contains extensive quotations of testimony that are completely consistent with the *Daily Times* account.

Hollow Horn Bear, Brule chief to whom Crow Dog surrendered after the killing of Spotted Tail

Crow Dog had submitted to traditional tribal authority, not to BIA police who were completely unable to arrest him. Before his arrest, Crow Dog had purified himself in a sweat lodge, shooting his rifle into sacred rocks four times to assuage the spirit of Spotted Tail.[35]

The speed with which Lelar acted in contravention of federal law seems to indicate that the BIA and the Justice Department had already developed

[35] Mary Crow Dog, *Lakota Woman*, 182.

Black Crow, who was arrested with Crow Dog as conspirator in the plot to assassinate Spotted Tail, held in jail until after Crow Dog was convicted and sentenced to hang, then released

a legal theory through which to extend federal criminal law to Indians and that they were only awaiting an appropriate test case. Evidence comes from a telegram to Agent Cook on August 15 from Hugh Campbell, U.S. attorney in Deadwood: "Is it desire of Indian Department that Crow Dog should be prosecuted criminally for murder of Spotted Tail? If so, where are witnesses and where is Crow Dog?"[36] This strangely offhand communication makes it evident that the U.S. attorney, ten days after the killing, had taken almost no interest in the case and was deferring the question of his jurisdiction to the BIA.

Three days before, on August 12, Campbell had wired Washington for instructions:

---

[36] Hugh Campbell to John Cook, August 15, 1881, Records of the BIA, Special Case 91, Record Group 75, National Archives.

> Crow Dog, Brule Sioux Indian, is reported to have killed Spotted Tail, Brule Chief, in this District about first August. Referring to article eight page two fifty six, vol. nineteen statutes at large and page three eighteen vol. eighteen statutes at large amendment to Revised Statutes twenty one forty six and sections twenty one forty six, revised statutes and the Indian amenable to U.S. laws and does the department think the court has jurisdiction and will a prosecution conflict with government policy as to treatment of Indians? Do provisions of page two fifty six, vol. nineteen statutes at large being later date control rather than section twenty one forty six Revised Statutes?[37]

This telegram was forwarded to the Interior Department on August 13, which responded on August 22 with a letter to the attorney general expressing the opinion "that it is perfectly competent for the United States courts for that territory to take cognizance of the alleged murder"[38] and requesting the attorney general to "examine the law on the subject."[39] The attorney general concurred with the Interior Department:

> It seems to me entirely clear that the conclusion that you have reached is correct. The treaty between the United States and the different tribes of Sioux Indians, proclaimed February 24, 1869/15 Statutes 635/ expressly provided in its first section that "if bad men among the Indians shall commit a wrong or depredation upon the person or property of anyone, white, black, or Indian, subject to the authority of the United States, and at peace therewith, the Indians herein named solemnly agree that they will, upon proof made to their agent and notice by him, deliver up the wrongdoer to the United States to be tried and punished according to the law.
>
> Article 8 of the subsequent agreement with the same Indians, approved by Act of Congress, February 28, 1877, expressly provides "the provisions of the said treaty of 1868 as herein modified, shall continue in full force, and that the provisions of this agreement shall apply to any country which may hereafter be occupied by the said Indians as a home, and Congress shall by appropriate legislation secure to them an orderly government they shall be subject to the laws of the United States, and each individual shall be protected in his rights of property, person, and life."[40]

[37] Attorney General to Secretary of the Interior S. J. Kirkwood, August 13 and 25, 1881. The second letter describes the contents of Campbell's August 22 letter, which has not been preserved. Both letters, together with some legal notes, are in Records of the BIA, Special Case 91, Record Group 75, National Archives.

[38] Here it is important to note that the BIA's willingness to cede its jurisdiction over the Brule Sioux to a territorial court is functionally the same thing as ceding it to a state court. Dakota Territory was self-governing under an organic act, preparing itself for statehood.

[39] Commissioner, BIA, to Attorney General, Special Case 91, Record Group 75, National Archives.

[40] Attorney General to BIA. Commissioner, in ibid.

These two treaty clauses provided the entire basis of the government's case in the constitutional argument before the Supreme Court – here fully developed via intercontinental telegraph less than twenty days after the killing, thirteen days after the local U.S. attorney asked for instructions, and ten days after that same official inquired of the Indian agent where the defendants and witnesses were. Furthermore, all parties were aware that they were making new law. What is the origin of the legal theory of the case? It was not uncovered in the legal research of U.S. Attorney Campbell in Deadwood, as we shall see, but already had a short and discredited history in the BIA.

Early BIA attempts to prosecute Indians under state or territorial law

While Crow Dog's case was in the process of trial and appeal, the BIA was involved in at least six parallel murder cases, each time attempting to extend some form of U.S. criminal law, either federal or state, to the tribes. The wide range of cases, which spanned the entire West, reveals that extension of criminal law to the tribes was a matter of BIA policy, and having been unable to induce the U.S. Congress to extend criminal jurisdiction over the tribes, the BIA was trying to induce state and territorial courts to do so in violation of its legal responsibility to defend the interests of the tribes. Moreover, the BIA prosecuted several of the cases simultaneously, using different approaches to gain criminal jurisdiction. Even if the agency was not certain of winning its desired result in *Crow Dog*, it had alternative cases ready for action.

The most important of these was the 1882 case of Johnson Foster, which, like that of Crow Dog, was ideal as a test, although for different reasons. *Crow Dog* involved the killing of an important chief under government protection and presented a direct confrontation of tribal law with U.S. law because Brule legal process had settled the issue. In the Foster case, because of legal anomalies in the Indian Territory, no court had jurisdiction over a cold-blooded killing, a perfect legal atrocity to force the federal courts or Congress to take some action.

Robert Poisal, an Arapaho, and his niece had journeyed across the Indian Territory to enroll their children in a government school. As they returned, passing through a wooded area on the Potawatomi Reservation, Johnson Foster, a Creek, appeared standing silently by a tree. Without saying a word, Foster fired a shot, instantly killing Poisal. His niece escaped.[41] Because

---

[41] John Miles, Indian agent, Cheyenne and Arapaho Agency, to Henry Price, Commissioner of Indian Affairs, September 20, 1882, in U.S. Congress, Senate, 48th Congress, 1st session, Ex. doc. 105 (1884).

both parties were Indians and the crime occurred in the Indian Territory, the matter was solely within the jurisdiction of the Potawatomi tribe. The Potawatomis, though possessing traditional legal mechanisms sufficient to deal with internal disputes, had no kind of legal process, either traditional or adopted Cherokee-style from a U.S. model, to prosecute a non-Potawatomi murder case.[42] Therefore, the tribe was unable or unwilling to take any action against Foster. The Arapahos were outraged and threatened extralegal action, but no tribe had any kind of extraterritorial jurisdiction over citizens of another tribe; hence Foster remained beyond their reach.[43]

The BIA proceeded exactly as it had in *Crow Dog*, relying on the same statutory grounds. The attorney general was persuaded to instruct U.S. Attorney Clayton of the Western District of Arkansas (with jurisdiction over the Indian Territory) to arrange for Foster's trial. The local U.S. attorney's refusal to bring the case was concurred in by J. R. Hallowell, the U.S. attorney for Kansas, and S. F. Phillips, the acting U.S. attorney general, and the case was not prosecuted.[44] In the BIA's 1883 annual report, covering the period when Crow Dog's case was on appeal, the Foster case was cited as an example of the kind of legal atrocity that could arise under the existing state of white criminal jurisdiction over the Indian tribes.[45]

The Foster case was not the only attempt of the BIA to extend U.S. law to reservation Indians at this time. In six contemporaneous cases, the BIA actively sought to have killings between Indians tried in state courts. In 1882, Yen-decker, a Nevada Shoshone, killed a Shoshone woman near Elko. Indian Agent John Mayhugh of Duck Valley Shoshone Reservation was instructed to turn the case over to the "proper legal authorities of the county."[46] Although Yen-decker was never indicted in Elko, this same BIA policy was applied a year later to Spanish Jim, another Nevada Shoshone. The decision

---

[42] The Potawatomis apparently had enacted a tribal code of laws in 1881 but, for either procedural or administrative reasons, could not apply it to Foster. BIA, *Annual Report of the Commission of Indian Affairs, 1881*, 102.

[43] While the major Indian nations in the Indian Territory had extradition treaties with each other, the federal government had removed dozens of smaller tribes to the Indian Territory as well. These tribes did not create the kind of hybrid legal systems of the Cherokees and Creeks, relying on traditional legal processes. Furthermore, the lack of police institutions made it impossible to find and arrest an accused criminal. Foster probably fled back to his people in the Creek Nation.

[44] Phillips issued a formal opinion, stating the Justice Department's analysis of its lack of jurisdiction over Foster. "Crimes Committed by Indians," 17 Op. A.G. 566 (1883).

[45] BIA, *Annual Report, 1883*, x–xv. The account of the Johnson Foster case ran to three full pages of small print – more attention than *Crow Dog* ever received in a BIA report.

[46] Letter from Henry Price, Commissioner of Indian Affairs, to John Mayhugh, Indian Agent at Duck Valley Reservation (September 29, 1882); letter from Price to Mayhugh (November 13, 1882) (both on file in vol. 37 of the "Letters Sent, Civilization Division" files of the BIA held in the National Archives. There are no county court records of the Yan-decker case (also spelled Yendecker), so it is not clear that the state took jurisdiction.

of the U.S. attorney to take the case to state court was initiated by BIA Commissioner Henry Price, indicating that the BIA at the highest levels wanted to impose any available criminal jurisdiction – federal or state – over the tribes. The U.S. attorney (who had legal responsibility to defend Jim's rights), joined the state's attorney in an appeal to the Nevada Supreme Court, arguing that Nevada had criminal jurisdiction over its Indian tribes, whether on or off the reservation. The Nevada Supreme Court rejected their argument, holding that states had no jurisdiction over tribal Indians because of exclusive federal authority in Indian affairs.[47] The next year the BIA commissioner reprimanded Peter Roman, Indian agent at Montana's Flathead Reservation for his decision that he lacked jurisdiction to prosecute François, a Flathead Indian, for a murder committed on the reservation. Roman was directed to provide the U.S. attorney with full information about the case that "the guilt or innocence" of François could "be tested before the proper legal tribunal," language that can only refer to bringing a criminal indictment against François in a territorial court, just as had been done against Crow Dog.[48]

Three parallel cases developed in Oregon at the same time in a concerted BIA effort to give Oregon criminal jurisdiction over reservation Indians. In the fall of 1882, Siletz Indians Kane Kelsey, Jack Kelsey, and Louie Dick complained to the secretary of war that they had been held as prisoners for two years without trial in Fort Vancouver. The secretary asked the BIA commissioner for an investigation, questioning his own legal authority to hold the three as military prisoners. The commissioner reported that the three had killed Tillamook George, a witch doctor who had taken money to cure Jim Cook. After Cook died, Kelsey, a tribal policeman who had already served two terms in the Oregon Penitentiary, induced his two partners to accompany him to George's camp, where they strangled him in July 1880. The BIA requested the army to hold them until the state took jurisdiction. A lengthy series of letters urged Indian Agent E. A. Swan to turn the three over to the state for trial.[49] He did not do so and the three must have been released from army custody because Kelsey was murdered in Tillamook the next year.[50] In March 1883, Tom Gilbert, a Grand Ronde

---

[47] *State v. McKenney*, 18 Nev. 1882 (1883). This case is fully discussed in Chapter 2, the section entitled "The North and West, 1835–80."

[48] BIA Commissioner to Peter Roman, Indian Agent, Flathead Agency, Montana, March 8, 1883. BIA, "Letters Sent" file, vol. 39, 45.

[49] The Kane Kelsey case is the subject of eight letters and telegrams from BIA Commissioner Henry Price to various military and BIA officials. These are found in BIA, "Letters Sent," file vols. 37 and 39, October 4, 13, 19 (two letters), 1882; March 14, April 14, 1883. Oregon county court records do not record the disposition of these cases.

[50] William E. Kent, *The Siletz Indian Reservation, 1855–1900* (Newport, Or.: Lincoln County Historical Society, 1977), 28.

Indian, was convicted in state court and sentenced to hang for the murder of two other Indians on the reservation.[51] This confusion extended to a third case when Ben Johnson, another Siletz Indian, was arrested for murder and taken to the county jail in Corvallis. Swan was instructed in a telegram from Washington to recommend that the state court appoint a lawyer to defend him – or to ask the U.S. attorney in Portland to do so.[52] The BIA requested an opinion from the attorney general, who, acknowledging that Congress had failed to take jurisdiction over such crimes, held that Oregon had criminal jurisdiction over reservation Indians because such jurisdiction was not specifically excepted upon Oregon's admission to the union.[53]

The BIA's willingness to turn reservation Indians over to states for trial was a parallel experiment to its *Crow Dog* test case, an attempt to find another method of extending the force of U.S. law to tribal Indians. State courts offered an attractive option in the face of the great reluctance of federal courts to acknowledge such authority. There was no doctrine of tribal sovereignty in state courts. Yet the BIA was surely not ignorant of fifty years of struggle between federal and state authorities concerning jurisdiction over the Indian tribes. The BIA willingness to reach out to state courts reflected a changed federal policy: forced assimilation required recourse to U.S. courts for the criminal punishment of tribal Indians. It did not matter whether the particular courts were state or federal.

The trial of Crow Dog

By the time Crow Dog was arraigned in territorial court in Deadwood in the spring of 1882, all parties were aware that they were participating in a test case and that it was bound for the U.S. Supreme Court.[54] Almost a

---

[51] Commissioner, BIA, to E. A. Swan, March 14, 1883, BIA, "Letters Sent" file, vol. 39, 133. The case file is held as *State v. Tom Gilbert*, case no. 1463, Oregon State Archives, Salem. Although both this letter and the original case file report that Gilbert's case was being appealed, the Oregon Supreme Court records contain no record of this case.

[52] Commissioner to E. A. Swan, [n.d. but obviously in 1882], BIA, "Letters Sent" file, vol. 37, 249.

[53] "Criminal Jurisdiction over Indian Reservations," 17 Op. A.G. 460, October 13, 1882. This reason relies on *United States v. McBratney*, 104 U.S. 621 (1882), decided the same year. This opinion is clearly wrong and never became law. To these six cases must be added *United States v. McBratney*, which arose at the same time and was a part of the same BIA strategy, although Indians were not parties to the case. *McBratney*, which involved a killing between whites on the Ute Reservation in Colorado, eroded tribal sovereignty more than any single case since *Worcester*. It held that the states had authority over whites on tribal land and thereby, like the Oregon and Nevada cases, extended state law into reservation lands. Such crimes were under federal court jurisdiction, traditionally recognizing federal authority over whites interacting with the Indian tribes. While the BIA could have taken an active role in defending tribal rights in the case, it did not, again yielding to the states.

[54] The territories were substantially self-governing, a process preparing them for statehood. Territorial courts were local courts, the equivalent of state courts. For an analysis of Dakota

month before the trial, Agent John Cook sent a telegram to the BIA asking
to split the cost of a court stenographer because the appeal was sure to go
to the Supreme Court; cooperation would save money for both the Interior
Department and the Justice Department.[55]

Although the trial proceeded in a sharply anti-Sioux climate, the initial
newspaper reporting in Deadwood's *Black Hills Daily Times* was balanced.
The change in federal Indian policy that led to charging Crow Dog with
murder was accurately related. The paper described the character of Brule
tribal law, giving full credence to Crow Dog's claim that he had settled the
killing according to Sioux law:

> In the case of Crow Dog, as in all other offenses of a like nature, the
> relatives of the deceased and his own meet together in council, talk the
> damages over until they come to some agreement as to what they should
> be, and have an understanding as to how much property shall be given
> to make peace. The pipe of peace and fellowship is then smoked, and
> the gifts distributed, and there the matter ends in harmony and
> fellowship.[56]

Since a white understanding of Sioux factionalism was at the heart of the
government's theory of the case, descriptions of tribal politics appeared in
the popular press and later in the government's opening statement. Reservation political factionalism, as described in anthropological literature, is
often a distortion of traditional Indian government. An economy of dependency introduced by whites and reliance on the Indian agent for sustenance
and political power produces sharp tribal divisions over how to maintain
tribal identity. The resulting pattern of tribal disagreement and division is
often oversimplified as a "treaty" faction versus a "traditional" faction, with
the treaty faction convinced that accommodation is the key to survival and
the traditionals opposed to many accommodationist actions.[57]

This oversimplification is embodied in two conflicting images of Spotted
Tail, a chief who drew his power from government recognition and who had
kept his people at peace through the Great Sioux Wars of 1868 and 1876.
Spotted Tail's rule was complex and not easily described in white political

territorial government, see Howard R. Lamar, *Dakota Territory: A Study in Frontier Politics,
1861–1889* (New Haven, Conn.: Yale University Press, 1956). Local interests appear to
have had nothing to do with the policy-making decisions behind the *Crow Dog* case.

[55] John Cook to Commissioner of Indian Affairs, February 28, 1882, Records of the BIA,
Special Case 91, Record Group 75, National Archives.

[56] *Black Hills Daily Times*, September 16, 1881.

[57] There is a substantial anthropological literature on factionalism on Indian reservations. See,
e.g., Robert F. Berkhofer, Jr., "Faith and Factionalism Among the Senecas: Theory and
Ethnohistory," *Ethnohistory* 12 (1965):99, and James A. Clifton, "Factional Conflict and the
Indian Community: The Prairie Potawatomie Case," in Stuart Levine and Nancy Lurie
(eds.), *The American Indian Today* (New York: Penguin, 1974), 184–211.

terms: his power was no longer derived from the traditional consensus model of the selection of Brule chiefs but, at least in part, was based on the army and the Indian agent. Lacking complete legitimacy, Spotted Tail had to rely on coercion and political maneuvering to maintain his authority. His appointment of Crow Dog as chief of police was a necessary compromise to include opposition subchiefs in his tribal government.[58]

Under the headline "Spot's Pleasantries," the *Black Hills Daily Times* ran an account of Spotted Tail's chieftainship on August 9, four days after his killing. The source for this article was Major A. D. Burt of the U.S. Army, who allegedly knew Spotted Tail well:

> He was a great chief and statesman among his people. He was strikingly handsome and manly, and a great friend of peace, but given to absolute authority over his minor chiefs. He was never timid, but was politic in his course towards the white.... He brooked no opposition to his commands and the fight probably arose from Old Spot's aggressiveness, he wanted no opposition from any of his people. He was fond of slipping out on the streets of his village with his Winchester rifle over his shoulder and was liable to command Mr. Red Dog, Mr. Rain-in-the-Sky, Mr. Crow Dog, or any other chief, to do so and so, and if the gentle savage opposed the old man's wishes, "Spot" would quietly cock his rifle, suggest that the order was not only quite imperative but the eyes of the Great Spirit were upon him and a little more delay might open to him a beautiful vista of the happy hunting ground.... General Crook selected Spotted Tail [to be sergeant in his famous corralling of Crazy Horse] because of the determination of his character and power to control this vicious element among his people.[59]

This matter-of-fact and utilitarian account of Spotted Tail neglects to mention that he had often enraged agents by his independent course. At the time of his death, he was something of a pariah among Indian reformers in the East because, on a visit to the Carlisle Indian School in June 1880, he had become enraged at the treatment of his children there and had taken them back to the reservation. This was a major setback for the reformers, and Spotted Tail was portrayed as violent and savage in the eastern press. Moreover, he had obstructed the construction of a railroad across the reservation, and at the time of his death, he was preparing for a trip to Washington to discuss railroad leases, another factor that had encouraged a rising level of dissent among his opponents.[60]

---

[58] George Hyde presents a laudatory view of Spotted Tail, portraying him as leading the Brule to a peaceful accommodation to the reality of U.S. power. Spotted Tail is still seen this way by many Brule people.

[59] *Black Hills Daily Times*, August 9, 1881, 1.

[60] Hyde, *Spotted Tail's Folk*, 321–5.

The prosecution, in its opening statement, offered yet another view of Spotted Tail:

> Deceased was chief of the Brule Sioux... by reason of a proclamation emanating from General Crook in 1876. He devoted himself and his utmost energy to an observance of all the treaty stipulations to be observed by his people. To this policy exception was taken by the more war-like element of the tribe, which faction became bitter and quite openly in defiance of the authority of the chief. A leading spirit in this faction was the defendant, Crow Dog. Each succeeding controversy became more bitter – finally to result in the death of the deceased. Attempts were frequently made to heal these differences, one step to this end being the appointment of the defendant as chief of police. Upon his refusal to abstain from further feuds defendant was dismissed from such service.[61]

This official picture of Spotted Tail and Crow Dog was put in the context of the Indian wars, with Crow Dog presented as a leader of a faction planning a continuation of those wars.

It is conceivable that the trial was lost in the jury selection, for there was no way to control the strong anti-Indian prejudice prevalent in Dakota Territory at the time, especially with the prosecution-created specter of an Indian war. When Crow Dog's court-appointed defense attorney, A. J. Plowman, asked one juror whether he could let the testimony of an Indian outweigh the testimony of a white, he got an honest answer: "I could not. The testimony of one white man would go further with me than that of a hundred Indians." Juror George Ayers was asked if he had ever had any fights with Indians. "I never have," he responded, "but I have been pretty badly scared by them." The jury was impaneled in a few hours.[62]

There were no surprises in the government's case. It is not insignificant that the lead prosecution witness was not an eyewitness but Agent John Cook, who, as already noted, had been in Chicago on private business when the killing occurred. He testified to the political factionalism prevalent at Rosebud and to Crow Dog's active role in undermining the authority of Spotted Tail. He Dog, a political ally, who had been riding slightly behind Spotted Tail, testified next, providing the factual basis of the government's case. He Dog was followed by more eyewitnesses and relatives, whose testimony generally served to establish that Crow Dog was present near the

[61] *Black Hills Daily Times*, March 17, 1882. There is no transcript of the trial extant. This discussion of the trial is based on a detailed, witness-by-witness account, published in the *Black Hills Daily Times*, running up to two newpaper pages a day and clearly based on a stenographic account kept by a reporter in the courtroom. For example, long passages of testimony were printed verbatim. While this account is not official, it is clearly essentially accurate. Obviously, a transcript was printed for the appeal, but it has been lost.

[62] Ibid.

council house at the time of the killing. Many witnesses were recalled – in anticipation of Crow Dog's claim of self-defense – and testified that they had not seen Spotted Tail draw his pistol before the shooting. Even so, the prosecution's case took only a day and a half.[63]

The defense was straightforward and based on a sharply different interpretation of the facts. According to Plowman, as Spotted Tail approached the wagon, Crow Dog, on the ground making repairs, was called by his wife, Pretty Camp. When he looked up, he saw Spotted Tail in the act of drawing a pistol. Crow Dog seized his rifle at the same time and fired, a classic case of self-defense.

After losing his request that Pretty Camp be permitted to testify (under territorial law the testimony of a wife could not be used either for or against her husband), Plowman called Brave Bear and asked the question, "Are you acquainted with the local laws and customs of the Brule tribe, for the punishment of offenses?" When the prosecution objected, Plowman argued that he intended to use the witness to show that Brule law was recognized by treaty and that Crow Dog had been "arraigned in keeping with custom, duly tried, and subjected to the penalties of such tribal laws." The court sustained the objection, and the witness retired. The defense raised the issue that tribal law governed the case but was not allowed to present evidence.[64]

Plowman then called Crow Dog, who told his own simple but eloquent story of the killing, recorded in the choppy syntax of a newspaper reporter's notes:

> I knew the deceased, Spotted Tail. I shot and killed Spotted Tail. Arrived at the scene of the tragedy on a wagon in company with my wife and child. There was no box on the wagon – two loose boards spanning the space between the bolsters. One of these had worked forward and dropped to the ground. Had got off to fix it. Had gone to horses to unwind a line when a person approached at a gallop, from the direction of the council lodge whom I recognized as Spotted Tail. [He] checked his horse into a walk. As he approached seemed to be searching for weapon in the vicinity of his hip. My wife said something which I did not understand. Saw from the facial expression of Spotted Tail that trouble was on hand. Deceased halted – drew his pistol – leveled it at me when I fired and killed him. [I] run around the wagon and was putting another cartridge – thinking I had missed him – when Iron Wing caught hold of me. ... I shot him without taking aim from a distance of fifteen feet. I was standing on the ground, my heart beating

[63] Ibid., March 17, 18, 1882.
[64] Ibid., March 20, 1882.

violently, as I was sure from demeanor of deceased that the time had come.[65]

Crow Dog admitted that there was hostility between himself and Spotted Tail but denied threatening to kill the chief. He testified that at the insistence of Spotted Tail, he had been removed as chief of police twice, the last time by the Indian agent, who had said he must "make up with Spotted Tail."

Deprived of the eyewitness account of Pretty Camp (which is preserved in affidavit form and corroborates Crow Dog's testimony), Plowman recalled a number of Brules who had earlier testified to Spotted Tail's violent character. Brave Bull remembered that Chasing Hawk, an eyewitness, had said to him: "Old man, I am going to tell you something. Spotted Tail had a pistol and I know it well, and if Crow Dog had not been quick Spotted Tail would have killed Crow Dog." Brave Bull further noted that Spotted Tail's reputation was "... not good. I never knew any good of him."[66]

Eagle Hawk, a member of the police force, told of having the same conversation with Chasing Hawk on a different occasion: "He said that Spotted Tail had a pistol and that he saw it; that he was going over to the Black Hills [to the trial] to testify and that he proposed to tell the truth about it this time; that we had agreed to tell the same story at the previous hearing, but he had made a fool of himself and told nothing concerning the pistol ...that he saw it lying beside the body of the deceased. I had another conversation with Thunder Hawk on the court house steps last Friday night in which he stated that he had not testified as he had said he would testify – that it was too late to rectify." Thunder Hawk was then called and corroborated "the material points of the conversation." This unsettling evidence of perjury ended the defense's case.[67]

The prosecution tried to recall Crow Dog in rebuttal, but Plowman successfully objected. Acting Agent Henry Lelar testified that Spotted Tail's reputation was good: "He was ever on the side of law and order, and was faithful in his observance of treaty stipulations." Plowman asked Lelar if he had heard that Spotted Tail had killed Big Mouth, a rival Brule chief Spotted Tail had shot in 1869.[68] Lelar responded that he had heard the story but

---

[65] Crow Dog testified at the end of the day on Monday, March 20, 1882. Ibid., March 21, 1882, 1.

[66] Ibid.

[67] Ibid., March 22, 1882. The defense took only two days to present its case, including most of one day spent on the Pretty Camp motion.

[68] Spotted Tail's killing of Big Mouth still divided the Brule along factional lines. Big Mouth was less willing to accommodate white demands for Brule territory than was Spotted Tail, who wanted to negotiate peace with the whites. Big Mouth invited Spotted Tail to a feast and, after consuming large quantities of liquor, began to insult Spotted Tail for his dealings with the whites. Spotted Tail left the feast but was confronted outside by Big Mouth. In

that both Indians were drunk at the time. H. L. Deer, John Cook, and Colonel Steele ended the prosecution's rebuttal, all testifying to the law-abiding character of Spotted Tail. On the character evidence of these three white men, the trial ended on the afternoon of the fifth day. The rest of the day was taken up with Plowman's argument, based on existing federal Indian law, that the court had no jurisdiction over crimes among the Brule.[69] The judge did not agree.

In his summary Plowman used the evidence to great effect in support of his self-defense argument. Regarding the alleged plot to replace Spotted Tail as chief with Black Crow, Plowman reminded the jury that a council meeting had been held on that very question with the agent attending; therefore, the opposition's desire was hardly as secretive and evil as the prosecution intimated. Plowman then asked a series of rhetorical questions designed to raise a "reasonable doubt" of Crow Dog's guilt in the minds of the jurors and to disparage the prosecution's "political assassination" theory. If Spotted Tail was unarmed, why did Crow Dog run around to the rear of the wagon after firing? If Spotted Tail did not stop his horse, why did the animal remain standing after the shooting? If Crow Dog was plotting to kill the deceased, why did he bring his wife and child along? Plowman ended with a plea not for mercy but for simple justice, asking jurors to put away their prejudices. Nor did he drop his appeal to the sovereignty of Brule tribal law. Having failed to convince the judge, he tried the argument on the jury:

> The race to which the defendant belongs has been driven east and west until here they are a mere remnant. Not only has his property been taken from him, but now we would cap the climax of his degradation and take away his local laws and customs for the trial of offenses and place him upon trial under laws in the making of which he has had no voice. It was upon the transcending of this God-given right that our forefathers made war upon the mother country.[70]

The jury, in spite of the complexity of the case, did not take long to render a verdict: it retired after hearing the judge's instructions at about 6:00 P.M. and returned a guilty verdict at 9:15 A.M. the next day. The judge thanked the jurors, remarking that their verdict was in keeping with the evidence

---

the altercation that followed, Big Mouth allegedly pointed a pistol at Spotted Tail, but it misfired. Spotted Tail then shot Big Mouth, who died hours later. For a few hours it appeared that the two factions might break out into a fight, but the dispute was settled with Spotted Tail agreeing to pay ten ponies to the family of Big Mouth. Hyde, *Spotted Tail's Folk*, 164–9. To the extent that Big Mouth was a serious rival chief of Spotted Tail, he would have represented the same traditional tribal interests that Crow Dog represented.

[69] *Black Hills Daily Times*, March 23, 1882.
[70] Ibid., March 24, 1882.

and that he did not see how they could have decided any other way. Plowman gave notice of a motion for a new trial, pointing out that the defendant had no funds for an appeal. The judge, prosecutor, and Agent Cook promised to do their utmost to help Plowman raise money and to petition the BIA for funds. The next week Judge Moody sentenced Crow Dog to death by hanging.[71] In an unheard of action in a capital case, the judge then allowed Crow Dog his freedom to return to Rosebud to await the outcome of his appeal.[72]

The conviction left many uneasy. The *Black Hills Daily Times* of March 25 reported: "We have conversed with a good many sensible people devoid of prejudice and feeling, and where we found one who approved of the verdict, a dozen equally as good men would disapprove it in the strongest terms.... The verdict...was received with great surprise by the entire community who had from the evidence believed that either acquittal or possible manslaughter would be the result."[73]

By the time the case reached Washington, Plowman had assembled a sheaf of affidavits that, while not usable in a Supreme Court appeal that turned on matters of law rather than fact, showed that the facts of the case were distorted by both the BIA and Spotted Tail's supporters. An affidavit of William Garnett, a half-blood Sioux, who had served as the official interpreter, stated that based on his acquaintance with the Brule, his "firm belief was that most of the evidence given by Indian witnesses for the prosecution were untruths and exaggerations." Valentine T. McGillycuddy, Indian agent at neighboring Pine Ridge Agency stated that, first, bribery and intimidation were used to coerce witnesses against Crow Dog at the trial; second, he had no doubt that Spotted Tail was armed at the time of his death and that it was "merely a matter of chance as to which should be killed first." William Henry Wright, a reporter for the *Black Hills Daily Times*, recorded his interview with an Indian woman called Woman-that-Carries-the-Shield, the fourth person to arrive on the scene of the killing. She confirmed that Spotted Tail had a pistol and that High Bear's wife had taken it and given it to Spotted Tail's son (also named Spotted Tail but designated "Junior" by whites). She also stated that when Hollow Horn Bear, He Dog, and Charley Jacket came back from Deadwood, Spotted Tail, Jr., had given

---

[71] Ibid., March 25, 1882.

[72] After Crow Dog was sentenced to hang, the court allowed him to return to the reservation to get his affairs in order. On the day agreed upon, he drove himself back to prison, accompanied by Pretty Camp. Peter Matthieson, *In the Spirit of Crazy Horse* (New York: Viking, 1983), 16. This account is also found in Vine Deloria, Jr., and Clifford Little, *American Indians, American Justice* (Austin, University of Texas Press, 1983), and in Mary Crow Dog, *Lakota Woman*, 182. Although this story has wide circulation, there is no reference to it in the *Daily Times'* thorough account of the trial. None of the correspondence regarding the trial makes any mention of either the imprisonment or release of Crow Dog.

[73] *Black Hills Daily Times*, March 25, 1882.

them each a horse for proving that Spotted Tail had no pistol. Another Brule, Bear's Head, admitted that he would not testify about the killing of Spotted Tail because he was afraid of Spotted Tail, Jr. Wright further stated that many Indians told him that Spotted Tail, Jr., called a council the night after his father was killed and told his people that they must all swear that the chief had been unarmed.[74]

Some of this evidence was legally inadmissible because the affidavits contained hearsay, but taken in their totality, the affidavits make it clear that much of the evidence was hidden from the court. This evidentiary confusion shows the injustice of imposing U.S. law over tribal law. The Deadwood trial failed to produce an accurate rendering of the facts, even if the white jury had the capacity to judge the evidence fairly, given local racism and a high level of miscommunication between two cultures. At best it seems clear that the jury was unable to get past the political assassination theory, which, in the context of an Indian war, made it impossible for them to comprehend the cultural complexity of the case.

Crow Dog's appeal

From the moment of Crow Dog's conviction, the BIA was willing to invest its resources in pushing the case speedily forward on appeal. Underscoring the trial's significance as a test case is the fact that the trial lawyer, the U.S. marshal for the Dakota Territory, the U.S. attorney, the Indian agent, the BIA, the secretary of the interior, and the Justice Department together engaged in a concerted effort to ensure adequate financing of the appeal and were instrumental in persuading Congress to pass a special appropriation of $1,000 for that purpose.

Although there are important doctrinal questions involved in Crow Dog's appeal, most of the existing correspondence discusses means of financing it, a not insignificant process in a case involving an indigent defendant in the days before any form of legal aid. On March 29, the day after Crow Dog was sentenced to hang, Attorney Plowman wrote to Samuel Kirkwood, secretary of the interior, to solicit funds for the appeal.

> Sir:
>   The trial of Crow Dog, a Sioux Indian indicted in the First District Court of Dakota Territory for the killing of Spotted Tail, also an Indian, has just resulted in a verdict of guilty of murder.
>   This is the first reported case where the United States has prosecuted

---

[74] These quotations are contained in unpaginated affidavits in the file, "Crow Dog Trial and Related Papers, Folder no. 3: Affidavits, 1883," South Dakota State Historical Society, Pierre. I have quoted from each of them, except one from Brave Bull that further testifies to Spotted Tail having a pistol in his hand.

one Indian for an offense committed upon another Indian and was brought under the provisions of the treaties made by the United States with the Sioux Nation of Indians, Statutes at Large, vol. 15, p. 635 and vol. 19, p. 254....

In view of this being the first case of the kind it is very much desired that the questions of law be passed upon by the Supreme Court, but the defendant is poor and unable to pay counsel in the costs necessary to make a review of the case. I therefore on behalf of the defendant respectfully apply to your department for the necessary funds.

Plowman enclosed a letter from A. S. Stewart, foreman of the jury, supporting Plowman's request for funds. Perhaps more revealingly, Stewart's letter indicates that the jury was unsettled about the state of the law relating to federal jurisdiction over the Sioux but had felt unable to consider the question because it was a matter of law that had been decided by the judge.[75]

The secretary was not especially sympathetic. He sent both letters to the commissioner of Indian affairs, stating that although he appreciated the importance of the matter, his department had no money for such purposes. Commissioner Henry Price, the federal official responsible for protecting the rights of Indians, had an idea where the money might come from. In a letter to Indian Agent Cook, he suggested that "the Sioux are rich having large possession in cattle and ponies and should be willing to provide the money to have their legal status decided by the courts." In the event the Sioux did not accept this logic, Plowman was to be informed that his fee depended entirely on an appropriation by Congress.[76]

Plowman, recognizing that money from Congress might be more certain than proceeds from pony sales, vigorously pursued his claims. With the money, serious questions of ethics were raised. In order to get the funds, Plowman felt it necessary to ask the BIA to approve the arguments he

[75] Plowman to Secretary Kirkwood, March 29, 1882. Records of the BIA, Special Case 91, Record Group 75, National Archives. There is not the slightest concern for Crow Dog's life expressed in any of these hundred-odd pages of letters by Plowman or anyone else.

[76] Henry Price to John Cook, April 27, 1882, in ibid. Plowman was the first, but not the only, person seeking money for work on the case. Frank Washabaugh, clerk of the territorial court in Deadwood, sought $150 for his part of "the work of preparing the Crow Dog case for the Supreme Court" in a letter to Agent John Cook. He also had two suggestions for raising the money. One was for Cook to write on his behalf to the secretary of the interior and the commissioner of Indian affairs, "informing them of the importance to the Indian Service to have the matter settled beyond doubt that the Indians may know and feel the responsibility which they owe to the white man's laws, and in as much as this is an appropriation made and set apart from the purpose of education and civilizing the Indians, this seems to me could consistently be taken from such fund as I know of no better way of educating or civilizing the Indians than making them feel their responsibility to the law of the Government. If the Department will not or cannot furnish the means, then it is but right to have the Indians on the Agency and particularly the friends of the department to raise the money and pay me by some means, either by selling some ponies, or any other way that they can raise it." Washabaugh to Cook, April 7, 1882, in ibid.

intended to make. On March 30, one day after his initial appeal for money and two days after Crow Dog's sentencing, Plowman, at the suggestion of U.S. Attorney Hugh Campbell, wrote Secretary of the Interior Kirkwood, detailing the legal questions he intended to put forward.[77] A month later, Congressman R. L. Pettigrew wrote Kirkwood on behalf of Plowman, suggesting that the Department of the Interior request an appropriation of $5,000 for the defense. Meanwhile, Plowman, in a letter to Commissioner Price, offered a detailed statement of his legal plans, estimating his actual costs of taking the case to the U.S. Supreme Court at $3,000 to $3,500 and modestly suggesting that "able counsel" in Deadwood had estimated the value of his services at $10,000.[78]

Ten months later, under the Sundry Civil Act of March 3, 1883, Congress appropriated $1,000, listed on the books of the BIA as "appeal Crow Dog case to U.S. Supreme Court." Plowman was appointed a special agent and gave bond in the amount of $1,000 for his work on the appeal. Meanwhile, an appeal had been taken to the territorial court, which had been totally ignored in all of the correspondence about money.[79]

If no one gave much consideration to the outcome of that intermediate appeal, it was both because all parties knew the case was ultimately headed for the U.S. Supreme Court and because Judge G. C. Moody, who had tried Crow Dog, sentenced him to death, and denied the original demurrer on jurisdictional grounds, also heard the appeal in October 1882.[80] Yet the perfunctory nature of the appeal does not mean that Plowman failed to take it seriously. His appellate brief testifies to the thoroughness of his work. He raised a variety of jurisdictional issues, challenged the sufficiency of the evidence, and alleged thirty-six errors in the court's jury instructions. Judge Moody addressed three of these issues. First, and most important, on the

[77] Plowman's disclosure of his arguments to the BIA and the Justice Department in order to get funding compromised Crow Dog's Sixth Amendment right to counsel.

[78] Plowman to Kirkwood, March 30, 1881; Plowman to Price, April 28, 1882, Records of the BIA, Special Case 91, Record Group 75, National Archives. The file contains seven letters from Plowman and three others specifically stating that they were written at his instigation, all requesting funds, although two also contain detailed discussions of the law as well. This involves all of Plowman's correspondence with the BIA.

[79] Commissioner of Indian Affairs Price to Secretary of the Interior Henry Teller, April 10, 1883; Teller to Price, June 1, 1883, Records of the BIA, Special Case 91, Record Group 75, National Archives.

[80] Appellate review by the trial judge was not uncommon in nineteenth-century criminal cases. Rather than the elaborate appellate review processes characterizing the late twentieth century, nineteenth-century appellate review was grounded in common law writs asking the court to examine its rulings on the ground of alleged errors. For a general discussion of the process, see David Rossman, "Were There No Appeal: The History of Review in American Criminal Courts," *Journal of Criminal Law and Criminology* 81 (1990):520–37. Crow Dog had no right to appeal his criminal conviction to the U.S. Supreme Court because of any errors made under territorial criminal law. Rather, the basis of his appeal was the violation of his treaty rights as a tribal Indian.

question of federal criminal jurisdiction over the Sioux he held as he had during the trial, following exactly the original argument of U.S. Attorney Campbell, formulated the week after the Spotted Tail killing: that the Sioux treaties of 1869 and 1877 had superseded federal recognition of tribal law in crimes between Indians. Second, Pretty Camp was not competent to testify for her husband Crow Dog. Third, the state's evidence was sufficient to prove murder because, the fact of the intentional killing having been proved, there was "a presumption of guilt . . . which must remain until proof sufficient to overcome such presumption shall be given by the defendant. . . . It is not enough to raise a reasonable doubt whether such justification . . . be proven, for the presumption still remains." The court then dismissed as "minor" all of Plowman's remaining points and remanded the case "with directions to carry the judgment into execution."[81]

The Supreme Court's decision

What is remarkable about the *Crow Dog* decision's recognition of tribal law as an inherent attribute of sovereignty is not that the Supreme Court had any respect for Brule law or even knew anything substantive about it. Characterizing the case as one of "red man's revenge," the Court hardly bothered to conceal its contempt for tribal institutions. Yet at the same time, *Crow Dog* upheld Marshall's recognition of tribal sovereignty in *Worcester*, a significant statement given the heightened Indian–white conflict fifty years later. Although the holding was based conservatively on narrow grounds – that congressional ratification of an 1877 Sioux treaty that contained general language securing "orderly government" and making the Sioux "subject to the laws of the United States" did not reverse a long-standing government policy toward Indians, "as declared in many statutes and treaties" – the Court went beyond the scope of the decision and offered important statements of late-nineteenth-century Indian policy. While accepting the justice and logic of recognizing the right of the tribes to maintain their own legal institutions, the Court also made it plain that it did not respect tribal institutions and that ultimately they must give way to "civilization." The case is memorable for both its strength and its weakness, as well as for the Court's fundamental inability to come to terms with the complexity of Indian–white relations or with a legal strategy to give effect to tribal sovereignty.

The unanimous opinion, written by Justice Stanley Matthews and delivered on December 17, 1883, fourteen months after the original appeal to

[81] Plowman's brief and argument before the territorial court are preserved in printed form: *Crow Dog Trial and Related Papers*, folder 1, 1882, South Dakota State Historical Society Archives, Pierre. The court's opinion is reported as *United States v. Kan-Gi-Shun-Ca*, 3 Dak. 106 (Oct. 28, 1882).

the territorial supreme court, was rooted in well-developed doctrines of Indian law.[82] It strongly supports the traditional conception that treaties are made between nations of people, and it interprets the Sioux treaties of 1869 and 1877 in ways that give greatest effect to tribal sovereignty. The *Crow Dog* opinion was a watershed, the legal divide where a traditional Indian policy that recognized the equality of tribal peoples and respected their national sovereignty last stood against the rise of the BIA policy of assimilation, which would dominate federal Indian policy for the next fifty years.

The Court's decision has two distinct parts. The first is a detailed analysis of the language of the treaties that formed the basis of the prosecution's case. The second is a statement of national policy regarding tribal sovereignty and the law of tribal people that was a central part of that sovereignty. The first of the treaty provisions orders that "if bad men among the Indians shall commit a wrong or depredation upon the person or property of any one, white, black, or Indian . . . the Indians herein named solemnly agree that they will . . . deliver up the wrongdoers to the United States to be tried and punished according to its laws." This clause, according to Justice Matthews, was taken out of context by the courts and needed to be read in conjunction with its preceding clause, which provides for punishment by the United States of any bad men among the whites who committed any wrongs upon the Indians. This was a common provision for the prosecution of crimes between Indians and persons of other races and was found in most of the treaties with Indian tribes. It did not refer to crimes committed between Indians of the same tribe.[83]

The second provision, from the treaty of 1877, involved the language "and Congress shall . . . secure to them an orderly government; they shall be sub-

---

[82] There is nothing in Matthew's career history to suggest any of the underlying motivations for the opinion. Stanley Matthews was a railroad attorney from Cincinnati, a Republican Party regular who had brokered Rutherford B. Haye's loss of the 1876 presidential election into the "compromise of 1877," leading Hayes to the presidency and ending southern reconstruction. Matthews controversial career, including service as a federal prosecutor of violators of the fugitive slave law and lobbyist for railroad interests, blocked his nomination for a time until he was finally confirmed by a margin of one vote. In judicial philosophy he was a conservative, advocating "strict adherence to the letter of the law," although as a senator he had supported free silver and opposed the Chinese Exclusion Act, very liberal positions for the day. His opinions range from very liberal to very conservative, with his support for Chinese laundrymen being run out of business by a racist San Francisco city ordinance in *Yick Wo v. Hopkins*, 118 U.S. 356 (1886), probably his most progressive opinion. On civil rights issues generally, he joined with the court to bury the federal civil rights legislation of the reconstruction era. Most likely, since the opinion was unanimous, he was assigned the task of writing the opinion, following a narrow doctrinal framework that was not particularly his own. Louis Filler, "Stanley Matthews," in Leon Friedman and Fred Israel (eds.), *The Justices of the United States Supreme Court, 1789–1969* (New York: Chelsea House, 1969).

[83] *Ex parte Crow Dog*, 109 U.S. 556 (1883), at 567–8.

ject to the laws of the United States, and each individual shall be protected in his rights of property, person and life." The Court took this statement to mean nearly the opposite of the interpretation given it by Judge Moody of the territorial court and the BIA:

> The pledge to secure to these people, with whom the United States was contracting as a distinct political body, an orderly government, by appropriate legislation thereafter to be framed and enacted, necessarily implies, having regard to all the circumstances attending the transaction, that among the arts of civilized life, which it was the very purpose of all these arrangements to introduce and naturalize among them, was the highest and best of all, that of self-government, the regulation by themselves of their own domestic affairs, the maintenance of order and peace among their own members by the administration of their own laws and customs.

The Court went on to describe this relationship in paternalistic terms: "as a dependent community who were in a state of pupilage, advancing from the condition of a savage tribe to that of a people who, through the discipline of labor and by education, it was hoped might become a self-supporting and self-governing society."[84] There is no denying the clear recognition of a contract between two political entities with equal sovereignty and of Indian tribes' natural right to maintain their own order and peace and to administer their own laws and customs.

Finally, the Court strongly stated the traditional reason for recognition of tribal law for Indian people:

> It is a case where ... that law ... is thought to be extended over aliens and strangers; over the members of a community, separated by race, by tradition, by the instincts of a free though savage life, from the authority and power which seeks to impose upon them the restraints of an external and unknown code, and to subject them to the responsibilities of civil conduct, according to rules and penalties of which they could have no previous warning; which judges them by a standard made by others and not for them, which takes no account of the conditions which should except them from its exactions, and makes no allowance for their inability to understand it. It tries them not by their peers, nor by the custom of their people, nor the law of their land, but by superiors of a different race, according to the law of a social state of which they have an imperfect conception, and which is opposed to the traditions of their history, to the habits of their lives, to the strongest prejudices of their savage nature; one which measures the red man's revenge by the maxim of the white man's morality.

[84] Ibid., 568–9.

A strong statement of the integrity of Sioux law emerges, one that could undermine the assimilationist policy of the BIA.[85]

Yet the language had changed since the Cherokee cases of the Marshall court. There was a strong tone of racism, combined with a clear message that tribal law was somehow transitory, a mechanism to assist in the inevitable transition from savagery to civilization. While adopting Marshall's legal theories, with their respect for tribal sovereignty, the Court also implicitly adopted the assimilationist ideology of the day.[86] The result was an unsatisfactory fit.

Although *Crow Dog* is always understood as a significant decision in Indian law, it may be ironic that the most important set of considerations in the case had nothing at all to do with the status of the Indian tribes. *Crow Dog* was also a capital criminal case. The U.S. Supreme Court, at the time, heard few criminal appeals. At the federal court level, there was no right of appeal at all of an ordinary federal criminal case until 1879 when a right of appeal to the circuit courts was created. It was 1889 before a criminal appeal could be taken to the U.S. Supreme Court. (Crow Dog's case, of course, could be appealed because it raised a constitutional question, that of treaty rights.) When the Supreme Court first came to hear criminal appeals, it reversed a great many of them, evidently appalled by the quality of criminal justice in many remote courts. To the Supreme Court, death penalty convictions had to show a level of integrity difficult for frontier justice.[87] Crow Dog's offense, committed with an uncertain mental element under an uncertain legal status, may simply not have warranted the death penalty in the eyes of the justices. Still, it seems the federal Indian law questions disposed of in the opinion are too elaborate to have been simply intended to save Crow Dog's life.

Crow Dog returned to the Rosebud Reservation to continue as a leader of the traditional faction, derisively labeled the "kickers" by the Indian agent. He left the reservation, leading Ghost Dancers into the Badlands in 1890. Later he was a leading opponent of allotment, refusing to accept his allotment until 1910, when he was seventy-eight years old. His agent repeatedly asked BIA authorities in Washington to remove Crow Dog from the reservation because he was a "troublemaker." According to the agent, the reversal of his conviction was responsible for his arrogant attitude.[88] This, of course,

---

[85] Ibid., 571.

[86] Russell Lawrence Barsh and James Youngblood Henderson, *The Road: Indian Tribes and Political Liberty* (Berkeley: University of California Press, 1980), 88.

[87] G. Byron Dobbs, "Murder in the Supreme Court: Appeals from the Hanging Judge," *Arkansas Law Review* 29 (1975):48, clearly shows the Supreme Court's critical approach to the quality of justice rendered in Judge Isaac Parker's Federal District Court for the Western District of Arkansas, including the Indian Territory.

[88] Information on Crow Dog's later activities comes from Richard Lee Clow, "The Rosebud Sioux: The Federal Government and the Reservation Years, 1878–1940," Ph.D. dissertation,

was not true. Crow Dog was deeply grounded in tradition, all his days a leader of traditonal Brule.

There is no record of the number of cases of Indian killings that were directly affected by the *Crow Dog* decision. Ironically, the only other Indian who was released from prison because of the Supreme Court's decision was Spotted Tail's son. On May 29, 1884, five months after the decision, Spotted Tail, Jr., Thunder Hawk, and Song Pumpkin had become involved in a dispute with White Thunder, an extension of the same factional struggle that gave rise to Crow Dog's case. Young Spotted Tail, unable to inherit his father's power within the tribe, went to the camp of White Thunder, a respected older chief, and took one of White Thunder's wives. White Thunder immediately responded by raiding Spotted Tail's camp and taking some prize ponies. As a further insult to Spotted Tail, White Thunder killed the ponies, a sign of great contempt. Spotted Tail gave chase and became enraged when he found several of his ponies shot by the side of the road. Upon arriving at White Thunder's camp, Spotted Tail and his friends opened fire. In the exchange, White Thunder and Song Pumpkin were killed and White Thunder's father fatally injured.[89]

Showing how little the doctrine of stare decicis penetrated the BIA, the Indian agent ordered Spotted Tail and Thunder Hawk to proceed to Fort Niobara and put themselves in the custody of the military. Both were locked in the guardhouse. There then followed an extended exchange of letters and telegrams between the agency and Washington over their disposition.[90]

While the BIA proceeded in a confused manner, the Sioux once more resolved the matter: the council met and decided to allow Spotted Tail and Thunder Hawk back on the reservation and agreed to take responsibility for their conduct. The council sent this information to the agent, who forwarded it to Washington along with a letter from Spotted Tail and Thunder Hawk requesting to be "paroled" from the guardhouse. On September 2, the commissioner of Indian affairs, citing *Crow Dog*, requested that the secretary of the interior order the release of the prisoners. This was done on October 4. Spotted Tail and Thunder Hawk had been illegally imprisoned in a

University of New Mexico, 1977, 47–50, 55–9, 69–70, 77, 81–2, 84, 89–91, 120–1. Clow adopts the BIA view of Crow Dog, characterizing him as having a "hostile and shiftless manner." It is more likely that Crow Dog was a powerful traditional leader, for he was active in the Ghost Dance movement of 1890 at the age of at least sixty.

[89] James Wright, Indian agent at Rosebud Reservation, to Commissioner of Indian Affairs Henry Price, May 30 and August 26, 1884, special file, "Spotted Tail, Junior, Murder Case," Record Group 75. National Archives, Wright never accepted Spotted Tail's version of the facts and was never sure of the cause of the killing. George Hyde published a similar account in *Spotted Tail's Folk*, at 343–4.

[90] Telegram from the Commanding Officer, Fort Niobara, Nebraska, to Adjutant General, Missouri Division, May 31, 1884, special file, "Spotted Tail, Junior, Murder Case," Record Group 75, National Archives.

military guardhouse for four months while the BIA reluctantly gave effect to the Supreme Court's holding.[91]

Law for the Indians: the Major Crimes Act

Since 1874, the BIA had been attempting to persuade Congress to extend federal jurisdiction over certain serious crimes committed among Indians but had been singularly unsuccessful. After 1880, this annual effort was joined by eastern Indian reformers, especially the Indian Rights Association (IRA), which advocated broad legislation that would make Indians subject to the same law as whites and, abandoning federal jurisdiction, make tribal Indians subject to full state or territorial criminal and civil law. The IRA was founded in Philadelphia in December 1882 by Henry Pancoast and Herbert Welsh. Where other Indian reform groups focused primarily on humanitarian aims, the IRA believed that Indians were capable of assuming full citizenship but had been held back by protective and paternalistic practices. The full extension of law and legal rights to the Indians became a central theme in IRA work, and the organization had considerable success lobbying in Congress. Many members' voices were added to the "popular outcry" over the *Crow Dog* decision.[92] Among the proposals before Congress in 1884 was an IRA draft "Act to Provide for the Establishment of Courts of Criminal Jurisdiction upon Indian Reservations."

The IRA proposal was much broader than the Major Crimes Act that Congress ultimately adopted. It would have created an "agency court" for each Indian agency, with the Indian agent serving as judge. This court was to apply the complete criminal law of the state or territory in which the reservation was located, except for capital offenses, which would be tried in U.S. circuit courts. Convicted felons would serve their sentences in guardhouses on the reservations or be turned over to U.S. marshals and treated as other federal prisoners. These courts would operate without juries; appeals could go only to the commissioner of Indian affairs, not to any federal court. Civil actions against Indians would be cognizable in "any court in the United States," including state courts.[93] This court structure would have put Indians under the complete legal force of U.S. law with few due process protections.

---

[91] Charging Thunder and eight others to the Secretary of War, July 30, 1884; Colonel John Gibbs, 7th Infantry, to Assistant Adjutant General, Division of Missouri, October 10, 1884, special file, "Spotted Tail, Junior, Murder Case."

[92] See Francis Paul Prucha, *The Great Father: The United States Government and the Indians* (Lincoln: University of Nebraska Press, 1984), 615. The best history of the IRA is John Hagan, *The Indian Rights Association: The Herbert Welsh Years, 1882–1904* (Tucson: University of Arizona Press, 1985).

[93] Indian Rights Association, Committee on Law "An Act to Provide for the Establishment of Courts of Criminal Jurisdiction upon Indian Reservations, to Define Their Powers and the

The logic behind this position was paternalistic: Indians needed to be protected by U.S. law but also to be held responsible under this law in order to prepare them as citizens. This reasoning was outlined in detail in a major IRA pamphlet, "The Indian Before the Law," by Henry Pancoast, published the year before the Major Crimes Act. After reviewing the legal status of the Indian, Pancoast went on to discuss different proposals for projecting U.S. law on Indian tribes. He opposed the BIA plan to extend a few criminal laws to the Indian tribes and try those crimes in local courts. Part of his reasoning was based on the practical difficulty in doing this, given the distances involved. Pancoast also wanted a far more repressive criminal justice apparatus to deal with misdemeanors and offenses against white standards of morality:

> In disturbances on an Indian reservation in particular there is the greatest
> necessity for a prompt, decided and inexpensive settlement of dispute
> ... some firm and consistent power on a reservation that shall system-
> atically and impartially enforce such simple rules of morality and justice
> as do not conflict too hardly with the primitive character of Indian customs
> or ideas, ... Side by side with the power of religion and the power of
> education to redeem the remnant of this people, there should stand the
> power of law.[94]

Such a system would have increased the power of the BIA over the tribes through its protectionist and paternalistic policies. However, the BIA neither needed nor desired such an expansive act to get the same measure of power. Already, it was experimenting with extralegal forces of Indian police under the control of Indian agents and informal "courts of Indian offenses" that were in no way restricted by the need for a formal statute. Moreover, the imposition of such a formal legal role on the Indian agents raised potential bureaucratic problems for the BIA that could be avoided by keeping the existing informal system for the agents and removing the "major crimes" to federal courts. Put bluntly, extending the full force of U.S. law to Indian reservations was likely to control the BIA as well as the Indians, and the BIA was unwilling to give up the extralegal power it held over the tribes.

The Senate had rejected the BIA's original 1874 proposal for a major crimes act because such legislation was inconsistent with existing notions of

Offenses of Which They May Take Cognizance, to Affix Penalties to the Commission of Such Offenses and for Other Purposes," IRA papers, document A18, 1883, microfilm copy, held in the Wisconsin State Historical Society, Madison. IRA, *First Annual Report, 1883.* Appendix A, 23–7, discloses a summary of this act, together with a questionnaire sent to Indian agents, and presumably many others, soliciting both comments on the draft bill and support.

[94] Henry Pancoast, "The Indian Before the Law," IRA pamphlet, 1883. Pancoast was the secretary of the Law Committee and one of the authors of the draft act.

tribal sovereignty.[95] Since the late 1870s, virtually every annual report of the secretary of the interior and of the commissioner of Indian affairs had advocated the passage of a major crimes act. Interior Secretary Carl Schurz wrote in his 1879 report:

> If the Indians are to be advanced in civilized habits, it is essential that they be accustomed to the government of law, with the restraints it imposes and the protection it affords. [A] bill was introduced at the last session of Congress providing ... that the laws of the respective States and Territories relative to certain crimes, shall be ... taken to be the law in force within such reservations, and the district courts of the United States ... shall have original jurisdiction over all such offenses committed within such reservations.[96]

The 1881 report of Schurz's successor, Samuel Kirkwood, written before the killing of Spotted Tail, repeated this argument and justified it with reference to "Apache outrages":

> Further legislation is, in my judgement, necessary for the definition and punishment of crime committed on reservations whether by Indians in their dealings with each other, by Indians on white men, or by white men on Indians. A good deal of uncertainty exists on these points, which should be removed. It is also important that the liability of Indians who engage in hostile acts against the government and our people should be declared more clearly and fully. During the present year the Apaches have committed many outrages in New Mexico and Arizona. ... Are they prisoners or war criminals? Should not the liability of Indians thus engaged be clearly defined? Should not all crimes committed on reservations be clearly defined, the punishment thereof fixed, and the trial therefor provided in the United States Courts?[97]

Henry M. Teller, who succeeded Kirkwood, repeated this request in his 1882 and 1883 annual reports. In the 1884 annual report, his successor, L. Q. C. Lamar, specifically used the *Crow Dog* case to justify the same measure and to misrepresent Sioux tribal law:

> I again desire to call attention to the necessity for legislation for the punishment of crimes on the Indian reservations. Since my last report, the Supreme Court of the United States decided in the case of *Ex parte*

---

[95] U.S. Congress, Senate, 43d Congress, 1st session, Report 367, 2 (1874).
[96] *Annual Report of the Secretary of the Interior* (1879), 12–13.
[97] Ibid., (1881), 7–8. Kirkwood also linked the destruction of Indian law with the necessity of destroying the tribal relation because it meant "communism": "The tribal relation is a hindrance to individual progress. It means communism so interferes with the administration of both civil and criminal law among the members of the tribe, and among members of the tribe and non-members. The Indians should learn both to know the law and to administer it. They will not become law-abiding citizens until they shall so learn" (7).

Crow Dog, indicted for murder, that the district court of South Dakota was without jurisdiction, when the crime was committed on the reservation by one Indian against another. If offenses of this character cannot be tried in the courts of the United States, there is no tribunal in which the crime of murder can be punished. . . . it will hardly do to leave the punishment of the crime of murder to a tribunal that exists only by the consent of the Indians of the reservation. If the murder is left to be punished according to the old Indian custom, it becomes the duty of the next of kin to avenge the death of his relative or some one of his kinsmen.[98]

Examples of Indians going unpunished for murder also produced a different interpretation of the savage character of tribal society and the inadequacy of tribal law. Bishop H. Hare, an Episcopal missionary among the Sioux, recognized the force of tribal law by reverse argument: because tribal law was being destroyed, the tribes were becoming disorderly:

Civilization has loosened . . . the bonds which regulate and hold together Indian society in its wild state, and has failed to give the people law and officers of justice in their place. Women are brutally beaten and outraged; men are murdered in cold blood; the Indians who are friendly to schools and churches are intimidated and preyed upon by the evil-disposed; children are molested on their way to school, and schools are dispersed by bands of vagabonds; but there is no redress. It is a disgrace to our land. . . . And . . . the efforts of civil agents, teachers, and missionaries are like the struggles of drowning men weighted with lead, as long as by the absence of law Indian society is left without a base.[99]

This language, quoted as part of the BIA commissioner's 1883 plea for such legislation, illustrates the relationship between the extension of criminal law to the Indians and the broad assimilationist goals of the Indian service: the work of teachers and missionaries needed to be protected by the criminal law.

Although the Major Crimes Act of 1885 was a clear departure from existing law, it was consistent with the move away from a policy based on treaty rights recognizing Indian sovereignty and toward one of dependency and forced assimilation. This policy shift, many years in the making, reflected broad national social and economic changes following from rapid westward expansion but was also bound within the contradictions of John Marshall's *Worcester* opinion. Even Marshall had assumed that given some protection of U.S. law, the tribes would ultimately assimilate into the mainstream of U.S. life. By the 1880s, it was obvious that the tribes would not cooperate,

[98] *Annual Report of the Secretary of the Interior* (1884), 9. See also ibid. (1882), 8, and (1883), xiii.
[99] BIA, *Annual Report, 1883,* xi.

that, on the contrary, traditional culture remained strong everywhere in tribal America. Crow Dog's case embodied the failure of federal Indian policy. Spotted Tail, a government-imposed chief, had not been willing to educate his children in a government school and had blocked the extension of railroad lines across his lands. Yet he was dead as a result of a factional conflict with traditional Brules who would yield nothing to the American nation, and his killer freely walked the Rosebud Reservation, challenging the authority of the government.

The Major Crimes Act was an easy solution to one piece of this problem: federal criminal law could be imposed on those who violated U.S. law. Congress had resisted such a policy since 1874, but the facts of *Crow Dog* gave the BIA a sharp tool with which to prod congressional action. Presented with a portrayal of Spotted Tail as a loyal and courageous chief leading his people into productive roles as U.S. citizens – and one of Crow Dog as a "savage" who would lead his people into a continuation of the Indian wars, a murderer freed by a U.S. Supreme Court applying an anachronistic Indian policy – Congress appeared to have no other choice.

The whole matter occupies fewer than five pages of the *Congressional Record*, and those pages are largely filled with confusion over language. The simultaneous consideration of a stronger federal law to prohibit the sale of liquor to Indians received far more detailed discussion. This lack of attention itself testifies that although the Major Crimes Act may have been a sharp departure from existing Indian law, it was consistent with existing Indian policy.[100]

The discussion in Congress cannot be called a debate. As presented by Congressman Cutcheon of Michigan for the Indian Affairs Committee, the bill's reasoning directly paralleled BIA policy and even borrowed language from the BIA commissioner's 1884 annual report:

> I believe it is not necessary for me to say that this amendment is in the direction of the thought of all who desire the advancement and civilization of the Indian tribes. It is recommended very strongly by the Secretary of the Interior in his annual report. I believe we all feel that an Indian, when he commits a crime, should be recognized as a criminal, and so treated under the laws of the land. I do not believe we shall ever succeed in civilizing the Indian race until we teach them regard to the law, but amenable to its penalties.
>
> We all remember the case of Crow Dog, who committed the murder of the celebrated chief Spotted Tail. He was arrested, tried by a Federal tribunal, and convicted of the murder, but the case being taken to the Supreme Court of the United States upon habeas corpus, it was there decided that the United States courts had no jurisdiction in any case

---

[100] *Congressional Record* (1885), 934–6.

where one reservation Indian committed a crime upon another. Thus, Crow Dog went free. He returned to his reservation, feeling, as the Commissioner says, a great deal more important than any of the chiefs of his tribe. The result was that another murder grew out of that – a murder committed by Spotted Tail, Jr., upon White Thunder. And so these things must go on unless we adopt proper legislation on the subject.

It is an infamy upon our civilization, a disgrace to this nation, that there should be anywhere within its boundaries a body of people who can, with absolute impunity, commit the crime of murder, there being no tribunal before which they can be brought for punishment. Under our present law, there is no penalty that can be inflicted except according to the custom of the tribe, which is simply that the "blood avenger" – that is, the next of kin of the person murdered – shall pursue the one who has been guilty of the crime and commit a new murder upon him.[101]

Congressman James Budd of California objected to including assault among the enumerated offenses, and it was agreed that courts of Indian offenses were adequate for such crimes. Some congressmen supported the IRA's desire to extend federal and state law to include all crimes among Indians, even misdemeanors. Others were concerned whether the law should be extended to include the tribes within the Indian Territory. The closest the matter came to policy debate is in an exchange that shows that Congress was aware of the threat the bill posed to traditional Indian policy, if not tribal sovereignty:

> *Mr. Hiscock:* I would like to inquire of the gentleman from Michigan if he believes that all of these Indian tribes are in such a condition of civilization as that they should be put under the criminal law?
> *Mr. Cutcheon:* I think if they are not in that condition they will be civilized a great deal sooner by being put under such laws and taught to regard life and the personal property of others.
> *Mr. Budd:* This provision is as much for the benefit of the Indians as it is for the whites; because now, as there is no law to punish for Indian depredations, the bordermen take the law into their own hands, which would not be the case if such provision as this was enacted into law.
> *Mr. Hiscock:* That may all be true; but when we bring in a bill here, year after year, appropriating many millions of dollars to support and care for these Indians, and treat them as irresponsible persons, it seems to me that policy is not in the line of the policy indicated by this amendment, which proposes to extend to them the harsh provisions of the criminal law.
> *Mr. Budd:* We would like to change the policy of the Government in that respect.

[101] Ibid., 934 (January 22); BIA, *Annual Report*, 1884, xiv–xv.

Mr. Hiscock: Then you had better defeat the present bill.

Mr. Budd: We can do it in the way we propose here without defeating the bill.

Mr. Cutcheon: We want to change the law a little in the direction of law and order.

Mr. Ryan: And civilization.

Mr. Cutcheon: Yes, and civilization.[102]

Budd was mistaken about the current state of Indian law in his remarks about the need for a major crimes act. "Indian depredations" came under the scope of the "bad Indian" extradition clauses that had been a feature of virtually all treaties. Nor, apparently, was he aware that the Major Crimes Act applied only to crimes committed between Indians while on a reservation. He was not the only congressman mistaken about the law.

Congressman Warner of Ohio asked whether the proposed amendment "conflicts with any treaty stipulations." Congressman Cutcheon incredibly answered, "Not that I am aware of." Warner responded, perhaps sarcastically: "I think that ought to be known positively." The discussion then went into financial matters. The whole appropriations bill passed on a vote of 240 to 7, with 77 members, including Hiscock, not voting. The Senate, after even less discussion, passed a narrower version. The two versions were reconciled in conference, and the bill became law on June 30, 1885. The Indian nations in Oklahoma, recognizing their special status, were excluded from the law, leaving them complete criminal jurisdiction over Indians within their territory.[103]

Though pleased that the final act followed closely their original proposal, BIA officials were concerned that without a substantial appropriation of funds, the legislation would have no impact. Local federal, state, and territorial authorities were often not interested in crimes on Indian reservations and might be deterred from pursuing felons under the act by the high cost of such prosecutions.[104] This was the reason that Kagama, whose case was the first under the Major Crimes Act to reach the U.S. Supreme Court, went free.

[102] *Congressional Record* (1885), 936.
[103] Ibid.
[104] Justice William E. Church of Dakota Territory wrote U.S. Attorney General A. H. Garland, complaining of the impossibility of enforcing the Major Crimes Act in the Dakota Territory, calling the effort "constant, expensive, difficult, and largely profitless." Letter, William E. Church to A. H. Garland, September 23, 1885, reprinted in "Communication from the Secretary of the Interior Relative to Trial of Indians Committing Certain Crimes," U.S. Congress, Senate, 49th Congress, 1st session, Ex. doc. 33, January 12, 1886. Congress then appropriated money to finance the prosecution of Indians under the Major Crimes Act.

Conclusion

The tragic facts of the killing of Spotted Tail give rise to a wide range of reactions. But these cannot obscure the central issue: Brule law was functioning and able to settle the dispute. The U.S. Supreme Court recognized tribal sovereignty and deferred to Brule law. That was the law in the United States of 1883. This law was based on a long tradition of recognizing tribal sovereignty. It also made sound policy sense: the tribes were best able to adjudicate intertribal disputes. This result does not depend on any taking of sides in the dispute between Spotted Tail and Crow Dog: whatever the underlying reasons for the killing, the Brule Sioux were in a better position to know and judge them. They had a right to do so. That is the essence of tribal sovereignty.

The desire of the BIA and U.S. Indian policymakers generally to destroy tribal sovereignty is well documented. Tribal law was an essential element of that sovereignty. The killing of Spotted Tail, a great chief, provided these people with an opportunity to defame Brule law – "red man's revenge" – so they could substitute U.S. law. The framework for this attack on Brule law was already in place, deriving from nearly a dozen attempts to try Indians for intertribal killings in the years immediately before and after 1881. But the killing of Spotted Tail was the perfect test case. Ironically, it was also an isolated case: in all the factional struggles sweeping two hundred reservations in the late nineteenth and early twentieth centuries no other chief was killed. This must testify to the capacity of tribal law to mediate and contain disputes. Clearly, the army and the BIA police lacked the capacity to serve as bodyguards to all the chiefs, no matter how much power the U.S. government was able to muster in Indian country.

5

Imposed law and forced assimilation

The legal impact of the Major Crimes Act and
the *Kagama* decision

If legal scholars are not in agreement about the meaning of *Crow Dog*, the
same cannot be said for *United States v. Kagama.* This case, decided on May
10, 1886, is known as the Supreme Court's first statement of the plenary
power doctrine, the principle that Congress's power over Indian affairs is
unlimited by treaty rights or tribal sovereignty. As one of the most important
cases in federal Indian law, *Kagama* stands for principles opposite those
advanced in *Crow Dog* and *Worcester.*[1] *Kagama* left Indian tribes mere "wards"
of the federal government, totally dependent on the will of Congress, which
could assert its political power even to their termination as tribes and the
expropriation of their lands without compensation.[2] *Kagama* is the judicial
embodiment of Congress's policy of forcing the assimilation of the tribes,
recognizing none of their sovereignty, none of their status as domestic
nations.

Kagama and *Crow Dog* are closely linked, not only as products of the same
Court, a little more than two years apart, but also doctrinally in that *Kagama*
represents the judicial approval of the Major Crimes Act, the congressional
restriction of the sovereignty of tribal law that the Court had recognized in
Crow Dog.[3] The Court itself in *Crow Dog* specifically stated that Congress
had the power to extend federal criminal law in Indian country if it chose

[1] Rotenberg, "American Indian Tribal Death – A Centennial Remembrance," *Miami Law
Review* 41 (1986):409. Rotenberg argues that in *Kagama* the Supreme Court – rather than
Congress, the Executive, or the cavalry – "killed" tribal sovereignty. I read the case in the
opposite way: in *Kagama* the Supreme Court upheld the intrusions of the other branches
into tribal sovereignty, refusing to intervene and protect the tribes as they had in *Crow Dog.*
[2] Nell Jessup Newton, "Federal Power over Indians: Its Sources, Scope, and Limitations,"
Pennsylvania Law Review 132 (1984):195, at 212–19.
[3] Clearly, it can be argued that the mere speed with which this legal restructuring of Indian–
white relations was achieved proves that the administration was devoting great effort to this
attack on tribal sovereignty. Crow Dog was convicted of murder in March 1882. His conviction
was overturned by the U.S. Supreme Court a year and a half later in December 1883. The
Major Crimes Act was passed a year and a half later, in June 1885. *Kagama*, the first case
to test the new law, was decided by the U.S. Supreme Court eleven months later, in May
1886, nine months before the passage of the Dawes Act in February 1887.

to do so, citing congressional extension of federal liquor laws to Indian country without the consent of the tribes in *United States v. Forty-three Gallons of Whiskey* (1876).[4] This duplicity may well have been intended: the Court may have made a strong sovereignty statement in *Crow Dog* to show Congress the danger this sovereignty posed to white interests; and just in case Congress missed the obvious solution to this problem, the Court directly stated that Congress had the power unilaterally to end tribal sovereignty. If this was indeed the Court's intention, then the first statement of the plenary power doctrine was not *Kagama*, but this dicta in *Crow Dog*.[5]

Moreover, both the Major Crimes Act and the *Kagama* decision occurred directly in the midst of Congress's most sweeping debate on Indian policy, a policy that led to the Dawes Act of February 8, 1887, providing for the forced allotment of Indian lands as a deliberate means of destroying "communistic" tribal culture and forcing the Indians to assimilate as farmers and ranchers into the mainstream of U.S. life.[6] The interconnections between these cases and Congress's legislation are obvious: the Dawes Act, for example, necessarily relied on the plenary power doctrine of *Kagama*. Perhaps even more obvious: the Indians could not be removed from their lands without federal criminal jurisdiction over them. Federal Indian law emerged as a distinct field of doctrine in the next twenty years as a number of unanswered questions in *Crow Dog*, *Kagama*, the Major Crimes Act, and the Dawes Act led to a great increase in the number of both state and federal decisions in the area of Indian law, many at the Supreme Court level.[7]

Doctrinally, *Kagama* pushed *Crow Dog* from the mainstream of federal Indian law for more than fifty years. In analyzing *Kagama*, however, it is important not to lose sight of the fact that the *Crow Dog* doctrine, recognition that tribal sovereignty protects the tribes' legal traditions, has survived dozens of court decisions, albeit with increasing limitations on the jurisdiction of Indian tribes. Congress was unwilling to extend full federal or state criminal jurisdiction to the Indian tribes, and the tribes have resisted the application

---

[4] *United States v. Forty-three Gallons of Whiskey*, 93 U.S. 188 (1876).

[5] 109 U.S. 556 (1883), at 567.

[6] D. S. Otis, *The Dawes Act and the Allotment of Indian Lands* (1934; Norman: University of Oklahoma Press, 1973), and J. P. Kinney, *A Continent Lost – A Civilization Won: Indian Land Tenure in America* (Baltimore: Johns Hopkins University Press, 1937). For an analysis of Congress's vision of the communalism of tribal society being the major obstacle to "civilization," see William T. Hagan, "Private Property: The Indians Door to Civilization," *Ethnohistory* 3 (Spring 1956):126–37.

[7] Well over a hundred major federal cases were decided between *Crow Dog* (1883) and *Lone Wolf* (1903), at least thirty by the U.S. Supreme Court. The entire nineteenth century up to 1883 had produced no more than twenty-five major federal cases, with perhaps a dozen decided by the U.S. Supreme Court. The role of the law in restructuring tribal society through forced assimilation is analyzed in Linda J. Lacey: "The White Man's Law and the American Indian Family in the Assimilation Era," *Arkansas Law Review* 40 (1986):327.

of U.S. criminal law. *Kagama*, therefore, does not overrule *Crow Dog*. Rather, it holds that Congress has the power, under the plenary power doctrine, to restrict tribal sovereignty and specifically upholds congressional action in doing so in the Major Crimes Act. Until Congress chooses to restrict tribal sovereignty, however, in direct and explicit terms, the tribes remain sovereign.[8] This doctrine primarily manifested itself, in the twenty years after *Crow Dog*, in the Supreme Court's insistence that tribal law governed in matters of civil and domestic law.[9]

A closer look at the early years of the plenary power doctrine shows that both the federal government and the states used it to impose U.S. law on tribal Indians in a variety of contexts. In general, federal courts rebuffed most of the state efforts, but federal legal domination of the tribes was achieved, and Indian country was transformed to a checkerboard country of farms and ranches, owned by both whites and Indians. Within this framework of federal legal domination, however, the tribes, for a variety of reasons, were able to preserve a great deal of their autonomy.

A Klamath killing under U.S. law

United States v. Kagama was decided one year after the passage of the Major Crimes Act and two and a half years after *Crow Dog*. The case arose out of the killing of Iyouse near the Hoopa Reservation in Northern California. The facts are depressingly common: an ordinary murder case arising from new patterns of conflict occurring on reservations as traditional social control and dispute resolution methods weakened in the face of rapid social change and factional struggle.[10] The Klamaths, dispersed on a number of reservations in Northern California and Oregon, were a poverty-stricken people without land or a reservation of their own.[11] The parties to the killing, all

[8] The plenary power doctrine can be read more broadly than this, holding that Congress has virtually total power over the tribes. This may have been the belief in the late nineteenth and early twentieth centuries, but it is clearly now the case that the plenary power doctrine is limited by competing doctrines. For a full discussion of these limitations, see Newton, "Federal Power over Indians."

[9] Felix Cohen, "Indian Rights and the Federal Courts," *Minnesota Law Review* 24 (1940):145, discusses the rights of tribal self-government that followed *Crow Dog*, including civil jurisdiction, the right to determine tribal membership, tribal regulation of inheritance, tribal taxation powers, control of tribal property, Indian domestic relations, and the determination of the form of tribal government.

[10] Agent Charles Porter's 1883 annual report describes the reservation as filled with internal dissention, citing this as a basis for his failure to organize either Indian police or courts of Indian offenses. BIA, *Annual Report of the Commissioner of Indian Affairs, 1883*, "Reports of Agents in California," 13,

[11] *Daily Alta California* (San Francisco), September 8, 1886, p. 1; September 9, 1886, p. 1. Leslie Spier, *Klamath Ethnography*, University of California Publications in American Archaeology and Ethnology, no. 30 (Berkeley: University of California Press, 1930), is the

Klamaths who had traditionally lived near the Hupa, had been involved for years in a dispute over some land. In tribal society, ownership of land was inconsistent with traditional law of land tenure, for tribal lands were held in common, but a U.S. survey had put two Klamath villages, Weitehpeck and Pactah, on the Hoopa Reservation. The legal rights of the Klamath who lived in these villages were unclear, and the Indian agent, Major Charles Porter, wrote Washington for instructions. Kagama, alias Pactah Billy, had lived all his life in Pactah and was, according to the agent, "quiet, sober, honest, and industrious." He supported his family and asked for no government assistance. Major Porter gave him the highest praise: Kagama "endeavors to live like a white man, and comes nearer being one – and a good one – in character and conduct than any Indian I have ever met. By his perseverance, industry and enterprise he has managed to accumulate some property and to clear and cultivate a few acres of land."[12]

Perhaps, ironically, Kagama's desire "to live like a white man" lay behind his killing of Iyouse. Kagama wanted to build a house but felt he could not do so until he got some kind of legal title to his land. But the land in question belonged to the Hoopa Reservation. Agent Porter wrote Washington, asking for some kind of authority to settle the matter. The BIA, which must have been inundated with many similar problems, did not respond. In the meantime, Kagama and his family had become embroiled in a dispute with Iyouse, a neighboring Klamath, over this land. The agent was called upon several times to mediated the dispute, the last time just a month before the killing.[13]

On the day of the killing, Kagama and his son Mahawaha, also called Ben, went to Iyouse's house to continue the dispute. No one knows exactly what happened, but angry words were exchanged and Kagama stabbed Iyouse twice, cutting his throat, while Mahawaha held back Iyouse's wife.[14] The Indian agent first referred the case to state authorities, who refused jurisdiction. The two Klamath were then arrested by federal authorities

standard ethnographic account of the Klamath; material on Klamath law and society is found at 21–41. Unfortunately, the *Alta California* account does not give us enough information about this dispute to understand it in the context of Klamath law. Obviously, a "dispute over land" already is indicative of the breakdown of traditional society. The killing occurred adjacent to the Hoopa reservation. Byron Nelson, *Our Home Forever: A Hupa Tribal History* (Salt Lake City: University of Utah Publication Service, 1978), the standard Hupa tribal history, does not contain any reference to the killing or any information that gives a clue to its motivation. The Hupa were deeply factionalized during this period (99), but it is not clear that this conflict affected the Klamath living among them. Note that Hupa is the tribal name, while Hoopa is the federal designation for the reservation.

[12] Major Charles Porter, Indian agent at Hoopa Valley, wrote two letters to the BIA commissioner, relating to the dispute between Kagama and Iyouse; Porter to commissioner, May 15, 1884, and June 25, 1885. Both are held in Records of the BIA, "Letters Received" file, Record Group 75, National Archives. The quotation is from the letter of May 15, 1884.

[13] Ibid.

[14] Ibid.

under the Major Crimes Act. While *Crow Dog* and *Worcester* had become test cases because of their compelling facts, Kagama's case was a mere fortuity: he killed Iyouse scarcely a month after passage of the Major Crimes Act, and his was the first of any number of arrests under the act to reach the high court.[15]

The case was brought before the federal district court in San Francisco barely two months after the Major Crimes Act became law. Kagama and Mahawaha's lawyer had one obvious defense in challenging the legality of the act, arguing that the federal government lacked power over the tribes. But he also made two other arguments, one of which proved to be more telling. First, he argued that there was no federal jurisdiction in the case because the crime occurred off the reservation and was thus under California's jurisdiction. Second, like Crow Dog's attorney, he claimed self-defense.[16]

The government, however, was in a hurry to bring the Major Crimes Act under Supreme Court review in order to clear up jurisdictional confusion in Indian country. The district court judge sent the question of whether the Major Crimes Act gave federal courts jurisdiction over a killing between two Indians on a reservation to the U.S. circuit court on an interlocutory appeal, that is, appealing the jurisdictional matter before the case was tried on its merits. The circuit court certified a division on this issue, permitting it to be appealed immediately to the U.S. Supreme Court. The Court decided the case with great speed, handing down an opinion in early 1886, seven months after the killing took place.[17]

The reasoning in the Supreme Court's decision contains no great insights into constitutional law. The logic of the decision is drawn straight from the contradictions that Marshall raised in *Worcester* and that caused difficulty for the *Crow Dog* decision. On the one hand, there was a powerful history of Indian sovereignty; on the other hand, the tribes were in a dependent relationship to the United States. However, instead of framing the opinion in the difficult policy of striking a balance, the Court announced a new doctrine for the governing of Indians: the plenary power doctrine. *Worcester* had been based on treaty rights, a system of relations that recognized a good measure of sovereignty to both parties. Federal Indian law had been fundamentally grounded in this reciprocal system of treaty rights and a negotiated relationship between nations, even if *Worcester* found that the Indian nations were not foreign nations or fully independent.[18]

---

[15] Ibid.

[16] This procedural history is found in the case file, *United States v. Kagama*, held in the Record Group 75, National Archives, San Bruno, Calif.

[17] The procedural history of the case can be found in the case file. It is held as Case no. 2096, Box 50, National Archives, San Francisco, Calif.

[18] On the origin and development of the plenary power doctrine, see Newton, "Federal Power over Indians," 207–28. Rotenberg, "American Indian Tribal Death," 409, correctly locates

The narrow result in *Kagama* was based on the ending of the treaty period. An act of Congress on March 3, 1871, formally and forever ended the making of treaties with Indian tribes:

> No Indian Nation or tribe, within the territory of the United States, shall be acknowledged, or recognized, as an independent Nation, Tribe, or power, with whom the United States may contract by treaty; but no obligation of any treaty lawfully made and ratified with any such Indian Nation or Tribe prior to March 3, 1871, shall be hearby invalidated or impaired.[19]

Although the last sentence recognizes existing treaty rights forever, Justice Samuel Miller held that, by passing the law, Congress had determined a "new departure, to govern [the tribes] by Acts of Congress."[20] The court's determination that the end of the treaty period signaled a "new departure" went directly to a denial of tribal sovereignty because that sovereignty right stemmed from the same status as "nations" that had been at the foundation of the treaty-based relationship between the United States and the Indian nations.

In the basic doctrinal core of nineteenth-century Indian law through *Crow Dog*, there was always a fragility to the balances struck in Indian policy decisions that reflected the striking contradiction between dependency and sovereignty. *Worcester* and *Crow Dog* both recognized the principle of tribal sovereignty. *Worcester* did so more strongly than *Crow Dog* on its face, but in *Crow Dog* the Court's result gave real meaning to tribal sovereignty. *Kagama* is a critical case because it, together with the later *Lone Wolf* decision (1903),[21] not only wiped out that balance, destroying sovereignty and making the tribes mere wards of the American nation, but also shifted the method of weighing tribal sovereignty from a complex balancing function in the federal courts to Congress's plenary power to simply do with the tribes whatever it chose.[22] Through *Kagama*, the right of Congress to abrogate treaty rights unilaterally was first established. At the same time, the case potentially deprived the tribes of the right to make laws to govern themselves, a critical aspect of their sovereignty and their ability to structure their own

---

the importance of *Kagama* in the formation of the plenary power doctrine but takes the case out of the context of other cases and political events.

[19] 2079 Revised Statutes, 1871. Quoted in *United States v. Kagama*, 118 U.S. 375 (1886), at 382, n. 1.

[20] Ibid., 382. Justice Samuel Miller served twenty-eight years on the U.S. Supreme Court. An Iowan, he was a typical late-nineteenth-century booster of western growth, another Republican lawyer in league with the railroad interests. Miller was also a strong promotor of federal power, although he did not consistently follow this through in civil rights and corporate cases.

[21] 187 U.S. 553 (1903). Newton, "Federal Power over Indians," 219–22.

[22] Newton, "Federal Power over Indians," 207–28.

societies. *Lone Wolf v. Hitchcock* completed this attack by ensuring that the tribes could be deprived of their lands in the same way.

Justice Miller's decision was rooted not in the framework of federal Indian law but rather in the political realities of U.S. expansionism of the day. Whatever Congress's motivation in ending its policy of treaty making – authorities on federal Indian law attribute it to rivalry between the House of Representatives and the Senate rather than to any change in Indian policy – it manifestly did not affect existing treaties or legal rights flowing from those treaties.[23] By the Court's *Crow Dog* logic in refusing to alter a treaty right by implication, it was incorrect to read an intention to create a new method of governing Indians into a congressional resolution and thereby change the treaty status of the tribes by implication. At the very least (although this result would not have supported tribal sovereignty), the Court should have left it to Congress to declare this new policy in explicit terms.[24]

The Court, however, with the same composition as at the time of *Crow Dog,* was making policy of its own. *Kagama* is filled with the language of dependency, perhaps the strongest to appear in any Supreme Court tribal rights case:

> These Indian tribes are the wards of the nation. They are communities dependent on the United States. Dependent largely for their daily food. Dependent for their political rights.... From their very weakness and helplessness ... there arises the duty of protection, and with it the power....
>
> The power of the General Government over these remnants of a race once powerful, now weak and diminished in numbers, is necessary for their protection, as well as to the safety of those among whom they dwell.[25]

Although the language of *Crow Dog* defended tribal sovereignty, there was virtually no litigation under its doctrine prior to *Kagama.* Thus, *Kagama*'s dependency language severely undercut any policy impact *Crow Dog* might have had – that is, if the Court ever intended that it should have any impact. *Kagama,* on the other hand, influenced policy in two distinct areas. First, it seriously undermined, although it did not extinguish, the concept of tribal sovereignty in U.S. law. Second, the plenary power doctrine, like *Worcester,* must be understood in the context of late-nineteenth-century federalism, representing the final victory of the national government over the states in

---

[23] Francis Paul Prucha, *Great Father: The U.S. Government and the Indians,* 2 vols. (Lincoln: University of Nebraska Press, 1984), 1:527–33, and F. Cohen, *Handbook of Federal Indian Law* (Washington, D.C.: U.S. Government Printing Office, 1942), 66–7.

[24] F. Cohen, *Handbook of Federal Indian Law,* 3d ed. (Charlottesville, Va.: Michie, 1982), 105–7, 127–8.

[25] *United States v. Kagama,* 113 U.S. 375 (1886), at 384.

the area of Indian affairs and remaining an important principle in the law of federalism. The plenary power doctrine gives the federal government, not the states, full power over the tribes.

State criminal jurisdiction after *Crow Dog* and *Kagama*

It should not be surprising that much of the litigation immediately following the *Kagama* decision concerned the rights of the states to enforce state laws on allotted tribal lands. While the Major Crimes Act and the plenary power doctrine might seem to have put an end to state claims of jurisdiction in Indian country, the Dawes Act allotting tribal lands also put tens of thousands of white farmers and ranchers in Indian country, living among tribal Indians with similar allotments. Thus, the whole meaning of Indian country, clearly spelled out in *Crow Dog*, was put in disarray by the Dawes Act. It would take the federal courts forty years to sort this confusion out.

The Court in its *Kagama* opinion must have had a sense of this impending jurisdictional conflict with the states because, unlike in *Crow Dog*, *Kagama* specifically dealt with the problem of the tribes relationship to the states, justifying the plenary power doctrine, at least in part, by the need of the federal government to protect the tribes from the hostility of local whites: "They owe no allegiance to the States, and receive from them no protection. Because of local ill feeling, the people of the States where they are found are often their deadliest enemies."[26]

Thus, the most important jurisdictional result of *Crow Dog*, its broad definition of "Indian country," was implicitly incorporated into *Kagama* to give the tribes protection against the states. This interpretation, coupled with the plenary power doctrine, greatly strengthened federal jurisdiction over the Indian tribes. This was the first time since *Worcester* that the Court had acknowledged that there was a serious conflict between the tribes and the states that required federal intervention. It also cannot be assumed that the Court's use of the phrase "deadliest enemies" was inadvertent: this was the first time the Court had acknowledged that it was making Indian law in the context of great violence and death.

In the early days of westward expansion, federal authority over the tribes had been largely illusory, both because the tribes functioned as independent nations and because few whites actually lived among Indians, but federal power became increasingly important as the few remaining territories (which were clearly under federal jurisdiction) became states and most Indian reservations were encompassed within them. While state jurisdiction over the tribes in the East and South had involved relatively small numbers of Indians,

[26] Ibid.

the admission of western states put hundreds of thousands of tribal Indians living within state boundaries. After the passage of the Dawes Act in 1887 and the allotment of tribal lands, many thousands of whites took up farms on reservations, further increasing state agitation for some measure of jurisdiction over tribal lands. This was true even though most of these statehoods were explicitly made conditional on the states' recognition of federal jurisdiction over the tribes.[27] Following *Kagama* it was up to the federal courts to decide the limits of state jurisdiction. With some legal confusion and jurisdictional chaos, the federal courts by and large kept the states from asserting jurisdiction over tribal allotments. But the states were persistent and ingenious in their attempts to do so. And although it was too late for the federal government to reclaim jurisdiction over tribes in Georgia, Alabama, and Tennessee, *Crow Dog* and *Kagama* were used for just that purpose in Wisconsin and New York, as well as to defeat state challenges to federal jurisdiction in the West.[28]

In applying the *Crow Dog* decision and the Major Crimes Act only to Indian country, the Court, while being firm about federal plenary power over Indians in Indian country, came to exclude most land within states from this definition:

> In our opinion that definition now applies to all country to which the Indian title has not been extinguished within the limits of the United States, even when not within a reservation . . . excluding, however, any territory embraced within the exterior geographical limits of a State, not excepted from its jurisdiction by treaty or by statute at the time of its admission into the Union.[29]

The reference to lands not excepted by treaty or by statute left unanswered many existing jurisdictional questions that had been repeatedly raised by state cases. Moreover, the *Kagama* decision could not anticipate the jurisdictional quagmire that allotment created, pitting the interests of federally protected Indians against local whites under state jurisdiction who lived interspersed with each other. The Court, consistent with its *McBratney* decision, clearly was trying to move beyond the seemingly absolute retention of jurisdiction by the federal government in *Worcester* and recognize that this had been politically untenable in a federal system, not only because the states

---

[27] For a discussion of South Dakota's agreement with the federal government on the state's recognition of federal jurisdiction over the tribes, see *State v. Nimrod*, 30 S.D. 239 (1912), at 243–6.

[28] See *State v. Rufus*, 237 N.W. 67 (1931), at 70, for the Wisconsin Supreme Court's decision. The case is briefly analyzed in Charles A. Riedl, "Criminal Law – Jurisdiction – Indians," *Marquette Law Review* 16 (1931):57. Cuthbert Pound, "Nationals Without a Nation: The New York State Tribal Indians" *Columbia Law Review* 29 (1922):97.

[29] *United States v. Kagama*, 118 U.S. 375, (1886), at 382.

did not accept it but also because, following allotment, it was an administrative nightmare. Thus, there was consistent pressure on the federal courts to concede criminal jurisdiction to the states in a wide variety of circumstances.

However, because there was both a clear policy of federal guardianship over the tribes and a federal court system willing to deny the states jurisdiction, the states fared worse under this system than they had under *Worcester*'s broader, but substantially unenforceable statement of federal power over states. In Wisconsin, for example, the federal courts consistently challenged state jurisdiction over Indian country. In 1894, within the boundaries of Lac Court Orreilles Reservation in Wisconsin, Michel Thomas, a Chippewa Indian, killed a fellow Chippewa. But the killing had occurred in one of the township sections set aside for school lands and therefore owned by the state for purposes of financing public education. Although this land was not excepted from Indian country by any "treaty or statute within the meaning of Crow Dog," the Supreme Court simply ignored this language and followed a policy of broad federal authority over the tribes. In upholding federal jurisdiction, the Court claimed what amounted to subject matter jurisdiction: all matters involving Indians within reservations were federal as a matter of national policy. This was a broader claim of federal authority than *Crow Dog*, which was based on treaty provisions and inherent tribal sovereignty, but it was consistent with the new plenary power doctrine.[30]

The greatest immediate problem was the vast stretches of the West that were customarily occupied by Indians, but not within the limits of the small reservations established in the late nineteenth century. Such lands were Indian country by custom, for Indians had traditionally lived there, but became juridically part of the national domain, "owned" by the federal government. The new western states jealously guarded their rights to this land, needed by their citizens for agriculture and commerce. The states argued that being admitted to the union "on an equal footing" with the original thirteen states, necessarily extinguished all tribal rights to this land, including treaty rights: essentially the same position that Georgia had taken in the Cherokee cases.[31] The Supreme Court in *Ward v. Race Horse* (1896) considered this issue in a Wyoming challenge to Bannock treaty rights to hunt on "unoccupied lands of the United States," holding that federal

---

[30] *United States v. Thomas*, 151 U.S. 577 (1894). Wisconsin was among the most determined states in exercising criminal jurisdiction over the tribes. See Chapter 2, the section entitled "The North and West, 1835–80."

[31] The settled law on this position is that treaty rights, entered into under the Constitution of the United States, are incorporated into the "law of the land" and therefore binding on the states under basic principles of federalism. Cohen, *Handbook of Federal Indian Law*, 1st ed., 117.

treaty rights in conflict with Wyoming's statehood act were terminated by statehood.[32]

Other states more readily yielded to federal authority, with state courts holding a lack of state jurisdiction. Minnesota had already carried this issue to its logical conclusion in an 1893 case involving a Chippewa and a non-Indian charged with committing adultery on White Earth Reservation. The state supreme court, properly deferring to the logic of a checkerboard criminal jurisdiction for a checkerboard reservation, found the Chippewa beyond the jurisdiction of state law but upheld the conviction of the non-Indian.[33] Big Sheep, a Crow Indian arrested in Montana in 1926 for possession of peyote, a crime under Montana law but not under Crow law, was held by the Montana Supreme Court to be beyond the jurisdiction of state law.[34] Both results are especially significant in that the decisions allowed Indian criminal defendants to go free, since the crimes involved were not among those given federal jurisdiction in the Major Crimes Act.

Other states did not so easily concede a matter seen as essential to state sovereignty. Perhaps the most ingenious legal route was taken by Iowa. Recognizing that it could not retain state criminal jurisdiction over the Sac and Fox Reservation, but unwilling to concede that the federal government had such authority, the state legislature in 1896 passed a law holding that it had such jurisdiction but ceding it to the federal government while retaining a right to exercise jurisdiction over crimes committed "against the laws of Iowa." A federal court later held, in dicta, that it did not think that the state of Iowa had ever held such authority; but as long as the state had ceased to exercise it, the conceit could not be challenged.[35]

South Dakota, also reluctant to accept federal criminal jurisdiction over reservation Indians within the state, tried another legal device to undermine

---

[32] *Ward v. Race Horse*, 163 U.S. 504 (1896). The Supreme Court reversed a circuit court opinion, *in re Race Horse*, 70 F. 598 (1895), that, in holding the opposite, accurately reflects the law. Race Horse, a Bannock hunter charged with killing seven elk in violation of Wyoming law, was in custody for nearly three months before the writ of habeas corpus was granted. Continued state efforts to enforce fish and game laws against tribal Indians led to increased violence, culminating in the "Lightning Creek fight" of 1903.

[33] *State v. Campbell*, 53 Minn. 354 (1893).

[34] *State v. Big Sheep* 243 P. 1067 (1926).

[35] *Peters v. Malin*, 111 Fed. Rep. 244 (1901). Like many state–federal disputes in Indian law, the Iowa case stemmed from a unique set of historical circumstances. Tribal rights were completely ceded to the federal government in a removal treaty, but a remnant of the tribe did not leave the state, falling under the protection of the state of Iowa. While the federal government soon reestablished a relationship with these Iowa Indians, some measure of state power continued to be exercised. A 1978 case, *Sac and Fox Tribe v. Licklider*, 576 F.2d 145 (8th Cir.), which holds that Iowa fish and game laws apply to Sac and Fox Indians on their reservation, appears to misread *Peters v. Malin* as holding that the state of Iowa could in fact exercise criminal jurisdiction over the Sac and Fox reservation. Another discussion of this jurisdictional history is found in *in re Lelah-Puc-Ka-Chee*, 98 F. 429 (1899).

federal authority. The state argued that federal jurisdiction under the Major Crimes Act was limited by statute to offenses by one Indian against the person or property of another Indian. Dennis Quiver, a Sioux living on a reservation, was arrested for adultery under state law on the theory that his was not an offense against the "person or property" of another Indian. Quiver's state conviction was appealed in 1916 to the U.S. Supreme Court, which rejected a narrow construction of the act and looked to the broad intent of Congress to take jurisdiction over crimes committed by Indians on reservations. According to the Court, it was clear that Congress intended for jurisdiction to be federal; thus Quiver's adultery was outside of state criminal jurisdiction.[36]

Ironically, the conflict between federal and local interests in applying criminal law to Indians also occurred between the federal government and its own territorial governments. While a territorial court operated under federal authority, it was a local court and applied a range of local laws, most often adopted from neighboring states, as well as federal laws. In 1889, the U.S. Supreme Court reversed the convictions of two Apaches convicted of murder – Gon-shay-ee, sentenced to hang, and Captain Jack, sentenced to thirty years in prison – because they were subjected to territorial court trials rather than federal court trials for killing white men. In doing so, the Supreme Court put an end to a BIA plan to bring the Apache wars under the jurisdiction of the Arizona Territorial Courts, a jurisdiction they received as long as the Apache warriors were outside of their reservations. The Apache cases involved rare attempts to bring Indian wars under the jurisdiction of the criminal law and to punish Indians as murderers rather than to treat them as warriors. The U.S. Supreme Court conceded that the territorial courts had applied the same substantive law that the federal courts would have applied but reversed on the narrow (but important) grounds that federal juries had to be drawn from the entire judicial district rather than the immediate locality of the territorial courts.[37]

The jurisdictional problems of land allotment

Land allotment caused a rush of litigation in Indian country in many areas of law, including criminal jurisdiction, confounding the already complex jurisdiction conflicts between the federal government and the states. The essence of allotment is that "surplus" Indian lands, that is, all lands not alloted in farm-sized parcels to Indians, was sold to whites, often at bargain prices. Thus, land ownership on many reservations assumed the checker-

---

[36] *United States v. Quiver*, 241 U.S. 604 (1915).
[37] *Ex parte Gon-shay-ee*, 130 U.S. 348 (1889). John U. Terrell, *Apache Chronicle* (Cleveland, Ohio: World Publishing, 1972), 370–1.

board pattern of today, with alternating plots owned variously by whites and Indians. There is no record in the congressional debates over the act that any thought was given to the jurisdictional chaos that would be created. Most congressmen apparently believed that state jurisdiction would shortly follow allotment. Section 6 of the Dawes Act directly dealt with this issue providing that at the completion of allotment, "every member of the respective . . . tribes of Indians to whom allotments have been made shall have the benefit and be subject to the laws, both civil and criminal of the state or territory in which they may reside."[38] It is not clear that Congress fully thought through the implications of this section. Initially some states argued that they held jurisdiction over the tribes at allotment, but the problem was put off for twenty-five years by Congress's language concerning the "completion" of allotments, or the actual patenting of the land. Until then, the allotted lands were held in trust by the government, extending the Indians' wardship status. But ultimately, that distinction disappeared as well, and the federal government never gave up jurisdiction on allotted lands on reservations.[39] This result appears to be inconsistent with the intent of Congress in the original allotment act and reflects the fact that allotment failed its purpose in forcing assimilation, defeating this attempt to cede jurisdiction over the tribes back to the states.

States already had jurisdiction over whites in Indian country, a line of cases beginning with *McBratney* (1881) and reinforced by *United States v. Draper* (1896).[40] But crimes by Indians on allotted lands or on reservation lands otherwise alienated were a common occurrence, and a number of states claimed criminal jurisdiction. North Dakota, South Dakota, and Washington were particularly aggressive in this respect.[41] There was strong precedent for such action: Kansas had argued since the 1860s that by taking lands in patent, Indians had given up their special status and become subject to state law.[42] The federal courts in that state had not decided the issue but acquiesced to the Kansas action.

Both North and South Dakota extended their criminal jurisdiction to Indians who had accepted allotments even within the boundaries of reser-

---

[38] Dawes Act, section 6.
[39] Felix Cohen, *Handbook of Federal Indian Law* (1942), 358–63.
[40] *United States v. McBratney*, 104 U.S. 629 (1881); *United States v. Draper*, 164 U.S. 240 (1896).
[41] See *State v. Denoyer*, 6 N.D. 586 (1897); *Farrell v. United States*, 110 Fed. 942 (1901); *United States v. Kiya*, 126 Fed. Rep. 879 (1903); *United States v. Pelican*, 232 U.S. 442 (1914); *United States v. Celestine*, 215 U.S. 278 (1909).
[42] *State v. Hunt*, 4 Kans. 65 (1866). Many eastern and midwestern tribes were removed to Kansas in the mid-nineteenth century and, in early allotment experiments, given individual title to their lands. Kansas took civil and criminal jurisdiction over such Indians. On the general history of Kansas Indians, see Clyde Milner and William Unran, *The End of Indian Kansas* (Lawrence: University of Kansas Press, 1978).

vations, arguing that allotment severed the tribal relation and made Indians full citizens of the states, fully accountable to state laws.[43] This action was upheld by the supreme courts of both states, as well as by federal district courts in *United States v. Kiya* and *United States v. Farrell* but was not to become national policy.[44] States were particularly inclined to take jurisdiction in criminal cases that fell outside of the Major Crimes Act, stepping into what they perceived as a jurisdictional void but what, under *Crow Dog,* remained under tribal jurisdiction. Many state laws had no parallels in traditional law. This was especially true in the area of consensual sex offenses as states tried to impose white marriage customs on Indians. Joseph Nimrod, a Yankton Sioux, was charged in a South Dakota county court with bigamy committed on his allotment on the Yankton Reservation. Nimrod demurred, arguing that the court lacked jurisdiction. The South Dakota Supreme Court held that while the federal government had jurisdiction over the offenses specified in the Major Crimes Act, the general criminal laws of South Dakota extended to all other offenses.[45]

In general, federal courts held allotted lands within reservations to be Indian country within the meaning of *Crow Dog.*[46] For a time, some courts believed that this definition held true only during the twenty-five-year period in which the federal government held title to the allotments "in trust" for individual Indians, but it was finally conclusively held that allotted lands within reservations were Indian country and under federal or tribal jurisdiction. Although this matter is now settled law,[47] the original decision did not resolve the issue, given the complexities of landholdings in the Dakotas. This confusion about the impact of state citizenship on federal warship status was so general that it ultimately led to the Supreme Court's own jurisdictional flip-flop on this issue, its cession of federal liquor control jurisdiction over allotted Indians to the states in *Heff* only to recover it ten years later in *Nice.*[48]

In 1911, Van Francis Moore, a Cheyenne River Sioux serving life in the South Dakota State Prison for killing Susan Tin Cup, another Sioux, appealed to federal court, arguing that he had been imprisoned unlawfully by the state since 1900 for an offense committed in Indian country on the allotment of Walking Eagle on the Cheyenne River Reservation. Illustrating the complexity of allotment, the court spent nearly two pages discussing reservation tracts and section lines before deciding that Walking Eagle's allotment was thirty miles from the nearest point on the Cheyenne River

---

[43] *State v. Denoyer,* 72 N.W. 1014 (1897); *State v. Nimrod* 30 S.D. 239 (1912).
[44] *United States v. Kiya,* 126 Fed. Rep. 879 (1903); *United States v. Farrell* 110 Fed. 942 (1901).
[45] *State v. Nimrod,* 30 S.D. 239 (1912).
[46] *United States v. Pelican,* 232 U.S. 442 (1914); *United States v. Celestine,* 215 U.S. 278 (1909).
[47] *Dick v. United States,* 208 U.S. 352 (1907), at 350.
[48] See a full discussion of these case at notes 74–85.

Reservation. But this did not end the matter. Walking Eagle had never lived on the reservation but had remained on traditional Sioux lands that were part of the Great Sioux Reservation until it was divided into smaller reservations in the years after 1876. A provision in the allotment law permitted tribal Indians who lived on federal lands to take their allotments anywhere, and Walking Eagle had done so, thus "Indian title" was arguably never extinguished from his allotment. Moore argued, first, that an Indian allotment anywhere on federal lands was Indian country within the meaning of *Crow Dog* and, second, that the original "Great Sioux Reservation," encompassing the western half of South Dakota, was entirely in Indian country. The court rejected both arguments, thereby restricting the scope of *Crow Dog* and effectively forcing those Indians who wished to be under federal jurisdiction to remove to reservations.[49]

The Paiute Indians of Nevada, by and large refusing to come in to their reservations, had, since *McKenney,* been under federal jurisdiction on the ground that their traditional lands were Indian country as long as they occupied them. After *Kagama* Nevada took jurisdiction over those Indians with the support and encouragement of the BIA, as part of a direct effort to force the Paiutes to remove themselves to reservations.[50] Ironically, for Buckaroo Jack, a Paiute who killed one Lotta, also a Paiute, being on a reservation may not have been enough. On appeal it was alleged that the killing had occurred at the house of Ox Sam, a quarter of a mile from the Indian school at McDermit. But the court held that there was nothing in the trial record showing that this property was on an Indian reservation and that the burden of proving this was on the defendant. Buckaroo Jack's death sentence was upheld.[51]

The state of Washington advanced similar jurisdictional claims that undermined the rights of tribal Indians to their own legal systems and disputed federal authority over reservation Indians. In *State v. Smokalem* (1905), a Puyallup living on his reservation, but with the reservation "having been abandoned, the lands allotted to the Indians in severalty, and the tribe having abandoned its tribal organizations, laws, habits, and customs, and the only parcel of reservation land retained by the government... for school purposes," was convicted in state court of manslaughter in the killing of his Puyallup wife on the reservation. The Washington Supreme Court held that the Major Crimes Act did not apply to Indians without tribal relations. But the court went beyond this in dicta that applied to all tribal law:

---

[49] *Ex parte Moore,* 133 N.W. 817 (1911). This case is the subject of a note: "Indians as Subject to State Regulation," Annual Cases, 1914B, at 652–4.
[50] *State v. Johnny,* 29 Nev. 203 (1906); *State v. Buckaroo Jack,* 30 Nev. 325 (1908).
[51] Ibid.

It is not to be supposed that Congress intended that the remnant of a band of Indians like the Puyallups, without tribal relations, without laws or customs, and without a government to administer them, should be left to prey on each other and upon society at large, without restraint, or fear of punishment from any source, unless they should commit one of the felonies enumerated in this act.[52]

Washington claimed jurisdiction over Indian allotments until *State v. Andy* in 1956.[53]

The idea that only Indians living with "tribal relations" were entitled to either federal protection or respect for their own laws and customs severely weakened the ability of *Crow Dog* to protect the traditions of the many small tribes that often needed such recognition and protection most.[54] Oregon adopted a similar position in dicta in *State v. Columbia George*, although coming to the opposite result on very different facts. While holding that Oregon did not have jurisdiction over a witch killing on an allotment on the Umatilla Reservation, it did adopt the view that "civilized" Indians on allotments, that is, those who gave up their tribal relations, might fall under state jurisdiction.[55]

Smokalem was as far as any state succeeded in seizing criminal jurisdiction over allotted lands. Had the case ever been appealed in the federal courts, it would almost certainly have been reversed. The state of Washington had no right to define the political status of the Puyallup. The process of state limitation of the rights of allotted Indians, begun with strong impetus in the Dakotas, was ended by the U.S. Supreme Court with two Washington cases, *United States v. Celestine* (1909) and *United States v. Pelican* (1914). Although these cases overruled *Smokalem* in their substance, the issue was never again raised for the Puyallups, whose tribal life was legally extinguished.

Celestine put a more decisive end to Washington's claims than had the

---

[52] *State v. Smokalem*, 79 Pac. 603 (1905), at 605. See also the case file, "State v. Smokalem," held by the Washington State Archives, Olympia.

[53] *Smokalem* was the third Washington case taking criminal jurisdiction over tribal Indians in Indian country. See also *State v. Williams*, 13 Wash. 335 (1895), and *State v. Howard*, 33 Wash. 250 (1903). Not only were these cases never taken to the federal courts, but Washington appears to have continued to take jurisdiction over its Indians until 1956. See *State v. Lindsey*, 133 Wash. 140 (1925), and *in re Andy*, 49 Wn. 2d. 449 (1956). See Allen Lane Carr and Stanley M. Johanson, "Extent of Washington Criminal Jurisdiction over Indians," *University of Washington Law Review* 33 (1958):289.

[54] There are also profound problems in defining what constitutes "tribal relations" and in determining whether a white court could identify such relations under any circumstances. A federal judge gave essentially the same question to a white jury in *Famous Smith v. United States*, 151 U.S. 50 (1893), at 54, a factor relevant in prompting the U.S. Supreme Court to reverse Smith's conviction. See the section entitled "The Racial Geography of Federal Indian law."

[55] *State v. Columbia George*, 65 P. 605 (1901), at 608–9.

federal courts in the Dakotas. Celestine killed a fellow Tulalip on the Tulalip Reservation. Both the defendant and the victim had taken allotments and become U.S. citizens. In a direct reversal of the issue in *Smokalem*, Celestine, already convicted in federal court, argued that he was a citizen of the state of Washington and entitled to the full protection of state law. The federal circuit court, believing Indians living as citizens on allotments to be under state jurisdiction, had sustained that argument. The U.S. Supreme Court reversed, holding that federal jurisdiction was not a matter of individual preference but of tribal jurisdiction. Therefore, it was not inconsistent for Celestine to have the full rights of a citizen of Washington as an individual but to be under the jurisdiction of the federal courts as a member of a tribe: it was for Congress to decide when to end federal jurisdiction over Indian tribes. This needed to be done directly and not by an implication drawn from Celestine's status as a citizen of Washington.[56]

This was not the limit of the problems of jurisdictional geography. The U.S. Supreme Court in *Crow Dog* finally decided on a definition of Indian country that included allotted lands but excluded lands where Indian title had been terminated. Many Indians, however, continued to live on their traditional lands after title had been extinguished, refusing to move within reservation boundaries; thus, many crimes between traditional Indians would come under state jurisdiction. Moreover, there are repeated cases of factual disputes concerning where crimes occurred, many of which may have been legal fictions designed to bring tribal Indians under state jurisdiction. In *State v. Thomas*, for example, even the U.S. Supreme Court, after holding that state school lands on a reservation were still Indian country and under federal jurisdiction, sent the case back to the state to determine where Thomas had committed his crime.[57] These fictions worked in both directions. Western states, with weak legal infrastructures, sometimes attempted to pass off crimes committed on state lands to federal jurisdiction by claiming they happened on reservations, or the legal authorities of white towns refused to become involved in crimes between Indians. At other times, as in the case of Kagama, the factual situation was so unclear that no court took jurisdiction.

Jurisdiction over railroad lands

The railroads were among the most powerful promotors of allotment policy and also its major beneficiaries.[58] Tribal sovereignty was directly in the way

---

[56] *United States v. Celestine*, 215 U.S. 278 (1909). Five years later, in *United States v. Pelican*, 232 U.S. 442 (1914), the Court held that allotted lands were "Indian country" and under federal jurisdiction.

[57] *State v. Thomas*, 151 U.S. 577 (1894).

[58] Otis, *Dawes Act*, 22–30.

of the railroads, keeping huge tracts and land, as well as large numbers of people, outside of the new economic order in the West that the railroads sought to create. Allotment changed all this: not only were extensive blocks of tribal land granted to railroads directly, but the population of the West provided a further economic basis for expanding railroads. These railroad land grants included not only thousands of miles of track, but also stations, stores, and towns, major meeting places and centers of commercial activity for both whites and Indians. In *State v. Tilden* (1915) a Nez Perce tribal police officer had ventured onto the railroad right of way that crossed his reservation to intercept a Nez Perce baseball team that he believed might be in possession of liquor while returning from a game in Washington. Officer Tilden had an encounter with Jackson, accompanying the team, in which Tilden shot Jackson, who died of his wounds. The court conceded state jurisdiction, holding that before entering into a treaty with the Nez Perce Indians, the government had conveyed the land to the railroad, thereby extinguishing Indian title to that land before the creation of the reservation. Accordingly, the homicide did not occur in Indian country and was under state jurisdiction.[59] This followed a U.S. Supreme Court ruling holding that the lands of the Northern Pacific Railroad had been completely withdrawn from the Flathead Reservation and were not in Indian country.[60]

The Court made clear in a later case, *United States v. Soldana* (1917), that railroads did not have a blanket exemption from laws governing Indian country. Rather, the nature of the railroad's title determined whether the Indian title had been extinguished or the railroad company had merely been granted a right of way over Indian lands. The court held that the railroad platform of the Chicago, Burlington, and Quincy Railroad at Crow Agency, Montana, was Indian country because the railroad merely possessed a right of way.[61]

The Wisconsin Supreme Court, in its ongoing jurisdictional conflict with federal authorities, took another approach. Not even looking to the legal status of the railroad lands, it looked to the nature of railroad travel itself, balancing the interests of an Indian agent in regulating the activities of Indians on a reservation with a national interest in the proper and safe conduct of rail travel. In *Deragon v. Sero*, a civil verdict won by an Indian against a tribal policeman for assaulting him in the course of his duties on the platform of a railroad at Odanah on the Bad River Reservation was upheld.[62]

[59] *State v. Tilden*, 147 P. 1056 (1915).
[60] *Clairmont v. United States*, 225 U.S. 551 (1912).
[61] *United States v. Soldana*, 246 U.S. 530 (1917).
[62] *Deragon v. Sero*, 137 Wis. 276 (1908).

Civil jurisdiction

Wisconsin's *Deragon* result was consistent with parallel efforts of other states
to seize civil jurisdiction, with most states simply not making any distinction
between civil and criminal jurisdiction over the tribes. Indeed, the original
early-nineteenth-century struggle between the states and the national government concerning jurisdiction over the tribes had similarly not made any
distinction between civil and criminal jurisdiction, for the logic of state
jurisdiction over the tribes applied to both. In addition, to the extent that
the real issue was state control over tribal lands, matters of land and eco-
nomics were primarily civil.

Crow Dog's holding that the tribal sovereignty included the right to apply
traditional law internally made no distinction between civil and criminal
law. Since the Major Crimes Act clearly did not reach civil law, such
issues, like the remaining criminal offenses not specified in the act, remained, under *Crow Dog*, a matter of tribal jurisdiction. Yet, since traditional tribal law covered traditional tribal activity, the imposition of new
forms of property and contract on the reservations created a jurisdictional
void: tribal law did not traditionally cover these problems, state law did
not reach Indian country, and the federal government lacked a legal basis
of civil jurisdiction. As allotment put more of these intratribal issues within
the reach of state courts, states persistently attempted to take civil jurisdiction over the tribes.

The states were more successful in the area of civil law than that of
criminal law. In part this was because the stakes were lower, and routine
Indian civil cases that were illegally decided in state courts were less likely
to be appealed than were routine criminal cases. But there were also legal
reasons. The logic of the Major Crimes Act and *Kagama* was largely that
the federal government had the power to exercise its jurisdiction in any
area of Indian affairs it wanted to and chose to do so in the area of major
crimes. At the same time it deliberately did not do so in the area of civil
jurisdiction, even though it could have. Thus, states willing to concede
that the federal government had preempted Indian criminal jurisdiction
could also argue that the federal government had left civil jurisdiction to
the states. This was true even though *Worcester* had clearly held that the
laws of Georgia had no effect in Indian country because it was a separate
political community.

This state interpretation, although clearly inconsistent with *Worcester*, was
strenghtened by a clear federal abandonment of civil jurisdiction by the U.S.
Supreme Court in *Felix v. Patrick* (1892), a legal atrocity of the first order
that represents the civil embodiment of *Kagama*, legitimating the wholesale

theft of Indian lands. Felix, a half-breed Sioux, had been issued a certificate of land scrip in 1857 under a Sioux treaty, with the express provision that "no transfer or conveyance of this scrip shall be valid."[63] In 1860 some persons by "wicked and fradulent means" induced Felix to execute both a power of attorney in blank and a quitclaim deed in blank to Patrick, who later transferred the property to himself, a process that would be repeated thousands of times in the West as allotments held by uneducated Indians were stolen by corrupt whites.[64]

For unclear reasons it was 1887 before Felix, through his heirs, was able to take legal action to protect his allotment. Patrick, through his heirs, responded with the common-law defense of laches, arguing that whatever the nature of the fraud, the twenty-seven-year delay in challenging it now meant that Felix was barred from doing so. Felix's attorney argued that, first, the suit was brought as soon as the fraud was discovered, and second, tribal Indians' lands were under the special protection of the government precisely because of their legal incapacity to protect their rights.[65]

The Supreme Court's opinion, by Justice Brown, began with the dependency language of *Kagama*, recognizing Indians as "wards of the nation, entitled to a special protection in its courts, and as persons in a state of pupilage." This language was extended, holding that "the conduct of Indians is not to be measured by the same standard which we apply to the conduct of other people."[66] But then the Court refused to follow the clear implication of this language that the Indian tribes could not be subjected to state civil jurisdiction. First, the court held that even though the federal courts were not open to Indians for civil matters, the state courts were, therefore Felix could have challenged Patrick's fraud. Second, the Court applied the common-law doctrine of equity to protect Patrick's title, arguing it was unfair to deprive his descendants of land "originally of the value of $150 . . . now worth over a million."[67]

Felix explicitly recognizes the nature of the problem of extending state civil jurisdiction over the tribes, that of wholesale fraud directed by local whites against tribal Indians with little access to courts, yet completely denies meaningful federal protection to the tribes, a protection that not only would have been provided through the dependency language of *Kagama*, but was

---

[63] *Felix v. Patrick*, 145 U.S. 317 (1892).
[64] Ibid., 328–9.
[65] Ibid., 322–3. There are obvious reasons for holding that the doctrine of laches does not apply to tribal Indians. The U.S. Supreme Court had held that laches did not stop the Oneida Nation from bringing a lawsuit for deprivation of their lands by the State of New York in the late eighteenth century. *Oneida Nation v. County of Oneida*, 414 U.S. 661 (1974).
[66] *Felix v. Patrick*, 145 U.S. 317 (1892), at 330.
[67] Ibid., 333.

specifically recognized there: "Because of local ill feeling, the people of the States where they are found are often their deadliest enemies" therefore necessitating a federal "duty of protection."[68]

In the wake of *Felix* there was no impediment to state extension of civil jurisdiction into Indian country. Such state action most often was de facto, not even requiring statutes, but simply following from the logic of state sovereignty. Wisconsin, typical of other states, in *Stacy et al. v. LaBelle* (1898) simply held that in the absence of a federal statute or treaty to the contrary, the state had civil jurisdiction over the tribes.[69] Although this case involved a contract between a white trader and a Menominee Indian, the same court in *Deragon v. Sero* extended state jurisdiction to civil actions between reservation Indians, a clear violation of the principles laid down in *Crow Dog*, but a violation ignored by the federal courts.[70] Ironically, the only area where federal courts held back the challenge of state jurisdiction over the tribes was in the area of tribal lands, including allotted lands, holding consistently that the state courts had no jurisdiction over such property.[71] The immense loss of those lands is testimony to the ineffectiveness of this effort.

Jurisdictional problems of liquor control

Since the original Indian Trade and Intercourse Act of 1834, federal control over the Indian liquor trade had been expansive. While the original "Indian country" language was contained in these laws, federal jurisdiction extended beyond the actual borders of Indian country because that jurisdiction concerned subject matter, not geography.[72] This specifically put counties with white populations near reservations under federal jurisdiction.[73] Whites had challenged these laws, making the Indian liquor trade one of the major subjects of nineteenth-century federal Indian law, including four U.S. Supreme Court decisions in the years before *Crow Dog*.[74]

---

[68] *United States v. Kagama*, 118 U.S. 375 (1886), at 384.
[69] *Stacy et al. v. LaBelle*, 75 N.W. 60 (1898). The U.S. Supreme Court in *Williams v. Lee*, 358 U.S. 217 (1959), finally recognized the interconnection between the tribal sovereignty issues of *Worcester* and *Crow Dog* and tribal jurisdiction over civil matters. The case holds that a national policy of encouraging tribal self-government requires that tribal courts have civil jurisdiction over matters arising on the reservation, including jurisdiction over both whites and Indians.
[70] *Deragon v. Sero*, 137 Wis. 276. (1898), is discussed at note 62.
[71] Cohen, *Handbook of Federal Indian Law*, 1st. ed., 379.
[72] The history of the Indian Trade and Intercourse Acts is traced in Francis Paul Prucha, *American Indian Policy in the Formative Years* (Cambridge, Mass.: Harvard University Press, 1962).
[73] *United States v. Forty Three Gallons of Whiskey*, 108 U.S. 491 (1883). This case concerned a local merchant in Crookston, Minnesota, in a county adjacent to the White Earth Reservation.
[74] *United States v. Holliday*, 3 Wall. 407 (1865); *Holden v. Joy*, 84 U.S. (17 Wall.) 1872; *United States v. Joseph*, 94 U.S. 614 (1877); *United States v. Forty Three Gallons of Whiskey*, 108 U.S. 491 (1883).

The history of the legal regulation of the Indian liquor trade has yet to be written. It begins with the recognition that white introduction of liquor into the Indian trade did great violence to the Indian people and produced the huge profits of the fur trade, as cheap liquor was used to purchase fur. The ethnographic accounts of tribal communities broken down by excessive use of liquor are too numerous to ignore.[75] At the same time, these accounts are often racist and paternalistic, describing the tribes wholly as victims and ignoring a literature that suggests that many tribes took a considerable amount of control over this trade and either restrained, or avoided altogether, the ravages of liquor.[76] To the extent that the federal government was free to use the criminal law to regulate the economic activity of its citizens, the use of liquor laws to regulate the fur trade primarily impacted on the activity of frontier whites, not Indians, for the tribes were free to regulate their own trade any way they wished. But the regulation of the liquor trade became a major area of federal criminal law enforcement by the end of the nineteenth century, leading to thousands of criminal charges a year, against both whites and Indians. This effort became a paternalistic intrusion into internal tribal matters.

While the Major Crimes Act did not include selling liquor to Indians as one of its enumerated "major crimes," the prosecution of Indians for intratribal liquor trading had been routine. In *United States v. Shaw-Mux* (1873) a Umatilla Indian was charged in federal court with disposing of spirituous liquor to Moo-los-le-wick. Shaw-Mux's attorney argued that the Indian Trade and Intercourse Act did not apply to crimes between Indians, a position that followed the predominant legal views of the day. Judge Matthew Deady, at the same time he was defeating tribal sovereignty for Alaska's Indians, held Shaw-Mux under federal jurisdiction. Deady's reasoning was straightforward. First, he held that the word "person" includes an Indian, whether "uncivilized" or otherwise, and that the burden is on the defendant to show that he is not intended to be covered by the statute.[77] Second, Deady held that Congress's power to regulate commerce "with the Indian tribes" includes trade between the tribes as well as trade between the tribes and whites.[78] Incredibly, Deady cited an earlier Oregon case, *United States v. Tom*, in which an Indian defendant was convicted of selling liquor to another Indian, arguing that although Tom did not challenge the court's jurisdiction, everybody knew he was an Indian, thus all were aware they were convicting him for a violation of the Indian Trade and Intercourse Act, therefore his

[75] Anastasia Shkilnyk, *A Poison Stronger than Love: The Destruction of an Ojibwa Community*. New Haven, Conn.: Yale University Press, 1985.
[76] Arthur Ray, *Indians in the Fur Trade*. Toronto: University of Toronto Press, 1974.
[77] *United States v. Shaw-Mux*, 27 Fed. Cas. 1049 (1873), at 1049.
[78] Ibid.

status as an Indian must have been thought immaterial.[79] Although this
decision was preposterous, it was never appealed and was cited thereafter
for the proposition that Indians could be prosecuted for violation of the
Indian Trade and Intercourse Act. For example, if "persons" meant Indians
unless specifically excluded, then all federal criminal laws applying to "persons" applied fully to Indians, a position that no one took in 1873. Similarly,
while one might construe the Indian Trade and Intercourse Act to regulate
the trade of the Indian tribes among each other, it simply did not do so in
the mid-nineteenth century. Beyond this, intertribal trade was distinctly
different from intratribal trade, a matter clearly under tribal sovereignty.

After allotment the situation became critical and enforcement efforts increased. Yet these laws were impossible to enforce. Federal laws prohibiting
the introduction of liquor into the Indian country applied to whites on
reservation lands that they owned in fee simple and on which they lived
under the jurisdiction of states often without parallel liquor laws. Huge
quantities of liquor flowed across these lands. Federal authorities made thousands of arrests, but the jurisdictional problems of trying these cases were
enormous.[80] Amid this patchwork system of land tenure coupled with increasingly common mixed-blood intermarriages, federal jurisdiction became
increasingly difficult to uphold. Still, federal courts generally held to the
position that neither mixed-blood status nor allotment ended federal wardship status over the tribes, thus preserving federal jurisdiction. These issues
came together in *Farrell v. United States*. Farrell, a white man, was sentenced
to sixty days in jail and a fine of $100 for selling liquor to Glode La Fram-
boise. He appealed, arguing that since La Framboise was a mixed-blood
and had a white paternal ancestor, he was a white man and that since he
had been allotted lands, he came under state jurisdiction, and the matter of
liquor regulation was a state matter. The circuit court of appeals took the
established federal position, holding La Framboise an Indian and allotment
irrelevant to his dependent status as a ward of the United States.[81]

But the U.S. Supreme Court, following an assimilationist policy and perhaps tired of the large number of minor federal cases these arrests generated,
was prepared to change this law and divest the federal government of its
jurisdiction over the liquor trade on the allotted lands. Heff, a white man,
was sentenced to four months in jail and fined $200 for selling two quarts
of beer to John Butler, a Kickapoo Indian living on an allotment. On appeal

---

[79] Ibid. *United States v. Tom*, 1 Ore. 26 (1853). In *Tom* Oregon Territorial Courts de facto
took jurisdiction over Indian country within the territory. Deady later applied *Tom* to Alaska,
extending territorial jurisdiction to crimes between Indians in Indian country. See Chapter
7. Deady's career is also discussed there.

[80] Cohen, *Handbook of Federal Indian Law*, 1st ed., chap. 17, "Indian Liquor Laws."

[81] *Farrell v. United States*, 110 F. 942 (1901).

Heff made two arguments. First, he argued that allotted Indians were state citizens and under the protection of state laws. Second, he argued that the police powers of the state extended to the regulation of liquor laws within state boundaries.[82]

Although the solicitor general ably represented the traditional position, the U.S. Supreme Court reversed Heff's conviction, holding that the new policy of assimilation, the breaking up of tribal relations, meant that it was contemplated that ultimately federal wardship over the tribes would end and that the conference of citizenship status on allottees necessarily changed that relationship, leaving allotted Indians subject to at least some of the police powers of the states, with the regulation of the distribution of liquor traditionally a part of the states' police power.[83]

It is fair to say that *Heff* caused immense jurisdictional confusion, with both federal and state authorities continuing to exercise jurisdiction over the liquor trade in Indian country. Although *Heff* was decided specifically in the context of the regulation of the liquor trade, its logic extended to other crimes as well, and for the next ten years state and federal authority were in conflict over criminal jurisdiction over allotted Indians in Indian country. As federal jurisdiction over those crimes was generally recognized under the Major Crimes Act, *Heff* became impossible to uphold and was even inconsistent with the Supreme Courts' *Hallowell v. United States* holding that citizenship was irrelevant in a federal prosecution for taking liquor onto an allotment in Nebraska.[84] The case stood for only ten years before the Court reversed itself in *United States v. Nice*. The *Nice* opinion is short, hardly saying more than that *Heff* was a mistake, in the process reiterating traditional dependency doctrine.[85] The federal government was clearly committed to a lengthy legal stewardship over its dependant wards, whether they were allotted small farmers and state citizens or not.

The racial geography of federal Indian law

Crow Dog, Kagama, and the Major Crimes Act continued a legal anomaly created by the Indian Trade and Intercourse Act half a century before: the existence of a distinct federal criminal jurisdiction applicable to several hundred thousand people, provided they (1) were Indians and (2) had committed their offenses within Indian country. Besides the obvious definitional problem of who an Indian is, there were significant factual problems: what is the burden of proof concerning the fact of being an Indian? States and

---

[82] *Matter of Heff,* 197 U.S. 488 (1904).
[83] Ibid., 503–6.
[84] *Hallowell v. United States,* 221 U.S. 317 (1911).
[85] *United States v. Nice,* 241 U.S. 591 (1915).

territories commonly took jurisdiction over cases in Indian country by falsely claiming that one of the parties was a non-Indian. Several of these cases reached the U.S. Supreme Court.

Famous Smith, a Cherokee, was convicted in federal court and sentenced to hang for the murder of James Gentry in the Cherokee Nation. Among Smith's defenses was that the federal court did not have jurisdiction because Gentry was also a Cherokee Indian and not a white man as the prosecution alleged. Contradictory evidence of Gentry's parentage and community relationships was introduced, although the weight of it tended toward proving he was a Cherokee. The judge gave the factual question of Gentry's race to the jury as a matter to be decided in weighing the evidence. As if this were not enough, the court instructed the jurors that they could find an Indian who goes out among white people and abandons tribal relations to be a "jurisdictional citizen" of the United States and under the protection of U.S. law. Not surprisingly, the jury found Gentry a white and Smith guilty of murder.

The U.S. Supreme Court reversed, holding that the trial court should have given the instruction that Gentry was an Indian and that therefore the court did not have jurisdiction. The Court further held that Gentry's race was a matter of law that the government was required to establish to a court, going to its jurisdiction, not a question of fact to be put to the jury. Obviously, there was a substantial danger to the tribes in letting local juries find race as a matter of fact in the process of deciding the guilt or innocence of Indian defendants.[86]

The federal courts decided dozens of cases in which the sole issue was whether the persons involved were Indian or white. Given several hundred years of intermarriage and intertribal migration, many mixed-blooded individuals were involved in crimes. On the one hand, it should have been clear from basic treaty law that tribal status was not primarily a racial status, but a political status, that of being recognized as a member of a tribe.[87] But the *Rogers* case had made it clear that race was clearly an element of tribal status, at least as far as legal recognition by the United States was concerned.[88] In addition, the late-nineteenth-century policy of forced assimilation was specifically aimed at destroying the tribes as political units and undermining the tribal identification of Indian people, making the courts less willing to defer to tribal custom in determining who was an Indian.[89] Finally, the period of the late nineteenth and early twentieth centuries was

[86] *Famous Smith v. United States*, 151 U.S. 50 (1893), at 54–5.
[87] Cohen, *Handbook of Federal Indian Law*, 1st. ed., 2–5.
[88] *United States v. Rogers*, 45 U.S. (4 How.) 567 (1846).
[89] Fred Hoxie, *A Final Promise: The Campaign to Assimilate Indians, 1880–1920* (Lincoln: University of Nebraska Press, 1984).

one of heightened white racism, with explicitly racial factors underlying many areas of national policy.[90] Many federal courts came up with simplistic racial formulas that did violence to the tribes and extended state jurisdiction.

In *Alberty v. United States* and *Lucas v. United States* – in which, not insignificantly, the parties were black – the U.S. Supreme Court undermined its own judgment in *Famous Smith*, handed down just three years before. While *Smith* had held that racial status was a matter of law for the judge and not to be given to a jury, it did not establish clear legal guidelines for determining the race of an Indian. Alberty was a black citizen of the Cherokee Nation who had killed Duncan, the child of a Choctaw man and a black woman, and, like Smith, faced the death penalty for killing an Indian on Cherokee lands. The Supreme Court, doubtlessly influenced by the racism of the day, held that Duncan's racial status followed from his mother, not from his father, defining him as a black.[91] Alberty fell in the same category as Rogers: although a citizen of the Cherokee Nation for its political purposes, he was not an Indian under U.S. law.

Lucas, a Choctaw Indian, fared much better. He was accused of killing Levy Kemp, a black man, in the Choctaw Nation. The trial judge instructed the jury that the federal authorities presumptively had jurisdiction over the case because Kemp, a black man, was presumptively not a Choctaw, going on to give the jury the task of determining whether Kemp was a negro and not an Indian as an essential element of federal jurisdiction.[92] The Supreme Court reversed, saying, in dicta, that if there was any such presumption, it was that a negro living among the Choctaws was a member of the Choctaw Nation. But it held that no presumption should apply and that it was up to the jury to find the legal status of the deceased as a question of fact from the evidence.[93] Thus, the trial court was wrong in instructing that the jury could presume Kemp's legal status as a member of the Choctaw Nation from the fact that his race was apparantly black and that the proper procedure was for the jury to find this fact from evidence presented. But this result defeated Famous Smith and put the matter of tribal jurisdiction back in the hands of a jury that could be strongly opposed to tribal sovereignty.

The matter of race was made even more complex because, as we have seen in *Alberty* and *Lucas*, a racial test had to be operationalized twice: once as to the race of the defendant and once regarding the race of the victim because only crimes between two Indians in Indian country fell under the

[90] On racism in late-nineteenth-century Indian policy, see Richard Drinnon, *Facing West: The Metaphysics of Indian Hating and Empire Building* (Minneapolis: University of Minnesota Press, 1980), pts. 4 and 5.

[91] *Alberty v. United States*, 162 U.S. 657 (1896); *Lucas v. United States*, 163 U.S. 612 (1896).

[92] Ibid., 615.

[93] Ibid., 616.

Major Crimes Act. It is not clear that racial status had the same meaning in both inquiries. Where a white man was the defendant, the courts followed *Rogers*, holding that U.S. citizenship controlled. But in *Nofire v. United States* the court found that a white man in the opposite position, as a victim, could still be considered an Indian, putting the crime under the jurisdiction of the Cherokee Nation and not the federal courts.[94] In this case full-blooded Cherokees had killed Rutherford, a white man who had become a citizen of the Cherokee Nation. A federal court convicted the defendants and they were sentenced to death. But the U.S. Supreme Court reversed, holding that "the courts of the Cherokee nation have jurisdiction over offenses committed by one Indian against another, and this includes . . . both Indians by birth and by adoption."[95] But it was also clear that once one of the parties was established to be non-Indian, the court did not need to inquire further, thus John Stevenson's Chickasaw citizenship was irrelevant as long as the person he killed was white.[96]

Where illegitimacy was not an issue, the status of the father was often controlling. This was especially true when the father was white, and federal courts were quick in such cases to define the offspring as white, not Indian, a policy going back to *Rogers* in denying white men the opportunity to abandon their white racial status and become Indians, even to the second generation.[97] But no policy could be consistently followed, especially in the face of the reality of tribal identification. To the extent that children of Indian women grew up in Indian country and were recognized as members of the tribe, the courts were forced to accord them tribal status because no other result made sense: such persons were Indians in every possible usage. But this does not mean that local jurisdictions did not make every effort to deny tribal status. Wisconsin's *et parte Pero* is illustrative. Pero was the child of a half-breed father and an Indian mother who grew up entirely on the Bad River Reservation and was still prosecuted and imprisoned as a white in state courts only to have a federal court hold, at a habeas corpus proceeding, that he was an Indian and under federal jurisdiction.[98] Similarly, a trial judge in Washington held that Brown, a mixed-blood, could not testify to the race of his parents because that testimony would be "hearsay," a decision that denied Brown the jurisdictional status of an Indian.[99] The Washington Su-

---

[94] *Nofire v. United States*, 164 U.S. 657 (1897).
[95] Ibid., 658. This deference to the jurisdiction of the Cherokee Nation, however, would not have been extended to tribes outside of the Indian Territory.
[96] *Stevenson v. United States*, 86 F. 106 (1898).
[97] *Ex parte Reynolds*, 20 Fed. Cas. no. 11719 (1879).
[98] *Ex parte Pero*, 99 F.2nd (1938).
[99] Hearsay, in the law of evidence, is inadmissible because it is merely what the witness has "heard" rather than what the witness has direct knowledge of. Since its truthfulness cannot be verified, it is seen as unreliable. The state also argued the "best evidence rule" from the

preme Court reversed this ruling, holding that while it could find no prec-edent, testifying as to the race of family members was similar to testifying to their age, a proposition for which there were numerous precedents.[100]

Issues of race and politics became more confused after allotment because racial definitions for determining allotment were sometimes different from those for determining criminal jurisdiction, although once a person was given an allotment as an Indian, that fact was controlling for criminal jurisdictional purposes. It was clear that a person needed some Indian blood for allotment purposes, hence white citizens of Indian tribes received nothing.[101] Beyond this the courts were more liberal than they were for criminal jurisdiction, generally finding that some quantity of Indian blood, coupled with tribal identification, was sufficient, no matter what the source. These same prin-ciples were applied in state attempts to tax mixed-blooded persons after allotment.[102] There is no question that many Indians were detribalized in the allotment process, with federal authorities refusing to recognize tradi-tional tribal rights to determine tribal membership. Such recognition would have been a simpler process than was ultimately applied. But the denial of tribal status was what was primary in this process: Indians as racial minorities could be individually assimilated. There was no place in the United States of the late nineteenth century for the political recognition of tribes or any status that derived from tribal membership.[103]

Cultural geography: inherent limits of the reach of U.S. law into tribal cultures

Related to matters of race were the cultural boundaries separating whites and Indians. The tribal cultures were little known by whites and even less understood. Tribal customs were denigrated and distorted in this highly ethnocentric period of U.S. nationalism. Appreciation for the diversity and complexity of tribal cultures, the tribes' rich religious heritage, and the deep humanity of Indian people was swept aside in an assimilationist vision that dismissed the tribes in the most racist terms as "barbaric" and worse. As white intrusion into Indian country became greater, U.S. law came more in

law of evidence. This rule requires that the best evidence must be introduced if it is available. Since Brown's parents were alive, the state argued that Brown should call them to testify to their race. Here there is an obvious problem with race: what evidence did Brown's parents have of *their* race other than "hearsay."

[100] *State of Washington v. John Rackich*, 12 Ann. Cas. 760 (1912), at 762.

[101] *Drapeau et al. v. United States*, 195 F. 130 (1912).

[102] *Sully et al. v. United States*, 195 F. 113 (1912); *United States v. Higgins*, 103 F. 348 (1900). The courts in these and in many other cases go into great depth describing the family histories of mixed-blood families.

[103] Cohen, *Handbook of Federal Indian Law*, 1st ed., chap. 14, "The Legal Status of Indian Tribes."

confrontation with unknown aspects of tribal cultures. The tribes used this unfamiliarity to shield their traditional cultures (discussed in Chapter 6).

The vast majority of the nineteenth-century laws with which the American nation intended to regulate the lives of tribal Indians failed to do so. Nowhere can this be seen more clearly than in the failure of U.S. criminal law after the Major Crimes Act to reach the killings that occurred on Indian reservations.

BIA annual reports record 147 killings between Indians, 37 killings of whites by Indians, and 28 killings of Indians by whites in the period 1875–1905. By and large, these killings exclude those that occurred during the Indian wars and describe almost entirely individual acts of violence either on a reservation or so immediately adjacent to one as to involve the BIA. Because of the patchwork criminal jurisdiction over reservation tribes, these cases involved tribal, state or territorial, or federal jurisdiction, depending on the actual location of the killing and the tribal membership of perpetrator and victim.[104]

It is clear from other sources that many killings were not included in these reports. Each agent reported what he thought was most important from his jurisdiction – customarily, but not always, matters involving general law and order, especially after the 1880s, when the uniformity of the agents' annual reports shows that BIA officials in Washington expected major criminal cases to be included in those reports, undoubtedly in response to the heightened interest in criminal law that followed from *Crow Dog* and the Major Crimes Act. Nevertheless, this large number of cases is broadly representative of the range of killings occurring on or near reservations and of the dispositions of those killings.

Significantly, for all this legal activity few killings between Indians were formally punished under U.S. law, even after *Crow Dog* and the Major Crimes Act. Of the 147 cases described in the BIA annual reports, fewer than 10 led to criminal convictions in U.S. courts, and only one definitely resulted in an execution.[105] Many other homicides went unsolved, with no evidence

---

[104] Robert N. Clinton, "Criminal Jurisdiction over Indian Lands: A Journey Through a Jurisdictional Maze," *Arizona Law Review* 18 (1976):503, provides a detailed analysis of the complexity of criminal jurisdiction over Indian tribes. Briefly, major criminal offenses between Indians are federal if they occur on a reservation (after the Major Crimes Act and *Kagama*) and state if they occur off the reservation. Minor criminal offenses are tribal, with tribal authorities having concurrent jurisdiction over major crimes with the federal government.

[105] Virtually all Indian murder cases that resulted in convictions were reduced to manslaughter because of evidentiary problems in proving intent. It is likely that this figure slightly underrepresents the actual number of convictions because crimes were usually reported in the year they occurred, and occasionally the accused was being held in prison awaiting trial. Therefore, a trial and sentence in the next year would not be reported. Still, the more common pattern was to hold Indians in prison for a year or more awaiting trial and then drop the case because no witnesses were available.

or witnesses to identify the killer or killers. Those involved in the killings fled, or tribal society surrounded the events with secrecy, refusing to give white authorities evidence or offering only misinformation. The tribes became adept at manipulating U.S. law to protect traditional ways.[106]

Even when suspected killers were brought to trial, the most minimal of formal requirements of evidence could not always be met: no motive, no witnesses, no physical evidence. An unusually large number of intra-Indian homicides were dismissed as "self-defense," often by Indian agents in declining to bring formal charges, but also by white juries.[107]

Indian agents often charged that Indians were uncooperative in legal proceedings or, much worse in their view, that they deliberately lied to obstruct justice and protect each other. An agent at the Siletz agency in Oregon put the matter clearly:

> Much disorder and crime have occurred at this agency during the present fiscal year...it is almost impossible to procure conviction in this agency because of the notorious untruthfullness of the Indians. Most of them openly manufacture evidence, swear to false statements for a financial consideration, friendship or revenge, and in this way defeat justice by raising a "reasonable" doubt in behalf of the prisoner.[108]

Added to the problem of evidence was the logistics of moving witnesses great distances, often making it "not worth the trouble" to prosecute. It is only through great determination that white authorities ever managed to convict any Indian of the murder of another Indian. But the BIA was determined to impose U.S. law on the tribes and, by the end of the century, there were hundreds of federal trials of Indians for offenses under the Major Crimes Act, clearly showing the effort the BIA invested in this goal.[109] The tribes resisted this intrusion.

---

[106] There is no systematic analysis of the process through which the tribes evaded the imposition of U.S. law, yet the noncooperation of the tribes in the BIA courts is legendary. One analysis of this process, and of white attempts to overcome it, is Sidney L. Harring, "The Rich Men of the Country: Canadian Law Comes to the Land of the Copper Inuit, 1914–1930," *Ottawa Law Review* 21 (1989):1.

[107] Of course, a large number of cases of self-defense may well have reflected cultural norms supporting violent interpersonal altercations, which, in turn, would give rise to a large number of legal cases in which "self-defense" was an issue. Or Indian agents, given the racism of the day, may have judged many Indian killings as not worth the trouble of prosecution, especially when the victim was seen as "uncivilized" or unworthy, in the same manner that many intraracial black killings were ignored or mitigated by racist white justice.

[108] BIA, *Annual Report, 1904*, 317. In the cases considered in this book for which a transcript is available, it is clear that Native Americans testified only reluctantly and withheld the most important information. We have already seen this in the discussions of *Crow Dog* and *Bill Whaley*. See also discussion of *Sah Quah* in Chapter 7.

[109] It is impossible to determine exactly how many tribal Indians were prosecuted under the Major Crimes Act. No statistics were kept by the BIA and most of the cases are unreported. By going through the case files of the individual federal district courts, a record of these

Among the most important of these trials was the 1888 prosecution of Bill Whaley, Pancho Francisco, Salt Lake Pete, and Juan Chino for the murder of Juan Baptista at Tule River Reservation in central California.[110] The case rates hardly more than a footnote in standard treatments of Indian law because the federal court rejected out of hand the defense that none of the Indians at Tule River had ever heard of the Major Crimes Act and therefore could not be prosecuted for committing a crime under that law.

Juan Baptista was a medicine man often called on to heal sick and dying people. A number of Yokuts under his care had died. Nevertheless, he was asked to cure Hunter Jim, the chief of the band that Bill Whaley and the others belonged to. For a fee of fifty dollars, he had treated Jim for two weeks, but Jim's condition had not improved. Baptista was both respected and feared for his power, so a council of the tribe, including Bill Whaley and perhaps ten others, decided to offer him fifty dollars more to cure Hunter Jim but to make it clear that they would kill him if he failed. Baptista accepted the money and promised to cure Jim. Two weeks later, Hunter Jim died.[111]

On the night of Jim's death, a tribal council attended by virtually all the men of the tribe decided to kill Baptista. The next morning, the four defendants went to the house of Baptista. Whaley and Francisco, armed with Winchester rifles, shot Baptista five times in the presence of the two others. No attempt was made to conceal the crime or the motivation behind it. To the Yokuts it was a legal witch killing, decided by the council according to traditional law.[112]

The Indian agent, C. G. Belknap, referred the case to state authorities. The four Indians were arrested and lodged in the county jail for a short time, then released because the state court held that it lacked jurisdiction over inter-Indian crimes occurring on the reservation. A year later, in May 1888, a federal grand jury in Los Angeles indicted the four for murder.[113] This was one of the first such prosecutions under the Major Crimes Act, following *Kagama* by little more than two years.

The attorneys for the four, perhaps more interested in framing a test case on jurisdictional grounds than in winning acquittals, erred in stipulating to the facts of the case and relying instead on a legal theory designed to weaken the scope of the Major Crimes Act. This argument centered on a lack of

cases can be made. Many tribal Indians were also sentenced in state courts, where records are less accessible.
[110] *United States v. Bill Whaley et al.*, 37 Fed. 145 (C.C.S.D. Cal. 1888).
[111] Trial transcript, 15–17. This transcript is contained in the case file *United States v. Bill Whaley et al.*, held in the National Archives, Los Angeles Branch.
[112] Ibid., 11–13.
[113] Annual report of C. G. Belknap, Indian Agent at Tule River Reservation, 1887, Record Group 75, National Archives, 14. The indictment was handed down on May 3, 1888, and is contained in the case file.

notice, even though, under the common law, such lack of notice is not a defense in criminal proceedings.[114] Given the large number of witnesses the government had subpoenaed and the openness with which the killing occurred, the attorneys may never have thought that the government could not carry its burden of proof because it could not induce any of its witnesses to give evidence. Visalia Bob, one of the government witnesses, for example, testified that he "heard" they were going to kill Baptista and that he was present at the council meeting but that he was "sleeping" and did not know what happened there. He clearly seems to have known that testifying to what he heard could not incriminate his chief and refused to offer any direct testimony that could have led to a murder conviction. No one knows what the other witnesses might have related because their testimony was limited to the jurisdictional issues left in dispute.[115]

Besides the issue of whether tribal Indians who did not speak English had any notice of the Major Crimes Act, the attorneys also raised again a potentially stronger version of *Kagama* as a test case on the issue of tribal sovereignty. They returned to Crow Dog's defense and argued that Baptista had been duly sentenced to death under the customary law of the Yokuts.[116] Here the attorneys had perhaps the clearest case possible. All the members of a tribe had acted together in a traditional way to punish a traditional offense. It had been twenty-two years since the last tribal witch killing, all of the people present knew of the previous case as precedent, and they acted according to tribal law. But a witch killing was not the right set of facts for inducing the federal courts to limit or modify the scope of the Major Crimes Act or the *Kagama* decision. Good-faith adherence to tribal custom in complete ignorance of U.S. law was no defense to prosecution under the Major Crimes Act. The course set by the Major Crimes Act and approved by the U.S. Supreme Court in *Kagama* was an irreversible statement of U.S. policy.

Bill Whaley, Pancho Francisco, Salt Lake Pete, and Juan Chino were convicted of manslaughter and sentenced to five years in San Quentin. In a show of generosity and in recognition of the unfairness of punishing Indians under a law they had never heard of, President Benjamin Harrison commuted their sentences. Three of the men were released after twenty-three months in prison, but Pancho Francisco had already died in captivity.

While the *Whaley* case was unique, involving the entire leadership of a tribe carrying out traditional justice, there were dozens of similar cases,

---

[114] The stipulation is in the transcript at 7 and 8. In fairness to the defense, this stipulation was a part of an agreement with the prosecution to have the president commute the sentences if the four were convicted. This bargain was not kept. In any case, the defense preserved the most important legal issue – the challenge to the reach of the *Kagama* decision.

[115] Ibid., 25–30.

[116] Ibid., 8, 9.

involving deeply held tribal traditions, that federal courts simply tried as ordinary criminal cases.

Conclusion

Crow Dog offers a prime example of how doctrine can be separated from the core matter of a case.[117] The main holding of the case is that, after one hundred years of living within the limits of the American nation, the tribes maintained their own laws as one attribute of their sovereignty. This had profound implications for the continued existence of Indian tribes in the United States, especially given the critical situation of Indian tribes in the late nineteenth century. But this policy carried within it notions of sovereignty and self-government that were inconsistent with the assimilationist policy prevailing after the early 1880s.

The holding that the Indian tribes had a right to their own law as an attribute of sovereignty was largely lost in both the racism and ethnocentrism of late-nineteenth-century U.S. law, as well as in the jurisdictional scramble that followed allotment. All legal scholars are aware of the richness of the balance that the Constitution struck between state and federal law. But the richness of including in that balance the legal traditions of the Creek, Cherokee, Iroquois, Sioux, Puyallup, Tlingit, and all of the other Indian peoples, while not altogether lost, was seriously weakened not only by the Major Crimes Act, but also by the actions of state and federal policymakers who moved to intervene in tribal life. This assault on the integrity and sovereignty of tribal law and government, combined with the alienation of Indian lands and the full application of a dependency model began the twentieth century with Indian people turning their legal traditions, along with other traditional ways, defensively inward.

The imposition of U.S. law on the Indian tribes was a profoundly legal process, involving hundreds of federal and state court cases immediately following *Kagama* and the Major Crimes Act. There is little doctrinal coherence to these cases, having in common little more than a desire to strip the tribes of their sovereignty. Even basic issues of federalism, all but settled at the time of *Crow Dog*, were reopened, as many federal courts were willing to cede federal power to the states. This time, however, the issue was not whether the federal government enjoyed plenary powers over the tribes. Rather, it was that the federal government could not exercise all the power it had acquired, leaving it willing to cede some of it, particularly in the area of civil and minor police matters, to the states on the basis of efficiency. This legal policy remained in force until *Williams v. Lee* (1959) reversed the federal courts abandonment of tribal sovereignty.

[117] Hoxie, *A Final Promise.*

6

Sitting Bull and Clapox

The application of BIA law to Indians outside of the Major Crimes Act

The legal history from *Crow Dog* to *Kagama* traces a relatively clear path: the U.S. Supreme Court interpreted federal Indian law to permit Congress to impose federal authority on Native Americans. Lower federal courts were then faced with dozens of individual problems calling for the application of this new law in a wide variety of legally, factually, and culturally complex situations.

This activity in the federal courts, however, documents only one aspect of the imposition of U.S. law on the tribes. Most of the intervention into the daily lives of Indian peoples took place beyond the reach of the Major Crimes Act – indeed, even beyond the reach of U.S. law in general – through the BIA's creation of two extralegal institutions. During the same period that the BIA was attempting to enact the Major Crimes Act, it established the "Indian police" in 1879 and the "courts of Indian offenses" in 1883. These were "police" and "courts" in name only. They could claim no legal status under either U.S. or tribal law. Rather, they were designed to perform important social control functions to force assimilation of the tribes under the authority of the BIA, through its Indian agents.

A major object of the imposition of this bureaucratic law at the reservation level was the destruction of tribal culture, including traditional law. Although the "law for the Indians" language of Indian reforms lay behind at least a part of the Major Crimes Act, the BIA resisted any idea of bringing the tribes under the applicable state and federal laws that governed white and black Americans. The BIA's claim that the tribes were not ready for the full responsibilities of U.S. citizenship thinly disguised the range of near-absolute administrative powers that it gave its agents – powers designed to be used to destroy tribal cultures. If private police forces and jails were not enough to enable agents to accomplish assimilation, U.S. Army troops stationed all over the West were at their ready call.

An understanding of the fate of Sioux law following *Crow Dog* requires an analysis of how the Indian police and the courts of Indian offenses were used on the various Sioux reservations and of how the Sioux people came to terms with imposed U.S. law. Not surprisingly, there was great resistance. There is no clearer illustration of the violence of this struggle than the killing of Sitting Bull, perhaps the greatest of the traditional Sioux leaders.

The arrest and killing of Sitting Bull

The killing of Sitting Bull was the culmination of the BIA's long effort to bring him under U.S. legal authority, a status that Sitting Bull, along with many other traditional Sioux refused to accept. The story paints a clear picture of the fate of the law of the traditional Sioux people only seven years after *Crow Dog*.

The Sioux in 1890 were still strong, not acting the part of a defeated, dependent people. They protested the repeated treaty violations by the United States, which had led to their impoverishment, and many of them defied the authority of the Indian agents.[1] In short, they behaved as any sovereign people might when their rights were being denied. Until well into the twentieth century, armed Sioux hunting parties pursued game across Wyoming and Montana, defying the authority of both Indian agents and local law enforcement.[2] Still, impoverishment and demoralization took a heavy toll.

The Ghost Dance, a nationalist and religious movement, offered hope and attracted a large following. Dakota whites found the dances unsettling, but there was no violence.[3] Indian agents, however, feared losing what marginal control they had on these reservations and began a campaign to criminalize the Ghost Dance. Indian dancing, while common, often had been prohibited by the order of agents, and punishing it was among the first objectives of the courts of Indian offenses after 1883.[4]

[1] The process of confining the Sioux to reservations is well documented because of the political attention that the Sioux had gained for the tribes' victory over General Custer and the rich cultural images Sioux warriors held. See, generally, George Hyde, *Spotted Tail's Folk: A History of the Brule Sioux* (Norman: University of Oklahoma Press, 1961); idem, *Red Cloud's Folk: A History of the Oglalla Sioux Indians* (Norman: University of Oklahoma Press, 1937); and the secondary works cited in this chapter.

[2] Barton Voigt, "The Lightning Creek Fight," *Annals of Wyoming* 49, no. 1, (1977):5–21. The legality of these off-reservation hunting parties reached the U.S. Supreme Court in *Ward v. Race Horse*, 163 U.S. 504 (1896). See discussion Chapter 5, the section entitled "State Criminal Jurisdiction After *Corn Dog* and *Kagama*."

[3] The best single study of the Ghost Dance is James Mooney, *The Ghost Dance Religion* (Chicago: University of Chicago Press, 1966). There are numerous nineteenth-century accounts of these events, including T. A. Bland, *A Brief History of the Late Military Invasion of the Home of the Sioux* (Washington, D.C.: Indian Defense Association, 1891); Willis F. Johnson, *The Red Record of the Sioux: Life of Sitting Bull and History of the Indian War of 1890–1891* (New York: Edgewood, 1891); Herbert Welsh, "The Meaning of the Dakota Outbreak," *Scribners* 9 (1891):429.

[4] *Annual Report of the Secretary of the Interior* (Henry M. Teller) 1883, House Ex. Doc. no. 1, pt. 5, vol. 1, 48th Congress, 1st session (Serial Set 2190), pp. xi–xii.

The Ghost Dance heightened the intensity of already deep factional divisions among the Sioux. By the fall of 1890, Washington was receiving a steady stream of complaints from agents whose Indian police were powerless against the dancers. Agent Palmer wrote from Cheyenne River Reservation:

> My police have been unable to prevent them from holding what they call Ghost Dances. These Indians are becoming very hostile to the police. Some of the police have resigned.... Nearly all of these Indians are in possession of Winchester rifles and the police say they are afraid of them, being armed only with revolvers.[5]

Palmer added two weeks later that his police still could not prevent the dances and that the traditionals were killing the reservation's cattle for feasts.[6]

The Ghost Dance had a substantial following by October, but it was threatening only in that it undermined official power. According to Agent Royer:

> As I understand it, I was sent here to advance these people as fast as possible on the road to self support and to suppress as far as it is in my power any inclination toward taking backward steps. The membership of this Ghost Dance is growing steadily each day and has, at this time, over half or nearly two-thirds of the Indian on the reserve [Pine Ridge].
>
> Some of the disadvantages originating from this Ghost Dance is the believers in it defy the law, threaten the police, take their children out of school, and if the police are sent after the children they simply stand ready to fight before they will give them up. When an Indian violates any law the first thing they do is to join the Ghost Dance and then they feel safe to defy the police, the law and the Agent.[7]

The Oglalla, who abandoned the agency at Pine Ridge, informed Royer that they would not give up the Ghost Dance. Indian Police Captain George Sword, according to Royer, had never seen "the Indians worked up in such a pitch of excitement and has never felt such uneasiness himself."[8]

The level of the resistance to the authority of the police can be gauged from a report by Special Agent Reynolds of Rosebud. He acknowledged that the Sioux were starving, yet he had been using the Indian police in attempts to stop them from killing agency cattle:

> They kill cows and oxen, issued to them for breeding and working purposes, and make no secret of doing so and openly defy arrest; they

---

[5] Palmer to BIA Commissioner Morgan, October 11, 1890. This letter, together with other correspondence on the Wounded Knee uprising, is found in the James McLaughlin papers, Record Group 75, National Archives.

[6] Ibid., October 25, 1890.

[7] Indian Agent Royer, Rosebud Agency, to R. V. Belt, Commissioner of Indian Affairs, October 30, 1890.

[8] Ibid.

say that the cattle were issued to them by the Great Father and that it is their right to do as they please with them. This evil is increasing daily. ... During the past week, it was reported to me that two Indians in the Red Leaf camp, on Black Pipe Creek, had killed their cows, for a feast at the Ghost Dance. I sent a policeman to bring them in; they refused to come.

The following day, I sent two officers and eight policemen and they returned without the men, reporting that after they arrived at the camp, they were surrounded by 75 or more Indians, well armed and with plenty of ammunition, and they unanimously agree that an attempt to arrest the offenders would have resulted in death to the entire posse.

On Friday, I sent the Chief of Police, with an interpreter, to explain matters and endeavor to bring the men in. They positively refused to come, and the Chief of Police reports that the matter is beyond the control of the police.[9]

Royer at Pine Ridge reported the same mass resistance:

Orders of constituted authority are daily violated and defied and I am powerless to enforce them.... Yesterday, in attempting to arrest an Indian for violation of regulations, the offender drew a butter knife on the police and in less than two minutes he was reinforced by two hundred Ghost Dancers, all armed and ready to fight. Consequently, the arrest was not made. Today, I received a communication from the offender stating that the policeman who attempted to enforce my order must be discharged.... I was given four weeks to do it. The police are overpowered and disheartened.[10]

At least one agent fared better. Agent Dixon at Crow Creek Reservation had his police arrest nine Ghost Dancers and lock them in the agency jail. This action, however, created another problem: "Agency jail now full. Additional quarters for prisoners needed. Cannot estimate strength of the movement."[11]

Royer at Pine Ridge outdid Dixon: he asked for troops to arrest the leaders and disarm the remainder. He sent the BIA commissioner a list of sixty-four Sioux at Pine Ridge to be arrested, including Red Cloud, the agency chief, who had not taken part in the Ghost Dance movement but was accused of "silently encouraging it." Red Cloud's real offense was that he led the traditional faction and interfered with the agent's control through Royer's handpicked, progressive chief.[12]

Sitting Bull had been a spiritual leader at Little Big Horn but not a war

---

[9] Special Agent Reynolds to Commissioner, November 10, 1890.
[10] Agent Royer to Commissioner, November 13, 1890.
[11] Agent Dixon to Commissioner, November 28, 1890.
[12] Agent Royer to Commissioner Best, November 25, 1890.

chief. The Sioux had a complex leadership structure, with different men leading in overlapping functions, such as warfare, buffalo hunts, and dispute resolution, but whites reduced tribal leadership to a matter of "chiefs." After the army victory and forced reservation settlement of the rest of the Sioux, Sitting Bull led a traditional contingent to Canada to escape U.S. authority. In 1882, he returned from Canada, was briefly interned in a military prison, and settled at the Standing Rock Reservation in 1883. There he lived among Sioux who would not accommodate the white power structure. His brief tour with Buffalo Bill's Wild West Show had made him famous.[13] Because of this prominence, however, both the BIA and the military saw him as the "leader" of the traditional Sioux: "Sitting Bull is high priest and leading apostle of this latest Indian absurdity."[14]

Like other Sioux, Sitting Bull was in defiance of the authority of the local agent, Major James McLaughlin, and his Indian police. McLaughlin described in detail Sitting Bull's activities two months before he was arrested and killed:

> [He gives] frequent feasts and holds councils, thus perpetuating the old time customs amongst the Indians and engrafting with their superstitious nature this additional absurdity of the "new messiah" ... [he] asserts himself a "high priest" here and ... is working upon the credulity of the superstitious and ignorant Indians and reaping a rich harvest of popularity.[15]

In fact, Sitting Bull was practicing his traditional role of medicine man and spiritual leader.

On October 9, Kicking Bear, a medicine man from the Cheyenne River Reservation, had come to Sitting Bull's camp to lead a Ghost Dance. McLaughlin acted at once, with predictable results:

> Upon learning of his arrival there, I sent a detachment of 13 policemen, including the Captain and 2nd Lieutenant to arrest and escort him from the reservation, but they returned without executing the order, both officers being in a "dazed" condition and fearing the powers of Kicking Bear's medicine. Several members of the force tried to induce the officers to permit them to make the arrest but the latter would not allow it but simply told Sitting Bull that it was the Agent's orders that Kicking Bear and his companions should leave the reservation and return to their agency. Sitting Bull was very insolent to the officers and made some threats against certain members of the force.

---

[13] BIA officials despised wild west shows, which, they believed, encouraged traditional Indians to cling to their old ways. The BIA attempted, unsuccessfully, through various regulations to keep Indians from participating in such shows.

[14] BIA, *Annual Report, of the Commissioner of Indian Affairs, 1891*, 329.

[15] McLaughlin to Commissioner, October 17, 1890.

McLaughlin, not about to let Sitting Bull undermine BIA authority, sent two men to notify Sitting Bull that "his insolence and bad behavior would not be tolerated and that the ghost dance must be discontinued." The two soldiers brought back Sitting Bull's message that he was determined to continue his Ghost Dance.[16]

McLaughlin had been urging the arrest of Sitting Bull since July 18. His reasons were direct: "Sitting Bull is a polygamist, libertine, habitual liar, active obstructionist, and a great obstacle in the civilization of those people, and he is so totally devoid of any of the nobler traits of character, and so wedded to the old Indian ways and superstitions that it is very doubtful if any change for the better will ever come over him."[17] The immediate decision to arrest the tribal leader, made by McLaughlin acting with military authorities in early December, was based on information that Sitting Bull and his band had readied their horses to leave the agency and join other Ghost Dancers in the Badlands.[18]

There were at least three choices concerning the form of the arrest: first, the military could move into Sitting Bull's camp and seize him; second, he could be arrested by the Indian police; third, he could be induced to come in and surrender himself. The decision to use the Indian police was deliberately manipulative: "For the salutory effect that it would have upon the Indians," McLaughlin "desired to have the arrest made by the agency police." He added that he wanted the Indians to see a strong show of force. It was also clear to McLaughlin that factional struggle among the Sioux – the same traditional versus progressive strife that had divided Crow Dog and Spotted Tail – would give the arrest of Sitting Bull special meaning to the Indian police.[19] Finally, well after the killing, McLaughlin claimed that he wanted the arrest made without violence and believed that the Indian police had the best chance of accomplishing that end.[20]

---

[16] Ibid., October 9, 1890.

[17] BIA, *Annual Report, 1891*, 329.

[18] This was always the rationale for the arrest of Sitting Bull. See James McLaughlin to Secretary of the Interior, December 30, 1890, in S. House of Representatives, Committee on Military Affairs, "Official Statements and Correspondence Relating to the Arrest and Killing of Chief Sitting Bull", January 6, 1891, H. Rep. 3375 (51-2)(Serial Set 2885), 4.

[19] "The police officers and others of the progressive Indians had been urging me for several weeks to permit them to arrest Sitting Bull and other leaders of disaffection who were engaged in fomenting mischief and participating in Ghost Dances, they, the Ghost Dancers having become so aggressive that the peaceably disposed Indians could not remain in that district or pass through the settlements without being subjected to insults from Sitting Bull or his followers." BIA, *Annual Report, 1890*, 334.

[20] IRA, *Annual Report, 1890*, 5. After the killing of Sitting Bull, McLaughlin spent a great deal of time explaining his actions. He always insisted that the arrest, which led to sixteen deaths, was a "success." Congress conducted its own investigation, and McLaughlin provided numerous explanations of his conduct. See his "Report of the Standing Rock Agency" in BIA,

The Indian police, however, were not to be entrusted alone with such an important task. Moreover, Sitting Bull had a large and angry band. Mc-Laughlin, therefore, decided to back up the Indian police with a full contingent of one hundred regular army troops on a hill a mile away, where they could train Gatling and Hotchkiss guns on Sitting Bull's camp.[21]

The Indian police operation was under the direct control of McLaughlin, who gave the orders and devised the tactics.[22] A force of forty-three Indian police were to capture Sitting Bull at daybreak and make a hurried retreat from the camp. The nearby presence of the army precluded pursuit by Sitting Bull's band. However simple, the plan quickly went awry, raising the question of whether the original motivation was to kill Sitting Bull, rather than capture him.[23]

What happened on the morning of December 15 in Sitting Bull's camp has never been established. The most straightforward version is that the Indian police, under Lieutenant Bull Head and Sergeant Shave Head, broke into Sitting Bull's house and shot him and his deaf son, Crow Foot. This version was reported in the press and believed by many Sioux. McLaughlin, however, vigorously denied it. In his version, Sitting Bull dressed slowly, stalling while his followers mobilized. As he was moved toward the transport wagon, he called out for help. A supporter, Catch the Bear, shot Bull Head, who in turn shot Sitting Bull. In the same instant, Shave Head, on the other side of Sitting Bull, was shot by Strike the Kettle and also shot the old medicine man. Violent hand-to-hand fighting followed, with the 43 Indian police pitted against Sitting Bull's force, estimated by the government at 150 men but probably not much larger than the police force in actual fighting strength. After a few minutes, Sitting Bull's followers retreated into a nearby woods, deserting their camp to the police. At this point, the military force opened fire on the Indian police; the firing was quickly stopped by a white flag, but it showed that the military dominated the action, and did not even care to distinguish between the Indian police and the "hostiles" they were sent to arrest. When the army troops arrived in the camp, the Indian police

Annual Report, 1890, 325–39, and a report he provided to the IRA: "Account of the Death of Sitting Bull" (1891). It is interesting to note that the IRA defended McLaughlin's actions, viewing Sitting Bull as a "troublemaker" who interfered with plans to assimilate the Sioux.

[21] Colonel E. G. Fechet, who was in command of the military force backing up the Indian police, wrote an account of the killing, "The Capture of Sitting Bull," South Dakota Historical Society, *Collections* 4 (1908):191.

[22] Major M. F. Steel, "Buffalo Bill's Bluff," South Dakota Historical Society, *Collections* 9 (1918):474.

[23] "The enthusiasm among the Indian police to make the arrest was so great that they neglected to take the wagon along, but went on horseback and rode boldly through the camp and up to Sitting Bull's house, where they dismounted just as daybreak began to appear." BIA, *Annual Report, 1890*, 335.

formed into columns and saluted. Sixteen people had died.[24] McLaughlin, responding to criticism of this operation, defended it as a fine example of police work, showing the loyalty of the Indian police.

The Indian police

The role of the Indian police in the killing of Sitting Bull reveals the contradictory nature of the force. The Indian police wore the uniform of army privates and had their roots in the army's Indian scouts. In the Sitting Bull killing, they acted as a front for the regular army, yet the form of the action was quite different from that of a military action. The event had been cast as a police action, with an arrest for an unnamed offense replacing the Indian battle. Indian warfare had been brought within the legal framework of U.S. society. Congress awarded medals to Bull Head, Shave Head, and their entire force and voted pensions for the widows of police who died in the action. These men epitomized the devotion to duty and obedience to authority that Indian agents came to laud in the Indian police. The incident persuaded Congress to support higher salaries for the Indian police and, from that time, the institution of the Indian police, although weak and ineffective, was introduced with renewed strength on reservations across the West.[25]

Very little is known about the motivations of the individuals who became Indian police officers. Their job was a difficult one, carried out in a complex cultural context. Normally, the men spent only a few days a month at the agency, a period that included standard military drill. The remainder of the time they were posted in the camps, where they had a broad range of administrative duties as well as police work to perform. In that capacity, they were often the only representatives of the BIA within long distances. Working in such isolation required a great deal of strength and self-discipline. The job was perhaps best described by Captain George Sword, long-time chief of the Indian police at Pine Ridge:

> We have a good deal of trouble among our people to get them to do what the government wishes them to do. I am in the service of the government. No matter what comes before me, I am willing to go ahead and do whatever the Government desires me to do.[26]

[24] BIA, *Annual Report, 1890*, 334–7; IRA, "Account of the Death of Sitting Bull" (Philadelphia, 1891), 5–7.

[25] BIA, *Annual Report, 1890*, 337, 338.

[26] U.S. Congress, Senate, "Report on the Condition of the Sioux and Crow Indians," 48th Congress, 1st session, Report no. 283 (1883). The Indian agents at Rosebud, Pine Ridge, and Standing Rock appear to have organized an effort to induce Congress to provide more support for the Indian police. At each agency they had numerous Indian police testify to essentially the same facts: that they worked very hard for low pay and that they deferred

The Indian police were often deeply involved in tribal factionalism on the side of the progressives. A significant part of their work centered on undermining traditional Sioux customs and policing and controlling the traditional Sioux out in their camps. Although this police role under white supervision necessarily tended toward the progressives' position in factional struggles, the original intention of the agents was to have police from all tribal factions, indeed even to overrepresent traditionals among the police in an effort to co-opt the most dangerous and threatening bands and bring them under the agent's authority. Often, important police jobs were offered to traditionals. Crow Dog, for example, had been appointed captain of the Indian police at Rosebud as part of an effort to incorporate the traditionals into the agent's governing system.[27]

Any attempt to incorporate all of the factions into the police had to fail, given the basic contradiction between traditional Sioux society and the work the police were routinely asked to do. Initially, both Spotted Tail at Rosebud and Red Cloud at Pine Ridge, the two most powerful Sioux chiefs, had accepted the Indian police idea, but only so long as the force would be under their personal control, as would be consistent with Sioux custom. All of the Plains warrior societies had well-established tribal traditions, and the Indian police could have been an extention of this tradition. But the agents insisted on keeping the police function under agency control. There was a struggle over this issue at both agencies in the early 1880s, and both chiefs lost.[28]

At Pine Ridge, Red Cloud attempted to take revenge by urging young men not to join the police force. The agent, Dr. Valentine R. McGillycuddy, reacted by cultivating a new leadership by supporting the progressive chief, Young Man Afraid of His Horses, who, in turn, suggested Man Who Carries the Sword as captain of police. George Sword, as he came to be known, was a young progressive who had also proven himself as a warrior by raiding enemy horse herds. When Sword had trouble recruiting the fifty young men that the Indian police force was authorized to have, McGillycuddy provided him with steers for a barbeque to attract potential members. The traditionals raided the event and made off with the beef. McGillycuddy provided more beef and suggested that Sword reschedule the event in a more isolated

completely to the authority of the agent. The quotation here is one of well over a dozen, all emphasizing loyalty to the government, although it must be clear that this authority was available to the Indian police only through the Indian agent. Sword's testimony was reprinted in BIA, *Annual Report, 1888*, xxviii.

[27] Hyde, *Spotted Tail's Folk*, 312.

[28] For Rosebud Reservation, see ibid., 319–21. The origins of the Indian police at Pine Ridge are discussed in Julia T. McGillycuddy, *McGillycuddy: Agent: A Biography of Dr. Valentine McGillycuddy* (Stanford: University of California Press, 1941), chap. 9. Both situations are discussed in William T. Hagan, *Indian Police and Judges: Experiments in Acculteration and Control* (New Haven, Conn.: Yale University Press, 1966), esp. chap. 5.

location. Sword acquired his full complement, for reasons that are not difficult to comprehend. The regular job, the money, and the power provided
clear incentives to police work on a reservation with no opportunities for
carrying on traditional hunting patterns and no other outlets for young men.
There was also a political rationale for progressive Sioux: if progress meant
adopting white ways and assimilating, the Indian police could speed along
that work and through that logic benefit the tribe.[29]

The Indian police also had a negative impact on many traditional aspects
of Sioux society, including the application of tribal law, and for that reason
met continuous resistance. The police constituted a strong force, with its
members routinely interfering in all phases of tribal life. This level of intervention was promoted by a code of agency law promulgated for the courts
of Indian offenses that was largely directed at Sioux customs.[30] It was also
encouraged by the direct rejection of the force of tribal law by Indian police,
who looked to the agents for their source of authority.

This deferral to agent authority is seen most clearly in the killing of Sitting
Bull, but there are other examples. Spotted Tail, a northern Cheyenne, stole
twenty-two Sioux horses from the band of Young Man Afraid of His Horses
and fled toward the northern Cheyenne agency with three warriors. Captain
Sword and nine Indian police gave chase and surrounded them. Spotted
Tail refused to surrender and threw off his blanket as a sign of defiance.
Sword shot him and delivered his corpse at the agency. Tribal elders, meeting
in council in the same tradition that mediated Crow Dog's case, decided
that the killing was unjustified and ordered Sword to pay fifteen ponies to
the family of the man he killed. Sword refused to pay and was backed by
McGillycuddy. Sioux tribal law was based on a common system of social
obligations, with general recognition of the power of chiefs and elders. It
could not survive overt conflict in a factional struggle induced by whites that
created two overlapping bases of power. When directly posed against the
power of the agent and his police, the traditional norms gave way. This does
not mean that those traditions were lost; rather, the tribal laws, like other
traditional ways, were driven underground.[31]

An agent, like George Sword, backed by fifty Indian policemen enjoyed
a great deal of power. Without that personal armed force, the agent had
little control. Yet as the killing of Sitting Bull demonstrates, the Indian police
did not guarantee effective police action, even though that incident at the

[29] McGillycuddy, *McGillycuddy*, 113.
[30] The annual reports of the Commissioner of Indian Affairs make it clear that the destruction
of customary law was a major objective of the courts of Indian offenses. See BIA, *Annual
Report, 1883*, xxi.
[31] Hagan, *Indian Police and Judges*, 93–4.

time was favorably compared with the military massacre at Wounded Knee, where 262 Ghost Dancers were killed. Agent McLaughlin best summed up the result of such actions: the killings would have a "salubratory effect" on the Sioux.[32]

The willingness of the Indian police to arrest and shoot Sitting Bull was the ultimate reflection of the conflict between tribal law and the imposition of U.S. law. This act was carried out in the context of a factional struggle between the progressive and traditional factions.[33] The Indian agents were aware that they had seized traditional tribal police structures and converted them to their own use. McGillycuddy was among the first to recognize this connection:

> The Indians generally recognize the police authority, for, from time immemorial, there has existed among the Sioux and other tribes, native soldier organizations, systematically governed by laws and regulations. Some of the strongest opposition encountered in endeavoring to organize the police force . . . was from these native organizations, for they at once recognized something in it strongly antagonistic to their ancient customs, namely a force at the command of the white man opposed to their own.[34]

Courts of Indian Offenses

What law had Sitting Bull broken? What law existed on the reservations after *Crow Dog*? Indian agents in the Dakota Territory had long believed that they had the power to arrest Sioux warriors for the general offense of "troublemaking." The Major Crimes Act of 1885 had no impact on such actions. Sitting Bull was never accused of any of the seven enumerated offenses that would have put him under the jurisdiction of federal criminal law.

There is no need to speculate on Agent McLaughlin's motive in ordering the arrest of Sitting Bull. He laid out the reasons for his superiors in Washington when he requested permission to make the arrest: in order to protect and encourage the agricultural pursuits of the Sioux, it was necessary to smash the Ghost Dance and all vestiges of traditional society, as well as to punish "evil doers and leaders of disaffection." Reservation agents, by using the law to punish Indians for nothing more than carrying on tribal traditions, could encourage the accommodationist activity of progressives. At the same time, some moderation in making arrests would

[32] James McLaughlin to Indian Rights Association. Quoted in IRA, *Annual Report*, 1890, 5.
[33] Doane Robinson, "A History of the Dakota or Sioux Indians," South Dakota Department of History, *Collections* 2 (1904):481–2.
[34] Hagan, *Indian Police and Judges*, 94, n. 5.

strengthen the legitimacy of the agents by making them and the government appear magnanimous.[35]

Under existing rules of the agency courts, first formally adopted in 1883 but previously informally applied, the agents had full authority to lock Indians in jail for a variety of "offenses." A major goal for these courts was the destruction of tribal law:

> Under date of April 10, 1883, the then Secretary of the Interior gave his official approval to certain rules prepared in this office for the establishment of a Court of Indian Offenses at each of the Indian agencies. ... It was found that the longer continuance of certain old heathen and barbarous customs, such as the sun-dance, scalp-dance, war-dance, polygamy, &c., were operating as a serious hindrance to the efforts of the Government for the civilization of the Indians. It was believed that in all the tribes many Indians would be found who could be relied upon to aid the Government in its efforts to abolish rites and customs so injurious and so contrary to civilization; hence these rules were formulated, looking toward the ultimate abolishment of the pernicious practices mentioned.
>
> There is [no special law authorizing the establishment of such a court] but authority is exercised under the general provisions of law giving this Department supervision of the Indians. The policy of the Government for many years past has been to destroy the tribal relations as fast as possible, and to use every endeavor to bring the Indians under [control] ...without such a court, many Indian reservations would be without law or order, and the laws of civilized life would be utterly disregarded.[36]

Violators of these offenses were brought into courts whose judges were appointed by and served at the pleasure of the agents. The judges were occasionally police officers, but often they were influential chiefs. The degree of apparent assimilation was a major criteria in the selection of judges, and agents' reports are replete with descriptions of them as "christian," "wearing white man's clothing," or "monogamous." The agents placed this legal process in the hands of progressive Sioux, factionalizing the Sioux legal system.[37] These legal rules were not a part of the corpus of criminal law.

---

[35] BIA, *Annual Report, 1890,* 332. The process that McLaughlin describes bears striking parallels to what Douglas Hay has argued was the primary function of eighteenth-century English criminal law. See his "Property, Authority and the Criminal Law," in Douglas Hay et al. (eds.), *Albion's Fatal Tree: Crime and Society in Eighteenth-Century England* (New York: Pantheon, 1975), 17–63.

[36] BIA, *Annual Report, 1883,* xxi.

[37] The BIA annual reports for the 1880s and 1890s contain short biographical statements about dozens of Indian court judges. The overwhelming majority are characterized as "progressive," and some are even claimed to support the alienation of Sioux lands occurring through the Dawes Act.

Rather, a single case, *United States v. Clapox* (1888), upheld the Indian courts as a valid exercise of the administrative power of the BIA.

Minnie, an Umatilla Indian, had been seized by the Indian police and locked in the reservation jail to await trial for the offense of adultery. Adultery was not a crime under the Major Crimes Act or any federal law, nor was it a violation of Umatilla tribal law. Rather, it was a rule promulgated for the Umatilla by the BIA, and its enforcement was ordered by the Indian agent. A number of Minnie's friends, including Clapox, attacked and "unlawfully and with force of arms" broke open the jail and set her free. Upon their arrest, all challenged the legality of the courts of Indian offenses. These "courts," they argued, were "not the constitutional courts provided for in Section 1 Article 3 [of the Constitution] which only Congress has the power to establish."[38]

Judge Matthew Deady of the federal district court in Oregon held that the Umatillas, by treaty, had agreed to submit to any rule that might be prescribed by the United States for their government, obviously including "the power to organize and maintain this Indian court and police, and to specify the acts or conduct concerning which it shall have jurisdiction." The courts of Indian offenses were not "Constitutional courts" within the meaning of Article 1, section 3, "but mere educational and disciplinary instrumentalities by which the government of the United States endeavor[s] to improve and elevate the condition of these dependent tribes to whom it sustains the relation of guardian." In fact, the reservation itself is in effect a school, and the Indians are gathered there, under the charge of an agent, "for the purpose of acquiring the habits, ideas, and aspirations that distinguish the civilized from the noncivilized man."[39] This opinion is still cited to uphold the constitutionality of the courts of Indian offenses. *Clapox* carried the plenary power doctrine of *Kagama* to the obscene conclusion that any tribal Indian could be held in jail at the whim of the agent with no due process whatever, not only because such power was necessary to "civilize" Indians, but also because the tribes had submitted to U.S. government authority and therefore had to accept anything that "authority" offered. By denying that a jail was an institution of punishment and holding it out, at least for tribal Indians, as a "school" meant that it was a fitting place to keep any tribal Indian who needed to "learn" to defer to white civilization. After *Clapox* no cases challenged the legality of the courts of Indian offenses.[40]

[38] *United States v. Clapox*, 34 Fed. Rep. 575 (1888).
[39] Ibid., 577.
[40] There are few statistics on the agents' use of arbitrary imprisonment to punish reservation Indians. This was done on an ad hoc basis, in makeshift jails often also serving as barns or

The courts of Indian offenses were not formal courts but merely disciplinary bodies. The BIA repeatedly acknowledged as much in its annual reports. The Board of Indian Commissioners in 1891 reduced them to the status of "so-called courts of Indian Offenses," noting that they were "more in the nature of courts martial than civil courts, and practically registered the decrees of the Indian agent."[41]

After years of trying to persuade Congress to pass specific legislation to authorize the courts, the BIA found solace in one sentence of the Indian Appropriation Act of June 29, 1888: "For compensation of judges of Indian courts, at such rate as may be fixed from time to time by the Secretary of the Interior, five thousand dollars, or as much thereof as may be necessary."[42] The 1890 annual report announced, "During the past two years, the reservation tribunals known as 'Courts of Indian Offenses' have been placed upon a quasi-legal basis for the pay of the judges of such courts."[43]

Among the Sioux, the reservation courts were established slowly and were not very effective, which implies a degree of resistance. The reports of the agents indicate that, before 1890, only the Standing Rock and Cheyenne River courts were fully functioning, although four other agencies had courts in operation: Crow Creek, Lower Brule, Pine Ridge, and Yankton. A report by Agent McLaughlin describes the general run of the Standing Rock court's business in 1890:

> There are 91 cases brought before the court during the year of a criminal nature: adultery, 8; assault, 9; attempt at rape, 10; taking second wife, 3; taking second husband, 2; elopement with another man's wife, 3; desertion of wife and family by husband, 7; desertion of husband and family by wife, 3; seduction, 1; resisting arrest by police, 6; abusive language, 2; maiming cattle, 3; malicious lying, 1; evil speaking, 1; wife beating, 1; offering insult to married women, 4; selling rations, 2; drunkenness, 2; larceny, 4; family quarrel, incompatibility, etc., 19. The punishment imposed was chiefly imprisonment in the agency guard house at hard labor during the day, from 10 to 90 days, according to the nature of the offense.[44]

McLaughlin went on to describe the character of the judges: John Grass, the head chief of the Blackfeet Sioux; Gall, who "bears a good general

sheds. There was no central reporting process, but it is clear that Indians were regularly locked up on many reservations.
41 Hagan, *Indian Police and Judges*, 110, n. 5.
42 BIA, *Annual Report, 1889*, 27.
43 BIA, *Annual Report, 1890*, p. lxxxiii.
44 Ibid., lxxxvi. It should be remembered that many of the most traditional Sioux at Standing Rock lived beyond the reach of the police.

character, favors the education of Indian children, and a progressive Indian in all respects"; and Standing Soldier, also "in favor of education and a progressive Indian." All were individually described as "wearing citizen's dress and conforming to the white man's ways." McLaughlin had just replaced the police officers who had been serving as judges and was proud of this step toward greater legality at Standing Rock.[45] Ironically, three years earlier, two of these judges had tried Sitting Bull for a quarrel with another man that had led to drawn weapons, and Sitting Bull had submitted to their authority by turning over his stone warclub.[46]

During the same year, the Cheyenne River Agency reported about 120 trials and 85 convictions for offenses similar to those handled at Standing Rock. The agent noted that the courts met regularly, tried to follow established procedures, and kept a record in the Sioux language. The penalties were prison terms of three days to three months, "no fines being imposed." The Crow Creek Reservation reported 20 cases.[47]

The opposite position among Sioux reservations was taken at Rosebud, which did not create a court of Indian offenses until well into the twentieth century. Agent James Wright laid out the reason in 1883, when he passed up the first opportunity to appoint a court. The reason did not change over the years:

> No nominations for judges of the Court of Indian Offenses have yet been submitted by me. I have studied over the matter, have talked it over with my Indians, and have not been able to select suitable persons for the position. From Indian standpoint, the offenses as set forth, and for which punishment was provided, are no offenses at all, and I doubt if one could be found willing to punish another for the offenses set forth in the rules governing such, and if willing or inclined would have the moral courage to do so. In my judgement, the checking of the so-called Indian offenses must be gradual, and done, if at all, by the agent.[48]

The limited language of the *Crow Dog* decision that held that the Sioux had a right to their own law did not give substance to that right. The administrative criminalization of many traditional practices, the dividing up of tribal lands, and the destruction of the power of the traditional chiefs undermined the same structures that provided the social base for tribal law.

---

[45] Ibid., lxxxvi.
[46] Stanley Vestal, *New Sources of Indian History, 1850–1891* (Norman: University of Oklahoma Press, 1934), 148–9. This altercation was a part of the factional struggle at Standing Rock.
[47] BIA, *Annual Report, 1890*, 46, 47.
[48] BIA, *Annual Report, 1883*, 42.

Indian court reform

The BIA issued new regulations in 1891 for the operation of the agency courts. The emphasis was on increased legality; hence, the most important change was formalization of procedure. The original regulations of 1883 had sufficiently broad sweep so that no greater substantive detail was needed, with one exception. The general incorporation of the misdemeanor codes of the states provided the Indian courts with a great deal of breadth, but the offense of vagrancy was specifically included to apply to Indian conditions: "If any Indian refuses or neglects to adopt habits of industry, or engage in civilized pursuits or employments, but habitually spends his time in idleness or loafing, he shall be deemed a vagrant."[49]

The BIA regulations of 1891 responded directly to the Indian reformers' demand for "law for the Indians." Henry Thayer and other reformers had long campaigned for state law to be applied to Indians as a necessary step in assimilating the tribes into white American life. The informal incorporation of many misdemeanors through the courts of Indian offenses held the Indians accountable for substantive violations of minor state laws but still left the BIA with full control through its agent-dominated court structure.[50]

Additional care was also taken with procedures to make the courts more closely resemble the form of other U.S. courts. Each reservation was divided into districts, with district judges sitting regularly to make sentencing more localized and efficient. A "court of general term," composed of all the district judges, was to meet less often to hear appeals from the district courts. A clerk was appointed to record the proceedings. Forms of practice and pleadings were to conform as nearly as possible to the courts of the state or territory in which the reservation was located. The agents had the power to compel witnesses to attend court and to order the police to enforce court orders.[51]

This emphasis on legal formality makes it clear that the Indian courts were heading toward the full incorporation of Indians into local state law,

---

[49] The 1891 codification listed six clear categories of Indian offenses, granted the courts power over state misdemeanors, and gave them the right to solemnize marriages (but not to grant divorces). The six categories were dances, polygamous marriages, practices of medicine men, destruction of the property of another Indian, immorality (prostitution), and intoxication or the introduction of intoxicants. BIA, *Annual Report, 1891*, 29–30.

[50] The commissioner of Indian affairs directly acknowledged the position of Thayer but argued that the new rules were the best compromise that could be made at the time. BIA, *Annual Report, 1891*, 25–7. Indian reformers opposed these courts on the ground that they denied the Indians due process.

[51] Ibid.

the position held by reformers of Indian law and the one eventually adopted in many states.[52] At the same time, the new regulations were primarily an exercise in form, not substance: the BIA retained full control of the courts and their work. The judges were appointed by the agents and could be removed at will. Each verdict could be modified by the agent. Hence, the courts were in no way "Indian courts" or even "tribal courts." What was applied was not "Indian law" but rather a set of BIA rules. Their purpose was to promote the assimilation of the Sioux by providing order on the reservations and by punishing traditional practices in order to force their abandonment. In fact, the traditional practices were driven underground, but the political power of the traditionals was broken in the process.

The courts of Indian offenses, in spite of their official backing by the BIA, never reached their full potential as social control institutions. The rules for Indian courts were revised twice, in 1891 and 1904, but the substance remained essentially that of the original 1883 rules. The thrust of the two revisions was in the direction of legality, focusing on improving procedures. Congress never gave the courts more recognition than it did in the renewal of the original 1888 appropriation. Hearings were held on the question several times, most extensively in 1926, but the courts failed to generate much support outside of the BIA. Indian reformers wanted to extend full rights and responsibilities to Indians, which meant putting reservation Indians under the authority of regular state law. The traditional Indians and some white allies objected to the arbitrary power of the agents and their hand-picked accommodationist judges and favored the preservation of tribal law. This latter policy won a number of adherents in 1926, but in time mainly to help the Pueblo and Navajo of the Southwest.[53] This does not mean that Sioux law was "lost." Rather its social base was undermined in the transformation of Sioux society, limiting its use to traditional people who kept their law from the eyes of the agent and his police.

The courts never achieved wide acceptance even on the reservations where they were adopted. No more than 50 of the more than 120 western reservations had such courts for any length of time. Many agents never bothered to create them.[54] In part agents did not need to because the rules for the

[52] Currently, the states have criminal jurisdiction over reservation Indians in all but eleven states, chiefly confined to the Great Plains and the Southwest. See Robert N. Clinton, "Criminal Jurisdiction over Indian Lands: A Journey Through a Jurisdictional Maze," *Arizona Law Review* 18 (1976):503, at 564–9, esp. the chart of criminal jurisdiction beginning at 577.

[53] For a variety of perspectives on the courts as they developed by 1926, see "Reservation Courts of Indian Offenses," hearings before the Committee on Indian Affairs, U.S. House of Representatives (Washington: Government Printing Office, 1926).

[54] As recently as 1978 a study of tribal courts financed by the American Bar Foundation could

courts had no more legal status than the BIA's general power to discipline and educate Indians. Each agent had exactly the same power with or without paying attention to the legal forms.

It is also clear that Indians often refused to participate in these institutions. Agent Charles Porter of the Hoopa Reservation reported it impossible to organize either Indian police or courts. Citing that "numerous internal quarrels and tensions" would mean that tribal issues would permeate these institutions and also that he could not get the necessary "unquestioned obediance" from the Hoopa, Porter dismissed the idea of tribal police as "impractical." The same concerns extended to the tribal courts, but to these Porter added that the "judicial character" was totally absent in Indians, also meaning that tribal prejudices and factionalism would pervade the court's decisions.[55]

Significantly, the legal status of the courts of offenses never went beyond the definition in *Clapox* and the congressional appropriations bill of 1888. In 1956, the circuit court of appeals for the Eighth Circuit upheld the legality of the courts, relying on no other basis than this plus the BIA Authorization Act of 1921, which provided for the expenditure of moneys "for the employment of inspectors, supervisors, superintendents, clerks, field matrons, farmers, physicians, Indian police, Indian judges, and other employees."[56]

The writ of habeas corpus and reservation Indians: the legal significance of *Standing Bear v. Crook*

During the early plenary power period when the tribes were being forced onto reservations to be held there until "civilized," the legal rights of Indians were not of concern to U.S. government authorities. The simplest form of social control was that the Indian agent, often through the military authorities that were usually near at hand, exercised extralegal authority to detain and punish Indians, to seize and hold rebellious Indians until they became cooperative. While the Indian police and the Courts of Indian Offenses were

not enumerate them, estimating their number at "60 to 120," depending on the definitions of "courts" and "reservations." Samuel J. Brakel, *American Indian Tribal Courts: The Costs of Separate Justice* (Chicago: American Bar Foundation, 1978), 5. The Indian Reorganization Act of 1934 (25 USC, sec. 476) gave individual tribes the authority to establish a wide range of institutions for the purpose of self-government, including "tribal courts." Gradually these tribal courts have succeeded the courts of Indian offenses. The tribal courts are distinct from the earlier ones in that they respond to the political process of tribal government rather than being guided by the authority of the Indian agent. At the same time, these tribal governments have often been very conservative, and the law applied by the tribal courts is strongly influenced by the courts of Indian offenses.

[55] BIA, *Annual Report, 1883*, "Reports of Indians in California," p. 13.
[56] *Iron Crow v. Oglalla Sioux Tribe of Pine Ridge Reservation*, 231 Fed. 2nd. 89 (1956), at 95.

convenient masks for the agent's unchecked exercise of authority, those institutions were completely an extension of the agent's power, and the agent was free to use such institutions or to ignore them. While all reservations had some form of police – the agent could not function without his capacity to use force – most lacked functioning courts of Indian offenses. The agent simply jailed whoever he wanted on his personal authority or asked the military to do so. There can be no question that many thousands of Indians were so detained for offenses ranging from murder to resisting allotment.[57]

It is doubtful that many lawyers in the United States in 1879, other than U.S. Attorney G. M. Lambertson of Omaha, believed that Roger Taney's infamous *Dred Scott* opinion stood for any proposition of U.S. law.[58] Still, Lambertson argued, on the basis of *Dred Scott*, that an Indian, not being a person, could not bring a habeas corpus action.

In fact, any noncitizen of the United States who falls into the custody of U.S. authorities has the right to challenge the legality of that custody through the writ of habeas corpus. And so the U.S. Supreme Court held in the case of Standing Bear. In actual practice, that right was not so obvious to government authorities, either before or after that decision, for the whole idea that the writ reached a reservation Indian undermined BIA authority there.[59]

Confusion over the availability of the writ of habeas corpus should not have followed merely from the contradictions inherent in federal Indian policy. The sovereignty model would have automatically extended the writ to the members of tribes held in government custody, just as foreign nationals enjoyed that right; the dependency model, while it left individual Indians in a much more ambiguous status, not unlike such other classes of dependents as children, paupers, and the mentally ill, still left Indians, like all other dependent categories of people, with full recourse to the writ.[60]

Complicating the issue was the argument that the military had authority over Indians because they remained within the United States after their defeat in the Indian wars as a conquered people subject to military discipline. No reported decision upholds this legal status. Moreover, there was a fiction that the tribes had voluntarily sold their lands in the East and had voluntarily relocated on reservations in the West under the protection of the U.S.

---

[57] See note 40.

[58] *Scott v. Sandford*, 60 U.S. (19 How.) 393 (1857). The case was rarely raised after the Civil Rights Acts. For a discussion of the application of the case after the 1870s, see Don Fehrenbacher, *The Dred Scott Case: Its Significance in American Law and Politics* (New York: Oxford University Press, 1978), 580–7.

[59] *United States ex rel. Standing Bear v. Crook*, 25 Fed. Cas. 695 (C.C.D. Neb., 1879).

[60] William F. Duker, *A Constitutional History of Habeas Corpus* (Westport, Conn.: Greenwood, 1980), is the major legal history of the writ in the United States. It contains no mention of any cases involving Native Americans.

government; the army was the institution that held the formal duty of that protection until the administration of President Ulysses Grant.[61]

The army exercised extensive extralegal authority over the tribes. A number of military trials of Indians were held, and a number of Indians were executed by military authority, but no court ever passed on the legality of these trials and executions.[62] The military also held a number of Indians in jail, sent there under the authority of Indian agents. Crow Dog had been arrested and sent to Fort Niobara, a process repeated with others involved in intra-Indian killings in the 1870s and 1880s. All of these actions occurred outside of legal authority.

Until *ex parte Standing Bear*, no Indian ever tested the legal status of such government action. The case developed from a set of facts typical of white exploitation of Indians in the United States of the mid-nineteenth century. Standing Bear and his Ponca people lived as farmers on a reservation in South Dakota, but local whites, clamoring for Indian land, forged an alliance with corrupt politicians and sold the Ponca lands, removing the Ponca to the Indian Territory in 1876. Standing Bear resisted from the outset, claiming that the Ponca owned their land in South Dakota. Visiting the Indian Territory to inspect the proposed new reservation, Standing Bear found the land "stoney" and not fit for cultivation. Nevertheless, the tribe was forcibly resettled there. The Poncas decided to return to South Dakota and, in the dead of winter, set out with no money and no food.[63] They made it as far as Fort Omaha, where they were taken into custody by the U.S. Army under General George Crook.[64]

The event attracted the attention of Indian reformers. Thomas Henry Tibbles, an Omaha editor, published a number of accounts of the Poncas' plight that were reprinted in newspapers across the country. General Crook himself argued that he did not have the authority to hold Standing Bear and

---

[61] Robert Wooster, *The Military and United States Indian Policy, 1865–1903* (New Haven, Conn.: Yale University Press, 1988).

[62] A complete listing of these trials and executions is impossible. The army tried 200 Sioux warriors after the Minnesota Sioux War, executing 18. Captain Jack and four of his aides were tried and hanged after the Modoc War. At least one Tlingit was tried and hanged at Wrangell, Alaska, in 1872. Finally, hundreds of Apaches were detained by the military following the Apache Wars.

[63] Raymond Powers, "Why the Northern Cheyenne Left Indian Territory in 1878: A Cultural Analysis," *Kansas Quarterly* 3 (Fall 1971):72–81, analyzes a parallel action from an ethnohistorical perspective. On the historical context of the original Ponca removal to the Indian Territory, see Earl W. Hayter, "The Ponca Removal," *North Dakota Historical Review* 6 (July 1932):262–75.

[64] For a general background of the case, see Thomas Henry Tibbles, *The Ponca Chiefs: An Account of the Trial of Standing Bear* (Lincoln: University of Nebraska Press, 1972). This is a reprint of a tract Tibbles published in 1879 to gain public sympathy for the Ponca. For more information on the activities of Tibbles and his group, see Stanley Clark, "Ponca Publicity," *Mississippi Valley Historical Review* 29 (March 1943):495–516.

assisted in framing a test case on the legal status of the Indian tribes. Local attorneys filed a writ of habeas corpus against General Crook, alleging that he lacked legal authority to confine the Ponca because they were not properly under the war powers of the army or held for any violation of U.S. law. General Crook returned the writ, responding that the Poncas had left a reservation in Oklahoma without the permission of their agent and that the secretary of the interior had issued an order for their arrest and return to the reservation. The legal issue was squarely framed as the right of Indians to defy the authority of the government to confine them to a reservation against their will.

The *Standing Bear* opinion, like the opinion in *Crow Dog* four years later, is a puzzling array of contradictions. At the outset, Judge Elmer Dundy couched Standing Bear's right to the writ on his status as an individual Indian who had renounced his tribal status. It is not clear that Judge Dundy would have done so had the Indians not alleged it in their petition; but for reasons that we no longer know, their lawyers gave up this critical point. The petition alleged in substance that

> the relators are Indians who have formerly belonged to the Ponca tribe of Indians ... that they had some time previously withdrawn from the tribe and completely severed their tribal relations therewith, and had adopted the general habits of the whites, and were then endeavoring to maintain themselves by their own exertions and without aid or assistance from the general government.[65]

This concession, although perhaps critical to the lawyers' attempt to gain the freedom of the particular Poncas in custody at Fort Omaha, was a potentially devastating setback to the legal status of the tribes. If adopted, the decision would have left both tribal Indians and Indians dependent on the government for sustenance without access to the writ.

What the decision actually meant for Indians who had not severed their tribal relations is unclear, for Judge Dundy's decision divides into two parts. The most important language in the case would seem not to have adopted any distinction between tribal and nontribal Indians in relation to their legal status as persons within the meaning of the federal law of habeas corpus. The court held that the writ was available to all "persons" and not merely "citizens." After quoting *Webster's Dictionary* on the definition of "person," the Court held that it refers to all members of the human race and not just white people. This definition renders any tribal relation not relevant and would allow tribal Indians full access to the writ. Such a decision would have greatly undermined the authority of the federal government to contain

---

[65] *United States ex rel. Standing Bear v. Crook*, 25 Fed. Cas 695 (C.C.D. Neb., 1879), at 695.

Indians on reservations and to discipline them there for violations of "Indian offenses."

However, the Court spent the second half of its opinion discussing both the history of Ponca–white relations and the right of Indians to sever tribal relations. This discussion is best characterized as confused. At the outset, the Court found that the Poncas had always been at peace with the whites and had signed several treaties, including one consenting to sell their lands in South Dakota and move to the Indian Territory. But the Court held that none of these treaties refer "to any right to arrest and remove" the Ponca. Here the unit of analysis is the Ponca as a tribe; hence, again, there is no basis for any distinction between tribal Indians and detribalized Indians: if the Ponca – as a tribe – did not consent to any right to be arrested and removed, then the Ponca – as a tribe – had the right to move freely to the Indian Territory, as well as to move back to Dakota.[66]

Only at this point does the idea of detribalization enter the opinion, when it is no longer necessary to support any part of the holding. In the analysis of the Court, after 20 percent of the tribe had died in a single winter in the Indian Territory, many of the others decided to sever their tribal relations, become self-supporting, and return to South Dakota. Taking the Indian tribes as sovereign nations, the court found that citizens of such nations could renounce their national status and transfer their allegiance to another sovereignty. This analysis recognized the sovereignty of the Ponca but was unnecessary to support the opinion that found that Indians could renounce their tribal status, something tens of thousands of eastern Indians had been doing for two hundred years on a de facto basis.[67]

The final part of the analysis is an inquiry into the legal basis of military power over the tribes. The Court seized on language in the Indian Trade and Intercourse Acts that permitted the commissioner of Indian affairs to order the army to remove from a "tribal reservation" any person held there without authority of law. The Court held that this language conferred a very broad authority properly on the army but also held that this same statute required all persons seized by the army to be turned over to the U.S. marshal and the appropriate civil authority. The court specifically determined that the army had no broad authority to hold Indians, or anyone else, seized on Indian reservations without full civilian due process.[68]

Standing Bear and twenty-five of his warriors were released from custody. Full adherence to the precedent would have transformed Indian–white relations all over the United States and undermined the authority of Indian agents on hundreds of reservations. But it did not: *Standing Bear* was largely

[66] Ibid., 698–9.
[67] Ibid., 698.
[68] Ibid., 699–700.

ignored as precedent. While Indians after *Crow Dog* regularly brought habeas corpus actions in federal courts to challenge state or territorial criminal convictions, few brought habeas corpus actions in federal court challenging the authority of their Indian agents. The government attempted to appeal *Standig Bear*, but Justice Miller refused to hear it on the grounds that Judge Dundy had released all the Poncas without bail; since no charges had ever been brought, there was no longer any case or controversy.[69] Three years later when Crow Dog became the first Indian to reach the U.S. Supreme Court on a writ of habeas corpus, the court did not even discuss the issue of whether the writ was available to tribal Indians, thus implicitly confirming at least the jurisdictional part of Judge Dundy's opinion.[70]

The habeas corpus writ was ineffective as a remedy for Indians against the abuses of U.S. government power. Even access to the writ required a good deal of support from some legal community, for the writ is meaningless when there is no knowledge of its existence. Even then, the time and expense of the writ made it ineffective. The use of the writ in the 1891 Kansas case of Wakwabashkok and Nibakwa, two Prairie Potawatomi, provides an example. The two had organized a large-scale Potawatomi resistance to allotment under the Dawes Act. They performed traditional rituals, stopped cooperating with the Indian agent, sent delegations to Washington to protest, and organized their own traditional police force to keep discipline and enforce traditional ways, including proscriptions against the sale of tribal lands. The agent had the two arrested by the cavalry and held in Fort Riley. With the help of Indian reformers and sympathetic ranchers who had an interest in blocking allotment because they were renting tribal lands for grazing, the two hired a lawyer and filed a writ of habeas corpus. The judge granted the writ and sent them home, where they continued their agitation against allotment.[71]

Lelah-puc-ka-chee, an Indian living on the Sac and Fox Reservation, brought a writ of habeas corpus against her Indian agent and the superintendent of the Indian residential school where she lived, arguing that she was held there against her will.[72] The Indian agent responded that she was a minor under his guardianship and had been induced by traditional Indians opposed to the school to leave and engage in a customary marriage with Ta-ta-pi-cha solely to undermine the authority of the agent to keep Indian "girls" – her age was testified to be either sixteen or eighteen – in school. The opinion was straightforward, holding that Indian customary marriages

---

[69] Ibid., 701.
[70] *Ex parte Crow Dog*, 109 U.S. 556 (1883), 557.
[71] The *Wakwabashkok* case is discussed in James Clinton, *The Prairie People* (Lawrence: University of Kansas Press, 1977), 395–7.
[72] *In re Lelah-puc-ka-chee*, 98 F. 429 (1899).

were legal and that the agent had no right to hold Indians in school against their will.[73] The writ was available to individual Indian "troublemakers" acting as members of their tribe; but considering that thousands of such Indians were jailed for all kinds of violations, it was not an effective remedy: tribal Indians often lacked access to lawyers and federal courts.

Bai-a-lil-le and the Indian Rights Association challenge to the "big stick" policy of Commissioner Leupp

It took more than thirty years for U.S. law to settle the question of the availability of the writ of habeas corpus to Indians locked up for resisting Indian agents' authority. The case of Bai-a-lil-le, a defiant Navajo medicine man arrested by the army in 1909, brought the issue to a close. Under the *Standing Bear* precedent, Bai-a-lil-le should not have been arrested at all.[74]

Bai-a-lil-le was one of the large number of traditional Indians then remaining on most western reservations. These people had retreated to the far corners of their lands, away from the authority of the Indian agents, and practiced their traditional ways. Some of these people lived quietly, preferring to be ignored. Others actively struggled against assimilation and the agents' authority. In the "progressive age," the perseverence of these people was a source of considerable embarrassment to the BIA, for it proved the failure of a large part of their assimilation efforts.

Living near Aneth, Utah, on a corner of the Navajo reservation never brought under government authority, Bai-a-lil-le's people were in open defiance of the agent's authority, refusing to send their children to school. The agent tried negotiating, but Bai-a-lil-le announced that he would "fight as he was an old man and prepared to die." The standoff that prevailed throughout the summer of 1908 ultimately required the attention of Commissioner of Indian Affairs Francis Leupp, who personally visited Shiprock, an agency forty miles from Aneth and made plans to arrest the rebellious Navajo.

Leupp, Theodore Roosevelt's appointee, had already become infamous among both tribes and Indian reformers for his "big stick" policy of coercion. In 1905, he had used troops to quell a Navajo disturbance at Fort Defiance and had sent seven Navajo without trial to a military prison at Alcatraz in an effort to show the tribes that any resistance would be futile. The next

---

[73] Ibid., 436–7.
[74] The *Bai-a-lil-le* case has produced a moderate literature, which is rare for an Indian case. See the pamphlet by J. Lee Correll, "Bai-a-Lil-le, Medicine Man or Witch," Navajo Historical Publications, Biographical Series, no. 3 (Window Rock, Ariz.: 1970), and Donald L. Parman, "The Big Stick in Indian Affairs: The Bai-a-lil-le Incident in 1909," *Arizona and the West* 20 (1978):343–60.

year he had also used troops to seize traditional Hopis in a factional dispute at Oraibi, again holding them in prison without trial.[75]

Bai-a-lil-le and his people became increasingly defiant, and they threatened witchcraft against Navajos who cooperated with the agent. The Navajo police refused to arrest him because they were afraid of his medicine. Two troops of cavalry were sent to arrest him and his followers. They took the traditionals' camp by surprise at dawn and captured Bai-a-lil-le and a number of followers asleep. The troops then proceeded to arrest all of the Navajo found in the area. Shooting broke out, and two young Navajos were killed.

Both Captain Harry Willard of the cavalry and the Indian agent wrote lengthy reports demanding long prison terms for the ten Navajo brought back under arrest. A number of serious charges were listed against them: disobedience, refusal to dip sheep, livestock theft, rape, kidnapping, polygamy, concealment of weapons, and intimidation of cooperative Navajo. Leupp ordered all ten held at Fort Huachuca, Arizona, at hard labor for an indefinite term.[76]

The event became a national issue, seized on by the IRA as a test case. The Senate was forced to conduct an investigation that led to a whitewash. The obvious *Standing Bear* precedent was not even raised in those hearings. The IRA, while advocating full assimilation of the Indian tribes, believed in a humane policy aimed at achieving those goals, one that respected the rights of Indian people. Not only were they outraged at the treatment of these traditional Navajo, but they believed that other Indian agents had taken this case as an example and were ordering the arrests of defiant Indians. Such a policy would leave Indians "slaves of the government." Legal action to extend the full rights of U.S. law to Bai-a-lil-le would not only win an important substantive issue for the IRA, but also embarrass the BIA and discredit its big stick policy.

An application for a writ of habeas corpus was filed by Bai-a-lil-le in the district court of the Second Judicial Circuit of Arizona Territory. As a territorial court, it held the power of federal courts within the territory and had habeas jurisdiction over army posts within Arizona. When the Navajos lost in a perfunctory opinion, they appealed to the Supreme Court of the Arizona Territory.[77]

The BIA based its case on two arguments. The first was simple: the BIA had the authority to "cause the removal of any Indian from an Indian reservation when he [the BIA commissioner] deems his presence therein to be detrimental to the peace and welfare of other Indians on the reservation." From this, the same statute used to justify holding Standing Bear, it followed

---

[75] Parman, "The Big Stick in Indian Affairs," 344–6.
[76] Ibid., 346–7.
[77] Ibid., 348–3.

that the BIA could hold a removed Indian in custody until he could be returned to the reservation. Another basis for its authority, the BIA argued, could be found in *United States v. Clapox,* where a federal district court had upheld the Courts of Indian Offenses and the punishment of Indians by those courts as "mere educational and disciplinary instrumentalities." *Lone Wolf v. Hitchcock* was also cited to explain that the full plenary authority over the tribes was a political one, governed by Congress and not by the courts, and justified a wide range of BIA actions governing "an ignorant and dependent race."

After citing other cases holding that it could remove "persons" from reservations, the BIA asked the Arizona court to "take cognizance of history": the BIA still held Geronimo and his band of Apaches at Fort Sill, Oklahoma, under the same authority that it held Bai-a-lil-le. This example was meant to alert the court to the still strong opinion in Arizona against the Apache. In sum, the BIA argued that it possessed "plenary power" to remove and hold in custody without trial Indians who defied government authority, a startling extension of the *Lone Wolf* doctrine.[78]

The BIA distinguished *Standing Bear* in two ways. First, it argued that no statute existed requiring Indians to live on reservations or authorizing their return if they left, the factual situation of *Standing Bear.* In contrast, Bai-a-lil-le was being held not for return to his tribal relation but because his presence was detrimental to the peace and good order of the reservation. Second, the BIA argued that U.S. policy was to encourage Indians to sever their tribal relations, a policy followed by the court in *Standing Bear.*[79]

Although the BIA must have believed that *Lone Wolf* was sufficient legal precedent, it made a second argument having a different foundation. Bai-a-lil-le's band was engaged in "hostilities and insurrection against the government of the United States" and therefore could be dealt with summarily under the articles of war. Here was cited an opinion of the attorney general that "it is not necessary to the existence of war that hostilities should have been formally proclaimed." The opinion looked to the case of *Marks v. United States,* where it was held that "to constitute an Indian war, it is sufficient that hostilities exist and that military operations are carried on." The Navajos were "prisoners of war," and no law governed when such prisoners should be released.

There was a stridency in the arguments of Attorney O. Gibson for the Navajo appellants. Reviewing the law of habeas corpus and the relevant

---

[78] The case file (*By-a-lil-le*) is found in the Arizona State Archives. It contains copies of all the lower court papers and briefs of both parties, along with other legal documents. This synopsis of the government's case is taken from the "Argument and Brief of Appellee," dated July 8, 1909, and contained in that file. Bai-a-lil-le was spelled a number of ways in the original court papers. I have followed the choice of both Parman and Correll.

[79] "Brief of Appellee," in ibid., 16–17.

statutes governing BIA actions, Gibson argued that arrest and imprisonment could not rest on historical usage in previous Indian wars or on BIA interpretations of its own power but could only be sanctioned by positive law.[80] For limits on military power, he looked to *ex parte Milligan*, which, although it derived from the immediate situation of the Civil War, contained clear language that "in a state where federal authority was always unopposed, and its courts always open to hear criminal accusations and redress grievances, no usage of war could sanction a military trial for any offense whatever, of a citizen in civil life. Congress could grant no such power. The right to trial by jury is preserved to every one accused of crime." The citizenship language clearly did not apply to the Navajo, but the general language referred to all persons and not merely citizens.[81]

Gibson could find only two other Indian habeas cases in the thirty years since *Standing Bear: Wiley v. Keokuk* and an application by an Omaha, William Walker, for a writ against an army officer holding him in custody. (He missed *Wakwabashkok*.) Remarkably, few Indians were able to take advantage of the writ in a period of extensive federal intervention into tribal life and many hundreds of restraints in custody. Keokuk's case was particularly egregious, but its facts offered no parallel to the case at hand. Keokuk, a famous Sac and Fox chief, wanted to go to Washington to speak to Congress about the mistreatment of his people. His agent refused to give him a pass to leave the reservation. As Keokuk prepared to go at his own expense, the agent ordered him arrested. This was not a difficult set of facts for a judge to seize on in granting a writ of habeas corpus. The case became a well-known example of the petty excesses of corrupt Indian agents.[82]

The *Walker* case occurred in 1907, immediately before *Bai-a-lil-le*. A captain of cavalry recommended to a superior officer that Walker be confined. When the Court of Indian Offenses of the Omaha reservation then ordered Walker detained, Walker filed a writ of habeas corpus. Federal District Judge Jacob Trieber issued a one-paragraph order:

> The establishment of a court exercising power to impose a sentence of imprisonment upon a person can only be done by an act of Congress, or, if done by the head of a Department, only express authority of an act of Congress. This is elementary and requires no citation of authorities. As there is no act of Congress authorizing the establishment of such a court as that which convicted petitioner and sentenced him to imprisonment, his detention is unlawful and absolutely void.

---

[80] "Brief on Behalf of Petitioners," contained in *By-a-lil-le* case file, in ibid., 1–7. It should be noted that Gibson, a prominent Arizona lawyer, had no sympathy for the imprisoned Navajos but agreed to take the case on behalf of the IRA because he believed their punishment too severe. Parman, "The Big Stick in Indian Affairs," 352.

[81] Ibid., 14–15.

[82] *Albert Wiley v. Keokuk*, 6 Kansas 94 (188). "Brief of Petitioners," 11–12.

Attorney Gibson provided the court with a certified copy of this order. Not only did Judge Trieber's statement of the elementary nature of the law involved support the strong language in the *Standing Bear* case, but it also held exactly the opposite of Judge Deady's often cited *Clapox* opinion, which found a broad general authority for Indian agents to imprison Indians as a part of their "education."[83]

The Arizona Supreme Court issued a unanimous opinion rejecting all of the government's arguments and releasing all the Navajos from custody. Although the court upheld BIA authority to remove troublesome persons from reservations, an authority granted by federal statute, it limited that authority to the act of removal itself and not to subsequent detention. Furthermore, it rejected the argument that the Navajos were prisoners of war. The court went on to follow Judge Trieber's reasoning and rejected any kind of broad-based plenary power doctrine justifying confinement of any sort. Rather, such confinement had to be specifically authorized by statute. In one final argument, the court held that the government had violated Navajo sovereignty guaranteed by the treaty of 1868, which specified that the tribe would turn over wrongdoers to the United States "to be punished by its laws."[84]

Commissioner Leupp remained unbowed by the Arizona court's rejection of every one of his arguments. He indicated that he had "discovered new authorities" and filed a notice of appeal to the U.S. Supreme Court. By that time Roosevelt's term of office had expired, and Leupp had become a lame duck Indian commissioner. In June, the acting Attorney General informed the new secretary of the interior that he had examined the Bai-a-lil-le case and was "somewhat at a loss to know on what ground an appeal could be maintained." The BIA "reluctantly" withdrew the appeal, and Bai-a-lil-le returned home.

As important as this victory was, the case has rarely been cited as precedent in Indian law. It marked the end of the BIA's "military option" of holding without trial Indians accused of crimes or offenses that, for various reasons, it was unable, or unwilling, to try under the Major Crimes Act. The decision closed a major extralegal mechanism used by the BIA to punish Indian "crime" and to extend the reach of U.S. law over the tribes.[85]

It had taken thirty years for a writ so basic under the common law as habeas corpus to have any effect for tribal Indians. By the time the military

---

[83] *In the Matter of William Walker for a Writ of Habeas Corpus*, U.S. Circuit Court, District of Nebraska, January 8, 1907, cited in "Brief of Petitioners," 13–14. A certified copy of the Walker decision is included in the *By-a-lil-le* file. Trieber's remarkable order is never cited in discussions of *Clapox* even though Trieber's court was a parallel federal court.

[84] *United States v. By-a-lil-le*, 12 Arizona 150 (1909).

[85] Parman, "The Big Stick in Indian Affairs," 359–60.

option was held to be extralegal by the courts, U.S. expansion had ended, the twentieth century had long since arrived, tribal lands were allotted, and the tribes were impoverished. There was no need for further military violence against them. However, hundreds of Apaches were still imprisoned at Fort Sill, Oklahoma, as military prisoners.

Indian citizenship

While individual Indians, especially in the East, had been granted U.S. citizenship through a number of treaty arrangements, this had not been extended to tribal Indians. The issue of the citizenship of tribal Indians, a legal right extended to Black Americans through the Fourteenth and Fifteenth amendments to the U.S. Constitution, was still unsettled in the 1880s. *Standing Bear*, legally establishing that an Indian was a "person" under U.S. law, paved the way for a test case, brought by the same people who had brought Standing Bear's case.[86] John Elk was a Winnebago who moved to Omaha in 1879, severing his tribal relations, living among whites, and attempting to vote in 1880. Denied this right, he sued. The U.S. Supreme Court decided *Elk v. Wilkins* in 1884, the year between *Crow Dog* and *Kagama*. Its holding, that tribal Indians were not citizens under the Fourteenth Amendment, was necessary to preserve the dependant, wardship status of the tribes that the Court soon put forth in the plenary power doctrine. Citing with approval the reasoning of federal district judge Matthew Deady of Oregon that being born a member of "an independent political community," a Chinook Indian was not born subject to the jurisdiction of the United States. Although an Indian might abandon tribal relations and adopt the "habits and manners of civilized people," this did not change his legal status. Citizenship was a privilege that must be directly bestowed by the United States in some form.[87]

This judgement produced a strong dissent, rare in U.S. Supreme Court Indian rights cases. Justices Harlan and Woods, conceding that "wild Indians who do not recognize the government of the United States and are not subject to our laws" were not citizens, argued that the phrase "Indians not taxed" in the U.S. Constitution conferred the rights of citizens on Indians who were taxed, thus voluntarily transferring their allegiance to the United States. Additionally, the plain language of the Fourteenth Amendment applied to all persons born within the limits of the United States.[88] Both

---

[86] Stephen D. Bodayla, "Can An Indian Vote? *Elk v. Wilkins*, A Setback for Indian Citizenship," *Nebraska History* 67, (1986):372–80.

[87] *Elk v. Wilkins*, 112 US 94 (1884), at 109. The Deady case quoted is *McKay v. Campbell*, 2 Sawyer 118 (1871), at 134.

[88] *Elk v. Wilkins*, 110–22.

opinions noted that many states had conferred state citizenship on Indians, the majority arguing that this had no impact on their federal status.[89] The Court's denial of citizenship in *Elk* was part of the foundation of the plenary power doctrine. However, like the idea of Indian citizenship generally, it was a side issue because tribal Indians did not want to be citizens. Whatever Elk's status as a resident of Omaha, the tribes were still held to be "independent political communities." When citizenship was ultimately conferred on the tribal Indians by legislative fiat in 1924, many Indians resisted, seeing the forced imposition of U.S. citizenship as denying the existence of their nations.[90]

The reservation as prison: forced confinement of Indians on reservations

The federal courts' refusal, following *Clapox,* to deal substantively with the injustice of the courts of Indian offenses and the abuse of power of Indian agents also led to the courts' refusal to deal with the legal status of the Indian living on the reservation. *Standing Bear* was ignored. Legally, the Indians there were dependent wards of the federal government in the process of being taught the skills necessary for civilization, allotment, and eventual state and federal citizenship. The Indian agent's authority was complete. Tribal Indians were prisoners in their own land, subject, as was Sitting Bull, to being killed by the agent's police to enforce their confinement.

The tribes resisted this confinement. The Sioux persisted in regular hunting and trading expeditions into Wyoming and Montana for at least twenty years after the Wounded Knee massacre. These hunting trips put the Sioux in direct conflict with both Indian agents and state law enforcement officers. Local whites bitterly resented Indian presence in their communities, accusing them of stealing livestock. Small-scale altercations between Indians and whites were common. The best known of these was Wyoming's "Lightning Creek fight." In the fall of 1903 two Oglalla Sioux hunting parties, totaling twenty to twenty-five men with their families, joined to return to the Pine Ridge Reservation. They were confronted by a Wyoming sheriff and his posse out to arrest Indians for hunting antelope in violation of Wyoming law.[91] The Sioux had resisted the imposition of Wyoming law on their traditional hunting grounds, finally losing the right in the U.S. Supreme Court in *Ward v. Race Horse,* an 1896 holding that Wyoming statehood had

---

[89] Ibid., 107–9.
[90] Clinton Rickard, *Fighting Tuscarora* (Syracuse, N.Y.: Syracuse University Press, 1973), 52–3.
[91] Barton Voigt, "The Lightning Creek Fight," *Annals of Wyoming* 49, no. 1 (1977):5–21.

extinguished tribal hunting rights.[92] Defying the law, the Sioux continued their hunt into the twentieth century.

Sheriff William Miller and his posse had been pursuing Sioux hunting parties for seven days before their attempted arrest at Lightning Creek. After arresting another party of nine Sioux, sending them, in custody, to Newcastle for trial, Miller finally caught up with the two Oglalla bands, led by Charlie Smith, a Carlisle Indian School graduate, and William Brown. When the sheriff showed Smith his arrest warrant, Smith was defiant: "I am no damn fool, and know more of the law than you do. I do not live in Newcastle, and I will not go there." The Oglallas then broke camp and headed toward Pine Ridge.[93]

Sheriff Miller, knowing that the Indians would not submit to arrest, went for reinforcements and confronted the bands the next day. Shooting broke out, leaving Sheriff Miller, one deputy, and five Indians dead. The Indians continued their return to Pine Ridge but were arrested by another posse and taken to Douglas for trial. All were discharged after their preliminary hearing when no witnesses could identify any Indian as having done any shooting.[94]

This was not the end of the case, however, as both Wyoming officials and the BIA pushed for a congressional investigation of the incident. The investigation that followed made it clear that the Wyoming posse exceeded its legal authority in attempting the arrest and was to blame for the violence that broke out. It was also confirmed that the agent's policy of granting permits was designed to placate restless Indians and was used for an illegal purpose – traditional hunting.[95] The real problems, however, were not reached in the investigation. The interests of the tribes and local whites had been put into direct conflict by federal government policies and expanded settlement, and as long as the tribes exercised their sovereignty in a context where their capacity to do so was restricted, conflict was inevitable.

Ultimately, demography was more successful than the Indian agents at keeping the tribes on the reservations. With increasing settlement, it became impossible to engage in traditional hunts. This left the tribes with no land but their reservations and no way to continue their hunts. The reservation over the next twenty years was converted from a "prison to a homeland" as tribal cultures adapted to the reality of reservation life. The forced assim-

---

[92] *Ward v. Race Horse*, 163 U.S. 504 (1896). The Supreme Court reversed a federal district court holding that the tribes retained their treaty rights to hunt after Wyoming statehood. *In re Race Horse*, 70 F. 598 (1895). Modern Indian law would agree with the lower court holding that treaty hunting rights survive after statehood.

[93] Voigt, "The Lightning Creek Fight," 7–8.

[94] Ibid., 11–12

[95] U.S. Congress, Senate "Encounter Between Sioux Indians of the Pine Ridge Agency and a Sheriff's Posse of Wyoming," 58th Congress, 2d session, 1903, Doc. 128.

ilation policy of the Major Crimes Act and the Dawes Act was defeated by the refusal of the tribes to assimilate.[96]

Conclusion

Concurrent with the Major Crimes Act and *Kagama*, the BIA created a substantial system of policing and punishment that was administrative rather than legal, therefore effectively beyond the reach of federal or state courts. Although federal courts clearly had habeas corpus jurisdiction over the actions of Indian agents, they rarely exercised it. The core of this process was the Indian agent, who enjoyed quasi-feudal powers on the reservation. As part of the efforts of the government to "civilize" the tribes, Indians who violated a wide range of rules were brought before the agent, or before a "court" of Indians handpicked by the agent, and punished, sometimes with fines, a burden on poor Indians, and often with jail terms served in filthy guardhouses. Sitting Bull was shot to death by Indian police for his determination to exercise his sovereignty by joining in the Ghost Dance. Clapox was jailed for breaking Minnie, his friend and lover, out of a dingy BIA cell, where she was held for violating the Indian agent's moral code. They represent many thousands of Indians killed or jailed for similar "offenses." There is no record of their exact number, but the impact of this arbitrary authority was deeply felt among reservation Indians.

At the same time this authority was arbitrary, it was also uneven and ineffective. Traditional Indians in remote corners of the reservation lived beyond the effective reach of tribal police. The tribal police themselves struck careful balancing acts between the authority of the agents and tribal law. Indian judges of the courts of Indian offenses balanced the agent's justice with tribal law.

The BIA knew this, but accepted the compromise. The BIA never intended to extend the full range of rights of U.S. citizens to tribal Indians; hence, it did not support extending either federal or state law to the reservations, except on a limited basis in specific areas, for example, with the Major Crimes Act. A BIA policy extending tribal Indians' legal rights would implicitly increase tribal sovereignty, interfering with efforts to force assimilation, a contradiction that grew more apparent in the twentieth century.

[96] There is an extensive literature on the transformation of the Indian reservation. See, e.g., Fred Hoxie, "From Prison to Homeland: The Cheyenne River Indian Reservation Before World War I," *South Dakota History* 10, 1 (Winter 1979):1–24; Carolyn Gilman and Mary Lane Schneider, *The Way to Independence: Memories of a Hidatsa Indian Family, 1840–1920* (St. Paul: Minnesota State Historical Society Press, 1987); and Frank Pommersheim, "The Reservation as Place: A South Dakota Essay, *South Dakota Law Review* 34 (1989):246.

7

The struggle for tribal sovereignty in Alaska, 1867–1900

The legal history of Indian–white relations in Alaska is substantially unrelated to parallel developments in the rest of the United States. While twentieth-century federal Indian law often applies to Alaska in the same manner as it does to the rest of the country, nineteenth-century law did not.[1] In fact, the major nineteenth-century federal Indian law cases had little impact in Alaska; few cases arose, both because courts came to Alaska only in 1884 and because there were so few whites. Moreover, no treaties were made with Alaskan natives, and many provisions of the Indian Trade and Intercourse Acts did not govern trade between whites and Alaska's tribes. In the nineteenth century, Alaskan natives lived under the same law as Alaskan whites. They were denied special status, either as tribal sovereigns or as wards dependent on federal protection. This reflected a deliberate decision by local whites, deferred to by federal courts and officials, who either desired to avoid the problems of the Indian law that existed in the rest of the United States or were simply unconcerned about Alaska because of its remoteness.

In order to provide a better understanding of both the history of federal Indian law and Alaska's unique situation, this chapter focuses on the legal incorporation of the Tlingit into U.S. law. The Tlingit occupied one thousand miles of coastline along the panhandle of southeast Alaska and bore most of the early impact of U.S. colonialism. First, I examine the development of a distinct legal status for Alaskan natives – a process of great importance when one considers the Alaskan native land crisis that followed the Native Claims Settlement Act of 1971. I then explore how the distinct legal status of Alaskan natives structured Tlingit–white relations in Alaska

---

[1] This situation is quite complex, in large part due to Alaska's distinct nineteenth-century history. Sybil R. Kisken, "The Uncertain Legal Status of Alaska Natives After *Native Village of Stevens v. Alaska Management and Planning:* Exposing the Fallacious Distinctions Between Alaska Natives and Lower 48 Indians," *Arizona Law Review* 31 (1989):404. David Case, *Alaska Natives and American Laws* (Fairbanks: University of Alaska Press, 1984), is an introduction to Alaskan Indians in relation to U.S. law.

in the late nineteenth century. Finally, I consider the impact of U.S. law on
Tlingit sovereignty.

Russian colonization and Tlingit sovereignty

Russian colonization strengthened Tlingit sovereignty, creating a powerful
Tlingit Indian nation where a culture of isolated fishing, hunting, and trading
villages had existed before. The sale of Alaska to the United States by the
Russians in 1867 could not be understood by native people: the Russians
had never tried to force the Tlingit to recognize that the Russian tsar
"owned" the land. Neither the Tlingit nor any other native Alaskan people
engaged in treaty making with the Russians or sold them any land. Moreover,
although the Russians had made territorial claims of ownership to England,
Spain, and the United States, they did not assert such claims to Alaskan
natives. An attempt to collect a tribute from the natives in the form of a tax
was abandoned because native resistance was so great as to undermine the
fur trade.[2]

The Russians never had effective control of the Tlingit and, without an
extensive military investment that they were unprepared to make, could not
gain sovereignty over the Tlingit. Thus, the Russians sold the United States
only their tenuous title. At the time of the Alaska purchase in 1867, there
were scarcely eight hundred Russians residing there, primarily in four fortified towns that they were most often afraid to leave for fear of Tlingit
attacks.[3]

The largest of these settlements, New Archangel, now Sitka, home to
most of the Russians in America, was visited in 1861 by Captain Pavel
Golovin of the Russian Navy. His journal reveals the strength of Tlingit
sovereignty in "Russian" America. Golovin described the heart of New
Archangel as "a large, ugly, two-story structure... painted yellow, surrounded by a wooden wall... with cannon embrasures and gun batteries."
In case of attack by "Kolosh" Indians, as the Tlingit were called by the
Russians, the citizens of the settlement could run under the protection of
the guns of the fort. Golovin described a small church for Tlingit services
but also noted that "services are rarely held there because the Kolosh simply
do not attend."[4] The failure of the Russians to extinguish Tlingit sovereignty
over their land was obvious to Golovin:

[2] James Gibson, "Russian Dependence upon the Natives of Alaska" and Liapunova, "Relations
with the Natives of Russian America," both in S. F. Starr (ed.), *Russia's American Colony*
(Durham, N.C.: Duke University Press, 1987).

[3] Hector Chevigny, *Russian America* (New York: Viking, 1965); Starr (ed.), *Russia's American
Colony.*

[4] Pavel Golovin, *Civil and Savage Encounters* (Portland: Oregon Historical Society, 1983), 81.

The Indians, of whom the closest neighbors to us are the Kolosh, are
... intelligent, warlike, and savage; they have a deep aversion to civilization of any kind. They work willingly if they know that their work will
be rewarded, but they also like to be lazy and lie around in idleness.
They are always armed with knives, and often have revolvers and guns.
... They are all very good shots and they are brave but they fear cannister
shot and balls. Some of the chief administrators have been very much
afraid of them, which has given the Kolosh much confidence. More
than once there has been fighting. There is no doubt that if firm measures had been taken they would long ago have been brought into
complete obedience and would be in fear of God, but unfortunately all
measures which have been undertaken up until now have been inade-
quate and indecisive. The result is that New Archangel is constantly in
a state of siege.

... Because the Kolosh are so dangerous, the Company has, for some
time, been thinking of banishing them from the settlement altogether,
but they are afraid that, in that case, there would be no fresh provisions
in New Archangel, because Russians do not go out in the forest.[5]

The Russian fear of the forest was a fear of disappearing when going
beyond the reach of the stockade. Russian trade with the Tlinglit occurred
in a stockaded market under the guns of the fort. Similarly, the Russians
were unable to explore their lands, confining their trips to the coastal areas
of Kodiak, Sitka, and a few of the larger islands.[6]

The Russians tried to extinguish Tlingit sovereignty but failed. It is simplistic to say that the Tlingit defeated the Russians, although surely the
Tlingit, and a number of other native peoples, did preserve their sovereignty
by defeating colonizing forces. In 1802, New Archangel, capital of Russian
America, was attacked and burned by the Tlingit. Virtually all of its Russian
inhabitants died. The Russians returned the next year and forcibly reestablished the base. Two years later the Tlingit attacked and destroyed the
Russian fort at Yakutat. Again, the Russians reestablished their fort there
the next year.[7]

The reestablishment of these forts with relatively small Russian forces
while the Tlingit forces of a thousand men failed to counterattack the next
year reveals that these events cannot be understood simply in their military
contexts. They do make sense, however, from the standpoint of Tlingit law.
Upon the arrival of the Russians, the Tlingit had no model for their incorporation into the Tlingit world other than Tlingit cultural norms. The Tlingit
were a prosperous fishing and trading people, making great profits trading

---

[5] Ibid., 84, 85.
[6] Ibid., 85.
[7] Frederica de Laguna, *Under Mount Saint Elias: The History and Culture of the Yakutat Tlingit*
(Washington, D.C.: Smithsonian Press, 1972), 1:170–6.

coastal goods to inland tribes. At first, Russian traders fit easily into this economic relationship, making the Tlingit rich middlemen buying furs cheaply from interior tribes and selling them to the Russians at high prices. Russians, however, did not understand that their roles in this arrangement were sharply circumscribed by the Tlingit: the Russians were not allowed to trade directly with these tribes, hence could not leave the trading posts. Nor could they get their own food: they had to buy food from the Tlingit. Some Tlingit *qwan*s (territorial bands) even charged Russian ships for fresh water.[8]

As the scale of Russian trade grew, the Russians objected to Tlingit control of the trade. However, Russian attempts to move beyond the narrow confines that the Tlingit held them in were likely to lead to violence. Russian violence against Tlingit people was treated just as internal Tlingit violence was: the *qwan*s met and required that the families of the injured be made whole through various kinds of payments. The Russians, undoubtedly, did not recognize either the justice or the existence of these Tlingit norms. Similarly, the Tlingit probably did not recognize Russian colonialism, racism, or ethnocentrism. It never occurred to them that the Russians thought they owned Alaska. Rather, Russian actions simply looked like greedy intrusions on Tlingit rights.

We know the reasons for this warring directly from Tlingit oral history. A Yakutat Tlingit, in 1954, listed six grievances against the Russians: they had failed to pay for the land they had taken for their fort, had promised to trade guns and ammunition but had not, had taken children for slaves, taken Tlingit women, threatened an Indian man who had taken copper nails from an old skiff to build a coffin for a shaman, and had put a gate across a creek.[9] The purpose of the Tlingit destruction of Sitka and Yakutat, two of the four Russian settlements in Alaska, was to restore a balance of power in the trading relationship between the Tlingit and the Russians but also to structure that relationship in a way more favorable to the Tlingit, putting the arrogant Russians back in the place that the Tlingit had accorded them.[10]

For the next sixty years, this relationship was tenuously maintained. There was a great deal of violence as Russian traders were regularly killed by the Tlingit and Tlingit were killed by Russians. It is unlikely that the Russians had any idea that there was a Tlingit social order that had changed to accommodate the increased trade with the Russians and that the sporadic

---

[8]   Gibson, "Russian Dependence upon the Natives of Alaska."

[9]   De Laguna, *Under Mount Saint Elias*, vol. 2, 260, 12.

[10]   The concept that native peoples used their laws as a basis to attempt to structure and control white colonialism is carefully developed in James Belich, *The New Zealand Wars* (Auckland: University of Auckland Press, 1986), and Henry Reynolds, *The Other Side of the Frontier* (Melbourne: Penguin, 1981).

Tlingit wars were the product of that changing social order. It is also unlikely that the Tlingit realized the nature of the Eurocentric view of the world that the Russians held. It seems likely that Tlingit sovereignty actually increased during this period, as newly prosperous trading families had more interests to protect and more resources to protect them with. Probably tribal institutions of social control became more complex: for example, surely the Tlingit never raised a thousand-man army before 1803, an effort that must have changed Tlingit social structure.

It is also clear that after the Tlingit revolts of 1802–6, the Russians made an effort to accommodate Tlingit sovereignty. For example, the Russians recognized *toions*, or local chiefs, accorded them Russian honors, medals, and other symbols of authority, and held banquets for them.[11] Families and *qwan*s with special access to the Russians had opportunities for massing greater wealth through the Russian trade than other Tlingits did, and Tlingit social structure, based on wealth and the potlatch, changed accordingly in ways that we still cannot recognize. Tlingit *qwan*s in proximity to the Russians, chiefly Sitka and Wrangell, grew in population with the Tlingit villages at those two towns, having populations of about a thousand by 1867, probably five times their traditional size.[12] This increased size and greater wealth made these *qwan*s proportionately more powerful in Tlingit society than they had previously been. It must also have sparked resentment from traditional Tlingit villages and destabilized preexisting *qwan* relationships.

The Tlingit lived in permanent villages composed of large wooden houses with totem poles in front, facing the ocean. By 1867 these villages had begun a process of consolidation, although several dozen distinct villages remained. The prosperity of the fur trade altered power and clan relationships in Tlingit society. The Tlingit had a hierarchical social order based on the accumulation of wealth and maintained a class system based on the inheritance of that wealth, unlike most other native societies in North America.[13] The original social organization of the Tlingit was based on two subdivisions, Raven and Eagle, each of which had perhaps twelve clans, named after animals. Offices in the clan were hereditary, but in avuncular Tlingit society the power of a chief passed to his sister's youngest son, the youngest nephew. Every clan was represented in thirteen *qwan*s. Each *qwan* consisted of a hundred to a thousand members, living in one to three permanent winter villages that occupied its own territory along a stretch of Pacific coastline.

[11] Golovin, 111, n. 16.
[12] L. A. Beardslee, *Reports Relative to Affairs in Alaska* Senate Ex. dic. no. 71, 47th Congress, 1st session, 1882, 13, estimated that 100–200 Tlingit lived in Sitka during the summer and 500–600 during the winter. A number of others lived in outlying villages near Sitka. J. Averkieva, "The Tlingit Indians," in E. Leacock and N. Lurie (eds.), *North American Indians in Historical Perspective* (1971), 325–9.
[13] De Laguna, *Under Mount Saint Elias*, 461–8.

Although whites often mistook these territorial units for tribes and therefore distinguished among different Tlingit *qwan*s, all were Tlingit people.[14]

Every Tlingit village had a number of chiefs of different ranks, based both on clan lineages and on wealth, with the wealthiest chief in each village having the highest rank. Some entire clans were wealthy, others were poor. Russian observers characterized wealthy Tlingits as "petty princes" and described the chief of Sitka as "so elated...with pride, that he made no use of his legs for walking, but was invariably carried on the shoulders of his attendants, even on the most trifling occasions." Many of these attendants, somewhere between 10 and 30 percent of Tlingit society in the mid-nineteenth century, were slaves, who were also property and could be inherited.[15]

Relations with the Russians were conducted at arm's length by parties that never trusted each other. Although this trading relationship was most often peaceful, each side punished the other for transgressions of their respective legal traditions, a process that involved a small-scale series of attacks and retaliations. Thus, at the time of U.S. acquisition of Alaska, the Tlingit had a long tradition of successfully defending their sovereignty against whites that they would not give up.

U.S. legal jurisdiction over Alaskan natives

There is probably no setting in which the extension of U.S. law over Native Americans can be studied in as much detail as in the Alaska panhandle during the early years of Alaska's incorporation into the United States. Because that process occurred very late in the history of U.S.–Indian relations and in a remote area with clearly defined populations, this meeting of two legal traditions can be reconstructed with great clarity. In addition, more extensive documentation of this process exists than for parallel situations in other parts of the United States.[16]

Until Alaska's Organic Act of 1884 provided some measure of local government, including a federal district court sitting at Sitka, Congress paid little attention to the legal status of either Alaska or the Indians living there. Alaska's original legal status under the United States, created by an act of Congress on July 27, 1868, was as a "customs district" occupied by two sets of U.S. authorities: customs collectors and a small military force. No distinct law for Alaska existed. Instead, all violations of law in Alaska were cognizable

---

[14] Ibid., 326–7.
[15] Ibid., 329–1.
[16] Perhaps the major reasons for this greater documentation were extensive government investigations in Alaska and the presence there of an active weekly press.

in any district court in the United States, a nearly meaningless process given the great distances involved.[17]

Nothing in the 1868 act made any provision for the administration of Indian affairs in Alaska or provided a legal basis for doing so. The third article of the treaty that ceded Alaska to the United States, however, twice raised the issue of the rights of "uncivilized tribes," once to exclude them from citizenship and once to make them prospectively "subject to such laws and regulations as the United States may from time to time adopt."[18] This language, while making clear that the uncivilized tribes were to be treated differently from whites, raised more questions than it answered. For example, it appeared to confer citizenship on Indians who were not members of "uncivilized" tribes. On the other hand, it seemed to promise those uncivilized tribes future laws regarding their status but left them without the protection of any existing laws governing Indian affairs. No language in the congressional debates on the treaty indicates that either of these issues was raised directly. Rather, the treaty consists of boilerplate provisions designed to leave the issues to future resolutions.[19]

The uncertainty regarding the tribes' status is more evident in light of an 1869 letter written by Secretary of State William Henry Seward to the secretary of war. Seward, quoting Chief Justice John Marshall's opinion in *Worcester v. Georgia*, stated that when new territory was added to the United States, existing laws fully governed there. In addition, Seward, citing Marshall's language concerning "dependent nations" and the "Indian commerce clause," concluded that these concepts applied to Alaska.[20] Seward's view was consistent with an 1855 attorney general's opinion that Indian country was not "limited by specific boundaries but includes generally all such portions of the acquired territory of the United States, as are in the actual occupation of the Indian tribes while the Indian title thereto is unextinguished." As a result of Seward's letter, the War Department exercised full

[17] The early legal status of Alaska is analyzed in G. Spicer, *The Constitutional Status and Government of Alaska*, Johns Hopkins University Studies in History and Political Science, no. 45, Baltimore, Md. (1927), 24–45.

[18] The treaty language is quoted from Lyman Knapp, "A Study upon the Legal and Political Status of Alaska," *American Law Register* 39 (1891):325–39, at 328. Knapp was governor of Alaska at the time he wrote this article.

[19] None of the major cases defining the status of Alaska natives appeared to turn on interpretations of the distinction between "civilized" and "uncivilized" tribes, evidently because all of the tribes were assumed to be uncivilized. Still, this language was often quoted by legal authorities. See *in re Sah Quah*, 31 F. 327 (D. Ct. Ak. 1886); *Kie v. United States*, 27 F. 353 (C.C.D. Or. 1886); *United States v. Kie*, 26 F. Cas. 776 (1885).

[20] Seward's letter is quoted in U.S. Congress, House of Representatives, "Brief on the Subject of the Jurisdiction of the War Department over the Territory of Alaska," Ex. doc. 135 (1876) (Serial Set, v. 1639, 5). This brief contains all known documents relating to the legal status of Alaska in 1876. Evidently it was compiled by the War Department to support its jurisdiction over Alaska.

Indian country jurisdiction over Alaska, forbidding the importation of liquor, regulating the sale of molasses to make liquor, and restricting the sale of firearms.[21]

The War Department policy was thrown into complete confusion, however, by Federal District Judge Matthew P. Deady's decision in *United States v. Seveloff* (1872), the first criminal case from Alaska to reach the federal courts. Military authorities had arrested Ferueta Seveloff, a Sitka Creole, on charges of selling liquor to "one John Doe, an Indian," and of distilling spirits without paying taxes. The government's theory of the case was simple: the U.S. attorney had properly indicted Seveloff for violating section 23 of the Indian Trade and Intercourse Act of 1834 by "introducing spirituous liquors, to wit, whiskey, into the Indian country, to wit, of Sitka, Alaska, United States of America." The government based its argument on the fact that Alaska was inhabited by Indians and on Seward's assertion that all acts of Congress applying to Indians extended to Alaska as soon as it was acquired from Russia.[22]

In his Portland, Oregon, courtroom, Judge Deady disagreed and held that Alaska was not Indian country.[23] For Deady, the mere fact that a country was inhabited or owned in whole or in part by Indians did not make it Indian country within the purview of the Trade and Intercourse Acts. Instead, the Indian Trade and Intercourse Act of 1834 was a "local act," applying only to those areas where Congress specifically extended it.

In his reasoning, Deady cited and generally followed an earlier Oregon Supreme Court case, *United States v. Tom* (1853), which held that the act

---

[21] 7 Op. Att'y Gen. 295 (1855), "Brief on Jurisdiction," 4–6. It is important to note that, no matter what the legal argument, the army acted as though Alaska was indeed "Indian country." Two further opinions of the attorney general clearly refer to Alaska as "Indian country" in the context of liquor sales. See 14 Op. Att'y Gen. 327 (1873), 16 Op. Att'y Gen. 141 (1878).

[22] *United States v. Seveloff*, 27 F. Cas. 1021 (D. Ore. 1872) (no. 16, 252). The term "Creole" was used in Alaska to refer to persons of mixed Russian and native ancestry. The majority of the 360 U.S. citizens in Sitka during this period were Creoles. See Beardslee, *Reports Relative to Affairs in Alaska*, 13, 17.

[23] Matthew Deady served more than forty years as federal district judge in Portland, Oregon, handing down a number of significant opinions in many areas of public policy unique to the West, including federal Indian law. For an analysis of his work generally, see Ralph James Moody, "Formalism and Fairness: Matthew Deady and Federal Public Land Law in the Early West," *Washington Law Review* 63 (1988):317, 370 and idem, "Matthew Deady and the Federal Judicial Response to Racism in the Early West," *Oregon Law Review* 63, 4 (1984):561–637. Moody's analysis of Deady's opinions, primarily in the area of the legal rights of Chinese immigrants, is inconsistent with the anti-Indian tenor of Deady's opinions. Deady's Alaska opinions are fully analyzed in Deborah Niedermeyer, "The True Interests of a White Population: The Alaska Indian Country Decisions of Judge Matthew P. Deady," *International Law and Politics* 21 (1988):195. A short biographical account of Deady is Sidney Teiser, "A Pioneer Judge of Oregon: Matthew P. Deady," *Oregon Historical Quarterly* 44 (1943):61–81.

of 1834 applied only to territory under the dominion of Congress at the time of its enactment. The justices noted that the western boundary of the United States ended at the Rocky Mountains until 1846. Therefore, they ruled that Oregon Territory was not Indian country under the Trade and Intercourse Act of 1834, and therefore Tom, although an Indian charged with selling liquor to another Indian, could be prosecuted under Oregon law. Adopting this rationale, Deady concluded that Alaska was not Indian country.[24]

The more difficult argument for Deady was Section 1 of the original Alaska Act of 1868, which extended "the laws of the United States relating to customs, commerce, and navigation" to Alaska. This language clearly appeared to embrace the 1834 act. Deady's reasoning began with the assertion that the act of 1834 applied unless there was evidence of a congressional intent not to extend it. Deady then fabricated an implicit intent not to apply the act to Alaska, based on two factors. First, he argued that Congress's use of "commerce" meant "commerce between foreign nations and several states" and not "as a sort of police regulation to preserve the Indians from the injurious consequences of unrestricted intercourse with the White population." Second, he pointed out that elsewhere, in the Alaska Act of 1868, Congress gave the president the power to regulate the importation of spirits into Alaska. This, Deady contended, was inconsistent with Congress's assumption that Alaska was already Indian country. Deady conceded that this view was "subject to correction" but noted that if Congress had intended the Indian Trade and Intercourse Act to apply to Alaska it should have expressed that intent in the Alaska Act of 1868.[25]

As to the second charge against Seveloff, that of distilling spirits without paying taxes, Deady's holding was again troubling. He reasoned that because only the laws regulating "customs, commerce and navigation" extended over Alaska, the court had no jurisdiction at all over the charged crime, which did not fall into any of these categories.[26] Deady's opinion meant there was no criminal law in effect in Alaska.

In response to the *Seveloff* decision, Congress passed a law in 1873 extending the liquor control provisions of the Indian Trade and Intercourse Act to Alaska. In addition, ten months later, Secretary of War William Belknap asked for clarification of the issue from Attorney General George Williams. Williams responded with an opinion holding that Alaska was indeed

---

[24] *United States v. Tom*, 1 Or. 27 (1853), 27–8. *Tom*, in turn, relied partially on *American Fur Company v. United States*, 27 U.S. 358 (Pet. 1829). For an analysis of U.S. Indian policy in Oregon at the time of *Tom*, see C. F. Coan, "The Adoption of the Reservation Policy in the Pacific Northwest 1853–1855," *Oregon Historical Society Quarterly* 23 (1922):1–38.

[25] *United States v. Seveloff*, 27 F. Cas. 1021 (D. Or. 1872), 1024.

[26] Ibid., 1025. Deady's decision is completely wrong: clearly, "distilling liquor" is covered by general laws regulating "customs, commerce and navigation." Indeed, federal liquor control regulations were explicitly under the "commerce clause" of the U.S. Constitution.

Indian country and that no spirituous liquor could be introduced there without War Department authority.[27] The resulting confusion left the military authorities in Sitka and Wrangell in the uncomfortable position of having orders to carry out liquor laws applicable to Indian country in the district of a federal judge who had held that the laws were inapplicable because Alaska was not Indian country. The military resolved this dilemma by acting extralegally: routine criminal matters were either punished summarily by short-term incarceration in the military lockup or left to tribal law.[28]

Between 1872 and 1875, the military in Sitka recorded "confinements" of 147 whites and Creoles and 200 Tlingits. This is a high number of jailings for a community of no more than 800 whites and Creoles and an equal number of Tlingit, although many of those arrested were repeat offenders.[29] Such military arrests were not merely symbolic assertions of power or routine police actions intended to remove people from drinking situations. They were highly intrusive in the daily life of the residents of Sitka, both Tlingit and white.

This state of affairs could not last. Military authorities arrested John A. Carr, the U.S. collector of customs in Wrangell, in September 1874 and charged him with introducing spirits into Alaska in violation of section 20 of the Indian Trade and Intercourse Act. The authorities kept Carr in a military jail until December 19, when the agent filed a writ of habeas corpus. Carr was then conveyed to Judge Deady's court in Portland. Deady found that Congress possessed the authority to extend the Indian Trade and Intercourse Act to Alaska and to empower the military authorities to enforce that law. Nevertheless, he concluded that when military personnel acted under this grant of congressional authority, they did so merely as "police officer[s], marshal[s], or constable[s]." They were civil officers acting pursuant to civil law, not military law. Civil law provided that a civilian in military custody had to be transferred to a civilian jurisdiction within five days of his arrest or be released. Since Carr had been in custody for more than ninety days, he had to be set free.[30]

---

[27] 7 Op. Att'y Gen. 295 (1855), "Brief on Jurisdiction," 8; 14 Op. Att'y Gen. 327 (1873).

[28] U.S. Congress, Senate, "Message from the President of the United States Re . . . Military Arrests in Alaska During the Past Five Years," 44th Congress, 1st session Ex. doc. 33 (1876; Serial Set, v. 1664). The army also generated its own law on the status of Alaska in the form of an opinion written by H. Clay Wood, assistant adjutant-general of the Department of the Columbia, which included Alaska. Wood concluded that Alaska was in fact "Indian country" and dismissed Deady's opinion in *Seveloff* as "fine, metaphysical, and vague reasoning." Wood to Brigadier General O. O. Howard, Dec. 16, 1875. U. S. Congress, House of Representatives, "Jurisdiction of the War Department over the Territory of Alaska," 44th Congress 1st session, Ex. doc. 135 (1876; Serial Set, v. 1689) 1–55, at 54.

[29] "Message from the President." Based on a population of eight hundred, the data reflect the jailing of about 12 percent of the population each year.

[30] *In re Carr*, 5 F. Cas. 115 (1875) (no. 2,432). This case raised again the issue of the legality

John Williams was the subject of another Deady opinion further limiting federal authority in Alaska. In a dispute with another man in 1880, Williams shot his victim five times. He was arrested by the Navy and sent to Portland for trial. Deady dismissed the charges, however, when he found no general laws of the United States prohibiting "assault with a deadly weapon." So long as Alaska was subject to the laws of no other jurisdiction, only federal criminal laws applying to the entire country had effect. Deady observed that sections 5,339 and 5,341 of the U.S. Code prohibited both murder and attempted murder "in any district or country under the exclusive jurisdiction of the United States" but that no corresponding statute covered assault with a deadly weapon.[31] Thus, Deady left Alaska with little protection of the criminal law.

Not surprisingly, Judge Deady's remarkable record of reversals did not extend to Tlingits brought before his court. The coincidence was not missed by the Tlingit, who took it as evidence of the bias of white justice. On January 1, 1879, on a bay not far from Sitka, Kot-ko-wot and Okh-kho-not shot Thomas Brown to death, evidently with robbery as the motive. The wheels of justice turned quickly, and the two received a one-day trial in Portland on April 15. After a short deliberation, the jury convicted Kot-ko-wot of murder and acquitted his partner. Deady then sentenced Kot-ko-wot to be hung and, afterward, to be dissected by a local medical school.[32] The execution proceeded as scheduled. Three years later, Ki-ta-tah, another Tlingit, met the same fate in Deady's court, again for the robbery and murder of two white men.[33]

These two murder cases involved Tlingits who killed whites. To deal with cases involving killings between Tlingits, the U.S. government, through the early 1880s, had a de facto policy of recognizing Tlingit law and leaving

of military law in Alaska and led to several congressional inquiries. See U.S. Congress, Senate, "Letter from the Secretary of War . . . Re. the Case of John A. Carr," 43d Congress, 2d session, Ex. doc. 24 (43–2), 1875 (Serial 1629).

[31] *United States v. John Williams*, 8 Sawy. (1880). The Williams case is described in detail in Beardslee, *Reports Relative to Affairs in Alaska*, 25–7. The file of the case is held as U.S. District Court, Oregon, case no. 865, Record Group 21, National Archives, Seattle Branch.

[32] *United States v. Kotkowot and Okh kho not*, judgment no. 487 (D. Or. 1879). This unreported case is held in U.S. District Court, Oregon, Record Group 21, National Archives, Seattle Branch. See also Beardslee, *Reports Relative to Affairs in Alaska*, 14–15. Judge Deady mentions the cases briefly in his diary, *Pharisee Among Philistines*, ed. M. Clark, Jr. (Portland: Oregon State Historical Society, 1975), 278–9.

[33] *United States v. Kitatah* (D. Or. 1882), judgment no. 640. This unreported case is held in U.S. District Court, Oregon, Record Group 21, National Archives, Seattle Branch. These were the only executions Deady ordered in his, at that time, thirty years on the federal bench. Both cases received matter-of-fact entries in the judge's personal diary. Kot-ko-wot, the first person Deady ever sentenced to death, was not even remembered by name. Ki-ta-tah's proper name made it into the diary, probably because Deady witnessed Kit-ta-tah's "mangled remains on the dissecting board" when the judge coincidentally went to the medical school to deliver a lecture.

such matters to tribal justice. For most military commanders this was a matter of simple expediency: sheer distances to Oregon courts, combined with the weakness of federal authorities in Alaska and the strength of the unconquered Tlingit, dictated such a policy.[34]

The confusion over the status of the Indian tribes in Alaska could not last indefinitely. Judge Deady had done everything within his power to limit the application of existing federal Indian law in Alaska, but he was not able to advance an alternative view of the legal status of the native peoples there. The case that gave him the opportunity to do so occurred in the context of the national debate about the right of Indian people to their own law that was occasioned by the *Crow Dog* decision. Prior to *Crow Dog*, neither Judge Deady nor any white Alaskan had recognized a right to sovereignty among Alaskan natives. For the Tlingit, however, the question of the formal recognition of their sovereignty by U.S. law was not an issue because U.S. authorities had never attempted to apply their law in intra-Tlingit matters. The *Kie* case of 1885 represented a change in this policy.

Charles Kie and his wife Nancy lived on the Indian "ranch" at the outskirts of Juneau.[35] Nancy began to spend more and more time in the white village, becoming friendly enough with whites to complain about Kie's treatment of her. Evidently incensed by Nancy's complaints and her general conduct with whites, Kie brutally stabbed her, leaving her dead in broad daylight in the middle of the Tlingit village. The Tlingits declined to punish Kie: under their tradition he had the right to kill her because her behavior constituted evidence of adultery. Local whites, however, were infuriated with Kie's cold-blooded conduct and his open defiance of U.S. law. They prevailed upon the U.S. marshal to arrest Kie and charge him with murder. Accordingly, Kie, old and syphilitic, was taken to Sitka for trial.

Kie's case, tried in the new federal district court created under the Organic Act of 1884, passed without incident, for the openness of the defendant's action left no question that he was guilty of some offense. A white jury convicted Kie of manslaughter, and he was sentenced to ten years in prison and fined $100. The jurisdictional issue, however, had been raised before the trial in the form of a demurrer. Kie's attorney, citing *Crow Dog*, argued that U.S. courts had no jurisdiction over crimes between Tlingits. Thus,

---

[34] Beardslee, *Reports Relative to Affairs in Alaska*, 11–27, provides the best report on local law enforcement in Alaska in 1880. The general demoralization and incapacity of the U.S. military in Alaska should be clear from the *Carr* case. See, generally, W. Hunt, *Distant Justice: Policing the Alaska Frontier* (Norman: University of Oklahoma Press, 1987), chaps. 1 and 2; and Claus Naske, "The Shaky Beginnings of Alaska's Judicial System," *Western Legal History* 1 (1988) 163.

[35] A Tlingit community adjacent to a white village was referred to as a "ranch" or "ranche" by local whites. Sitka, Wrangell, and Juneau were all located next to Tlingit *qwans*, which grew with the increased commercial activity of the white settlements.

United States v. Kie was contemporaneous with *Kagama*, the first case after the *Crow Dog* decision to place the issue of the extent of Indian criminal jurisdiction squarely before a court.[36]

In a poorly reasoned opinion, Judge Ward McAllister, Jr., newly appointed as Alaska's first federal district judge, closely adhered to Judge Deady's four preceding cases and defined the question solely as "whether Alaska was Indian country." In deciding that Alaska was not, Judge McAllister ignored Supreme Court Justice Stanley Matthews's expansive definition of Indian country in his *Crow Dog* opinion. According to Justice Matthews, Indian country included "all the country to which the Indian title has not been extinguished within the limits of the United States, even when not within a reservation ... and notwithstanding the formal definition in that act has been dropped from statutes."[37] Here Matthews addressed the formalistic rules of statutory construction that Judge Deady had previously used to hold that Alaska was not Indian country. The U.S. Supreme Court's broad definition was a deliberate attempt to curtail the ability of local courts, including federal district courts and territorial courts, to weaken the *Crow Dog* doctrine by limiting the extent of Indian country.

Even though Judge McAllister overlooked the fact that *Crow Dog*'s definition of Indian country directly threatened the underpinnings of Judge Deady's early reasoning, Deady himself, hearing *Kie* on appeal in 1886, did not. He recognized the direct challenge to his Indian country decisions and, in an opinion that still has a negative impact on the rights of Alaskan natives, retraced all of his old steps. He first addressed the Supreme Court's departure from the limitations imposed by the definition of Indian country in the Indian Trade and Intercourse Act of 1834. Deady observed that the Court's new definition was even more narrow and would always leave Alaska law distinct from the rest of U.S. law. Falling back on territorial determinism, Deady argued that *Crow Dog* "arose in Dakota, a territory acquired from France in 1803, while the anomalous condition of Alaska was not probably considered by the court." Deady further observed that the Court always treated Alaska separately from other states in all references to Indian law unless it took direct cognizance of the Alaskan situation.[38] Since the Court had never taken a case from Alaska or directly passed on Alaska's status, this argument was dishonest.

Deady addressed the question of Indian title to Alaska for the first time, seizing on the language of Justice Matthews, which required the Indian title

[36] *United States v. Charles Kie*, 26 F. Cas. 776 (Court 1885). The court files of the case, Criminal case 1 of Sitka Federal District Court are held in Record Group 21, National Archives, Anchorage.

[37] *Crow Dog*, 109 U.S. 556 (1883), 561–2.

[38] *Kie v. United States*, 27 F. 353 (C.C.D.Or. 1886).

to be "unextinguished." Deady began by pointing out that the United States acquired title to Alaska from the Russians, who had not made treaties with the Indians. Rather, "at the date of this cession, Russia owned this country as completely as it now does the opposite Asiatic shore." Thus, Alaska failed to meet the two conditions that would constitute it as Indian country: first, the language of the Trade and Intercourse Act did not apply to it; second, the United States acquired the Russian title to the land, thereby extinguishing the Indian title.

Perhaps knowing, however, that his reasoning would not stand the scrutiny of higher courts, Deady mooted the case to prevent an appeal: he remanded on the grounds that Kie's sentence had been miscalculated. The Alaska District Court later sentenced Kie to a seven-year prison term, but there is no record that he was ever imprisoned.[39]

Alaskan natives felt the impact of Deady's holding in the most direct way: they were deprived of their sovereign right to apply their own laws to disputes between native peoples and were made subject to all of the same laws that governed whites in the Territory of Alaska.[40] At the same time, however, they were deprived of most of the protections afforded other tribes under federal Indian law, which, because it was based on either treaty rights or the Indian Trade and Intercourse Act, did not apply to Alaska. With no special federal protection, or even recognition of their status as members of native tribes, Alaskan natives were fully exposed to local law and legal institutions. These laws could be applied unimpeded to natives in all situations and could be used as powerful weapons in the process of assimilation, as well as for broader purposes of social control and land deprivation. Judge Deady, certainly knowledgeable of the political burden of Indian sovereignty in the territories, dealt a terrible blow to the rights of the Alaskan natives by using federal law to deprive them of their sovereign right to be ruled by their own law.[41]

Tlingit law meets U.S. law

Although whites characterized Tlingit law, as well as other native law, as based on revenge, the truth is quite the opposite. The Tlingit regularly used

[39] Kie's name does not appear in the official register of prisoners at McNeil Island Federal Prison, where all Alaska prisoners were sent. This list appears to be complete. It is possible that Kie served a short term in the local jail at Sitka.

[40] Only a few federal laws were applied to Alaska in the 1870s. The Organic Act changed this situation by bringing the laws of the state of Oregon to Alaska. Thus, after 1884 the Tlingit faced a full range of white laws governing all aspects of social life.

[41] What motivated Deady's determination to withhold "Indian country" status from Alaskan natives is unknown. As a longtime resident of Oregon, however, Deady was fully aware of similar debates over the extension of "Indian country" status to Oregon in the 1850s. From his perspective, such status adversely affected white settlement. For an analysis of Deady in

peace ceremonies to settle both local and interclan disputes that might lead to feuds or warfare. These ceremonies were initiated along clan lines by men married to women of the clan or family involved in the dispute. Thus, attempts to negotiate peace began with a recognition of the interrelatedness of all Tlingit peoples.[42]

The men who served as peace negotiators for each clan were charged with determining what compensation the other side demanded. They then carried the message back to their own clan and arranged for the actual performance of the agreement, in either goods or human lives. Within the *qwan*, the settlement of disputes always took the form of an exchange of property and never involved blood.[43]

The Tlingit had a very definite sense of peace and justice and believed that such notions of justice should extend to the whites who came into their land. Accordingly, a pattern developed in Tlingit and white relations. The Tlingit tried repeatedly to restore their traditional sense of justice through their own laws but were frustrated by continual white interference. This conflict often led to violence. This violence, in turn, undermined the legitimacy of the military government in Alaska, leading to congressional intervention and, ultimately, the installation of a civilian government. At first, a series of small incidents had been ignored; ultimately, the unrest in Alaska led to national and international embarrassment for the United States.

Two of the best-known conflicts between the Tlingit and Americans led to the shelling of Tlingit villages by the U.S. Navy. In the first incident, in 1870, a white laundress at Fort Wrangell intervened in a dispute between a Tlingit man, Si-wau, and his wife. Angry at this interference, Si-wau seized the woman's hand and bit off her finger. An army lieutenant, with a detachment of twenty men, was sent to bring in Si-wau. A Tlingit named Scutd-doo directed them to a house where Si-wau was waiting with several other Tlingit. Si-wau refused to go with the officers, rushed the line, and tried to take a gun from a soldier. The officer hit Si-wau in the head with his sword to stun him. In the process, however, the soldier inadvertently gave a prearranged signal to fire. Si-wau was killed instantly, and another Tlingit, Esteen, was badly wounded. After an altercation with Tow-ye-at, a subchief, the soldiers removed Si-wau and Esteen to the military fort. Unfortunately, detailed records of this encounter were not made, but it seems

the context of racial cases, see Ralph Mooney, "Matthew Deady and the Federal Judicial Response to Racism in the Early West," *Oregon Law Review* 63, no. 4 (1984):584–6.

[42] De Laguna, *Under Mount Saint Elias*, 592–3, provides an outline of the principles of Tlingit law.

[43] Ibid., 593: "Peace does not mean cessation of fighting, the imposition and acceptance of conditions of surrender; it means restoration of lawful relationships, settlement of claims for loss and injury, and reestablishment of equity." This is a central theme of Oberg, "Crime and Punishment in Tlingit Society," *American Anthropologist* 36 (1934):145–56.

probable in light of later events that Tow-ye-at demanded payment for the death.[44]

Within an hour of this altercation, residents heard gunfire and found Leon Smith, a trader, shot to death in front of his store. A detachment of troops was sent under a flag of truce to demand that the Tlingit village turn over Scutd-doo, the killer, for punishment. The troops were met by Tow-ye-at in paint and a fighting costume. He refused to turn over the murderer. Several hours later, after the deadline for the surrender of the killer passed, the army opened fire on the Tlingit village with two cannon, one from the fort and one from the hills behind the fort. The Tlingit returned the fire with muskets.[45]

The bombardment ceased the next day when Scutd-doo's wife and sub-chief were turned over as hostages. A few hours later, the killer surrendered. Scutd-doo was given a military trial and hung three days later. Although the military chose to treat the incident under U.S. law as an individual act of killing, there is no question that Scutd-doo had acted for his clan in killing Smith, probably to impress upon the whites the importance of respecting Tlingit law.

The U.S. military command in Sitka managed to become involved in a parallel situation and also destroyed a Tlingit village. A visiting Chilcat chief was received at dinner by the U.S. commander General Jefferson Davis and was given a present of two bottles of whiskey. On the chief's way back to his camp, a sentry challenged him, kicking him when he refused to yield. The chief then kicked the sentry and took his rifle back to his camp. A detachment of soldiers was sent to arrest the chief but was repulsed in a skirmish. The chief later submitted to U.S. authority and was locked in jail. In the meantime, a Kake canoe entered Sitka harbor, and a sentry, acting under orders imposing a curfew on Indians in Sitka during this trouble, fired on the canoe, killing two Kake warriors.[46]

The Tlingit demanded payment for both of these affronts. The Chilcat affair was settled easily when a Sitka trader was seized in Chilcat territory. The Chilcats demanded payment, in money or in life, for their injury in Sitka. The trader, after acting as a peacemaker and trying to mediate with General Davis, paid thirteen blankets and a coat, settling the matter amicably. The Kake, however, failing to receive compensation, killed two white traders. General Davis proceeded to Kake and attacked and burned the village, destroying twenty-nine houses and a number of canoes.[47]

---

[44] U.S. Congress, Senate, 41st Congress 2d session, Ex. docs. 67 and 68 (1870; Serial Set, 1406). Another account of this event can be found in Sherwood, "Ardent Spirits: Hooch and the Osprey. Affair at Sitka," *Journal of the West* 4, 3 (1965):301–44.
[45] U.S. Senate, Ex. doc. 67; Sherwood, "Ardent Spirits," 309–10.
[46] Sherwood, "Ardent Spirits," 308–10.
[47] Ibid., 310, 311.

In the following years, such situations occurred with increasing frequency. Although whites usually did not pay for violations of Tlingit law, they sometimes did, implicitly recognizing Tlingit law. Because white payment was most often problematic, these events always created tension. One 1872 incident put the entire Sitka garrison under arms and on full alert over compensation for the value of an egg broken by a soldier.[48]

The corruption and incompetence of army rule became obvious, both because of these instances of violence and because of the spectacle presented by the *Carr* and *Waters* cases, which featured military officers involved in the fur-trading business. Therefore, the army was withdrawn from Alaska in 1877, and the Treasury Department took administrative control in Sitka and Wrangell. Alaska, for all legal purposes, became a customs district. The Tlingit did not fail to understand the significance of this change: they pulled down the military stockades in Sitka and Wrangell and burned them for firewood.[49]

The low point in Tlingit and U.S. relations came with the "Sitka affair." In 1879, Sitka was a very rough place, more or less under Tlingit control. Its population included no more than 80 whites and 200 Creoles, whereas the Indian population numbered about 800 and was the center of an active trading circle that often attracted more Tlingit to Sitka.[50] For all practical purposes, the Tlingit did not respect the sovereignty of the United States, but believed they existed as coequal peoples in a trading relationship.

Liquor, however, corrupted the equality of this exchange process. Although Alaska was officially dry, there was liquor smuggling and widespread manufacture of "hooch," named after the Hoochinoo Tlingit, a local people demoralized by the product. Hooch was made in crude stills from molasses and almost any other available ingredient. Federal raids often destroyed forty stills in a single village without affecting the trade at all.[51]

Because of the power inequality, Tlingit law prevailed amid this disorder, and events unsettling to local whites often occurred. When, on one occasion, a white and a Tlingit got so drunk that the Tlingit died, his family demanded retribution from both the drinking partner and the merchant who sold the liquor. After negotiation, the Tlingit were paid $250 and liquor. In a killing between Tlingits, Indians searched various houses owned by whites looking for the killer. The execution of a Tlingit witch, carried out in plain view of

[48] Ibid.
[49] Beardslee, *Reports Relative to Affairs in Alaska*, 13–15.
[50] Ibid., 13–27.
[51] Morgan Sherwood, "Ardent Spirits," details the history of hooch manufacture in the Sitka area. See also E. Lemert, *Alcohol and the Northwest Coast Indians*, University of California Publications in Culture and Society, vol. 2, no. 2 (Berkeley: 1954), a pioneering sociological analysis for the effect of liquor on Northwest Coast Indians (although not specifically the Tlingit) that includes some historical background.

white society but with no regard for white law or custom, distressed local whites even more.[52]

Two events precipitated the Sitka affair. In the first, members of Kiksati, an aggressive Tlingit *qwan* that did not defer to U.S. authority, killed a white resident of Hot Springs, a nearby settlement. Indian policemen sent by Chief Annahootz of Sitka arrested two men from the second most powerful Kiksati clan. In a second, unrelated incident, a Kiksati tried to collect compensation for the drowning of five fellow Kiksati crewmen on a trading vessel. When the ship's owners in San Francisco refused, he returned home and demanded the back wages of the five men from local authorities, who were also unwilling to make restitution.[53]

From the Kiksati standpoint, two of their men were in jail for killing one white man, while five of their men were dead with no compensation. The exchange between the two peoples was not in balance. Chief Katlean threatened to kill five shopkeepers in Sitka unless the money was paid. When a drunken brawl later ensued in the Sitka Tlingit ranch, word spread among whites that Katlean's men were attacking the local Tlingit. A small Kiksati party aiming to free the Kiksati murder suspects was repulsed with one Tlingit injured. Alarmed residents met the next day and, recognizing the military weakness of the United States in the Northwest and not expecting the U.S. government to come to their aid, sent a message asking for British help. Happy to embarrass their rival, the British dispatched the man-of-war *Osprey* from Victoria with six cannon and 141 men. A few weeks later, the *Osprey* was reinforced by the U.S. Navy. The whole affair was an overreaction on the part of local whites to their powerlessness at the hands of the Tlingit.

In the aftermath of the Sitka affair, the United States tried another tactic. Although the Treasury Department remained in administrative control, U.S. Navy Captain Beardslee was sent to restore orderly relations with the Tlingit. Conflict with the Tlingit was interfering with the fur trade, the mainstay of the Alaska economy, and thus undermining the whole colonial enterprise. Beardslee, taking a lesson from the Russian experience, and realizing that he could not control eight thousand heavily armed Indians along one thousand miles of rough coastline without their cooperation, came ready to recognize Tlingit sovereignty as the price of living among them.

Arriving in Sitka in 1880, Beardslee carried important and upsetting news of the execution and dissection of Kot-ko-wot. The Tlingit were not angry about the execution – Kot-ko-wot had killed another man and that man's people were entitled to retribution – but they were distressed by the circumstances of the trial and by the dissection of the body. The Tlingit

[52] Sherwood, "Ardent Spirits," 324–5.
[53] Ibid., 327–8.

reasoned that the presence of one's family and clan at the settlement of the offense was necessary to ensure justice; no one represented Kot-ko-wot's people at his trial. Nevertheless, Kot-ko-wot's execution, by Tlingit standards, ended the matter, as both sides were even. But dissection injured Kot-ko-wot in his afterlife, a punishment that went beyond his offense.[54]

Beardslee was unimpressed with the Creole population at Sitka, calling them vile characters and emphasizing their dishonesty, laziness, and drunkenness.[55] Following in the footsteps of military commanders before him, he recognized that although he had no legal power to arrest a citizen or inflict punishment, he had no choice but to assume responsibility for doing both. This put Beardslee squarely at odds with Judge Deady's various rulings on the legality of such arrests, but he also knew that few Alaskans could reach the federal court in Oregon.[56]

Beardslee spent much of his time trying to form a civil government for Sitka's white community, while maintaining the belief that the Tlingit community was well governed by Chief Annahootz. For Beardslee, the failure of U.S. law to punish several violent white assaults was irreconcilable with the conviction and hanging of Kot-ko-wot and made it impossible to explain U.S. law to the Tlingit. As a result of this experience, Beardslee decided that he had no choice but to conduct his work in Alaska under Indian country statutes. The general laws of the United States applied to Indian country but not to crimes committed between Indians. In effect, Beardslee adopted a course directly opposite Judge Deady's opinions and set about to support and strengthen Tlingit tribal law as the most efficient way to ensure order in Alaska. The use of force under such conditions would not work because the Tlingit were so strong and independent. Moreover, in Beardslee's view, the violence of the previous year had been caused by whites ignoring Tlingit law.[57]

In the Sitka area, Beardslee's policy led to the immediate appointment of Chief Annahootz and four other tribal leaders as policemen for the Tlingit ranch. They were to preserve order by arresting all drunken Tlingit who entered the adjacent white village. These Tlingit police, however, were

---

[54] Beardslee, *Reports Relative to Affairs in Alaska*, 15–16.

[55] "According to Indian law, the man who gets another drunk is responsible for the acts committed by him while in that state and for his life if he dies or is killed. Thus, at the very root of the difficulty, I found the acts of bad white men." Ibid., 45.

[56] Ibid., 13.

[57] Ibid., 43–8. Beardslee sets forth this position with considerable clarity and a remarkable sense of Tlingit ethnography. He clearly knew that he was acting inconsistently with Deady's decisions but never acknowledged that he was acting illegally. Rather, he based his decisions on his own interpretation of the federal law contained in the "Indian country" statues. For a history of federal criminal jurisdiction in "Indian country," a doctrine originating in 1790 and surviving to this day, see Robert Clinton, "Criminal Jurisdiction over Indian Lands: A Journey Through a Jurisdictional Maze," *Arizona Law Review* 18 (1976):503–83.

forbidden to arrest whites or to collect rewards for catching deserters in order to avoid inciting resentment by white citizens. The police thereafter kept order on the ranch without white assistance.[58]

Beardslee also focused on the source of much Indian crime. With three Tlingit policemen and no military assistance, he raided three Tlingit ranches at nearby Hunter's Bay, destroying forty stills. About twenty Tlingit joined the effort, and the crowd grew larger as the owner of each smashed still joined in to smash the stills of his competitors. Beardslee, pleased with the success of this raid, overlooked the fact that by joining in the destruction of smaller stills, the Tlingit protected larger ones. Thus, it appears that the Tlingit seized on a part of the form of white law, in this case the police function, to protect tribal activities.

Beardslee was not above the raw use of U.S. law in a show of power in violation of his own policy. Big Charlie, a well-known Tlingit who was often drunk and dangerous, had raped a Tlingit woman. The Tlingit did not take cognizance of the crime. Moreover, Charlie had tried to kill a military sentry several years before in retaliation for being punished by General Davis. For Beardslee, this indicated a lack of respect for U.S. government authority and a more general feeling among the Tlingit that the white were afraid of them. Beardslee summoned the chiefs to a council and tried Charlie. After the tribal council convicted him, it imposed "severe punishment," a term in the local jail. When Charlie had served his time, he was given a job with the Navy and became "one of the best behaved Indians in Sitka." Word of the trial spread far and wide among the Tlingit, and U.S. justice became more respected.[59]

When murder pushed his authority to the limit, however, Beardslee hedged. One Tlingit caught another in an adulterous relationship with his wife and shot the man to death. On hearing this, a brother of the dead man sought out and killed his brother's murderer. White authorities seized the killer and an accomplice, but Beardslee declined either to try the case or to send the accused to Oregon for trial. The two deaths left the two families even.

Beardslee's decision not to invoke U.S. law in a murder case was not only a conscious and important choice; it was the logical outcome of his policies. The Tlingit knew that whites were weak, so Beardslee limited the scope of his intervention. He used Tlingit police to keep order in the Indian ranch because it was more efficient and less inflammatory than sending marines there and because he did not particularly care what disposition the Tlingit police made. Riot and disorder were common in the Tlingit ranch, but

[58] Beardslee, *Reports Relative to Affairs in Alaska*, 46.
[59] Ibid., 48.

whites were most concerned with drunken Indians in their own village.[60] Although Beardslee might intervene in an Indian rape, punish Creole wife-beaters with imprisonment on bread and water, and occasionally smash stills, he treaded very lightly on Tlingit sovereignty.

This was the situation in Sitka, the seat of white Alaskan power. Elsewhere in Alaska, Tlingit political authority went almost unchallenged. Major events in both Wrangell and Juneau, then named Harrisburg, show the fragility of U.S. authority.[61]

A group of Kootznoo Tlingits visited Wrangell on a trading expedition and began to manufacture hooch for trade in the interior. Sticheen Tlingits tried to suppress this traffic by force, and several were killed and wounded on both sides. The Kootznoos sent back to their village for reinforcements, while local whites set up a "committee of safety" and barricaded themselves in their town.

A missionary sent a Sticheen policeman to arrest the Kootznoos, who did not recognize his authority and beat him up. The injured police officer's clan then set about to avenge the beating, and the Kootznoos sent a young man to receive a beating to set matters right. Unfortunately, angry Sticheens beat the young man too severely, and when the Kootznoos rushed to his rescue a general fight broke out. After the Kootznoos retreated, their village, used as a trading residence by visiting tribes generally, was burned by the Sticheens.[62]

To Beardslee the whole affair was the fault of local whites, who incited the Sticheens to violence in an effort to further their interest in weakening trading competition. The destruction of the village angered all local tribes, who thereafter avoided Wrangell for trading. Beardslee believed that whites should learn more about and interfere less in Tlingit local customs. He evidently felt that the Kootznoos possessed a traditional right to use the trading village and believed that the Sticheens had no authority to regulate Kootznoo affairs. Beardslee later visited the Kootznoo village and threatened to punish the tribe if they renewed the trouble in Wrangell, even though he

---

[60] Ibid., 46. The single most important cause of the *Osprey* affair was aggressive U.S. antiliquor patrols through the Tlingit village. See Sherwood, "Ardent Spirits," 328.

[61] Beardslee, *Reports Relative to Affairs in Alaska*, 44–5. The fragility of U.S. authority was one of Beardslee's major themes: "If by a mistake we won the ill-will of the Indians, it would have been impossible for me, with the force at my disposal, to prevent outrages or punish the perpetrators.... Fully conscious that, should our course in handling them be such as to excite the opposition of the Indians, our physical force would not prove equal to the task of subduing them, it was deemed advisable that our efforts should be directed to obtain control of them with their good will and consent, instead of trying to do so against it, and to avoid taking any steps which would redound to the injury of whites at Sitka if left again without protection, or which would tend to increase the dangers to such men as sought the interior on prospecting trips" (44).

[62] Ibid., 50–4.

believed the trouble was not their fault. The Kootznoos agreed to this, on the condition they be allowed to fight the Sticheens if they came to Kootznoo territory.[63]

Beardslee's most complex mediation was between the Chilcats and Chilcoots, who were in conflict not only with each other but also with a growing population of white miners on the mainland. A series of shootings between the tribes left many scores to settle, both with each other and with the whites. In addition, increasing exposure to corrupt and brutal traders and miners destabilized relations on the northern reaches of Tlingit land.

Beardslee assembled Chilcat and Chilcoot chiefs to resolve the dispute. Klotz-Kutch, chief of the Chilcats, declared that it was right to settle, claiming that he "would rather pay two hundred blankets than have a long war about a bad man not worth a hundred." But the trouble could not be ended without the consent of the families of the dead men. Finally, the chiefs agreed that they would personally pay whatever amount was finally decided, and this concluded the matter.[64]

Beardslee's work lasted only a year and a half, the final period of military rule before the Alaska Organic Act extended a measure of self-government. His policy of stabilizing authority in the Alaska panhandle by building a foundation of honorable relations between whites and Tlingits and his deferral to Tlingit authority as much as possible proved to be highly successful practices. Clearly, contradictions existed in this policy, but Beardslee struck what appeared to be the only responsible compromise possible under the circumstances. He sent no criminal cases south to Judge Deady's court. Moreover, he recognized Tlingit law de facto in cases between Tlingits. Because of the great distance to Judge Deady's court and the few resources of the small and poor white population in Alaska, Beardslee's extralegal recognition of Tlingit law escaped legal challenge. While there was a well-developed legal doctrine prior to 1884 that denied the Tlingit any legal rights in their own country, there was also a very clear set of government actions ignoring that law and recognizing Tlingit sovereignty. Both of these inconsistent policies were passed on to Alaskan authorities with the arrival of self-government in 1884.

Ironically, perhaps the most famous conflict between Tlingits and whites occurred as a direct result of Beardslee's policy of recognizing and deferring to Tlingit law. The new U.S. Navy commander, Captain E. C. Merriman, apparently decided that the Tlingit were behaving too much as a sovereign people and needed to be put in their place. On a U.S. whaling ship in the bay at Angoon, one of the bombs used in whaling exploded by accident,

[63] Ibid., 54–5, 69.
[64] Ibid., 71–3.

killing a Tlingit shaman employed by the whaling company as a crewman. Outraged Tlingit demanded compensation of two hundred blankets and seized one of the whaling boats, some equipment, and two whites as hostages until payment could be arranged. The seizure of hostages in such cases was in keeping with Tlingit law, and the Tlingit treated them honorably to demonstrate the good will of the clan. The captain of the whaling fleet, however, was not interested in settling the matter according to Tlingit tribal law and fled in a tugboat to Sitka, calling upon the U.S. Navy to "teach the Tlingit a lesson."[65]

Captain Merriman, it seems, had been looking for just such an opportunity, so he took a company of marines, a howitzer, and a Gatling gun and sailed to Angoon. As soon as Merriman anchored in the harbor, the Tlingit released the hostages and the property. Merriman, in turn, captured some Tlingit "ringleaders" and demanded four hundred blankets in tribute. When the Tlingit refused, Merriman responded first by destroying forty canoes and later by burning the village. The Navy expedition then shelled a nearby village, and a landing party burned all the houses, except for a few belonging to Indians known to the Navy as "friendly."[66]

William Morris, a collector of customs who accompanied the expedition, filed a report on the incident. He made clear that the action was aimed at stopping the Tlingit from applying their laws to whites. Tlingit custom had, in his view, forced whites to pay for a number of Tlingit deaths. Morris went on to emphasize that the Tlingit were surly, impertinent, insolent, "saucy toward Whites," and did not fear the authority of the government. As a result, the insistence of the Tlingit on applying their laws to whites who worked among them became a major issue in the struggle for political domination of Alaska.[67]

Merriman's actions were not without controversy. The image of the Navy shelling an Indian village had a powerful impact all across the country. Congressman James Budd of California characterized these actions as "pro-

[65] U.S. Congress, House of Representatives, "Letter from the Secretary of the Treasury in Response to . . . the Alleged Shelling of Two Villages in Alaska," 47th Congress, 2d session, Ex. doc. 9, pts. 1–4 (1882), pt. 1, 1–3; pt. 2, 1–2; pt. 3, 1–4; pt. 4, 1–2.

[66] Ibid.

[67] Ibid., pt. 2, 1–2: "Whilst an Indian was cutting down a tree for the Northwest Trading Company . . . the tree fell and killed him. Immediately, a certain number of blankets were levied as a fine upon the company by his relatives, and payment demanded. The company refused, of course. Matters remained at a status quo until Captain Merriman arrived . . . and complaint was made by the superintendent of the company. He informed the Indians that in future no such payments should either be demanded or enforced as far as white men were concerned; that if they persisted he would punish them severely, and that, in this instance, the company would and should not pay. They submitted in bad grace." Thus, Tlingit law was seen as a threat to U.S. economic interests. U.S. companies that employed Tlingit workers faced liability for accidental deaths under Tlingit law but not under U.S. law.

ceedings unworthy of a drum-head court martial" and accused the Navy of making and executing laws: Merriman was "judge, jury, and sheriff."[68]

Tlingit law under the purview of U.S. courts

The Angoon incident marked the end of the joint rule of Alaska by the U.S. Navy and the Treasury Department. While cavalry attacks on Indian tribes had become a part of white folklore, the image of Navy gunboats bombarding a Tlingit village was a negative one, inducing Congress to demand changes in the administration of Alaska. At the same time, the still small white population there was lobbying for local self-government. The passage of the Alaska Organic Act in 1884 made the full application of U.S. law there possible for the first time. In addition to an administrative apparatus headed by an appointed governor, the act supplied a federal legal apparatus in the form of a U.S. district court and supporting officials, all located in Sitka, still a community of not more than three hundred U.S. citizens, two hundred of whom were Creoles.[69]

The creation of a federal legal institution in Alaska was the result of a well-organized campaign by Alaskan businessmen and missionaries, who viewed the "Indian problem" as part of a larger "law and order problem." Missionary Sheldon Jackson and the Presbyterian hierarchy wanted legal protection for their mission work. Alaskan businessmen, like those in the Indian Territory, regarded the routine disorder of Sitka and other Alaskan towns as a major obstacle to the expansion of commerce.[70] The great distance to Oregon made it impossible to continue to subsume Alaska within the federal district of Oregon, while the rising value of gold and other natural resources further heightened the importance of a local legal institution. The twin scandals of the "Sitka affair" and the "Alaska ring," a corrupt monopoly

---

[68] James Budd, "Alaska: Needed Indian Policy," in "Papers on Alaska," a bound volume of miscellaneous documents on Alaska, Newberry Library, Chicago. Budd's remarks were made on the floor of the House of Representatives on May 13, 1884.

[69] Portions of the debate over Alaska's Organic Act can be found in U.S. Congress, Senate, "Report of the Committee on Territories," 47th Congress, 2d session, Report no. 457 (1882; Serial Set, v. 2006). On the role of the Organic Act in creating Alaska's judicial system, see Spicer, *Constitutional Status and Government of Alaska.*

[70] J. Paddock, *Alaska: A History of Its Administration, Exploitation, and Underdevelopment,* (Cleveland, Ohio: Arthur H. Clark, 1924), 65–113, describes these lobbying efforts. At the same time, there occurred parallel debates over the extension of federal laws to the Indian Territory. See Morris L. Wardell, *A Political History of the Cherokee Nation, 1838–1907* (Norman: University of Oklahoma Press, 1938), 308–11. Although no direct connection can be made between these situations, it seems clear that where local whites saw Indians with political and legal power, the "law and order" issue was raised.

on fur trading in western Alaska, contributed toward making law and order for the territory a major issue.[71]

In its debates on Alaskan self-government, Congress was aware of the legal position of the Indians there. In the report of the Committee on Territories, Senator Manning Butler explained precisely why the language of the law did not distinguish the Indians' legal status from that of whites: the Indians in Alaska were "industrious and well disposed," and "no different treatment of them was advised." Butler went on to observe that the policy of giving Indians the same status as whites was working well in British Columbia.[72]

As congressional discussion continued, it is clear that a new Indian policy was being formulated, not only for Alaska but for the entire United States. In the debate on the Organic Act, Congressman Budd strongly advocated a policy of alienating Indian land and of holding Indians fully accountable under U.S. law.[73] Congress, divided by its debates regarding Indian policy in the rest of the United States, decided to keep Alaskan natives under the same law as whites. Congress thus avoided the difficult legal and moral issues raised by the sovereign legal status of Indians in its policy for Indians throughout the rest of the United States.

Budd's view, the same as that of the IRA, was never wholly adopted by Congress, but a substantial body of congressional opinion favored the extension of U.S. law to Indians. Unable to incorporate that viewpoint into the law for the rest of the United States, Congress achieved this result in Alaska virtually by default. By simply avoiding recognition of the sovereignty of Alaskan natives and their tribal law, Congress made these people fully subject to U.S. criminal law.[74]

Legal affairs in Sitka soon degenerated into a maze of incompetence and

---

[71] Sherwood, "Ardent Spirits;" Naske, "Shaky Beginnings of Alaska's Judicial System."

[72] "Report of the Committee on Territories," 4.

[73] Budd, "Alaska: Needed Indian Policy," 3.

[74] See J. Thayer, "A People Without Law," *Atlantic Monthly* 68 (Oct. 1891):682–83, 686–7, for the classic statement of the position of the IRA. Thayer, a professor at Harvard Law School, drafted several bills for the Friends of the Indian, a reform group whose goal was to extend U.S. law to the Indian tribes as a means of "civilizing" them. Congressman Budd's view was informed by this assimilationist vision: "Certainly no one can deny the fact that the white citizens of Alaska are the only persons up there who can have the least appreciation or understanding of our legislative, executive, and judicial system of law and order, and they are the only ones to whom we can intelligently apply these legal provisions. Any one at all acquainted with Indians and their life will at once admit the futility of attempting to treat those people to courts of justice or trials by jury.... It is the 250 white citizens of Alaska only who are deprived of those legal rights and privileges and protection that the committee must keep in mind as they frame a bill for the establishment of additional courts." U.S. Congress, House of Representatives, "Courts of Justice in Alaska," 46th Congress, 2d session, Report no. 754 (Serial Set, v. 1936).

corruption, the result of both presidential patronage and conflict among local whites over the legal allocation of Tlingit property. The first major Tlingit case handed down by the new federal district court directly challenged the authority of the Presbyterian mission school in Sitka to hold Tlingit children for educational purposes.

U.S. Attorney Haskett encouraged a number of Creoles to sue the Presbyterian mission, charging that the mission took land belonging to the community. When the Organic Act granted 640 acres to the Presbyterian mission, Sheldon Jackson had appropriated the best land in Sitka and blocked expansion of the village in one direction in order to create a large mission and school. In the process, the missionaries – outsiders and Protestants – alienated the local Russian Orthodox Creoles.[75]

Rivalry quickly escalated, as local political forces aligned with the Creoles. Jackson was subpoenaed to appear before a grand jury just as he was planning to leave Sitka; he was arrested boarding a ship and held just long enough for the ship to depart. The district court then began to issue writs of habeas corpus on behalf of Tlingit families seeking to remove their children from the mission school, without allowing school officials to be heard. Judge McAllister issued a far-reaching ruling providing (1) that verbal contracts to enroll students in the school were not binding, (2) that Indians could not make contracts with whites, and (3) that the school had no right to restrain students there for any reason.[76] The ruling destroyed discipline at the school: any child "corrected" by the missionaries could simply leave. Many Tlingit parents took advantage of this opportunity to take their children out of school, evidently encouraged to do so by local whites.[77]

Jackson then exercised his political connections, which led directly to the White House both through marriage and through the powerful Presbyterian hierarchy, in a successful campaign to remove the whole Organic Act government and replace it with one more amenable to his wishes. In the process, Jackson's attitude toward Tlingit society became well known. He regarded it as inherently evil and felt that salvation for the Tlingit lay in separating children from their parents and superstition-ridden communities and giving them a white education. The swift dismissal of the old government put

---

[75] Sheldon Jackson, *A Statement of Facts Concerning the Difficulties in Sitka, Alaska, in 1885* (Washington, D.C.: Thomas McGill, 1886), 1–3. Jackson's *Statement of Facts* and newspaper reports in the *Alaskan* are the only remaining accounts of this dispute. Both Jackson and the *Alaskan* were opposed to the existing court officials. Jackson also kept a scrapbook of clippings on the incident; it is held in the Sheldon Jackson Papers, Presbyterian Historical Society, Philadelphia.

[76] Criminal case no. 10, *Con-ah-clan-et v. Sheldon Jackson*, Record Group 21, National Archives, Anchorage. Although this is not a criminal case, habeas corpus cases are routinely so classified.

[77] Jackson, *Statement of Facts*, 1–3, 13. It seems that Judge McAllister was clearly wrong about the first two points and probably right about the third.

control of Indian policy in Sitka in the hands of a group of whites who favored using local law to force the assimilation of the Tlingit. The former policy that emphasized a trading relationship between two sovereign societies and a minimal white effort to dominate Tlingit society was replaced by a program that required the destruction of Tlingit social, economic, cultural, and political institutions as a necessary step in the incorporation of the Tlingit people as menial workers into the white Alaskan economy. Jackson and other Presbyterians led the effort to enforce the policy of assimilation.[78]

Jackson also popularized a number of stories about witchcraft and slavery that were used to justify both a closed school system and legal intervention into Tlingit society, including the imposition of U.S. law over the Tlingit and the corresponding destruction of Tlingit law. Whites found Tlingit treatment of those accused of witchcraft abhorrent and regularly rescued witches. A few Tlingit executions of witches were reported in the press and held out as examples of the evil of Tlingit society and the need for stronger measures to repress tribal traditions, but such incidents seldom came to the attention of the courts.[79] A Tlingit slavery case, however, the only one in North America to come before the courts, played an important role in defining Tlingit society as immoral, uncivilized, barbaric, and fit only for extermination.

Ex parte Sah Quah (1886) was among the boldest of U.S. legal attacks on the tribal law of Native Americans. Although not significant for its doctrine, *Sah Quah* represented a major white intrusion into Tlingit society and reveals the changing internal dynamics of Tlingit society in the face of the extension of white authority. With *United States v. Kie* having already established that Native Americans in Alaska had no sovereign right to their own laws, *Sah Quah* was an easy case: the district court had no trouble finding that the traditional right of Tlingits to take and hold slaves violated the Thirteenth Amendment.[80]

The origin of *Sah Quah* is obscure, but it appears to have been a carefully

---

[78] The campaign to replace the government appears in part in Jackson, *Statement of Facts*, in the form of letters written by powerful people in support of Jackson. The rise of the reform Presbyterian group to domination of Alaskan politics can be seen in T. Hinckley, *Alaskan John G. Brady, Missionary, Businessman, Judge and Governor, 1878–1918* (Miami, Ohio: Ohio University Press, 1982). Not surprisingly, the law of habeas corpus as applied to Tlingit children in missionary boarding schools changed under the new administration.

[79] Jackson, *Statement of Facts*, 11; *Alaskan*, June 30, 1886, 3; July 14, 1888, 4; July 13, 1889, 4; Feb. 28, 1891, 4.

[80] Here it is important to note that even if the court had applied *Crow Dog* to Alaska in the *Kie* case, U.S. law would have applied to *Sah Quah* since the Thirteenth Amendment forbids "persons" from holding slaves anywhere in the United States. Because Indians were clearly "persons" and Indian country was "within the United States," it followed that Indians could not hold slaves. What remains is the culturally complex question, Was Sah Quah a slave within the meaning of the Thirteenth Amendment?

chosen test case deeply rooted in the assimilationist policies of the leading white members of the Sitka community. Just as the Creoles used Tlingit grievances against missionaries in their own struggle for political and economic recognition in Sitka, white reformers seized on a pitiful Tlingit plaintiff, Sah Quah, to force the local court to write a condemnation of Tlingit society and culture so strong that it would attract national attention. Surely, the specter of Tlingit slavery was the most potent point of condemnation possible in post–Civil War United States, more compelling than witchcraft or murder.[81]

On the stand, Sah Quah claimed to be a Haida, kidnapped as a boy by Flatheads, who took him to British Columbia and then sold him to Chilcats, who sold him yet again. He described a life of poverty until a man took pity on him and brought him to Sitka. In response to the direct question, "Are you the slave of this man?" Sah Quah answered, "He is my father." Attorney W. Clark followed up, "Is he your master, also?" Sah Quah replied, "He is my father." Clark tried again, "Is he really your father?" Sah Quah answered unequivocally, "Yes, sir." Clark, nevertheless, continued, "How does it happen you are a Haida if your father is a Sitka Indian?" Sah Quah responded, "The White man is same as Indian; they adopt children." After several more queries, Clark tried a more direct approach: "Have you considered yourself a slave of this man?" Sah Quah replied, "No."[82]

The rest of the case was not much easier. Clark called Marchia, a Tlingit woman. She admitted to being a slave as a little girl, but claimed not to know how she became a slave. Nor did she know when she had become free, but thought it was about two years earlier, after her master finished building a house.

The last witness was Chief Annahootz. Indicative of the political ends of the case, the initial inquiry of Annahootz focused on Tlingit political life and whether the Tlingit political structure was tribal or familial. Annahootz was asked if a chief was chief of the tribe or of his family only, to which

[81] *Sah Quah* had all the makings of a collusive case. Sah Quah appeared in court represented by attorneys W. Clark and Major M. P. Berry, a local politician and former collector of customs. Sah Quah appears to have taken no interest in the case: he would not fully admit to being a slave and did not appear to want to change his status. His alleged owner, Nah-ki-klan, refused to defend his ownership, but Federal Judge Lafayette Dawson would not let the lack of a party stand in the way of this landmark case. He appointed the U.S. attorney, M. D. Ball, to represent Nah-ki-klan. Ball conceded that Sah Quah was held as a slave, a fact that was not proved in court. The alleged owner did not testify. Sah Quah's habeas corpus hearing is summarized in the *Alaskan*, May 8, 1886, 1, 4.

[82] The unpaginated transcript is held as Civ. case no. 35, Record Group 21, Alaska District Court, National Archives, Anchorage. Why a transcript was made remains unclear. No appeal of the court's order was taken, and Nah-ki-klan, because he was represented by the U.S. attorney, had no control over whether an appeal would be taken. In all likelihood the transcript was made because an appeal was contemplated.

Annahootz correctly claimed to be chief only of his family. Status in a tribe was based not on political position but on prestige as head of the richest family. Following this line of questioning was an inquiry into Tlingit justice: if a person was killed, did the tribe or the family pay? Again, the answer was the family.

Annahootz was then asked whether slavery existed. He admitted that it had, but claimed it existed "a long time ago." He described a system of constant warfare and testified that it was formerly the custom to identify slaves by putting out their eyes. He vehemently denied that the Tlingit continued to hold slaves.

The evidence was weak and had little to do with the legal arguments of either side. Clark presented an elaborate argument that had three distinct focuses. First, he advocated the imposition of U.S. law as a means of advancing the Tlingits to civilization. Second, he argued that the Thirteenth Amendment forbade slavery anywhere in the United States, among any people. Third, recognizing that both *Crow Dog* and the Major Crimes Act contained language respecting the sovereignty of Indian tribes, Clark tried to distinguish between the family and the tribe to show that the Alaskan Indians were outside of the scope of federal Indian law because they were families and not tribes.[83]

U.S. Attorney Ball made the only credible argument possible for the Tlingit accused as Sah Quah's owner. He based his case on two issues. First, the Thirteenth Amendment was never intended to apply to Indian tribes; second, the "uncivilized tribes" of Alaska were left by the treaty of acquisition to be provided for in future laws enacted by Congress, and no laws had altered their status. The Major Crimes Act, according to Ball, applied to Alaska and, by specifically enumerating several crimes, had purposefully omitted slavery.[84]

None of these arguments should have been necessary, because *Kie* clearly established that all U.S. laws fully applied to Alaska natives. That the U.S. attorney would argue that the Thirteenth Amendment did not apply to Indians approaches unreality. But this case was a collusive one, and Ball was playing his part. Someone had to represent Sah Quah's Tlingit owner, and the U.S. attorney had the responsibility of representing the interests of Indians. Local whites wanted a strong statement of Tlingit legal rights and of the nature of Tlingit law and social institutions. In their view, *Kie* did not go far enough, and its facts, those of an ordinary murder case, were not as compelling as those of *Sah Quah*.

Judge Dawson's opinion contained no surprises. He rejected both of Ball's

[83] *Alaskan*, May 8, 1886, p. 1.
[84] Ibid., pp. 1, 4.

arguments in an opinion focused on two basic and unrelated issues. First, he once again traced the short history of Indian country legislation for Alaska and held, consistent with Judge Deady's opinions, that *Crow Dog* and the Major Crimes Act never applied there. Second, in a holding that broke new ground and is still unique in federal Indian law, he held that the Thirteenth Amendment applied to the Indian tribes because Congress clearly pronounced its intention to abolish slavery within the territorial limits of the United States. Judge Dawson then granted the writ, and Sah Quah was set free.[85]

In retrospect, the *Sah Quah* decision presented a great distortion of Tlingit society. Even if slavery was the most vulnerable of Tlingit institutions in the eyes of whites, it was so different from black slavery in the United States that it could not be realistically compared. The institution was based on Tlingit family hierarchies of wealth and power and was rooted in a long tradition of raiding neighboring villages. Although slavery was extensive among these peoples in the early 1800s – in some estimates amounting to 30 percent of the total population – it was dying out by the end of the century.[86] Some estimates put the slave population in the 1880s at 10 percent of the Tlingit population, but that figure is almost certainly too high. For those remaining slaves, it was not even clear that being a slave had much meaning. Rather, the slaves functioned as adopted members of families who could not easily be turned away.[87]

Ex parte Sah Quah made it clear that Alaskan whites were deeply involved in a struggle to destroy Tlingit society and assimilate its people as useful citizens of the white community of Alaska. The powerful image of a "slave society" was the most strikingly negative image of the Tlingit that local whites could muster, an image that justified almost any white intrusion into Tlingit society. The court in *Sah Quah* dug up this sad remnant of

---

[85] The full text of the opinion was printed in the *Alaskan*, May 8, 1886, p. 4.

[86] J. Averkieva, *Slavery Among the North American Indians* (Victoria: Victoria College, 1966). De Laguna, *Under Mount Saint Elias*, 469–75, analyzes changes in Tlingit slavery over time. She believes that the last slaves in Yakutat, a far more remote place than Sitka, were freed about 1900 (470).

[87] In his census of Sitka in 1880, Commander Henry Glass noted a slave population of 17 among a total Tlingit population of 721, or 2 percent; quoted in Sherwood, "Ardent Spirits," 302. In 1861, Lieutenant Wehrman of the Russian Navy reported 49 slaves at Yakutat among a total Tlingit population of 380, or about 12 percent. It is probable that both counts are inaccurate, for the Tlingit social structure was complex and slavery difficult to see. For example, Sah Quah did not live in his master's house and evidently provided no labor for him; *Alaskan*, October 23, 1886, 4. What, then, did slavery mean under such conditions? See also R. Olson, *Social Structure and Social Life of the Tlingit Indians in Alaska* (Berkeley: University of California Anthropological Records, 1967), 26. 53 (estimate of 10 percent); Averkieva, "The Tlingit Indians," in E. Leacock and N. Lurie, eds., *North American Indians in Historical Perspective* (New York: Random House, 1971), 329 (range of estimates from 10 to 30 percent).

a great and complex native society to prove that the Tlingit community was barbarous beyond redemption, in desperate need of the civilizing influence of U.S. law.

The accelerating imposition of U.S. law, 1886–1900

The *Kie* and *Sah Quah* cases were the first in which Alaska's district court considered the status of the Indians living in the territory. Both occurred within the first year and a half of the operation of that court. During the next fifteen years, over one hundred more criminal cases were brought against Tlingit in federal district court, fully extending U.S. criminal law to all Tlingit in Alaska without reference to the Major Crimes Act.[88] Hundreds of minor criminal cases against Tlingit were tried in local, justice of the peace courts.[89]

These developments tracked the rapid white migration to Alaska. By the mid-1890s, the Tlingit were a minority in their own land. As the economy shifted from fishing and commercial activity to gold mining, the most extensive interaction between whites and Tlingits moved from Sitka to the gold rush area north of Juneau and Skagway, the land of the Chilcats. The presence of the federal district court in Sitka meant that this difficult period in Indian–white relations was perhaps more legally structured than any similar experience in the United States. Alaska fully applied the "law for the Indians" policy that Indian reformers argued was the key to solving the Indian problem in the United States of the late nineteenth century. The Tlingit still resisted the application of U.S. law.[90]

The murder of a Tlingit by a white in a whiskey riot on Douglas Island occurred soon after the *Kie* case. The ensuing series of events illustrates a great deal about the legal structuring of Tlingit–white relations at the time,

[88] An examination of the original criminal case files held in Record Group 21, National Archives, Anchorage, making racial determinations by name, or by reference to "Indian" in the court records, reveals 108 criminal cases between Kie in 1884 and 1900. These cases are more fully discussed in Chapter 8.

[89] The records of only one of these courts remains, the journal of the U.S. Commissioner's Court for Sitka for 1885–6, when John G. Brady was commissioner. It is held in Record Group 506, Alaska State Archives, Juneau. An analysis of Sitka jail records in 1898, 1899, and 1900 reveals a monthly Indian population ranging from 6 to 25, mostly short-term offenders, which would indicate the jailing of perhaps 100 Tlingit a year in Sitka at that time, perhaps 10 percent of the population. Sitka Jail Sentence Book, held in the Alaska State Archives, Juneau, Record Group 505.

[90] Ward McAllister, Jr., was appointed the first federal district judge for Alaska on July 15, 1884, and arrived in Sitka several months later; Naske, "Shaky Beginnings of Alaska's Judicial System," 168–71. *Kie* was decided in May 1885 and *Sah Quah* in May 1886. The legal foundation for white intervention in Tlingit society was entirely laid out in *Kie* and not changed thereafter.

revealing both the limits of imposed U.S. law and the continuing force of Tlingit law.

Newtown, a small white settlement, developed on Douglas Island around a mine. An Indian ranch spread out nearby, supplying some labor to the mine. When an illegal music hall opened there, "orgies attended by drunken Indians and frequently drunken Whites" occurred. One night, several Tlingits became drunk and demanded more liquor from the proprietor, William Pierce. When he refused, he was hit in the head and face, but the Tlingits were forcibly ejected in the process. A few minutes later, these Tlingits returned and stormed the building, throwing stones at the front and breaking all the windows.[91]

In the midst of this melee, two pistol shots were fired. One struck Kluskeetz, a quiet Tlingit man not involved in the affair, killing him instantly. The other struck a white tug captain, who, hearing the noise, had stepped out in front of a nearby saloon. Pierce escaped to Juneau by boat, raised a posse of a dozen miners, and returned. By then, the situation had quieted down, although a deputy with the posse arrested one man for selling beer.

Although five Tlingits claimed they saw Pierce fire shots out of the window of his saloon, a coroner's jury composed of Pierce's white neighbors found that the shots were fired by "parties unknown." By then, however, the event was notorious throughout southeastern Alaska, and the legal authorities brought eleven cases stemming from the incident, including a charge of murder against Pierce.

The legal principles under which Newton's Kake *qwan* lived were the subject of considerable speculation among whites. Of all the Tlingit peoples, the Kakes were still among the most removed from U.S. government authority. Moreover, the Kakes distrusted white justice and did not expect Pierce to be punished for his crime. Neither did the local press. The *Alaskan* remarked that "whatever the evidence, it may not be possible to convict Pierce of murder in the first degree."[92]

It was immediately clear that, under Tlingit law, some white man must pay for the white murder of a Tlingit. A brother of Kluskeetz was heard by local whites to say that unless Pierce was executed for the murder, he would kill a white. The brother reportedly hired a lawyer, John F. Maloney, to make sure that Pierce was prosecuted. U.S. legal process was explained to Kluskeetz's brother, but he apparently thought it too slow. Pierce also hired Maloney to represent him. Judge Dawson reprimanded Maloney for attempting to represent both sides of the case and ordered him to return the Tlingit's fee.[93]

[91] *Alaskan*, October 29, 1886, 4.
[92] Ibid.; see also the *Alaskan*, December 4, 1886, 4.
[93] Ibid.

Several days after Kluskeetz's brother's remark was overheard, Jack Welch, a miner and carpenter, disappeared. No trace of him was ever found. At the same time, the brother also disappeared, and among local whites there was no doubt that Welch had been killed by the Tlingit. In white terms, such a killing was explained with a simple revenge analysis, but for the Tlingit this kind of action was intended to restore a natural balance.

A Kake delegation went to Sitka to see the governor about the case, concerned that Pierce might be punished less severely than a Tlingit would be. The leader of the delegation put the matter simply: "When an Indian kills a White man you hang him; now a White man kills an Indian. If you want to prove to us that your laws are just and intended to protect as well as punish us, you must hang this White man who killed our brother." The *Alaskan* pointed out the dilemma: the court was considering releasing Pierce on his own recognizance while he awaited trial, and few in Sitka thought a white man could be convicted on the testimony of five Indian witnesses. The paper urged that no effort be spared in the prosecution of this case because Pierce's acquittal could leave the Tlingit with only one opinion about white justice.[94]

Under U.S. law, Pierce's due process rights could not be abridged. However, the operation of that same system could not provide true equality of justice because Alaskan whites would not hold each other legally accountable for crimes against Tlingits. At Pierce's trial nearly a year later, the jury acquitted him after deliberating for twenty-three minutes.[95]

Another major case involving crime against a Tlingit ended the same way as the Pierce trial did, but was partially saved by a plea bargain. F. L. Bangs, a trader, arrived in Wrangell in a small sloop carrying twelve boxes that contained 400 blankets and numerous Tlingit artifacts worth a fortune in Tlingit society. Suspicions were aroused, and the property turned out to belong to Tai-ka-et, an old man who had cached the items for a potlatch. Bangs and two accomplices were arrested and sent to Juneau for trial. Judge Dawson's charge to the jury made it clear that the Tlingit had property rights in cached goods recognized under U.S. law. The jury acquitted one defendant but deadlocked on two others. As a result, the U.S. attorney made a deal with the defendants: if they would restore 250 blankets and pay Tai-ka-et $100, he would nolle prosse the case. Although Tai-ka-et had filed a civil suit to recover the blankets, he could not post sufficient bond for the court to hold the articles pending trial. Under the circumstances, both the

---

[94] Ibid. The *Alaskan* sympathetically noted that the Kake were in a difficult position: on the one hand, they were held rigidly accountable for violations of U.S. law they had little understanding of and knew to be prejudiced against them; on the other hand, they had never seen the fair application of U.S. law against someone who had injured Tlingits.

[95] *Alaskan*, November 26, 1887, 4.

defendants and Tai-ka-et agreed to the plea bargain. Moreover, Tai-ka-et was reportedly pleased that the U.S. government authorities restored a good part of his property. The case shows that authorities were willing to protect Tlingit property rights when they could, even if this meant resorting to some extralegal compromise.[96]

One might have expected U.S. law to be actively involved in Tlingit–whites relations, but U.S. law also intervened directly in Tlingit life. By the late 1880s, there arose some very clear examples of the extension of the policy first developed in *Kie*. Perhaps the most revealing example is the case of Jim, of the Auk *qwan*, who killed his wife, Jenny, in their village sixty miles north of Juneau in 1887.[97]

In many ways the circumstances repeated those of the *Kie* case. Jim seized Jenny in broad daylight in the center of their summer camp, in the presence of two white miners, and stabbed her for adultery. The case probably would have gone unnoticed by U.S. law, but the miners reported the events in Juneau, and a deputy marshal set out to investigate. Upon landing at the Auk camp, the interpreter revealed the purpose of his mission. The Auks then seized rifles and fled to a longhouse on a hill. Jim, on being asked to surrender, responded: "No, the whole matter is settled. It is none of the white man's business." After some negotiations, the Auks agreed to return to Juneau in their own canoes, and the two parties proceeded down the coast. As they passed the main Auk village near Juneau, however, the Tlingits went ashore "to get new clothing." Once ashore, they refused to return to their canoes.

The deputy marshal reappeared with the marshal, who took up the matter with the chief. The chief adamantly refused to surrender Jim even after the marshal threatened to take him with force. The marshal returned to Juneau and held a public meeting. It was decided that an attack by a small group of men would be risky and that the whole village, en masse, should proceed to the Tlingit village the next day and take Jim. At their request, the Alaska Mill and Foundry Company mine across the bay sent thirty rifles and a thousand rounds of ammunition.

After Auk women and children had been evacuated, some sixty or seventy members of the tribe remained fortified in their village. As many as 125 whites surrounded it and gave the Auks ten minutes to surrender Jim. The Tlingits remained defiant, but as the white vigilantes moved in from all sides, the Tlingits surrendered. Jim was sent to Sitka for trial.

The Auks reported that Jenny might have been kicked by Jim but that he did not stab her. Her body was cremated, so no further evidence existed.

[96] *Alaskan*, October 30, 1886, 1.
[97] *Alaskan*, August 6, 1887, 1; July 30, 1887, 4.

Jim was sentenced to seven years in the federal prison at McNeil Island, Washington, but was pardoned by the president in the spring of 1889, after serving about a year and a half for his crime.[98] Jim was not the only Tlingit sent to prison in this case. Tom-kook-ish and Squeet were both charged with perjury. They had testified for Jim, stating that they had examined Jenny's body and that it did not contain stab wounds. Both were convicted and sentenced to five years in prison.[99]

Jim's case illustrates much more than a symbolic resistance of the Tlingits to the imposition of U.S. law on intratribal matters. The spectacle of an entire white town, fully armed, surrounding an Indian village to seize a prisoner conjures up a vivid picture of the dynamics of power relations in Alaska at that time.

A case of white intervention in a witchcraft incident in Juneau illustrates once again the Tlingits' attempts to defend their law and also the simple lack of communication between the two legal systems. An Indian policeman, Joe, found an old man tied up as a witch and arrested two men for the crime. The men were fined twenty dollars in the magistrate's court and given a lecture. The next day the old man disappeared, and the two men were brought back into court. Joe recovered the old man from a dead house in an old Auk village some miles from Juneau. In court, the old man claimed he was a witch and that Joe's wife had joined with him in doing harm to people. Joe's wife then tried to hang herself but was cut down before she died. The two men who had tied up the old witch told the court that they had each paid twenty dollars for the privilege of punishing the witch and they wanted to do it right. They were sent to jail.[100] A similar use of the federal court to protect accused witches from retribution under tribal law occurred in a more minor context in Juneau of 1898, illustrating the U.S. legal penetration of Tlingit culture. Kah-oo-lee-key was indicted for "disturbing the peace" for charging Skoon-tah-aht with witchcraft. The indictment went on to allege that this charge was the "most odious and infamous" charge that can be made against one Indian by another as well as to allege that "the charge was false" but was believed by "said Indians"

---

[98] The pardon is reported in the *Alaskan*, June 15, 1889, 3. Indians held in prison were often pardoned, for two reasons. First, even whites who strongly wanted to apply U.S. law fully to Indians realized that there was an injustice because Indians did not ordinarily have the same mens rea, the intent to commit a crime, as whites did. Rather, they acted within accepted traditional norms. Second, since most Indians appear to have died in prison, their early release was often granted on humanitarian grounds; otherwise, every prison sentence was a death sentence. In fact, the goal of applying the full coercive impact of U.S. law was served as soon as an Indian was given a sentence and taken off to prison.

[99] U.S. District Court, Sitka, criminal case no. 168, *United States v. Squeet*, November 30, 1888; *United States v. Tom Kook-ish*, criminal case no. 169. Record Group 21, U.S. District Court, Sitka, held in the National Archives, Anchorage.

[100] *Alaskan*, April 20, 1889, 4.

who threatened to drive Skoon-tah-aht from the village and do her "great bodily harm."[101] An assault on a boy arising out of a witchcraft charge at Kake in 1900 was of such concern that the deputy marshal at Wrangell took the local judge to the village, both to save time and to deal with the problem of bringing large numbers of Tlingit witnesses many miles to court.[102] Anatolii Kamenskii, the Russian Orthodox priest at Sitka, reported that there were five or six cases of witches being beaten, tied up, or killed every fall and that white efforts to repress the practices were ineffectual.[103]

Just as Tlingit witchcraft continued despite the interference of U.S. law, so did other forms of Tlingit tribal law. This is perhaps best illustrated by white attempts to settle a fourteen-year-old dispute between the Sitkas and Takous. In a disagreement over liquor at a tribal gathering at Wrangell sometime around 1877, a Sitka was killed and a Takou was wounded. The Takous paid sixty blankets at the time to settle the matter. In 1891, however, just before a Takou journey to Sitka, the Takou man injured fourteen years earlier died. Arriving in Sitka, the Takou argued that the man had died of injuries sustained in the earlier conflict. Thus, the two tribes were even, and the Sitkas should return the sixty blankets.[104]

Governor Knapp, anxious to avoid trouble and to assert the supremacy of U.S. law in resolving all conflicts, sent an Indian policeman to mediate the matter. Not surprisingly, this policeman, who held no legitimacy in tribal law, upheld the status quo. He found that the Sitkas owed the Takous nothing and told the Takous not to enter the village on threat of jail sentences. The Takou sailed a short distance down the coast and landed at a Ko-kwanton village beyond the jurisdiction of the Sitka police. Once outside of the punitive authority of U.S. law and with the mediation of a neutral village, the Sitkas and Takous negotiated a settlement. The sixty blankets were returned, minus five kept in payment for another injured Sitka for whom no payment had been received. After the exchange was completed, a dance was held and the Takous returned home without incident. Thus, despite white interference in the case, the Tlingit settled the matter in accord with tribal law.[105]

The trial and conviction of Scun-doo, a Chilcat witch killer, epitomizes

---

[101] U.S. District Court, Sitka, Criminal file no. 1020, *United States v. Kah-oo-lee-Key* or George Hunter, October 18, 1898. National Archives, Anchorage, Record Group 21.

[102] Letter, February 10, 1900, William Grant, Deputy U.S. Marshal, to James Shoup, U.S. Marshal. "Letters Received" file, U.S. Marshal at Sitka, Record Group 505, Series 115, 116, 117, box 4397, Alaska State Archives, Juneau.

[103] Anatolii Kamenskii, *Tlingit Indians of Alaska*, (1906; Fairbanks: University of Alaska Press, 1985), 118.

[104] *Alaskan*, May 21, 1891, 3.

[105] Ibid. The fact that Governor Knapp was confronted with this Tlingit dispute and two large, armed bands of Tlingit in Alaska's capital seven years after the Organic Act is testimony to the continued strength of Tlingit sovereignty.

Scun-doo, Chilcat Indian doctor, convicted of a witch killing and sentenced to three years in San Quentin

the use of U.S. criminal law for a purpose that merged both immediate political needs and long-range assimilationist goals. The Chilcat lived at the head of the water route from North America to the Klondike gold fields. They strongly defended their lands, and by the mid-1870s there were many confrontations with miners and with U.S. government authorities. Gunboats were sent several times, but the Chilcats, unlike most of the Tlingit peoples, had access to the interior and could escape.

Scun-doo was known to government authorities as one of the most powerful Chilcats. He possessed great wealth, supposedly from payments in blankets for his services as a witch killer. Moreover, he was a strong defender

Scun-doo, in traditional dress

of traditional Chilcat culture and opposed every extension of white authority over the Tlingit. Somehow, word got out of a woman he had identified as a witch and ordered starved to death. Scun-doo fled into the interior, but on returning home some time later in 1895, he was arrested and taken to Juneau for trial, where he was convicted of manslaughter and sentenced to three years in San Quentin.[106]

---

[106] *Alaskan*, February 9, 1895, 3. Although the *Alaskan* thought that San Quentin might be a bit hard on him, there was no question of the necessity of the sentence: "He threatened the miners of Chilicoot and the Chilkat Pass, and was a disturber. Besides, it was felt an example had to be made of him to the other Tlingit."

One early Tlingit criminal case, from the 1890s, reached the U.S. Supreme Court. In *United States v. Tla-koo-yel-lee*, the defendant was convicted of murder and twice sentenced to hang by a federal district court in Sitka. Although the only evidence against the defendant consisted of statements from his wife, Tlak-Sha, and another man, Ke-Tinch, the trial court refused to permit a line of questioning establishing that Ke-Tinch and Tlak-Sha had become lovers as soon as Tal-koo-yel-lee was arrested and that their relationship might have provided them with a reason to perjure themselves to convict the defendant. The Supreme Court reversed on evidentiary grounds, observing that "the mind is oppressed with a painful doubt as to the soundness of the verdict rendered by the jury." When on retrial the prosecution could not produce additional witnesses, the case was dismissed.[107]

Although this case was decided on narrow grounds, it cannot be separated from its cultural context. Criminal cases against Indians, as we have already seen in the confusion over the facts in *Crow Dog*, occurred in complex cultural contexts that were often impossible to present in U.S. courtrooms. The U.S. Supreme Court rarely overturned ordinary criminal convictions on narrow evidentiary grounds. But here, as in *Crow Dog*, the Court seems to have recognized, albeit too late for the Tlingit, the danger of injustice in the imposition of U.S. criminal law on the Tlingit, especially when the death penalty was at stake.

Most symbolic of the extent to which U.S. law invaded Tlingit culture was the federal district court's unsuccessful intervention in a dispute about the ownership of a frog totem. Tlingit totems represented stories that were the property of the individual clans. When some Sitka Tlingit proclaimed the frog as their clan emblem, this offended Kiksatis, who also claimed the frog. The two competing claims of ownership of the frog totem wound up in federal court. Federal judge Johnson sat on the case for two years before holding that the court had no legal right to intervene in this dispute, effectively denying the protection of U.S. law to this form of Tlingit property. Soon thereafter nine Kiksati, using a specially constructed ladder, attacked the frog and chopped it to pieces. The nine were arrested on a charge of "riot" and held in jail on $1,000 bond. The severity of this response was a calculated effort to stop the trouble.[108]

Now that U.S. law had terminated any notion of Tlingit sovereignty and established a complete set of legal institutions, with the full capacity to

---

[107] *United States v. Tla-koo-yel-lee*, 167 U.S. 274 (1897); see 275–7 for details of the case. See also *Alaskan*, June 11, 1897, 1. There is evidence that due process standards were systematically violated by the Alaska courts where Tlingit were concerned.

[108] Anatolii Kamenskii, "The Frog Case," *Russian Orthodox Messinger* 5, no. 10 (1901):208–10. This account is reprinted as in idem, *Tlingit Indians of Alaska*, 117–22.

intervene in Tlingit tribal life, the path was cleared for the forced assimilation of the Tlingit into Alaskan life. But Alaska was still different from the rest of the country by virtue of its size, isolation, and lack of resources. Harry, a Tlingit sentenced to three years in prison for larceny and shipped to McNeil Island, Washington, to serve his sentence, was sent back by the U.S. marshal in Tacoma. The accompanying letter explained that Harry had been pardoned by the president because "he is suffering from tuberculosis and was a menace to the institution."[109]

The development of an assimilationist policy for the Tlingit

Governor James Brady represents an anomaly in Alaskan politics. Appointed by President William McKinley in 1897, Brady served three terms as governor of Alaska and was credited with providing a stable administrative framework for the territory. In dealings with the Tlingit, Brady was committed to a policy of assimilation, much like the Indian reformers of the era. Unlike those reformers, however, Brady had complete political authority over Alaskan natives, for there were no BIA officials or Indian agents in Alaska.

Brady's familiarity with the Tlingit came from his experiences as a Presbyterian minister, a trader, and a federal magistrate in Sitka. As magistrate, Brady learned firsthand of the problems of ranch Indians when he sentenced hundreds to jail terms. His commitment to a policy of assimilation was all-embracing. In a letter to the secretary of the interior in 1902, Brady argued for organizing the Tlingit into militia companies. In support of his proposal, he cited the degree to which the Tlingit were integrated into full legal relations with whites. His courts not only decided civil matters between Tlingits, but also granted divorces. Similarly, Brady insisted that Tlingit children attend the same schools as white children in spite of white opposition to the practice.[110]

Brady also knew that the Tlingit were hesitant to give up traditional ways. When he heard that a young witch was staked out on the beach to drown in the tide, he personally took a revenue cutter to Hoonah, cut the witch

[109] Letter, C. W. Ide, U.S. Marshal, Tacoma, Washington, to James Shoup, U.S. Marshal, Sitka, Alaska. "Letters Received" file, U.S. Marshal, Sitka. Record Group 505, Series 115, 116, 117, Box 4397, Alaska State Archives, Juneau. Harry's case file, Criminal case no. 1341, *United States v. Jack #1 and Harry*, 15 July, 1899, reveals that the two were convicted of stealing $80 in gold and sentenced to three years in prison. The file is held in Record Group 21, National Archives, Anchorage.

[110] T. Hinckley, "We Are More Truly Heathen than the Natives: John G. Brady and the Assimilation of Alaska's Tlingit Indians," *Western Historical Quarterly* 11 (1980):37, 44–5, 50–51.

loose, and took him home with him. Twice, he took a gunboat to Yakutat to rid the village of a troublesome shaman, but both times the man was shielded by the village, clearly indicating a degree of Tlingit solidarity.[111] Brady described his second trip, in August 1901, claiming that the village was "lawless," leaving missionaries "afraid for their lives" because of heavy drinking. The governor's party included a judge, who kept the court open for two days and a night, resulting in eight criminal convictions, concluding that "the cost of inflicting these punishments is comparatively small" and would "give those people peace for some time." The governor pointed out that he had talked to the Yakutat and made it clear to them what their situation was but that punishment would have more emphasis than talk. The prisoners were taken to jail at Sitka on the Brady boat.[112]

Claiming that the regular potlatch ceremonies were wasteful, Brady vigorously condemned the institution. Nevertheless, in 1904, he used government funds to throw a giant potlatch on the condition that it be the last. Brady also tried to get one of the old Tlingit villages protected under the 1906 Antiquities Act, although the notion that a decaying Tlingit village represented an important part of U.S. heritage was too much for Congress. In addition, he pushed for the abolition of Alaska's prohibition on the ground that it was a total failure.[113]

The depth of Brady's belief in the assimilationist view is demonstrated in the transcript of a meeting between the governor and Tlingit chiefs at Juneau in late 1898. It is a remarkable document because it presents two competing visions of the Tlingits' future. Brady insisted on the need for assimilation and often cited a comparison with the dependent, decaying Indian cultures in the rest of the United States. Whereas those comparisons may have been powerful for Brady, they were meaningless to the Tlingit, who knew nothing of other native tribes and whose history was sovereign and independent.[114]

The Tlingit chiefs consistently observed that although they were not as powerful as white people, they had laws, traditions, families, and a way of life they wanted respected. They were willing to let the whites live in Alaska, but they wanted some land where they could continue their traditions and be left in control of their own lives. The Tlingit chiefs pointed out that this was not a lot to ask but only what was reasonable. The Tlingit thus attempted

[111] Ibid., 48.
[112] Letter, John G. Brady to Secretary of Interior, August 19, 1901. Copy found in "Letters Received" file, U.S. Marshal, Sitka. Record Group 505, Series 115, 116, 117, Box 4397.
[113] Ibid., 51, 52.
[114] T. Hinckley, "The Canoe Rocks – We Do Not Know What Will Become of Us: The Complete Transcript of a Meeting Between Governor John Green Brady of Alaska and a Group of Tlingit Chiefs, Juneau, December 14, 1898," *Western Historical Quarterly* 7 (1970):265–90.

to negotiate a workable legal framework with Brady, but they had already seen that no white legal principles remained consistent.[115]

All the Tlingits told similar stories. Shoo-we-kah recounted how, in 1880, he lived at Juneau and that when white authorities came to Sitka, he went over to them and was given a paper. White men would come among the Tlingit, and the Tlingit agreed to take good care of them. The Tlingit expected the white men to take good care of them in return. The white men, however, did not act as expected. Instead, they took the land, cut down the trees, killed or stole dogs, and hired Tlingit as policemen but did not pay them. Charlie, also of Juneau, pointed out that all the creeks with salmon were claimed by whites, and every creek where Tlingits lived was claimed by the Treadwell Gold Mining Company. "Our people feel bad about the way the White men act. They never tell us what they are going to do, and they put notices on the premises. And if you make a complaint and go into court, we are notified that it is too late now, that the paper is recorded and nothing can be done."[116]

Brady did not want to hear any of this. He berated the Tlingits for wanting to hold on to their old customs and asked them if they wanted to be put on an island under the authority of an Indian agent "to keep them straight," or whether they wanted to live among the whites, "obey White man's law; have all the privileges he has?" Then revealing his ignorance of the crime even then occurring with the lands of the Five Civilized Tribes, Brady gave the Tlingit a brief lecture on Alaskan land laws: "Anybody can buy a mine. ... The land commissioner has decided that an Indian can take up a quartz claim, record it, and hold it." Similarly, if any Tlingit would take and improve land – plow the ground, make fences, build a home – then he would hold that land too. But the Indians could not hold the whole district. For Brady, these land laws were fair and neutral and would equally protect the rights of the Tlingit. Brady's speech concluded, the meeting ended.[117]

The two sides did not understand each other. No one can believe that the Tlingit left thinking that they could hold land according to the white man's law or, if they could, that it would give them a meaningful existence. Nothing in the subsequent history of the Tlingit in Alaska indicates that they were wrong.

Conclusion

The doctrine of tribal sovereignty, which played a critical role in shaping federal Indian policy until the end of the nineteenth century, had no impact

[115] Ibid., 278.
[116] Ibid., 277–9, 281–2.
[117] Ibid., 283–7.

in Alaska. Nor did the federal legislation that applied to Indian country under the Indian Trade and Intercourse Act. The reason for the Alaskan exception was not initially grounded in federal Indian policy in Washington but in Northwest territorial politics. The national government took little interest in Alaska, and northwesterners had enough recent experience in territorial government to recognize that any special Indian country status for Alaskan natives was a liability to local whites. By the 1880s, however, this locally based policy of keeping the Tlingit distinct in status from other natives in the United States merged with the assimilationist policy of Indian reformers who sought to extend the full force of U.S. law to Indians all over the United States. Alaska, to which Indian country jurisdiction had been removed, therefore became one place where the Indian reformers did not have to fight to change existing law.

Judge Matthew Deady of the federal district court in Portland, with jurisdiction over Alaska until 1884, singlehandedly determined the legal status of Alaskan natives with a series of rulings inconsistent with both existing federal Indian policy and the actual intent of the Department of Interior regarding that status. None of Deady's rulings were ever appealed to the U.S. Supreme Court. No Alaskan native had sufficient resources or confidence in U.S. legal institutions to do so.

As a result, Alaskan native policy became largely territorial in its content and control. Instead of having Indian agents administer the Indian police, authority over these important forces fell to the territorial governor. The Indian ranches that grew up alongside white towns were under the direct control of local whites. Distant Indian villages were ordinarily outside the reach of white authority, but armed parties of local miners were occasionally raised to augment regular police forces in imposing U.S. law on even the most remote Tlingit villages.

The Tlingit of southeastern Alaska possessed a strong social order and the ability to resist white intrusions into their institutions. Much of the trading relationship with both Russians and Americans was on Tlingit terms. Moreover, the Tlingit remained undefeated and were a military threat to the Alaskan whites until well into the 1890s. Similarly, the Tlingit regularly sought to punish whites for violations of Tlingit law, a rare occurrence in the rest of the United States outside of the Indian wars.

A comparative analysis of the fate of the Tlingit because of their unique legal status as Alaskan natives and the fate of Indians in the rest of the United States remains to be written. The long delay in resolving the legal status of Alaskan Indians in the twentieth century is itself testimony to both the power of white territorial politics and the Tlingits' ability to resist attacks on their traditional institutions. The Tlingit became impoverished in relation to Alaskan whites, but the prosperity of the commercial fishing industry, which employed Alaskan natives from the 1880s, left the Tlingits wealthy compared to American Indians in general.

In any case, there can be no question that the Tlingits wrote a good part of their own legal history, on their own terms. The legal history of the incorporation of the Tlingit under U.S. law cannot be written only in terms of the cases that Judge Deady decided. It must also be written from the standpoint of the Tlingits who passed their own laws on white cases and then resisted the imposition of U.S. law on their society. Even without a formally recognized federal legal doctrine of tribal sovereignty, the Tlingit were sovereign and repeatedly acted as a sovereign people.

8

The legal structuring of violence

U.S. law and the Indian wars

In a very real sense this whole inquiry is anomalous: every schoolchild in this country knows that the history of the incorporation of the Indian tribes into the United States was one of great violence and illegality. If anything, the real history is worse: the popular images are of parties of armed warriors combating troops of cavalry, not the genocide of starvation, smallpox, tuberculosis, the shooting of villages full of women and children. This genocide is beyond the scope of legal history, but in reality such events reflect U.S. legal choices. The Indian wars were legal events from two perspectives. First, U.S. policymakers' decision to permit settlers to continue pushing back the Indian frontier was the most direct cause of the Indian wars. In its failure to police the frontier effectively, the federal government left a lawless void, whereas Canada, for example, almost entirely avoided Indian warfare by policing frontier whites.[1] Second, the Indians fought wars against whites to enforce their law and protect their legal rights against white illegality.[2] The Indian wars do not reflect "villainy" on the part of the tribes as Justice William Rehnquist asserts in a dissent (conceding "greed, cupidity, and other less than admirable behavior" on the part of the government), disagreeing with the U.S. Supreme Court's weak attempt to redress wrongs committed by the United States against the Sioux in illegally seizing the Black Hills.[3]

The study of legal history requires thinking about law in two ways. First

---

[1] Olive Patricia Dickason, *Canada's First Nations: A History of Founding Peoples from Earliest Times* (Toronto: McClelland and Stewart, 1993), 280–3.

[2] We are just beginning to see an ethnohistorical analysis of the American Indian wars; see Kenneth Morrison, "The Bias of Colonial Law: English Paranoia and the Abenaki Arena of King Philip's War, 1675–1678," *New England Quarterly* 53 (1980):363. Such a literature exists describing other native resistance to colonialism. See James Belich, *The New Zealand Wars and the Victorian Interpretation of Racial Conflict* (Auckland: Auckland University Press, 1986), and Gordon Reid, *A Nest of Hornets: The Massacre of the Fraser Family at Hornet Bank Station, Central Queensland, 1857, and Related Events* (Melbourne: Oxford University Press, 1982).

[3] *United States v. Sioux Nation*, 448 U.S. 371 (1980), at 435. It is instructive to note that "villainy" clearly refers to criminal violence on the part of the Sioux, while "greed, cupidity, and other less than admirable behavior" attributes only general immorality to whites.

is the study of the law itself: its structure, scope, and impact on people's lives. Second is the study of what the law does not do, the places that law cannot reach, revealing much about the place of law in society. This is especially true when an alien law is imposed on an unwilling native people. Although Indian resistance to imposed law can be seen in the study of laws and legal processes, the tribes often chose extralegal options in dealing with U.S. law. Even the U.S. choice of law as an appropriate method of structuring a complex social relationship was opportunistic, and the law was employed in some situations and not in others. In any case, U.S. legal choices were not those of native people. On the contrary, Indians viewed U.S. law with a mixture of distrust and confusion, occasionally using it but most often avoiding it to the extent that they could.

This study of the legal structuring of the violence of Indian–white contact faces problems of definition and scope. Whites killed Indians with virtual impunity in a wide range of situations. Indians themselves used violence in various settings, defying simplistic classifying schemes. The following sections discuss some forms of this violence. The Indian wars loom large in U.S. history and legend but were never a significant legal issue. Still, the ways that U.S. courts dealt with these wars reveals a great deal about both the function and limits of law in the United States of the nineteenth century. Beyond the specter of Indian wars, there was a substantial level of intra-Indian violence that U.S. courts, mostly through the Major Crimes Act, attempted to reach. Much of this violence was every bit as much the product of collective tribal action as the Indian wars were. U.S. law, however, an instrument of the policy of forced assimilation, focused criminal responsibility on individuals.

The legal recognition of Indian wars: the Indian Depredations Act of 1891

By 1891 the Indian wars were over. There had been more than a hundred, making these wars a routine U.S. means of taking Indian land.[4] This history, dreadful as it is, conceals the fact that most tribes negotiated treaties with the United States. However, even those treaties were negotiated in a context

---

[4] There is no commonly agreed on figure for the number of Indian wars fought in the United States. One hundred is my own estimate. There is an extensive literature on the Indian wars, but most of the studies describe only one war in great detail. For a general overview of the western wars, see Robert Utley, *Frontier Regulars: The United States Army and the Indian, 1866–1891* (New York: Macmillan, 1973); idem, *Frontiersmen in Blue: The United States Army and the Indian, 1848–1865* (New York: Macmillan, 1967); and idem, *The Indian Frontier of the American West, 1846–1890* (Albuquerque: University of New Mexico Press, 1984); and Robert Wooster, *The Military and United States Indian Policy, 1865–1903* (New Haven, Conn.: Yale University Press, 1988).

where all parties knew war might well be the alternative. The proof of this is that many tribes negotiated treaties, fought when the treaties were routinely broken, then negotiated new treaties, always settling for less. This history is largely kept separate from the history of Indian law. None of the major federal cases decided before the 1890s directly concerned an Indian war, and the Indian wars had no legal recognition at all. Other than *Kagama's* oblique reference to the people of the states being the "deadliest enemies" of the tribes, no federal judicial language even refers to these wars.[5] The state courts occasionally followed the reasoning of *Corn Tassel*, arguing that since Congress never declared war against an Indian tribe, it followed that the tribes were not "nations."

The passage of the Indian Depredations Act of 1891 brought hundreds of claims for damage to property from Indian "depredations" to the U.S. Court of Claims, a number of which reached the U.S. Supreme Court on appeal. Among the issues litigated in these cases was that of whether the "tribe or band" committing the depredation was "in amity" with the United States, forcing the courts to define the parameters of an Indian war.[6]

The act of 1891, providing that the U.S. government pay western settlers for damages to their property occurring from attacks of Indians under the protection of the federal authorities, had a long history in U.S. law, going back to the administration of George Washington. The basic theory of federal responsibility was the recognition that once a tribe made peace with the United States and came under federal protection, residents of the states were prohibited from entering tribal lands. While a white bandit might be followed anywhere and stolen property recovered, the same was not true for Indians who engaged in similar actions. Once they returned to federal protection, state residents could not pursue them. The federal government, therefore, had a responsibility both to protect residents of the states from Indian attack and, it followed in failing to do so, to pay for the damages. Until the Civil War many such claims were presented to the government and paid. Congress, in 1859, passed a law refusing to pay such claims unless moneys were specifically appropriated. Thereafter, depredations claims were paid by private bill, requiring an act of Congress for each individual claim, a cumbersome process that, by 1891, left more than seven thousand claims totaling more than $20 million unsettled, many dating back to the 1850s.[7] The problems with private bills were legion: besides being inefficient, the

---

[5] *Ex parte Kagama*, 118 U.S. 375 (1886), at 394; *State v. George Tassels*, I Dud. 229 (1830), at 233.
[6] *United States Statutes at Large*, Act of March 3, 1891, 26 Statutes, 851–2. *Montoya v. United States*, 180 U.S. 261 (1901).
[7] The history of Indian depredations claims is discussed in U.S. Congress, Senate, Report no. 1016, "Claims Arising from Indian Depredations," May 16, 1890, 51st Congress, 1st session (Serial Set, 2709), Congressional Record, House, 1890, 482.

bills were unimportant as legislation and did not receive the regular attention of Congress. This provoked considerable frustration in the West. Senator Teller of Colorado, protesting the refusal of Congress to appropriate $4,000 to pay the 1879 victims of a Ute uprising that led to the killing of their Indian agent and the wrecking of their agency, sarcastically referred to the Utes as "pets" of the government, protected in spite of their violent behavior.[8]

The congressional debate was, at times, acrimonious, with a group of westerners presenting the image of pioneers who, facing great dangers, had opened up the riches of the West only to be abandoned by the federal government. Countering this view was an argument that these settlers had knowingly taken a few risks and been rewarded with the great wealth of cheap lands, made available by the federal government's acquisition of those lands from the tribes.[9] Of a number of proposals for settling these claims, Congress chose to turn them over to existing federal courts, giving jurisdiction to the courts of claims and federal district courts as well as creating inspectors to investigate the claims and special assistant attorneys general to represent the government and the tribes.[10]

The tribes became parties in these lawsuits because the act made the tribes legally responsible for depredations they were found to have committed and required them to pay the claims from annuities and treaty moneys due them. This provision was at the core of the act, intending to punish the tribes for not controlling rebellious factions among them, to force the tribes to maintain internal order to protect local whites, and probably not inconsequentially, to deprive the tribes of much of the money they were to receive from the allotment of their lands.[11] The tribes, as parties in all of these four thousand lawsuits, were forced to prove they had not been involved in depredations going back forty years, an unwieldly legal process. Early versions of the act undermined the tribes' capacity to defend themselves in these suits by providing that the testimony of Indians was not admissible unless corroborated. A number of congressmen objected, pointing to the impossible position this put the tribes in: being held legally accountable for millions of dollars in damages without being competent witnesses in the cases.[12] Ultimately, this provision was replaced by a provision that "any Indian . . . interested in the proceedings may appear and defend . . . if he or they shall choose so to do," with the approval of the Indian agent.[13]

The claims were factually complex, with many claimants not even sure

---

[8] U.S. Congress, House of Representatives, "Claims for Depredations Committed by the Ute Indians," 48th Congress, 1st session, March 7, 1884.
[9] Congressional Record, House, 1890, 481–6.
[10] Ibid.
[11] Ibid.
[12] Congressional Record, House, 1890, 485.
[13] Act of March 3, 1891, 26 Statutes 851, section 4.

which Indian band or tribe attacked them. John Taylor, for example, claimed $2,025 for the 1856 loss of a pack train in the Siskiyou mountains to unknown Indians, ultimately settling for $1,725.[14] Making matters more complex, individual Indians were entitled to make depredations claims. Many of these claims were of members of one tribe against another tribe, but some were intratribal claims, with one faction claiming damages from the depredations of another. The Ghost Dance "disturbance" resulted in 754 claims totalling $201,455, mostly filed by Sioux. Ten claims were disallowed by the investigator on, among others, grounds that the claimants were, in fact, hostiles, but $100,000 in claims was paid.[15]

This legal process was so efficient and so many claims were granted that it came to conflict with the BIA's assimilation policy: so much tribal money was being allocated to pay for depredations that the program to civilize the Indians was undermined. The BIA warned of violence if the impoverishment of the tribes continued. In asking Congress for an amendment to the law to relieve the tribes of their obligation to pay for the depredations from moneys due them, the BIA included data showing that many tribes were buried in potential debt from these claims, pointing out that most of the depredations occurred in previous generations so that the policy was "punishing children for crimes committed by their ancestors."[16] The Comanche tribe led the list, with 1,307 claims totaling over $4,056,000, with the Apache's having fewer claims – 986 – but totaling $4,186,000. Creeks, Cheyennes, Sioux, Navajos, and Kiowas each had over $1 million dollars in claims, with forty-eight other tribes subject to smaller claims – all told 7,434 claims for a total of $23,726,322.[17] To remedy this problem the secretary of the interior was given the authority to release money if "imperatively demanded" for "support, education, or civilization."[18]

In this context the federal courts heard these thousands of claims, with ten reaching the U.S. Supreme Court. Among the most complex of the legal issues was the requirement that the depredations be committed by Indians "in amity" with the United States. This requirement limited the scope of the act and was based on the theory that the federal government's responsibility for the tribes did not begin until after they were subdued. The claimant could not simply prove that Indians had committed the depreda-

[14] U.S. Congress, House of Representatives, 51st Congress, 1st session, Ex. doc. no. 123, January 16, 1890, "Papers in the Claim of John Taylor."
[15] U.S. Congress, Senate, 52d Congress, 2d session, Ex. doc. 93, February 27, 1893, "Letter from the Secretary of the Interior" (Serial Set, v. 3062). This report contains an individual listing of the moneys paid each Indian.
[16] U.S. Congress, Senate, 52d Congress, 1st session, Ex. doc. 117, June 17, 1892, "Letter from the Secretary of the Interior," 10 (Serial Set, v. 2915).
[17] Ibid., 9.
[18] Ibid., Report no. 903.

tions, but also had to establish the political status of the particular Indians involved. The courts were faced with difficult inquiries into the internal politics of tribes involved in Indian wars. The simplest situation was beyond the scope of the act. At the very least "in amity" meant that the tribe had to have entered into some political relationship with the United States, so initial warfare between a tribe and the United States was beyond the scope of the act and no one was responsible for the damages. The U.S. Supreme Court in *Marks v. United States* set out the basic statement of the legal nature of Indian wars under the Indian Depredations Act. Noting that ordinarily there was never a formal declaration of an Indian war, the court distinguished the phrase "in amity with" from meaning the same thing as "under treaty." According to the Court, "in amity with" meant "friendship, actual peace" while "under treaty" meant having "political relations." The court held that the mere existence of a treaty did not put a tribe in amity with the government of the United States. Rather, the Court had to inquire whether actual peace existed at the time of the depredation. If a depredation was committed by a single individual or a few individuals, without the consent of the tribe, then a claim might lie. But if the whole tribe, as a tribe, engaged in actual hostilities, it was not in amity with the United States. The court affirmed a court of claims dismissal of Marks's $8,000 claim against the Bannock for property destroyed during an uprising in Happy Valley, Oregon in 1878.[19] Included in the record are dozens of documents defining the course of the Bannock War, revealing that the Court took a close look at the actual conduct of the Bannock uprising in reaching its decision.[20]

Underlying the Court's simple reasoning was a complex dispute about the nature of Indians under federal authority. In *Marks* as well as two companion cases, *Johnson v. United States* and *Leighton v. United States*, the tribes involved had entered into peace treaties with the United States and moved to reservations under the control of an Indian agent. They were obviously in amity with the United States at that time.[21] Later, common to many Indian uprisings in the West, the tribes rebelled against federal authority, left the reservation, and engaged in warfare to protect tribal rights. For local whites it was the initial federal assumption of responsibility for the tribes that gave rise to federal responsibility for damages following from Indian depredations. Once a tribe was in amity with the United States through treaty relations, the federal government was responsible for protecting local whites who might settle nearby.

The Bannock War was an effort of the Bannock to push white "intruders

---

[19] *Marks v. United States*, 161 U.S. 297 (1895), at 302–3.

[20] *Marks v. United States*, Appellate case file, Case no. 15542, Record Group 267, National Archives.

[21] *Johnson v. United States*, 160 U.S. 546 (1896); *Leighton v. United States*, 161 U.S. 291 (1895).

and tresspassers" off tribal lands. Initially, whites treated these Bannock actions as crimes, arresting the perpetrators. One Bannock had left the reservation and shot two white teamsters. He was jailed by the agent and handed over to civil authorities for trial. The Bannock were angry at this violation of their sovereignty, and a friend of the arrested man shot the agency butcher to death. Troops were called and the killer was seized by the military, later tried, and hung. The Bannock spent the winter preparing for war stockpiling guns and feeding their horses well. Troops, aware of the preparations, made several attempts to seize the weapons but failed because the Bannock anticipated their actions. In early June five hundred Bannock left the reservation, raiding white ranches for hundreds of miles, burning buildings and running off livestock.[22] While, under this framework, the actions of individual Indians breaking off from a tribe in amity would fall within the scope of the act, the concerted military effort of the tribe did not.

The court's straightforward analysis in *Marks* turned on a traditional definition of an Indian tribe and did not begin to come to terms with the complexity of rapidly changing Indian political organization in the assimilationist era. Treaty relations and forced removal to reservations split most tribes into factions. The Indian Depredations Act anticipated this, stating that the depredations must have been committed by Indians belonging to any "band, tribe or nation" in amity with the United States. Neither "tribe," "band," nor "nation" was the subject of precise legal definition at the time of the act. The U.S. Supreme Court confronted this definitional problem in *Montoya v. United States*. The Court held that the terms "were used almost interchangeably," then, in dicta unnecessary to deciding the case, dismissed the idea that there could be Indian "nations":

> The North American Indians do not and never have constituted "nations" as that word is used by writers upon international law, although in a great number of treaties they are designated "nations" as well as "tribes."... As they had no established laws, no recognized method of choosing their sovereigns by inheritance or election, no officers with defined powers, their governments in their original state were nothing more than a temporary submission to an intellectual or physical superior. ... In short, the word "nation" as applied to the uncivilized Indians is so much of a misnomer as to be little more than a compliment.[23]

The court then turned to the real issue, distinguishing between a "band" and a "tribe." In the case at hand, Victoria, an Apache chief, had refused to remain on the Mescalero Reservation, leading a traditional band to war.

---

[22] *Marks v. United States*, Case file 15542, at 8–10.

[23] *Montoya v. United States*, 1 U.S. 261 (1900), at 265. It seems likely that this statement was aimed at denying the legitimacy of the Indian nations of Oklahoma.

The court applied a functional test: whether a "collection of marauders" was a band was determined not by their numbers, but by their purpose. If part of a "hostile demonstration against the government," then they were a band not in amity with the United States. However, if primarily organized for "individual plunder" they were not a band, but rather a collection of individuals split off from the main tribe, and such depredations would fall within the scope of the act. Victoria's band was in the former category, therefore the Montoya's $3,000 claim for lost stock was denied.[24] Similarly, when Dull Knife's band of Northern Cheyenne separated themselves from the main body of the tribe on a reservation in the Indian Territory and fought their way north toward their traditional lands they were a band not in amity with the United States, and settlers injured by the band could not recover under the act.[25] Perhaps ironically, bands and tribes not in amity with the United States – those exercising their traditional sovereignty – were beyond the scope of the act and not legally responsible for any damage resulting from their exercise of sovereignty. This provision had nothing to do with the tribes. Rather, it was a simple move by Congress to limit the claims. It had the effect of finally moving the federal courts to legally recognize the Indian wars as extensions of tribal political sovereignty distinguished from individual criminal actions.

The Indian war as a criminal defense: the trial of Plenty Horses

This same reasoning did not reach the criminal liability of Indians for killings committed in Indian wars until the 1891 trial of the Brule Sioux warrior Plenty Horses for the killing of Army Lieutenant Edward Casey. Casey had been shot in the back of the head while negotiating the return of a large band of Ghost Dancers from the Badlands, where they had fled following the army massacre at Wounded Knee. Plenty Horses admitted the killing, done in front of many witnesses, but claimed he shot Casey to prevent him from further injuring his people:

> You can understand my state of mind at hearing we were to suffer more because we arose to demand the food and clothing the government owed us. All this passed before my mind and then I thought that right at my side road a spy from our enemy who was boldly announcing his determination to come back and do us still further injury.[26]

---

[24] Ibid., 266. Many of the documents pertaining to the Montoya claim are printed in U.S. Congress, House of Representatives, 51st Congress, 1st session, Ex. doc. 127, January 18, 1890, "Papers in the Indian Depredation Claim of E. Montoya & Sons."

[25] *Connors v. United States*, 1 U.S. 271 (1900).

[26] Robert Utley, "The Ordeal of Plenty Horses," *American Heritage* 26, no. 1 (December 1974):15–19, 82–6, at 86.

Plenty Horses was charged with murder in Federal District Court in Sioux Falls. Local lawyers, hired for his defense with funds provided by the IRA, argued that the killing occurred between belligerents in a war and was therefore beyond the reach of the courts. Although this argument had been raised before when Indians were criminally charged for acts occurring during Indian wars, it had never been recognized by a court. The prosecution resisted the raising of the issue, objecting to questions about the state of mind of the Sioux or conditions in the Sioux camps. The court ruled that it held jurisdiction but allowed the evidence to be introduced as a "mitigating circumstance" that would reduce murder to manslaughter.[27]

Plenty Horses was unable to tell his own story. He took the stand in his own defense but testified in the Brule language. The prosecution objected, pointing out that Plenty Horses had studied at Carlisle Institute, a BIA boarding school in Pennsylvania for five years, and spoke English. The prosecution's underlying reasons are obvious: Plenty Horses, less than twenty years old, was a product of the BIA's assimilationist policy. He had grown up on the Rosebud Reservation and been removed from his people for "training" at a BIA school in the East. Therefore, he was fully responsible to U.S. law. As in the case of Crow Dog, the popular press presented sharply different images of Plenty Horses. One was that of a wastrel who chain-smoked cigarettes and, although trained as a farmer, never took up the occupation because it was "too much work."[28]

The defense strategy placed Plenty Horses in the context of the Ghost Dance and traditional Brule resistance to forced assimilation. When the court ruled for the prosecution, Plenty Horse left the witness stand, never testifying in his defense. Later he told newspaper reporters: "I wanted to tell them I am not guilty of murder. If they do not care to hear me I am satisfied. Probably it is better that way."[29]

The judge instructed the jury that "although the Sioux did not constitute an independent nation with legal authority to declare war, they still had the power to go to war." Therefore, following the same reasoning as in the Indian Depredation Act cases, if the jury found "that a war existed in actual if not legal fact," they should acquit. If there was no war in progress and Plenty Horses acted with malice and deliberation, they should convict of murder. Finally, if the killing occurred in a state of mental excitement and without premeditation, the jury should convict for manslaughter. The jury deadlocked six votes for murder and six votes for manslaughter, rejecting Plenty Horses "act of war" defense.[30]

[27] Ibid., 83–4.
[28] *Argus Leader* (Sioux Falls), April 8, 1891, 2.
[29] Ibid., 84.
[30] Ibid.

Plenty Horses, acquitted of killing Lieutenant Casey after the Wounded Knee uprising of 1890 on an "act of war" defense

The government lost no time retrying the case, impaneling another jury three weeks later. However, this time aware that it had to address the "act of war" defense, it requested that the army send a witness to testify that no war existed. Here the interests of two powerful federal institutions collided: General Nelson Miles, who had fought many Indian wars, responded that it was certainly a war and that he would not reduce the dignity of his campaign to a "dress parade." Captain Frank Baldwin, a friend of Casey, was sent to Sioux Falls as the army's witness, testifying that the army viewed the event in which Casey was killed as a war. Judge Shiras stopped the trial, directing a verdict of acquittal and freeing Plenty Horses. Shiras explained that unless

The trial of Plenty Horses

there was a state of war, the soldiers involved in Wounded Knee were guilty of murder. Extending this argument, he pointed out that if Lieutenant Casey had killed Plenty Horses, he would not be on trial, so the opposite also had to hold true. The bewildered jury later told reporters they would have convicted of manslaughter.[31]

Throughout the trial, the Brule had stood behind Plenty Horses. While his chief, American Horse, did not condone the killing, he made it clear that the young man had been driven to this reaction by starvation and oppression. The day after the trial, as the Sioux boarded a train to return to the Rosebud, American Horse addressed reporters: "What must the Indian do? Die, starve or fight? We ask not much. The spot of snow is melting. Soon the Indian will be no more. Give us a chance, keep your treaty."[32] Plenty Horses himself, in a newspaper interview, elaborated on the legal basis of the Sioux wars, comparing the open and fair way the Sioux had engaged Custer with the cowardly attack on Big Foot's band at Wounded Knee.[33]

Government authorities never had a consistent policy toward Indian warriors accused of criminal acts occurring during warfare. In the late nineteenth

[31] Ibid.
[32] Ibid., 85. The phrase "keep your treaty" probably refers to the keeping of treaty promises to recognize tribal sovereignty and provide a reasonable level of support for Brule efforts to reconstitute tribal society on the Rosebud Reservation.
[33] *Argus Leader* (Sioux Falls), April 28, 1891, 1.

century alone Sisseton Sioux, Tlingit, and Modoc warriors were given military trials for killings occurring in war against whites and were hung.[34] Four hundred Sioux warriors were given a military trial for their acts committed in the Minnesota Sioux uprising of 1862. Three hundred and three were given death penalties, while only eighteen were sentenced to imprisonment.[35] President Abraham Lincoln, coldly intending some executions for their deterrent effect, commuted the sentences of all but thirty-seven, who went to their deaths together on one large gallows, singing their death songs.[36] Kiowa warriors were turned over by the army to state of Texas authorities, tried, and hung for similar killings.[37] Thousands of other warriors were detained as prisoners of war in military prisons and camps, often a thousand miles or more from home and without any legal process whatever.[38] Other tribes were forcibly returned to their reservations and kept in virtual imprisonment by military detachments.[39] U.S. law did not extend to the Indian wars until after they were over. The Indian Depredations Act attempted to force the tribes to pay for property damages, largely to local whites. The acquittal of Plenty Horses was an anomaly.

U.S. law and Indian crime: the legal structuring of intra-Indian violence

To this point, a long list of cases and incidents has been described in which U.S. law was applied to Indian tribes. These are the cases that came to the attention of white authorities, who attempted to intervene. That makes them atypical, for most tribal matters in the nineteenth century were often kept private by Indians and remained beyond the scope of U.S. law. This appears to have been true both before and after the Major Crimes Act and the

---

[34] The Tlingit case is discussed in Chapter 7, the section entitled "Tlingit Law Meets U.S. Law." The Modoc trials and executions are discussed in Keith Murray, *The Modocs and their War* (Norman: University of Oklahoma Press, 1959).

[35] Isaac Heard, *History of the Sioux War* (New York: Harper and Brothers, 1864), 251–71.

[36] Ibid., 272–95; Roy Nichols, *Lincoln and His Indian Policy* (Columbia: University of Missouri Press, 1978). Lincoln seems to have been considerably anguished trying to determine how many executions were needed to deter Indian uprisings. The ultimate result of 37 was a compromise between a much larger number and only a few. The executions were so badly organized that one Indian, responding to a mispronounced Indian name, was hanged by mistake.

[37] Utley, "Ordeal of Plenty Horses," 85

[38] The IRA carried out a long, largely unsuccessful campaign to free several hundred Apache warriors, including Geronimo, from military imprisonment (without trial), first in Florida, later in Oklahoma. Indian Rights Association, *Fifth Annual Report*, 1887, 27–32.

[39] Each Sioux reservation had a detachment of troops nearby, which figured prominently in agency affairs.

Kagama decision, although as the nineteenth century drew to a close tribal society was increasingly vulnerable to the imposition of U.S. law.[40]

The majority of the nineteenth-century laws with which the United States intended to regulate tribal life failed to do so. Nowhere can this be seen more clearly than in the failure of U.S. criminal law to reach the killings that occurred on Indian reservations. The annual reports of the BIA record 147 killings between Indians, 37 killings of whites by Indians, and 28 of Indians by whites in the period 1875–1905. By and large, these exclude killings that occurred during the Indian wars and describe individual acts of violence either on a reservation or so immediately adjacent to one as to involve the BIA. Because of the patchwork criminal jurisdiction over reservation tribes, these cases involved tribal, state or territorial, or federal jurisdiction, depending on the actual location of the killing and the tribal membership of perpetrator and victim.[41]

It is clear from other sources that many killings were not included in these reports. Each agent reported what he thought was most important from his jurisdiction – customarily, but not always, matters involving general law and order, especially after the 1880s, when the uniformity of the agents' annual reports shows that BIA officials in Washington expected major criminal cases to be included in those reports, undoubtedly in response to the heightened interest in criminal law that followed from *Crow Dog* and the Major Crimes Act. Nevertheless, this large number of cases is representative of the range of killings occurring on or near reservations and their dispositions.

Few killings between Indians were punished under U.S. law, even after *Kagama* and the Major Crimes Act. The BIA collected minimal crime statistics on reservations, especially concerning homicide cases. This effort began in the late 1870s, probably to generate data to bolster its case in Congress for an extension of criminal jurisdiction to the tribes on the ground that Indians were "uncivilized," the Indian reservations harboring unpunished criminals. Of the 147 cases described in the BIA annual reports, fewer than 20 led to criminal convictions in U.S. courts, and apparently only one resulted in an execution.[42] A Sioux convicted of raping a woman and then

---

[40] The capacity of U.S. law to intervene in tribal life dates in the West only from the late 1870s, based on (1) the Indian agents' access to their own Indian police forces, (2) the *Kagama* case and its legal basis for intervention, and (3) the full assimilationist policy underlying the Dawes Act, which provided ideological reason to intervene in intertribal crimes.

[41] Robert N. Clinton, "Criminal Jurisdiction over Indian Lands: A Journey Through a Jurisdictional Maze," *Arizona Law Review* 18 (1976):503, provides a detailed analysis of the complexity of criminal jurisdiction over Indian tribes. Briefly, major criminal offenses between Indians are federal if they occur on a reservation (after the Major Crimes Act and *Kagama*) and state if they occur off the reservation. Minor criminal offenses are tribal, with tribal authorities having concurrent jurisdiction over major crimes with the federal government.

[42] This listing was derived from a study of BIA annual reports, relying heavily on indices to the annual reports. There is no question that these records are incomplete, but the listing

killing her and her small child with a rock received a ten-year sentence.[43] William Black and Pancho, two Mescalero Apaches, were given five-year sentences for killing Joe Treas.[44] Old Man Rock was given a ten-year sentence for manslaughter in the "cold-blooded" killing of his wife on the Fort Peck Reservation.[45] A murder resulting from a "drunken brawl" among the Winnebagos resulted in a four-year sentence.[46] These sentences were typical, reflecting a sentencing pattern already seen in the witch-killing cases. It seems that the BIA was not intent on death penalties for intra-Indian killings. Rather, the function of the imposition of criminal law on tribal Indians was the destruction of tribal legal institutions.

The only Indian in the BIA annual reports reported to receive the death sentence was Pablo, a Ute Indian who had killed two Ute companions and the wife of one of them a few miles from the reservation. He was hunted down by a party composed of both whites and Utes, confessing his guilt to Chief Severo, who testified against him. Because the killing occurred a few miles off the reservation, he was tried in a Colorado state court, a court more likely to sentence him to death than a federal court.[47] Pablo's case was further unique in that he was executed for killing Indians.

Indians were more frequently executed for killing whites, offenses that did not fall under the Major Crimes Act. If committed in Indian country, such killings were under federal jurisdiction, but many of these crimes were committed in local towns, under state jurisdiction, putting Indians at the mercy of local judges and juries.[48] The 1906 Nevada executions of Johnny, a Shoshone, and Ibapah, a Goshute, for their drunken killing and robbery

---

does provide a framework for analyzing Indian crime. Virtually all Indian murder cases that resulted in convictions were reduced to manslaughter, primarily because of evidentiary problems in proving intent. It is likely that this figure underrepresents the actual number of convictions because crimes were usually reported in the year they occurred, when the accused were being held in prison awaiting trial. Therefore, a trial and sentence in the next year would not always be reported. Still, the more common pattern was to hold Indians in prison for a year or more awaiting trial and then drop the case because no witnesses were available.

[43] BIA, *Annual Report of the Commissioner of Indian Affairs, 1895,* 297.

[44] BIA, *Annual Report, 1902,* 253.

[45] BIA, *Report, 1893,* 193.

[46] BIA, *Annual Report, 1903,* 203.

[47] BIA, *Annual Report, 1896,* 134. The case is reported as *Pablo v. the People,* 23 Col. 134 (1896). The case file, including a transcript, is held as case no. 3656, Colorado State Archives, Denver. Other Indians were certainly executed by the states for crimes that the BIA took no notice of. Columbia George and Toy Toy, 39 Ore. 604 (1900) and Buckaroo Jack, 30, Nev. 325 (1908), received the death sentence in state courts but were not executed.

[48] An analysis of the complex nature of state jurisdiction over Indians who crossed into state jurisdiction is Judith Royster and Rory Snow Arrow Fausett, "Fresh Pursuit onto Native American Reservations: State Rights 'to Pursue Savage Hostile Indian Marauders Across the Border': An Analysis of the Limits of State Intrusion into Tribal Sovereignty," *University of Colorado Law Review* 59 (1988):191.

of a tramp occurred in the context of great local prejudice.[49] Similarly, South Dakota's 1882 hanging of Brave Bear, a Sioux warrior, for the murder of a white trader was explicitly in response to fears of Indian violence.[50] Indian Joe, a Mission Indian, was hung in 1893 on questionable evidence for the murder of a German farmer and his wife near San Diego, California.[51] New Mexico's hanging two years later of the Mescalero Apache Carpio Monte was part of a major effort by citizens of New Mexico and Arizona to punish severely "renegade" Apaches, those who left their reservations and engaged in attacks on whites.[52]

The Indian Territory, previously discussed, presented a wide range of interracial conflicts. Of the seventy-nine executions of prisoners sentenced in Judge Isaac Parker's federal district court in Fort Smith between 1875 and 1896, at least eleven were clearly Indians, not a large proportion given the total population of the territory, but a large number of Indian executions nevertheless.[53] Smoker Mankiller, a Cherokee, had killed a white neighbor.[54] Sinker Wilson killed Datus Cowan, also in the Cherokee Nation.[55] Isham Seely and Gibson Ishtanubbee, both Choctaws, killed and robbed a white farmer and his servant.[56] John Postoak killed a white man and his wife in the Creek Nation.[57] Amos and Abner Manley, two Creek brothers, arose in the middle of the night and killed a white farmer who had given them refuge, evidently intending to rob him.[58] Tualisto, a Creek who needed money to attend a green corn dance, ambushed and killed a white traveller.[59] Silas Hampton, a Cherokee, killed a white farmer, robbing him of $7.50 and a pocketknife.[60] Webber Isaacs had killed a white peddlar who had come to his house in the Cherokee Nation to sell his wares.[61] Rufus Buck, a Creek, together with four others, was executed for the gang rape of two white

[49] *State v. Johnny et al.*, 29 Nev. 203 (1906).
[50] Louis Pfaller, "The Brave Bear Murder Case," *North Dakota History* 36 (1969):121.
[51] Clare V. McKanna, Jr., "Four Hundred Dollars Worth of Justice: The Trial and Execution of Indian Joe, 1892–93," *Journal of San Diego History* (1988):197–212.
[52] *United States v. Monte*, 3 N.M. 126 (1884).
[53] Glenn Shirley, *Law West of Fort Smith*, and S.W. Harmon, *Hell on the Border*, both contain detailed accounts of most of the death penalty trials in Parker's court including many personal details and the race of the offenders and victims. While this information is not complete, local information about matters of race was probably highly accurate, and it is clear that few Indians were hung after trials at Fort Smith.
[54] Harmon, *Hell on the Border*, 76.
[55] Ibid., 92.
[56] Ibid., 87.
[57] Ibid., 93.
[58] Ibid., 96–7.
[59] Shirley, *Law West of Fort Smith*, 217.
[60] Ibid., 222.
[61] *Isaacs v. United States* 159 U.S. 487 (1895).

women. He was the leader of an outlaw gang, primarily composed of Black Creeks, that had committed numerous crimes in the Indian Territory.[62] At least several others executed at Fort Smith were "part" Indian, but it is impossible to assess the extent to which these men identified as Indian. Crawford Goldsby, for example, better known as the outlaw "Cherokee Bill" had been born in Texas, the son of a soldier who was "of Mexican extraction, mixed with white and Sioux," and a mother who was "half Negro, one fourth white, one fourth Cherokee." In a shoot out with deputies as he was attempting to escape prison, "every time the outlaw fired, he gobbled. It was an unearthly sound, halfway between the bark of a coyote and the gobble of a turkey cock. It was the death cry among the territory Indians."[63] Samuel Fooy, "less than half Cherokee and nearly white," killed and robbed a white schoolteacher.[64]

Indians convicted of murder almost always had their convictions reversed if they went to the U.S. Supreme Court, regardless of the race of their victim. The Court heard the appeals of eighteen Indian murder convictions between 1883 and 1900.[65] Six of these (all previously discussed), *Crow Dog, Kagama, Thomas, Talton, Famous Smith,* and *Lucas,* involved Indian victims, and turned on jurisdictional issues.[66] In four of those cases, the Court held that tribal courts had jurisdiction, rather than federal courts, a clear victory for the tribe involved, although the decision in *Talton* went against the individual defendant. *Kagama* was a test of the power of Congress to pass the Major Crimes Act. *Thomas,* like *Kagama,* primarily concerns issues of federalism, turning on whether an intratribal killing on state school lands within a reservation was under state or federal jurisdiction.

The remaining eleven homicide cases involved non-Indian victims. Nine of these were reversed, most often on the grounds of highly technical errors in their original trials, a high rate of reversal in death penalty cases.[67] Only

---

[62] Shirley, *Law West of Fort Smith,* 159–74.

[63] Ibid., 122, 130. Goldsby was executed on March 17, 1896 (134–6).

[64] Harmon, *Hell on the Border,* 80–1.

[65] Other than *Corn Tassell,* no homicide conviction of an Indian was appealed to the U.S. Supreme Court before *Crow Dog* in 1883. These nineteen convictions involved only seventeen defendants: Sam Hickory and Henry Starr each appealed two convictions.

[66] *Ex parte Crow Dog* 109 U.S. 556 (1883); *United States v. Kagama* 118 U.S. 375 (1885); *United States v. Thomas* 151 U.S. 577 (1894); *Talton v. Mayes* 163 U.S. 376 (1896); *Famous Smith v. United States* 151 U.S. 50 (1894); *Lucas v. United States* 163 U.S. 612 (1896). All of these defendants lived, except Bob Talton. Ironically, he had been sentenced to death by a Cherokee court. The U.S. Supreme Court, in upholding Cherokee jurisdiction, left the nation free to hang Talton.

[67] *Gon shay ee, Petitioner* 130 U.S. 343 (1889); *Captain Jack, Petitioner* 130 U.S. 353 (1889); *Hicks v. United States* 150 U.S. 442 (1893); *Hickory v. United States* 151 U.S. 303 (1894); *Hickory v. United States* 160 U.S. 408 (1896); *Starr v. United States* 153 U.S. 614 (1894); *Starr v. United States* 164 U.S. 627 (1897); *Alberty v. United States* 162 U.S. 499 (1896);

the death penalty convictions of Webber Isaacs, a Cherokee, and Rufus Buck, a Creek, were affirmed.[68] Thus, even in cases involving non-Indian victims, the U.S. Supreme Court was reluctant to execute Indian murderers.

Many killings went unsolved, with no evidence or witnesses to identify the killer or killers, who often fled. Tribal society frequently surrounded the killing with secrecy, refusing to give white authorities evidence or offering only misinformation. The tribes became adept at manipulating U.S. law to protect traditional ways.[69]

Even when suspected killers were brought to trial, the most minimal of the formal requirements of evidence could not be met: no motive, no witnesses, no physical evidence. A large number of intra-Indian killings were dismissed as "self-defense," often by Indian agents in declining to bring formal charges, but also by white judges and juries.

Indian agents often charged that Indians were uncooperative in legal proceedings or, much worse in their view, that they deliberately lied to obstruct justice and protect each other. An agent at the Siletz agency in Oregon put the matter directly:

> Much disorder and crime have occurred at this agency during the present fiscal year...it is almost impossible to procure conviction in this agency because of the notorious untruthfullness of the Indians. Most of them openly manufacture evidence, swear to false statements for a financial consideration, friendship or revenge, and in this way defeat justice by raising a "reasonable" doubt in behalf of the prisoner.[70]

The same view was held by Agent Charles Porter of the Hoopa Reservation. He wrote in his 1883 annual report, the year before the *Kagama* case arose under his jurisdiction, that "in investigating complaints made by them against one another I have...the greatest difficulty in discovering the true state of affairs, and have not always succeeded owing to the cloud of falsehood which surrounds all the circumstances."[71]

Added to the problem of evidence was the logistics of moving witnesses

---

Rowe v. United States 164 U.S. 546 (1896); *Tla Koo Yel Lee v. United States* 167 U.S. 274 (1897); and *John Bad Elk v. United States* 177 U.S. 529 (1900).

[68] *Isaacs v. United States* 159 U.S. 487 (1895). *Buck v. United States* 163 U.S. 678 (1896).

[69] There is no systematic analysis of the process through which the tribes evaded the imposition of U.S. law, yet the noncooperation of the tribes in the BIA courts is legendary. One analysis of this process, and of white attempts to overcome it, is Sidney L. Harring, "The Rich Men of the Country: Canadian Law Comes to the Land of the Copper Inuit, 1914–1930," *Ottawa Law Review* 21 (1989):1–64.

[70] BIA, *Annual Report, 1904*, 317. In the cases considered in this book for which transcripts are available, it is clear that Native Americans testified only reluctantly and withheld the most important information. We have already seen this in the discussions of *Crow Dog*, *Whaley*, and *Sah Quah*.

[71] BIA, *Annual Report, 1883*, "Reports of Agents in California," 13.

great distances, often making it "not worth the trouble" to prosecute. Under such conditions it might seem remarkable that white authorities ever managed to convict any Indian of the murder of another Indian, but both the tribes lack of power off the reservation and the weak legal protection afforded Indian defendants, made many convictions inevitable. By the end of the century, there were many hundreds of formal trials of Indians for offenses under the Major Crimes Act, clearly showing the effort the BIA invested in the attempt to impose U.S. law.

An analysis of the patterns of prosecution of typical types of Indian murder cases reveals much about the scope of the BIA effort to prosecute Indians for violations of U.S. criminal law and also the clear efforts of the tribes to limit the reach of U.S. law in order to protect tribal sovereignty. Nowhere is this clearer than in the failure of government efforts to prosecute three types of intratribal killings specifically related to the changing social life of reservations: killings of witchs and various authority figures imposed on reservation society, as well as those resulting from drunkenness.

Witch killings

The frequency of witch killings, as well as the related practice of traditional medicine, was a source of great embarrassment to the BIA, especially after the turn of the twentieth century. Of the 147 murder cases reported in the BIA annual reports, 17, or about 12 percent, were known witch killings, and many others must have been concealed. These cases have special importance here because the continuation of witch killings demonstrates the depth of traditional belief systems in tribal communities. The prosecution of witch killings, although legally no more difficult than those resulting from drinking and fighting, was more embarrassing to the government because such trials revealed images of Indian life at odds with official reports of a smoothly progressing assimilation process.[72]

Little is known about the practice of witch killing before the imposition of U.S. law, so we do not know the extent to which the witch killings of the late nineteenth and early twentieth century were traditional or were adaptations of tribal society to forced assimilation.[73] The incidence of witch killings may have increased in reaction to the forces cataclysmically transforming tribal society. For example, the previously described witch killing

---

[72] Sidney L. Harring, "Red Lilac of the Cayugas," *New York History* 73 (Jan. 1992), 1:65–94, describes the trial of a Cayuga witch killer in Buffalo, New York, in 1931, focusing on the different meanings that white society placed on the event and the evidentiary problems raised by introducing a witchcraft defense at a white trial.

[73] This has been suggested to have been the case in some African societies.

at the Tule River Reservation occurred in a tribe that was a small remnant of its former existence, a few old people who had been repeatedly removed by the government, trying very hard to maintain their tribal life.[74] Both early ethnologists and Indian agents were confused about the nature of traditional medicine among the tribes and collectively described a wide range of traditional ceremonial practices they did not understand as "witchcraft." In its preferred usage, the term "witch" should be applied only to one who injures or kills another through magic and not to traditional healers, even though the skills involved often overlapped.[75] Much traditional healing consisted of driving out the evil spirits that were injuring the victim.

Undoubtedly most witch killings were concealed, the known ones representing only a small proportion of the actual number. Similarly, the evidence that Indians gave in witch-killing trials was often distorted to protect tribal traditions and values as well as to limit the involvement of others in the tribe to protect them from prosecution.

The Yakima Agency had two witch killings in 1887. Dick Wyneco shot and killed an Indian "doctor" named Wynocks. The agent learned of the killing through other Indians. When Wyneco was arrested, he admitted his action, stating that he believed that Wynocks was causing the death of his child. A number of Yakima came to hold council with the agent, demanding to know what would become of Wyneco. When the agent told them of the Major Crimes Act of 1885 and that he believed that the killing of a witch doctor was a crime, the Yakima responded that they had never heard this before. They indicated that they would not object to being held accountable to this law in the future but implied that it was not fair to hold Wyneco accountable to a law he did not know.[76] While Wyneco was in jail awaiting trial, Dan Plan-o-ple-o-pike shot and killed an Indian doctor named Waltose. The motive was similar: Waltose was believed to be killing relatives of Plan-o-ple-o-pike. As proof that the Indians accepted the new law that was

---

[74] The *Bill Whaley et al.* case is discussed Chapter 5, the section entitled "Cultural Geography."

[75] There is no universal terminology describing witchcraft. A wide range of behaviors involved in the practice of traditional medicine were often falsely categorized as "witchcraft" by Indian agents and other whites, either by mistake or as part of a deliberate effort to discredit the practice of such medicine. Accordingly, some of the killings described here are witch killings, whereas others resulted from the practice of traditional medicine. Often the two are difficult to separate because some of those called on to practice traditional medicine were believed to possess extraordinary powers, including the power to call up evil spirits to do harm. There is a vast literature on the practice of Native American witchcraft among the different tribes. The best known of these studies is Clyde Kluckholn, *Navajo Witchcraft* (Boston: Beacon Press, 1962). An introduction to this literature is Deward Walker, Jr., *Witchcraft and Sorcery of the American Native Peoples* (Moscow: University of Idaho Press, 1989).

[76] BIA, *Annual Report, 1888*, 232. *Territory of Washington v. Wineco*, Yakima Superior Court, Criminal case 211, April 21, 1888.

imposed on them, the agent cited the fact that none of the friends of either defendant had resisted their arrests.[77] In an effort to show the force of the Major Crimes Act, the agent had the Indian police take the two accused to the territorial jail in North Yakima in the middle of the day, having announced the time that the transfer would be made so that the tribe would see them removed from the reservation to face white justice.[78] The two were convicted of manslaughter in separate trials and given one-year jail sentences. The sentences were light because these killings were among the first committed under the Major Crimes Act, and both Indians claimed to be acting under tribal authority with complete ignorance of the act.[79]

The most significant direct intervention into tribal witch killings was a series of indictments of a society of Zuni priests in 1897, coupled with the military occupation of the Zuni Pueblo to stop a series of witch killings and beatings. As in most of the recorded witch killings, and unlike the remarkable record left by the Tule River case, there is little information on the meaning or context of the Zuni cases. The immediate event that provoked government response was the hanging of Marita, an old woman:

> They threw her off the house, took her to a corral, where they tied her wrists behind her back and pulled her up on a beam, with her feet from the ground. They kept her hanging nearly all day, and while she was hanging they tortured her in every way. I hear four or five Zunis were implicated in the torture, and there were many spectators. It is only the poor ones, who have not enough friends to protect them that are accused and tried.
>
> The woman is the fourth one since last summer; the others they didn't tie up on account of friends interfering.[80]

The agent further reported that "crimes of this character have been frequent among these Indians," alleging that two witches had been killed "only a few years ago" and also that a Carlisle Indian School graduate had been brutally beaten. He demanded severe punishment in an effort to stop this outbreak.

Lacking an Indian police or any other means of intervening in Zuni life, the agent got the assistance of a troop of cavalry and two cannon. The captain demanded to confer with tribal leaders about the witchcraft hangings, but the tribe refused to meet with him, showing that the activities of the priests were protected as traditional practices. When the army sent more cavalry,

[77] Ibid. *Territory of Washington v. Dan Planopleopike*, Yakima Superior Court, Criminal case 212.

[78] Letter, Thomas Priestly to BIA Commissioner, April 31, 1888, Record Group, 75, BIA, Yakima, Box 12, "Letters to Commissioner," National Archives, Seattle.

[79] Letter, Thomas Priestly, Indian Agent at Yakima reservation to BIA Commissioner, August 31, 1888, in ibid.

[80] BIA, *Annual Report, 1897*, 62.

the governor of the pueblo agreed to meet with them. As a result of this discussion, four priests of the Bow, a traditional society, were turned over to the army, which in turn presented them to territorial authorities.[81] They, together with an unnamed "John Doe," were indicted for felony assault in the territorial court in Valencia County and held in jail on $5,000 bond. The army stayed on at Zuni because local whites were afraid the tribe would retaliate. The priests were held in jail for at least a year before being transferred to a federal court. Since no record of their trial exists, it is likely that they were freed for lack of witnesses.[82]

An 1886 witch killing on Warm Springs Reservation in Oregon ended the same way. The father of a sick child summoned a traditional doctor. With the father's belief that the doctor was not curing the child, the doctor was "made away with over the night and his body appeared the next day, with his throat slit from ear to ear." A four-day investigation was held by the agent, but no evidence was found. No one would testify, but all informants revealed that they believed in traditional medicine. One Indian policeman stated that he believed that he would die if he arrested a medicine man but that it was his duty and he would do it.[83]

The most complex of the late-nineteenth-century Indian witch-killing cases, and the only one taken to the U.S. Supreme Court, arose on the Umatilla Reservation in 1900. Columbia George and Toy Toy poisoned Anna Edna, an elderly woman witch doctor they believed had killed Toy Toy's father. George, while drunk, gave Anna twenty-five cents worth of coyote poison, mixed with whiskey in a small flask. They were tried for murder in Umatilla County Court. Their lawyer, faced with George's confession, mounted a jurisdictional defense, arguing that the killing had occurred on an allotment on the reservation. When the defense attorney offered to call as witnesses a number of Indians to testify that George and Toy Toy were traditional Indian headmen who believed they had a right to kill Anna under

---

[81] Report, Colonel [signature illegible], 2d Cavalry, Fort Wingate, New Mexico, to Governor Bradford Prince, January 19, 1893. A copy of this report is contained in the Territorial Archives of New Mexico, New Mexico State Archives, Santa Fe. The 1893 date is inexplicable: there can be no question that the events described are the witchcraft events of 1897, properly dated by the BIA annual reports and the court records for the four Zuni priests sent for trial on assault charges.

[82] A search of both federal and territorial court records produced one case file, *New Mexico v. Nynche et al.*, an indictment for assault filed in Valencia County in February 1898. The file is held as Criminal case 511, Valencia County, in the New Mexico State Center and Archives, Santa Fe. The facts alleged in the indictment name Nynche, three others, and John Doe and describe the beating of "Maoriorita." Further papers include an order transferring custody of the four to Bernadillo County. No disposition can be found. Here I might add that this is a common outcome in Indian cases for two reasons: the first has to do with poor or lost records; the second involves the fact that Indian cases were frequently dropped for procedural reasons, most often for lack of evidence or lack of complaining witnesses.

[83] BIA *Annual Report, 1886*, 223.

tribal law, the judge held such testimony irrelevant and refused to allow it in evidence. The county court held that it had jurisdiction on tribal allotments, convicted the men, and sentenced them to hang.[84]

Both convictions, however, were overturned by the Oregon Supreme Court on the ground that the state courts did not have jurisdiction over intra-Indian killings on reservations, one of the few state supreme court opinions that denied state jurisdiction over Indian allotments. Toy Toy's lawyer at trial did not challenge the jurisdiction of the county court over the Umatilla Reservation, legally waiving this issue. Fortunately, Toy Toy's appeal was heard together with Columbia George's, otherwise he might have been hung.[85] The two were tried a second time in federal district court in Portland, convicted of murder, and given life sentences. The defense that they were traditional headmen, carrying out a lawful tribal execution, was rejected, consistent with *Whaley* and the Major Crimes Act.[86] Both later appealed to the U.S. Supreme Court, arguing that their convictions should be reversed because, the killing being committed on allotments, the federal courts lacked jurisdiction. This was too much for the Court, which delivered a stinging rebuke.[87]

It is not possible to make sense of witch killings within the framework of twentieth-century U.S. law, nor could Indian agents or federal judges do so in the nineteenth century. This is true for a number of reasons. First, neither the agents nor the courts ever had the real facts of any of the cases before them. The tribes concealed most of the cases from any form of recognition by white authorities. Second, even when the agents and courts recognized that a "crime" had occurred under U.S. law, they were most often powerless to prosecute it. The formal requirements of evidence, for example, could not be met when tribal members protected their traditional medicine by giving partial and false evidence. *Whaley* and *Columbia George* were exceptions, successful prosecutions only because the defendants forthrightly admitted the killings. The overall meaning of this is that tribal sovereignty was protected by the capacity of the tribes to isolate their own traditions from U.S. law. The Major Crimes Act and the *Kagama* decision gave U.S. courts a juridical power over the tribes; but no matter how much the BIA wanted

---

[84] Transcript, *State v. Columbia George*, held in the Archives Division, Office of the Secretary of State, Salem, Oregon. The two were tried separately, although their appeal was decided together.

[85] *State v. Columbia George*, 39 Oreg. 127 (July 1901). BIA, *Annual Report 1901*, 353; *Annual Report, 1902*, 323. Transcript, *State v. Toy Toy*, Archives Division, Office of the Secretary of State, Salem, Oregon.

[86] *United States v. Columbia George and Toy Toy*, Record Group 21, Box 253, Case no. 2568, National Archives, Seattle.

[87] 201 U.S. 641 (1906) (cert. denied); Toy Toy alone continued the appeal thereafter, finally losing in *Toy Toy v. Hopkins*, 212 U.S. 542 (1909), at 548.

to prosecute as part of their effort to force the assimilation of the tribes, neither the agents nor the courts had the actual power to do so.

The killing of authority figures

The killing of tribal leaders was almost unknown in native society. Leadership structures differed substantially among tribes but were fluid relationships based on accomplishment and complex internal political traditions. Leadership was socially accountable to a tribal body, and chiefs could be removed for a wide variety of reasons. Tribal authority structures had a high degree of legitimacy in traditional society.[88] An attack on these structures approached the unthinkable.

All that changed in the age of BIA-nominated chiefs or co-opted traditional chiefs. One need look no farther than Crow Dog's killing of Spotted Tail to see the conflict that such authority structures not only faced but actually created. There were no longer legitimate traditional models, and a wide variety of factional conflicts emerged. The standard progressive versus traditional model of factional struggle that many anthropologists and historians have identified represents a simplistic reaffirmation of how the Indian agents of the 1880s and 1890s described the divisions they saw on virtually every reservation: a "progressive" faction cooperated with the agent, accepted allotment, participated in the agent's courts of Indian offenses, went to church, and sent their children to the agency school; a "traditional" faction – called by such names as "kickers" or "blanket Indians" – retreated to far corners of the reservation, did not cooperate with the agent, resisted sending their children to schools, refused to accept the jurisdiction of the agent's courts, and fought allotment.

This model, however, casts tribal politics in white terms and ignores the political consciousness of late-nineteenth-century native peoples. These struggles were deeply rooted in traditional tribal political life, turned on carefully thought-out strategies designed to protect tribal society from the continuing onslaught of "Americanization," and involved a much larger and more complex array of beliefs than are conceptualized in the labels "progressive" and "traditional." For example, it seems clear that all native belief systems were deeply based on traditional views of the world and that all were geared to meeting the changes imposed by white society. Belonging to a church and sending children to school, for example, were important adaptive mechanisms accepted by many who belonged to a traditional faction. The agent was thrown a few symbolic and visible measures of tribal acqui-

---

[88] In traditional legal systems, conceptions of leadership merge with the totality of the normative system that encompasses the law. E. A. Hoebel, *The Law of Primitive Man* (Cambridge: Oxford University Press, 1964).

escence to white authority in an effort to protect more important traditional institutions and values. The long struggle to outlaw traditional dancing illustrates this. After most Indian agents outlawed traditional rituals and enforced this ban with arrests by tribal police, tribes used every possible white-sanctioned occasion for traditional rituals, including cattle fairs, church services, and Fourth of July celebrations.[89]

These adaptions to white authority were not uniform or understood in the same way by all members of the tribe. The result was a high level of conflict on many reservations that produced a number of killings. It is important to recognize, however, that the actual number of killings in factional struggle was very low, which suggests that traditional mechanisms of social control continued to have a much stronger hold than the popular "social disorganization" theories of reservation life would suggest.

Still, at least 15 percent of the 147 intra-Indian killings on reservations were political in that they stemmed directly from conflicts introduced by white pressure to assimilate. A number of other killings undoubtedly resulted from the same source, but the nature of the conflict was either unknown to the Indian agent or went unreported to Washington. An "absense of factional strife" made an individual agent appear to be effective, and so agents felt some pressure to falsify the issues underlying such killings.[90]

Often the victims were Indian police. Their role was a tenuous one in tribal society, for they acted for the Indian agent in enforcing a wide range of reservation rules that violated tribal rights and offended traditionals, including compulsory school attendance, prohibition of religious ceremonials, and the forced cutting of the long hair of males. The political importance of the tribal police to the Indian agent might lead one to expect vigorous prosecution of the killers, but again, the Major Crimes Act failed to reach them.[91]

---

[89] The best critique of simplistic theories of tribal factionalism is found in Peter Whiteley, *Deliberate Acts: Changing Hopi Culture Through the Oraibi Split* (Tucson: University of Arizona Press, 1988). Fred Hoxie, *Final Promise: The Campaign to Assimilate the Indians, 1880–1920* (Lincoln: University of Nebraska Press, 1984) discusses tribal means of co-opting U.S. holidays. BIA annual reports are replete with complaints from Indian agents that traditional dancing was dangerous and held back assimilationist efforts but that it was impossible to stop.

[90] In general, Indian agents always minimized the factionalism occurring on their reservations, both because it undermined their effectiveness and because it was largely invisible to them. It is significant that most of the major cases directly involved intratribal political conflict, including *Crow Dog, Kagama, Whaley, Crazy Snake,* and *Clapox.*

[91] William T. Hagan, *Indian Police and Judges: Experiments in Acculturation and Control* (New Haven, Conn.: Yale University Press, 1966), is the standard account of the tribal police institution. While there was some struggle between Indian agents and tribal leadership over control of the police, especially, as seen in Chapters 4 and 5, on the Pine Ridge and Rosebud reservations, by the 1890s the agents were dominant.

John Seepo, also called See-po-wa-sa-moah, was a member of the police force at the Sac and Fox Agency in Iowa. He was "heartily disliked by certain members of the tribe who trained with the retrogressive element," according to William Malin, the Indian agent. As Seepo sat with a woman on the banks of a river, a young man approached him from behind and threw him in the water, where he drowned. The agent immediately proceeded to the scene, took the woman into custody, had her identify the perpetrator, wired a U.S. marshal, arrested the perpetrator, and secured his indictment for murder by a federal grand jury on the testimony of the witness. Malin took great pains to deny the crime had anything to do with Seepo's unpopular police work but blamed it on "personal jealousy." At the trial, the woman refused to identify the perpetrator, and he went free.[92]

Similarly, four Indians on the Tulalip Reservation killed tribal judge David Teuse. Two were bound over to the grand jury by a U.S. magistrate; but the grand jury, after a week-long investigation, refused to indict. In spite of the organized nature of the killing, the agent did not have any idea of the roots of the crime.[93]

Two Colorado River Reservation police were knocked down and stabbed by an Apache/Mohave man and his brother while in the act of removing the man's twelve-year-old son to the agency school. Both police officers lived, so no charges could be brought in federal court because felony assault was not one of the seven offenses enumerated by the Major Crimes Act. This omission created an obvious danger to tribal police: they could be injured with impunity without the protection of federal law. Agent L. A. Wright of the San Jacinto agency in California lamented that two of his Indian police officers had been seriously shot. One died, and the murderer was in jail awaiting trial in the federal courts. The other was still alive, although very seriously injured; unless he died within a year, Wright pointed out, the perpetrator could not be punished.[94]

The fact that the Five Civilized Tribes were not included in the Major Crimes Act created an anomaly. white courts had no jurisdiction over killings of Indian police by Indians. A widely cited Cherokee Nation case involved some young Cherokee men arrested for shooting at deputy U.S. marshals. Their defense was that they thought "they were only shooting at Indian police." Sam Sixkiller, a Cherokee who served as a captain of Indian police at Union Agency, was killed in cold blood in downtown Muskogee in 1887. One of the killers was arrested by U.S. marshals; lacking jurisdiction, they placed him in the custody of Creek officers. The Creeks, however, had no

[92] BIA, *Annual Report, 1904*, 210.
[93] BIA, *Annual Report, 1901*, 391.
[94] BIA, *Annual Report, 1898*, 114.

jails, and the young man escaped and was never tried. Both instances were used to discredit tribal legal institutions.[95]

A number of other killings of Indian police involved drunks resisting arrest. The politics of these situations is difficult to sort out, but at least some of them must have turned on traditional resistance to police interference in traditional ways. At Mescalero Agency, the police force was active in breaking up traditional camps making *tiswin*, a native-brewed beer. Still, the agent pointed out, many influential Apaches were involved in the making of *tiswin*, and the police, either because of their own love for *tiswin* or in response to tribal pressure, did not report or destroy many of the camps.[96]

Zacate had previously had his *tiswin* and the utensils for making it destroyed. Therefore, as two police approached him and his son Tomas, he attacked them, stabbing one fatally. The other police officer shot Tomas. Enraged, Zacate seized a rifle and announced that he would kill all the police and everyone in the village, and he shot a woman and her two children before they could escape. He fled into the mountains but was captured a week later by a posse of Indians, who, according to the agent, would have killed Zacate outright but for the promise of a reward for him alive. He was tried and convicted in federal court. Five months later, the mother-in-law of one of the officers killed was stabbed to death by the mother of the other. Both were drunk, but the killing was thought to be an extension of the dispute.[97]

As shown by the case of Zacate, any study of intra-Indian killing must take account of the killings by Indian police. Under tribal law, killings by Indian police were often no more legitimate than they were under federal law. The killing of Sitting Bull by tribal police exemplifies that two distinct sets of legitimate authority structures engaged in a direct and violent altercation. In other cases, traditional Sioux attempted to hold Indian police accountable for killings that violated tribal law. The Cherokee tried and sentenced to death a Cherokee police officer of Union Agency who killed another Cherokee within the Cherokee Nation; a white marshal who had accompanied him was acquitted of murder in the federal court in Fort Smith.[98]

A Northern Cheyenne Indian police officer was sent out to arrest a young Cheyenne for stealing the wife of another, an offense in the eyes of the Indian agent but one with no parallel in Cheyenne law. The young man resisted arrest, and the traditional camp rallied to support him. His father attacked the police with a knife and was killed. There was considerable agitation in the village for months, as other members of the band feared

[95] BIA, *Annual Report, 1887*, 118.
[96] BIA, *Annual Report, 1881*, 10–11.
[97] BIA, *Annual Report, 1888*, 187.
[98] Ibid.

being killed by the police. The agent reported that the overall effect was positive, believing the event taught the Indians that the police must be obeyed.[99]

Most of the authority figures killed were police, but several interpreters, a few chiefs, and members of their families were also killed. Ko-sho-way, a chief on the Sac and Fox Reservation, was killed on a semiannual annuity day and his body thrown in the river. The parties were arrested but could not be prosecuted because the killing occurred in the summer of 1884, prior to the passage of the Major Crimes Act.[100]

The wife of a Pawnee chief was shot and killed while drying corn. The crime was never solved.[101] Apache chief Diablo was killed by three Apaches of another band. When his band sought to kill the perpetrators, the agent ordered his scouts to separate the bands. A few months later, the perpetrators were killed in family feuds, probably bringing a closure to the case by traditional law.[102]

To sum up the meaning of these killings is not an easy matter. U.S. law did not have much impact in the prosecution of these cases. Yet there was also less killing than we might expect, given how violently U.S. law was imposed on Indians. Although this might be true because of the overwhelming power of U.S. law and BIA institutions, the situation was little different where white power was weak and tribal power strong, for example, in the Creek and Hopi nations. It is likely that traditional tribal law held a great deal more sway than the Indian agents believed, in ways that were invisible to whites. Within the matrix of traditional law, even in an era of great factional struggle, there was great respect for leadership. In the context of the violent assimilation process that tribal peoples were subjected to – often with the collusion of their leaders – comparatively few authority figures were killed.

Drinking and fighting

A number of stereotypes arose on the frontier concerning the character of intra-Indian violence. These center on images of Indians being "uncontrollable" and violent after the consumption of alcohol.[103] This simplistic categorization distorts the nature of the conflicts that underlay tribal society. The introduction of alcohol would not have changed the underlying motivations for killing if rooted in political conflict or in controversy over land.

Analysis of the large number of killings attributed by agents to alcohol,

---

[99] BIA, *Annual Report, 1887*, 41.
[100] BIA, *Annual Report, 1884*, 102.
[101] BIA, *Annual Report, 1875*, 322.
[102] BIA, *Annual Report, 1881*, 10.
[103] BIA, *Annual Report, 1896*, 312.

usually in the context of "drinking and fighting," reveals another dimension of the reach of U.S. law into tribal life. At least half of all intra-Indian killings were alcohol related. They were the least planned and most difficult to cover up and therefore should have been among the easiest cases for prosecution under U.S. law. Such cases received matter-of-fact notice in BIA reports. Agents were often cold-bloodedly dismissive of the killings. A Papago living on the Pima Reservation stabbed and killed a Pima allottee while both were in a state of "deep intoxication." J. M. Berger, "farmer in charge" of the reservation, was elated: "Fortunately, this death befell the greatest drunkard and mischiefmaker upon the reservation, who was also the leader of the few malcontents."[104]

Indian agents seized on alcohol as a cause of Indian crime, not as a symptom of oppression, overlaid with all other results of tribal disorganization and rapid social change. Alcohol became a convenient, readily visible symbol of what the impact of white society had done to the tribes, a symbol that deflected attention from the massive white theft of land and the herding of the tribes onto impoverished reservations.

Official reports were filled with lurid descriptions of drunkenness and death, sometimes racist in tone and always portraying the Indians as savages needing the civilizing effect of U.S. law. W. A. Sprole, acting agent at the Fort Peck Reservation, reported that "an Indian buck had killed his squaw ... because she was not successful at bringing the lazy hulk some provisions which he sent her to beg from the agency." Sprole recommended hanging this Indian on the reservation in the spot where the crime was committed as a lesson to the rest of the tribe.[105] On the Rosebud Reservation, two men drunk from liquor procured off the reservation induced a married woman and her six-year-old child to accompany them to a canyon, where they attacked the woman and stoned her and her child to death.[106]

Atypical only because of the large number of deaths is the report of Yakima agent L. T. Erwin:

> I find the greatest hindrance of Indian prosperity is whisky. There is an immense traffic in alcohol and vile decoctions carried on with these Indians. At the federal court in Walla Walla, in December last, 70 men were convicted for selling spirituous liquors to the Yakima Indians. In May, there were 12 or 15 more convicted, and I am informed that there are 12 or 15 more in jail in Yakima now, awaiting trial for the same offenses.

---

[104] BIA, *Annual Report, 1893*, 119. The BIA appointed farmers to train Indians in white agricultural methods. Occasionally, these farmers were placed in charge of reservations when there was no resident agent.

[105] BIA, *Annual Report, 1895*, 195.

[106] Ibid., 297. One man committed suicide, the other received a ten-year sentence.

The murder and three violent deaths among the Indians during the past year are chargeable to these offenses. Only a few weeks [have passed] since Zalzaltan, the chief of the Yakimas, died from an overdose of alcohol and extract of lemon. In March, Cayuse Jack was killed the same way. A few weeks since Bill Sequey, an Indian from this reservation, was arrested at Roslyn and placed in jail for being drunk. He set fire to the jail and was burned to death. On December 24, Pimps and Smuskin...were drunk together. The next morning Smuskin was missing. He was afterwards found in the Yakima River with his head crushed...Last October, one of the "Wild Blanket" Yakimas was arrested in North Yakima for stealing a pair of shoes. The next morning, he was found dead, having hung himself with a scarf to the jail bars during the night. A few weeks ago, Wild Man, a leader among the Yakimas, was found hanging to a tree. He was cut down and...resuscitated. He has never given a reason for the rash act.[107]

All this mayhem is matter-of-factly contained in a report for one year for a reservation with a population of about two thousand adults. Although most of the hundred or so men sent to jail for selling liquor to the Yakima were white, these prosecutions, like the whole effort to police the sale of liquor to Indians, were ineffective.[108] The Yakima agent reported a large number of arrests and jailings for selling liquor to Indians. The nearby Umatilla agent reported in 1884 sending six whites, four Indians, and one Chinese to Portland for trial for selling liquor to Indians. All pleaded guilty, claiming "ignorance of the law," and were fined between $5 and $25. The agent complained that it cost the government at least $100 to send a prisoner from the agency to Portland, arguing that liquor sales would never be eradicated without more severe penalties.[109]

Moreover, as the suicides of Yakimas in prison show, nearly as many Yakima were killed by white intervention into their drinking patterns as were killed by alcohol-related violence itself. This form of official violence, the numerous deaths of Indians in white prisons, primarily attributed to suicide or tuberculosis, is beyond the purview of U.S. law. To the tribes, the white practice of locking people in cages was a cruel assault on the human spirit and caused two of the four drink-related deaths at the Yakima agency.[110]

[107] BIA, *Annual Report, 1894*, 327. An analysis of the allotment process and the resulting impoverishment of the Yakima is Barbara Leibhardt, "Allotment Policy in an Incongruous Legal System: The Yakima Indian Nation as a Case Study, 1887–1934," *Agricultural History* 65, no. 4 (1991):78–103.

[108] The Inmate Register, McNeil Island Federal Prison, National Archives, Seattle, has personnel data on all the men sent there for selling liquor to Indians, largely from Yakima. Only a few were Indians.

[109] BIA, *Annual Report, 1884*, 148.

[110] The problem of Indian deaths in white custody has never been analyzed in the United States. A major Australian investigation, including research on the historical dimensions of

At reservation after reservation, parallel stories were told in the agent's reports. All of these were described in impassive language that belied the parallel violence of U.S. Indian policy. U.S. law did not punish the vast majority of the perpetrators of these homicides for much the same reasons that it failed to punish most other Indian killers. The tribes kept their killings to themselves, not trusting U.S. law and effectively blocking the extension of the Major Crimes Act to reservation Indians.

Indian property crime

Most of the white violence, both legal and extralegal, visited on the Indian tribes was rooted in property relations, both in white efforts to take control of Indian property and, later, in white attempts to transform the "communistic" tribal cultures by imposing Anglo-American property laws on the tribes. The tribes responded to these changing ideas of property in a number of ways, ranging from accommodation to resistance. By the 1890s tribal Indians were occasionally being arrested for trading in forged bank notes and writing bad checks. Jimmie, a Tlingit Indian, received two years in federal prison in 1892 for forgery. He had forged the name of a packing company official on a receipt for salmon, then exchanged the note for goods at a store. The case file contains the forged note, revealing it to be skillfully done.[111] Tlingit arrests for burglary were not uncommon in Alaska and were probably alcohol related.[112]

On the opposite end of the scale were the efforts of Indian agents to transform property relations of reservation Indians. Agent Joseph McMaster of the Nevada Agency reported that Paiutes treated potatoes planted and cultivated by any person as communal, digging and eating them "without scruple" wherever found. McMaster thought he could lock potato thieves up for a day or two, except that he lacked either police or a jail, and pointed out that he had requested funds for such institutions and hoped that he could begin enforcing these "laws" soon.[113] Similarly, the major property crime on many reservations was that Indians, given seed and breeding stock to start small farms, simply ate everything as food, defeating government efforts to turn them into farmers.[114] Such matters were the object of the

---

the problem, is reported in Royal Commission on Aboriginal Deaths in Custody, Final Report, Canberra, 1991.
[111] *United States v. Jimmie*, Criminal case no. 327, Federal District Court, Sitka, September 26, 1892, Record Group 21, National Archives, Anchorage.
[112] *United States v. Tom*, Criminal case no. 357, Federal District Court, Sitka, June 5, 1893. Record Group 21, National Archives, Anchorage.
[113] BIA, *Annual Report, 1881*, 131.
[114] Richard Clow, "The Rosebud Sioux: The Federal Government and the Reservation Years, 1878–1940," Ph.D. diss., University of New Mexico, 1977.

agents' courts of Indian offenses, but were not brought to federal court because they did not fall under the Major Crimes Act. Few property crimes were prosecuted under the act, although larceny and burglary were both included. Probably, the costs involved made such prosecutions not worth the time and effort involved, leaving reservation property crimes to the Indian agents' courts.

Conclusion

The failure of U.S. courts to reach the broad range of Indian killings that occurred after the Major Crimes Act illustrates that the act alone could not extend federal authority to the tribes. Much Indian behavior was protected by the tribes, with many Indian agents acquiescing out of self-interest, preserving the myth that their reservations were orderly, well-managed places. As traditional tribal legal mechanisms broke down, intratribal violence may have become more frequent, although reservations were as orderly as frontier communities generally. An analysis of intratribal homicides, however, reveals that their fundamental nature was hidden from federal authorities to protect traditional people from the intrusion of U.S. law. In turn such law was applied to Indians with little regard for procedural due process, often basing convictions on questionable confessions. Even with little evidence, convictions were regularly obtained.

The Indian wars that resulted from the wholesale breakdown of agent authority were beyond the scope of U.S. law until the 1890s. Only then were these wars made the subject of judicial inquiry, expressly for the purposes of assessing what damages the tribes or the the federal government might be responsible for. This judicial inquiry recognized the sovereign political status of the tribes, a recognition inherent to the distinction between individual crimes and concerted military activity perpetrated by a tribe, acting under traditional tribal leadership. Even tribes that had signed treaties and come under federal authority could, by their actions, renounce those treaties and go to war, retaining their sovereign political status for the purposes of waging war.

9

Conclusion

No one knows what moved Crow Dog to shoot Spotted Tail on the Dakota prairie. The Brule Sioux even today are divided in their opinions. Spotted Tail is seen by many in the tribe as a heroic figure, a man who kept the tribe together in difficult times in the 1870s, protecting his people's interests. Crow Dog's people still live on the Rosebud Reservation; they are respected traditional leaders still opposed to tribal policies seen as too accommodative of U.S. interests. Crow Dog was among the leaders of the Ghost Dance movement, leading his people north from the Rosebud to the Badlands to await their rebirth. Spotted Tail's people still run the Rosebud Reservation, and Sinte Gleska College, the reservation's community college named after Spotted Tail, is one of the Brule's most vital institutions. A full understanding of the differences between the two men requires an understanding of Brule culture that white Americans simply do not have. Crow Dog's case involves two completely distinct cultural contexts, one the legal culture of the Indian tribes, the other nineteenth-century U.S. legal culture.

Toward an ethnolegal history of Indian law

Only Brule law could penetrate this unknowable world, come to an under-standing of Crow Dog's case, and settle it in a way that preserved the integrity of the Brule people. Crow Dog's motives for killing Spotted Tail were intricately bound up in his humanity and cultural identity. He and Spotted Tail were both Brule leaders involved in a complex struggle to shape the Rosebud Reservation as a homeland for Brule people and their tribal culture. While whites characterized this struggle in simple terms as a struggle between progressive and traditional factions, this view oversimplified and distorted the reality of the dispute. Both Crow Dog and Spotted Tail embodied progressive and traditional values and made striking political compromises to carry out their own particular visions of that strategy. Brule law was one cultural force in shaping this internal struggle.

Brule law, intact and strong in the early 1880s, had survived the defeat of the Sioux peoples and their removal to small tracts of their traditional homelands. The reservation cultures that were created, under the supervision of Indian agents, re-created a large part of the cultural world of the Brule people. That was the issue that brought U.S. policymakers to choose a strategy of forced assimilation, one embodied in the extension of U.S. law to these reservations through the Major Crimes Act, a compromise with a broader proposal to fully extend U.S. law, either federal or state, to the tribes.

The Dawes Act, allotting Indian lands to individuals, was the second element of this legal solution to the Indian "problem." This act embodied two separate attacks on tribal culture: first, the individual allotment of Indian lands destroyed the "communistic" land tenure of the tribes, transforming their communal social orders into copies of rural white counties, complete with plat maps. Second, this allotment alienated most of the land of the tribes as "surplus," land beyond the individual plots that the tribes needed that was sold to whites by the federal government. The money from these sales was put into trust funds to be used to finance the assimilation of the tribes, forcing the Indians to pay for their own impoverishment.

These assimilationist policies, embodied in U.S. law and originating federal Indian law as a new field of doctrine, were a deliberate effort to transform the social world of the Brule Sioux, a world represented symbolically – and imperfectly – in the U.S. Supreme Court's *Crow Dog* opinion. While Brule justice there was dismissed as "a case of red men's revenge," it was clear that even if the "red men" had a different legal order that the Court did not respect, it was their right to have such an order, for only Brule tribal law could effectively structure the new cultural contexts that inevitably arose as tribal culture changed in the face of U.S. authority. Crow Dog's people, following their traditional law, abandoned the Rosebud Reservation for the Badlands in the Ghost Dance uprising of 1890. The Brule Sioux there were joined by other Sioux peoples but were hunted down and killed by the U.S. Army. While the motives of Plenty Horses in shooting Lieutenant Casey are buried in the same cultural complexity that characterizes Crow Dog's motives, there can be no question that he believed he acted under tribal law.

In the years following *Crow Dog*, U.S. legal institutions attempted to bury tribal law. Just as the U.S. Supreme Court had mischaracterized the nature of Brule tribal law, the very existence of tribal law was denied. The tribal law that the Supreme Court recognized in 1883 became incomprehensible within the sphere of U.S. law and jurisprudence, as can be seen in congressional hearings in 1926 on the Leavitt bill. This bill, the successor of the IRA efforts in the 1880s to extend the full measure of U.S. law to Indians, was introduced by Congressman Scott Leavitt of Montana, head of the House Committee on Indian Affairs. Briefly, the bill proposed to extend the full range of civil and criminal laws of the United States to tribal Indians, give formal legal status to the courts of Indian offenses, and abolish customary Indian marriages and divorces, a direct attack on one of the last visible vestiges of tribal tradition.

The testimony shows clearly that Congress had no idea at all that tribal law even existed. When F. C. Campbell, a veteran of thirty-six years of service on the Northern Plains as a BIA district superintendent, was asked if any Indians opposed the present BIA court system, he responded that "there is no organized opposition." Yet he went on to admit that "there are Indians who oppose it . . . we have Indians who oppose constituted authority." Congressman Knutson then inquired about the "so-called blanket Indians," or "less progressive Indians." Campbell responded that 80 percent of the "long-haired Indians" objected to the Indian courts. Chairman Leavitt then interrupted, asking what those Indians wanted in place of the tribal courts. Campbell testified that he did not know. Forty years after traditional tribal law had settled a complex Brule killing and had been accorded legal recognition by the highest U.S. court, its existence was completely unknown in a congressional hearing on the legal status of Indians under U.S. law.[1]

To the extent that Crow Dog's case represents the legal conflict between tribal law and U.S. law in the forced assimilation of the plains tribes, the Creeks and Tlingits were in very different positions with respect to federal law. Both tribes protected and defended their tribal laws. The Creeks, like the rest of the Five Civilized Tribes in the Indian Territory, constructed a complex legal world with two parallel tribal legal orders, one traditional, one adaptive, incorporating many of the features of U.S. law. For thirty years these two laws were repeatedly in tension, reflecting factional struggles within the tribe over very difficult political and social choices posed by increasing white intrusion into Creek society. Creek law, and the legal orders of the other Five Civilized Tribes, survived the Major Crimes Act by fifteen years. These tribes were not included with the act because white policymakers recognized that those tribes, like the territories, had achieved a remarkable measure of self-government, including elaborate systems of law that functioned within the federal system. Creek and Cherokee death sentences survived legal challenge in federal courts as late as 1898. Ultimately, in a complete recognition of the racist, land-grabbing forces behind federal Indian policy, after several years of efforts to negotiate the termination of the special legal status of the Five Civilized Tribes, the United States acted unilaterally – and illegally – to terminate their national governments.

---

[1] U.S. Congress, House of Representatives, Committee on Indian Affairs, "Reservation Courts of Indian Offenses," hearings on H.R. 7826.

The traditional Creeks, standing firmly on their fully preserved legal order, not only refused to abandon their national government, but reconstituted it and asserted its power against the government of the United States. While the legal context of Crow Dog's killing of Spotted Tail can only be inferred, Crazy Snake was as clear and direct in his actions as anyone could be. He stood on the "old law" of the Creek people, a leader of a faction so large that more than two hundred Creek men were criminally indicted with him. After being freed in a plea bargain on a charge of "purporting" to organize the government of the Creek Nation, Crazy Snake ignored his agreement and repeated his action. This time, like Sitting Bull, he was attacked and shot in his own home, but he escaped into the Oklahoma hills where he was sheltered by traditional Indian people for the rest of his life, still under traditional law and beyond the reach of U.S. law.

The Tlingit did not act with the collective strength of the Creeks, for their tradition of sovereignty was based in isolated villages, traditionally in a competitive relationship with each other. These villages, however, maintained their own traditions of sovereignty that openly defied federal law. There can be no greater symbolization of this than Governor John Brady steaming down to a Tlingit village to cut loose a witch tied in the tidal zone to await execution by drowning. Clearly such an act represents the traditional village law being put into effect, so much in the open that news of the event reaches U.S. authorities. The Angoon, Yakutat, and Sticheen *qwan*s were so openly defiant that U.S. authorities regularly went to discipline whole communities.

More difficult is an understanding of the motives of individual Tlingits. Tla-coo-yel-lee reached the U.S. Supreme Court as a convicted murderer and robber. Yet we have no way of knowing his real motivation for killing and looting a white trader. Such actions were regularly employed to redress white attacks on the Tlingit, but the legal underpinnings of Tlingit action were ignored by U.S. courts. Sah Quah, allegedly a slave, lied to the court about his status, comparing Tlingit slavery to white adoption. In so doing he may have been trying to protect the culture of his adopted people from the intervention of U.S. courts. We simply cannot tell.

Beyond these three tribes, the hundreds of Indian tribes in the United States faced many forms of imposed U.S. law and responded in myriad ways as well. Assertions of tribal sovereignty through tribal law were common, perhaps universal. These events take individual Indian actions out of a cultural context that is difficult or impossible to know. In some cases events can clearly be understood as legal events. Bill Whaley and Pancho Francisco's killing of Juan Baptista was a desperate action, carried out by agreement of the last twenty males of a tribe decimated by California whites, reduced in size from thousands to only a hundred people. Nynche was indicted along with a number of members of a secret Zuni society for its punishment of a witch, a traditional function under Zuni law.

For individual Indians often the offenses cannot be so easily understood in their tribal legal context. The actions of Clapox, Columbia George, Toy Toy, Charles Kie, Spanish Jim, Buckaroo Jack, Yen-decker, Jim Easy, Johnson Foster, and the Apache Kid all straddle a line between western badmen and traditional Indians acting in accord with tribal laws. The cultural reality of these cases is unknowable, reflecting individual Indian's adaptations to changing tribal cultures. Human matters that should have been easily resolved under tribal law moved increasingly into the interstices of the two cultures. It was at one of these points that Crow Dog killed Spotted Tail.

The tribal tradition of acting sovereign – forcing U.S. law either to recognize this sovereignty or at least to confront the reality of its repression – kept sovereignty alive in the plenary power years and characterizes American Indian legal culture. A devotion to the law, not as an abstract body of doctrines, but as a fundamental core value in shaping the human world, still characterizes American Indian legal culture. This legal tradition is lived, rather than argued, as can be seen in countless twentieth-century actions defending tribal sovereignty.[2]

Chief Clinton Rickard, the "fighting Tuscarora," wrote of his poverty as his fall crops rotted because he was in a Canadian jail for his activism in organizing Canadian and American Iroquois to defend their treaty rights. The Iroquois Nation, divided by the Revolutionary War between the two countries, held the treaty right to cross the international border freely, a right necessary to maintain the unity of their nation. Later Rickard and other Iroquois, having failed to get either country to honor that right, organized massive marches of Iroquois through the border posts of both countries at Niagara Falls. These legal border crossings, without adhering to the customs formalities of the United States and Canada, were the only way that the Iroquois could get U.S. and Canadian law changed.[3] The legal events discussed, most directly connected to appellate cases, represent only a few of the uncounted examples of individual and group assertion of tribal sovereignty. Most such events escape formal notice. These stories need to be told, for more than doctrine, they define tribal sovereignty in U.S. law.

The tribes not only have refused to give up their traditional law but have seized on U.S. law as a tool to defend tribal rights. Huge sums of tribal money have been spent hiring the best legal talent available to bring lawsuit

---

[2] Stephen Cornell, *The Return of the Native: American Indian Political Resurgence* (New York: Oxford University Press, 1988).

[3] Clinton Rickard, *Fighting Tuscarora* (Syracuse, N.Y.: Syracuse University Press, 1973), 69–114.

after lawsuit against those who have taken Indian land, chiefly the government of the United States. These challenges have became part of the legal cultures of the tribes. Whole tribes can recite the history of these legal struggles, with old people knowing United States statutes by number. The Tlingit efforts to regain their lands took fifty years. Conversations in villages in the 1920s went on in the Native Brotherhoods, where early discussions of lit-igation were conducted. By the 1930s Washington lawyers were working on litigation strategies. When twenty years of litigation was swept away by the U.S. Supreme Court in *Tee-Hit-Ton Indians v. United States* in 1955, the tribe, undaunted, developed other legal approaches, finally culminating in the Alaska Native Claims Settlement Act of 1971.[4] Losing a case in the Supreme Court is not taken by the tribes as a decision of the highest court, because U.S. courts are understood to represent a chaotic body of law reflecting conflicting white interests. Lost cases mean that the tribes develop another way to challenge the offending laws.

These events should be included in our modern understanding of the doctrine of Indian law. This can be done without romanticizing the diffi-culties and contradictions of tribal law, problems exaggerated by twentieth-century factional conflict. To the extent that some BIA-installed tribal gov-ernments became corrupt copies of U.S. governments, tribal law became corrupted as well. Tribes often divided into factions, with a more traditional law preserved in a conservative faction that is still mischaracterized by U.S. policymakers. Even without overt factional struggle, tribal law evolved to meet changing social and economic conditions. Traditional tribal institutions were also strained or even broken by the imposition of U.S. law via the direct BIA assault on tribal cultures. There is no question that large parts of this legal history, a history that, like Crazy Snake, went underground, are unknowable and therefore cannot be written. It is also clear that much of this history of tribal law and its evolution in relation to U.S. law can be described in a variety of ways. This law was used to shape Indian America, becoming a major force in the preservation of the tribes. American Indian legal history is a part of our nation's legal culture in its own terms, as tribal law, a jurisprudence wholly independent of U.S. law.

American Indian law

The tribes have also used the other Indian law – federal and state Indian law – to structure tribal–federal relations. Tribal sovereignty has repeatedly been asserted in U.S. law, primarily by the tribes, ever since *Corn Tassel*.

---

[4] 348 U.S. 272 (1955); Act of December 18, 1971, Pub. L., no. 92–203. Duane Champaigne, *American Indian Societies: Strategies and Conditions for Political and Cultural Survival* (Cam-bridge, Mass: Cultural Survival, 1989), documents the Tlingit struggle for their land.

But a consistent doctrine of tribal sovereignty never emerged under federal Indian law. After stripping the tribes of their sovereign right to their lands in *Johnson v. McIntosh,* the U.S. Supreme Court in the Cherokee cases defined a "domestic dependent nation" legal status for the tribes. While this formulation advanced U.S. national interests by bringing the tribes under federal and not state jurisdiction, it left their sovereignty in an ambiguous status. Not only did this formulation fail to work in its immediate context, as the Five Civilized Tribes were forced to abandon their lands and were removed to the Indian Territory, but it failed either to protect tribal sovereignty or to define adequately the legal relationship between the United States and the Indian nations.

Crow Dog unambiguously defined the extent of tribal sovereignty after fifty years of dodging the issue. This sovereignty was broad in its scope, thus becoming the foundation of the next fifty years of federal Indian law, but it was ultimately limited by the power of the U.S. government, which could be exercised without limitation. Not only did this formulation effectively limit tribal sovereignty, but it set up a weighted "balancing test" that still characterizes federal Indian law. The doctrine of tribal sovereignty direct from *Worcester* and *Crow Dog* is at the core of federal Indian law, but it is weighed against U.S. national interests, a complex process applying several other doctrines that severely limit tribal sovereignty, including a "new federalism" doctrine that gives the states rights over the tribes that U.S. courts consistently denied the states in the nineteenth century.

Nineteenth-century Indian law, in its own terms, lacked a coherent doctrinal base as federal and state courts vied for control over the tribes on a case-by-case basis. The courts decisions were "adventitious and temporary," as an Alabama court had falsely defined Creek law, with Indian law not becoming a body of legal doctrine until the 1880s and 1890s, the period when federal political control over the tribes was consolidated. This consolidation produced a unitary body of law under the plenary power doctrine. This doctrine, while simple on its face, created many local problems that increased both the number and complexity of Indian law cases, as local white and tribal interests collided in a wide spectrum of social contexts.

The concept of tribal sovereignty survived the plenary power doctrine for reasons beyond the tribes powerful defense of that doctrine. Ironically, the plenary power doctrine was rooted in the doctrine of tribal sovereignty, just as Chief Justice Marshall's domestic, dependant nations formulation was. For federal power over the tribes to be plenary, both the power and special nation-to-nation status of the tribes were implicitly recognized. The framework of the relationship of the federal government to the tribes was a political, not a legal, matter. The doctrine of tribal sovereignty was the counterweight of the plenary power doctrine as federal and state courts balanced both to dispose of the thousands of legal problems that arose from the imposition of U.S. law on the tribes and the settling of millions of whites on and near Indian reservations. Moreover, the doctrine of tribal sovereignty was used by federal courts to give weight to local tribal interests against local white interests, problems that the broad plenary power doctrine – recognizing federal supremacy as a theoretical matter but failing to give it concrete form in the case of local problems – failed to reach. Tribal sovereignty at the end of the nineteenth century, just as in midcentury, remained one of the bulwarks of the doctrine of federal Indian law, necessary to formulate a complete system of legal doctrine protecting both federal and tribal interests against the states.

American Indian law is best understood politically rather than doctrinally, which is not to say that Indian law has no doctrines. The doctrine of tribal sovereignty reemerged as a dominant doctrine in federal Indian law in *Williams v. Lee* (1959), brought back to the federal courts not by the BIA or the states but by the tribes.[5] There, Justice Hugo Black held that the Navajo possessed the "right to govern themselves," a right that the state of Arizona could not infringe on by enforcing state civil law on the reservation. Moreover, the right to self-government in this case turned specifically on the fact that denying the tribal courts jurisdiction over a lawsuit between a white trader and a Navajo would "undermine the authority of the tribal courts, thereby infringing on the right of the Indians to govern themselves." Tribal law was, once again, inseparable from tribal sovereignty.

Though the doctrine of federal Indian law now continues to mask difficult political choices behind a package of competing doctrines, as in the nineteenth century, tribal sovereignty is still at the core of the doctrine of American Indian law. The plenary power doctrine still coexists with tribal sovereignty, which, in legal theory at least, can be limited at any point by the political will of Congress. The courts, however, have limited the plenary power doctrine, holding the federal government, under the trust doctrine, to discharge its guardianship responsibly over the tribes. A "new federalism" doctrine is gradually ceding tribal powers to the states. This system of doctrinal choices faces each court deciding an Indian case. In this scheme tribal sovereignty is somehow balanced against other doctrines.

This leaves tribal sovereignty poorly protected in federal Indian law. A simple example of the failure of this protection can be seen in one case, Chief Justice William Rehnquist's disingenuous use of logic and history in his opinion in *Oliphant v. Suquamish Indian Tribe* (1978), a case in which

[5] 358 U.S. 217 (1959).

tribal sovereignty could have been simply upheld with few costs to other interests.[6] Oliphant, a young white man, was arrested by tribal police for drinking and fighting on the Suquamish reservation, common forms of criminal activity against which Justice Rehnquist regularly advances many arguments to extend the scope of the law's capacity to repress. Oliphant challenged the jurisdiction of tribal courts over white people. Justice Black's holding in *Williams* should have led to a simple and equitable decision for the tribe: Suquamish tribal courts need jurisdiction over reservation lands in order to protect tribal sovereignty. Such a simple upholding of tribal sovereignty would offend no U.S. values, even in a simplistic "balancing" analysis: every locality in the United States has its own misdemeanor court that punishes minor criminal offenses, even by strangers passing through. Rehnquist's analysis did not begin with tribal sovereignty; rather, he followed a long and highly selective history of federal restrictions of tribal sovereignty, emphasizing the dependence of the tribes and the fact that they often did not have jurisdiction over whites. Finally, turning the methodology of *Crow Dog* on its head – allowing no repeal of a treaty right by implication – the chief justice held that "by acknowledging their dependence on the United States . . . the Suquamish were in all probability recognizing that the United States would arrest and try non-Indian intruders who came within their reservation" – a wild leap of logic that reads Rehnquist's twentieth-century meaning into the Suquamish understanding of their own treaty and allows a dependent status to infer a loss of sovereignty in a treaty that is silent on such matters.

In the middle of his opinion, Rehnquist acknowledges Indian law, but then, because historically "few Indian tribes maintained any semblance of a formal court system," he dismisses traditional tribal law as having no relevancy at all. "Offenses by one Indian against another were usually handled by social and religious pressure and not be formal judicial processes; emphasis was on restitution rather than punishment." In support of this proposition, the chief justice cites a patently erroneous 1834 Report of the Commissioner of Indian Affairs stating, "The Indian tribes are without laws, and the chiefs without much authority to exercise any restraint."[7]

Thus, *Oliphant* is simply another case grounded in the dependency theory

---

[6] 435 U.S. 191 (1978).

[7] Ibid., 197. Chief Justice Rehnquist's cite is to H.R. Report, no. 474, 23rd Cong. 1st session, 91 (1834). This same reasoning is used in *Duro v. Reina* 110 S.Ct. 2053 (1990), 2061. There Justice Anthony Kennedy cites Rehnquist's use of history in *Oliphant* in holding that the Pima-Maricopa Tribe of the Salt River Reservation did not have criminal jurisdiction over a Cahuilla Mission Indian living on their reservation. There is simply no relationship between the jurisdictional history of Indian/white relations and of inter-tribal relations. Rather, Justice Kennedy's cite to Rehnquist's history is used to deny that the Pima-Maricopa tribe has any legal history at all.

of *Kagama* and denies the concept of tribal sovereignty. The real questions that any case involving the tribes should begin with are: Who are the Suquamish people? What is their history? What can the courts of the United States do to recognize their sovereignty and to help increase their exercise of self-government?

Obviously, Justice Rehnquist did not ask these questions, because he did not see the issue in this way. There is no question that, in a traditional white sense, the Indian tribes did not arrest and try white criminal offenders. But that was not their way. They resisted white intrusions on their lands and their sovereignty in the form of overt wars but also in more subtle forms. This resistance was structured by Suquamish notions of law and justice. Tribal law had its impact in the life of the tribe and was not intended to dominate other peoples. In the Indian view, these other peoples were responsible to their own law. The modern Suquamish tribe had both the law and the legal institutions to punish a drunken troublemaker like Oliphant and would have done so without offense to any domestic or international human rights values. Rehnquist saved Oliphant from the specter of ignominious punishment by the Suquamish exactly as the 1832 Alabama Supreme Court saved Caldwell from Creek justice.[8] The law-and-order ideology of the chief justice does not extend to respecting the law and order of the Indian tribes.

Toward a new Indian legal history

That the nineteenth-century Indian tribes were transformed by the process of forced assimilation is beyond question. The role of the law in shaping that transformation provides a rich field for study. The survival of tribal cultures is nothing less than miraculous, given the violence of the process of forced acculturation. We know little of how the tribes structured this change. It seems clear, as a starting point, that the tribes made use of both tribal and U.S. law to adapt their cultures to the social change induced by forced assimilation. Tribal law continued to govern tribal life long after white intrusion, changing in form and ability to resolve new types of disputes.

Tribal law also structured the tribe's reception of U.S. law. There can be no question that the constitutional legal order of the Creek Nation was structured by the nation's traditional law. Similarly, the tribal police and tribal court systems of the Plains reservations incorporated tribal law into both their structures and their decision-making processes. The Tlingit even

---

[8] There is another ironic reversal to point out here. While the Alabama Supreme Court saved Caldwell from an "ignomious" death at the hands of Creek justice, it is now Chief Justice Rehnquist who must frequently stay up late at night at the center of U.S. legal order backlogged by two thousand executions, "ignomious" deaths at the hands of U.S. justice.

used tribal law in an attempt to impose some order on the Klondike Gold Rush.

At the same time, it is obvious that U.S. law and the imposed law of the courts of Indian offenses has never permeated the legal consciousness of Indian peoples. Rather, they retain whole systems of legal understanding that are significantly evolved from their traditional ways, reflecting a century of innovation and social change, but that are nevertheless distinct. This Indian law is deeply embedded in the legal culture of the United States, even if it is not found in legal scholarship or, all too rarely, in the practice of federal or state Indian law. This rich legal tradition does not exist because it was recognized by the courts, either before or after *Crow Dog*, but rather because the tribes never ceased to act as sovereign peoples and never gave up their "old law."

The task for legal scholars is not to remind the tribes that this is so. They do not need this arrogance. Rather, it is to infuse into federal Indian law an "original understanding" of its first principles. Any analysis of the rights of Indian people under U.S. law must begin with a careful analysis of tribal sovereignty, with great weight given to the widest possible recognition of that sovereignty. In the process, we not only do justice to the tribes, but we also enrich U.S. law with tribal law, a process Robert Williams called "Americanizing American law."[9] We have always paid lip service to a pluralist legal tradition in U.S. law, but we have failed to allow it to sink very deeply into the consciousness of judges, lawyers, and the people of the United States.

Many of the cases analyzed here do not appear in any of our modern law books because they do not stand for currently recognized principles of the doctrine of federal Indian law. However, we cannot frame these issues in such a narrow context. The vitality of nineteenth-century Indian law lies in the reality that the tribes never let their sovereignty be determined by any case or trusted that question to any judge. The way that the federal courts analyzed the doctrine of federal Indian law was of great concern to the tribes, but they never let those outcomes define tribal sovereignty. The tribes have resisted in every conceivable way. They lost very often and lost badly. Many of the Indian individuals named in these cases went to jail; a few were executed. Were it not for their cases, they would be anonymous figures in the white culture of the United States. And except for *Crow Dog* and *Kagama*, their cases remain uncited precedents in federal Indian law. But these cases do not have to be cited as precedents in U.S. law to have legal meaning to Indian people. These cases are remembered: the people who remember them know that they stand for tribal sovereignty.

[9] This is the central theme of Robert Williams, "Algebra of Indian Law."

Index

293